WORLD STUDIES

FOURTH EDITION

Dennis Bollinger

bju press®

Greenville, South Carolina

Note: The fact that materials produced by other publishers may be referred to in this volume does not constitute an endorsement of the content or theological position of materials produced by such publishers. Any references and ancillary materials are listed as an aid to the student or the teacher and in an attempt to maintain the accepted academic standards of the publishing industry.

WORLD STUDIES
Fourth Edition

Dennis Bollinger, PhD

Editor
Manda Kalagayan, MEd

Bible Integration
Brian Collins, PhD
Bryan Smith, PhD

Cover Design
Drew Fields

Book Design
Steve Mitchell

Page Layout
Jessica Johnson

Page Design
Dan Van Leeuwen

Project Coordinator
Dan Berger

Illustration
Paula Cheadle
Preston Gravely Jr.
Del Thompson

Permissions
Sylvia Gass
Sarah Gundlach
Meg Jones
Carrie Walker

Photo credits are listed on pages 409–11.

© 2017 BJU Press
Greenville, South Carolina 29614

First Edition © 1985 BJU Press
Second Edition © 1998, 2000 BJU Press
Third Edition © 2011 BJU Press

Printed in the United States of America

ISBN 978-1-60682-983-7

15 14 13 12 11 10 9 8 7 6 5 4 3 2 1

CONTENTS

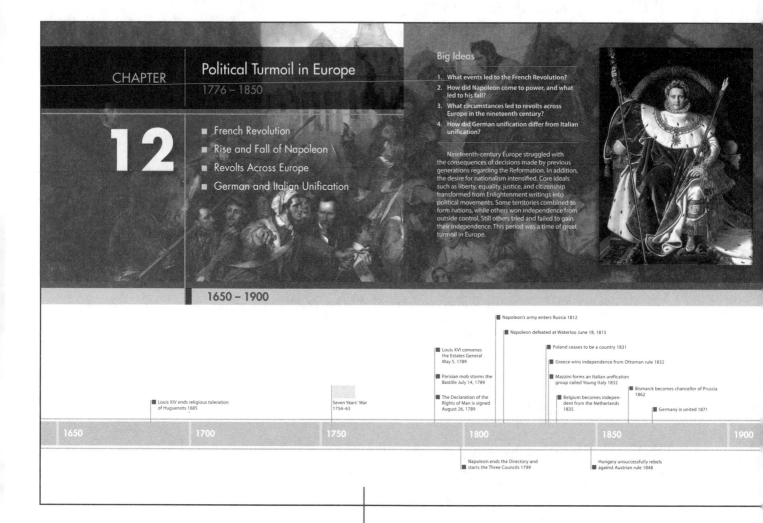

CHAPTER

Political Turmoil in Europe
1776 – 1850

12

- French Revolution
- Rise and Fall of Napoleon
- Revolts Across Europe
- German and Italian Unification

Big Ideas

1. What events led to the French Revolution?
2. How did Napoleon come to power, and what led to his fall?
3. What circumstances led to revolts across Europe in the nineteenth century?
4. How did German unification differ from Italian unification?

Nineteenth-century Europe struggled with the consequences of decisions made by previous generations regarding the Reformation. In addition, the desire for nationalism intensified. Core ideals such as liberty, equality, justice, and citizenship transformed from Enlightenment writings into political movements. Some territories combined to form nations, while others won independence from outside control. Still others tried and failed to gain their independence. This period was a time of great turmoil in Europe.

1650 – 1900

- Napoleon's army enters Russia 1812
- Napoleon defeated at Waterloo June 18, 1815
- Louis XVI convenes the Estates General May 5, 1789
- Poland ceases to be a country 1831
- Greece wins independence from Ottoman rule 1832
- Parisian mob storms the Bastille July 14, 1789
- Mazzini forms an Italian unification group called Young Italy 1832
- Louis XIV ends religious toleration of Huguenots 1685
- Seven Years' War 1754–63
- The Declaration of the Rights of Man is signed August 26, 1789
- Belgium becomes independent from the Netherlands 1835
- Bismarck becomes chancellor of Prussia 1862
- Germany is united 1871

1650	1700	1750	1800	1850	1900

- Napoleon ends the Directory and starts the Three Councils 1799
- Hungary unsuccessfully rebels against Austrian rule 1848

Chapter openers offer a glimpse of major events with a photo or painting and a timeline. In addition, the chapter outline lists the major topics that will be covered.

Margin info boxes offer interesting bits of extra information.

Terms in bold type draw attention to important facts, ideas, people, or definitions.

General feature boxes provide a more detailed look at a person, event, or concept mentioned in the text.

ing fibers and rags with water. The mixture was pressed and then allowed to dry. The Chinese used paper for wrapping, padding, and writing. By the sixth century, the Chinese had developed toilet paper. Later they folded and sewed paper into bags to protect the flavor of tea. During the Song dynasty, the Chinese issued the first known paper money for general use.

Compass

Lodestone, a magnetic mineral, aligns itself with the earth's magnetic field. The Chinese were among the first people to discover this. However, the Chinese probably first used the **compass** as a novelty, or possibly to determine the will of their gods. Records indicate that during the Song dynasty the Chinese learned to use compasses for finding direction.

Gunpowder

For centuries the Chinese mixed ingredients with saltpeter to make items such as medicines. In the ninth century the Chinese discovered **gunpowder** by accident. They were trying to create a substance that would give them eternal life. The Chinese quickly developed many weapons with gunpowder, including flame-throwers, rockets, and crude bombs. They developed guns or firearms around the time of the Ming dynasty in the fourteenth century.

Printing

During the third century, the Chinese became the first to develop woodblock **printing**. They carved images into a block of wood and then applied ink or paint. The woodblock was then pressed against paper or cloth. A reversed image of the carving would be imprinted on the material.

The Chinese also developed a method of printing that uses movable characters. This method, known as movable-type printing, was first developed in China around 1041. The characters were made out of ceramic. Although the Chinese invented this technology, they made little use of it. The Chinese language is very complicated, and p... ng with this method involved a great amount of ... nberg, around 1450, was the first known person ... with great success. However, he was German,

Saltpeter

This is another name for a mixture of sulfur, charcoal, and potassium nitrate. It is commonly referred to as gunpowder. It burns rapidly and produces hot solids and gases. These gases can be used to propel a bullet or to launch and create beautiful fireworks displays.

Early Chinese rocket

... stries developed, and these industries em- ... The Chinese were also among the first to ... rocess would not be used in Europe for an- ... e sale of iron products brought great wealth ... ss in China.

... ast Asia and Other Lands

... ed that merchants brought gold, ivory, ... frica to China as early as 500 BC. Camel ... ross Central Asia from China to Europe. ... ods between nations in Southeast Asia ... These ships worked out of ports in ... erchants served as an important link to ... turies.

Cast Iron

Cast iron is formed when iron ore and a small amount of carbon and silicon are heated to about 1200°C. At this temperature the iron becomes a liquid and can be poured into a mold. Iron in this form has several advantages, including increased hardness, durability, a lower melting point (about 300°C lower than pure iron), and the ability to be cast into almost any shape. Cast iron has been used to make bridges, columns for buildings, machine parts, weapons, cooking utensils, and many other products. Archaeologists have found hundreds of molds for casting iron in China.

Chapter 2

Guiding Questions

1. What contributions did the Abbasid dynasty make to mathematics, science, literature, philosophy, and technology?

2. How did Islam win converts among culturally diverse peoples?

■ III. The Culture of Islam

In 750 the Islamic Empire came under new leadership with the defeat of the Umayyads. This dynasty became known as the **Abbassid** (ah BASS id) Caliphate. The capital was moved to **Baghdad** in Iraq. This move reflected a growing influence by Persians on the Muslim Empire. The emphasis of this dynasty shifted from conquest to learning and culture.

Beginning in the eighth century, Islam achieved a golden age. Many non-Muslim scholars who lived under Islamic rule preserved knowledge from earlier civilizations, including Egypt, Rome, and Greece. In addition, they worked with Muslim scholars to develop important advances in science, math, and medicine. Much of this knowledge had been lost in Europe. Baghdad became the intellectual center, and many works of antiquity were initially translated

Historical Perspectives

Bernard Lewis and Rodney Stark are two historians who have written about the early development of Islam. Read the following summaries that follow. Keep in mind that neither author is making up facts, but they are arguing for a different conclusion. (Look at the title of each book for a hint.)

Bernard Lewis points out that Islamic civilization, at a certain point in the Middle Ages, was among the most advanced cultures in the world. Islam's military power was clear as it spread east, west, north, and south. It had the most active economy of the time. It had trading relationships with Asia, Europe, and Africa. It adopted the knowledge of Greece and Persia upon conquest, and it imported knowledge from India and China and built upon this knowledge. For instance, it combined Indian numbers with knowledge of mathematics gained from other civilizations. It encouraged additional scientific experiments and added to scientific knowledge. But at some point the advance of scholarship in the Muslim world stopped while that of Europe leaped forward.

Bernard Lewis, *What Went Wrong? Western Impact and Middle Eastern Response* (New York: Oxford University Press, 2002), 3-7

Rodney Stark argues that Islamic culture never was superior to European culture. He says that Muslims learned from the people they conquered. They learned about science, math, shipbuilding, and philosophy this way. He admits that they knew more Greek philosophy than Europeans. Stark says that Europe was not trapped in the Dark Ages. He points out that Europe had many advances in the Middle Ages. Europeans developed better harnesses. This meant they could use horses for plowing. Horses could also draw wagons. This helped their armies move equipment. They developed better plows and methods of crop rotation. This made Europeans healthier. They wore better armor than the Muslims. For this reason European armies won in the First Crusade and sustained others.

Rodney Stark, *God's Battalions: The Case for the Crusades* (New York: HarperOne, 2009), 56-76.

1. What is Lewis's point?

2. What is Stark's point?

3. How do they select facts to bolster their point of view?

Averroës—Muslim scholar who preserved Aristotle's Greek philosophy

Transition in Sub-Saharan Africa

Sahel

Flaxseed (left) and millet (right) that will be ground into flour

in the **Sahel** (sah HEL; a narrow strip of land between the Sahara and the savannah). Crops such as finger millet, peas, and flax took hold in Ethiopia.

Livestock

Africans raised a variety of animals, including sheep, goats, and cattle. However, they prized these animals and seldom killed them. The animals provided milk and other benefits (such as wool) for their masters. Cattle especially were considered a sign of wealth.

Ankole Watusi cattle in the plains of Uganda

41

Amazing color photographs and artwork help the students "see" the sites, people, and events discussed in the text.

...y is found in Genesis 4–11. If ...u see the beginnings of civili-...and Eve's sons, moved to the ...er of a group of people who ...ation. The first city mentioned ...7). The division of labor ...d on by Cain's descendants. ...an. Jubal labored in the arts, ...-Cain worked in industry,

...a civilization twisted by ...wanted to worship God ...ction of his sacrifice, he ...built away from the ...rt from God. It was the ...ning the seed of the

...a of the woman, those loyal to God, was at first main-tained in the line of Seth, another of Adam and Eve's sons. But the Sethites did not remain true to God. Even righteous people die. Therefore, a godly culture cannot remain godly unless it passes on its love for God to each new generation. At some point in their history, the Sethites allowed their children to marry Cainites (Gen. 6:2). Eventually the Sethites were no different from the Cainites (6:5).

Grieved by the great sinfulness of the human race, God determined to judge His world. He would cover the whole earth with a great flood. But God chose to show favor to one member of the Sethite line (Gen. 6:8). God instructed Noah to build a massive ark. Noah was to take his family and representatives of the animal kingdom into the ark, where they would be safe. God held back His judgment for 120 years (Gen. 6:3). But in the end Noah, his wife, his three sons, and their wives were the only people to enter the ark. Then the "fountains of the great deep" were broken up, and rain fell (7:11). Eventually the entire earth was under water. The Creator had caused the earth to return to its original state: once again it was "without form, and void" (1:2).

The Rise of Nations

After the Flood, God repeated the Creation Mandate to Noah and his descendants (Gen. 9:1-7). But instead of spreading out to fill the earth and subdue it, humans gathered to build a great tower (Babel). They were going to build a civilization on their own terms. Fallen man could use civilization-building abilities God gave him for evil. God chose to restrain mankind's ability to do evil by confusing the people's languages. Unable to communicate and work together, the people were forced to scatter and fill the earth.

7

The Chapter Review asks students to think in terms of higher learning, including understanding, analyzing, evaluating, and creating.

CHAPTER REVIEW

■ Making Connections

1. What impact did the invention of the compass from lodestone have on China?

2. Why were merchants prevented from serving in government in China prior to the Song dynasty?

3. Why did Japan descend into feudalism?

4. How did the rise of the warrior class in Japan affect Japanese culture?

5. Why were Japanese warriors trained in history, literature, and writing?

6. How did silk shirts minimize the damage to a Mongol soldier from an arrow strike?

■ Developing History Skills

1. Go to your local library or go on the Internet to discover the various raw materials that have been used to record written information. Organize them in chronological order. Compare your list with lists of others in the class.

2. Construct a timeline that includes early Chinese history through the time of the Mongol invasions and that includes the rise of the Ming Dynasty. (This assignment may require outside reading or Internet research.)

■ Thinking Critically

1. Evaluate traditional Mongol religion in light of God's Word (using passages such as Exodus 20:4–5 and Romans 1:23).

2. When Islam becomes dominant, as it did in the Mongol empire, how are other religions, especially Christianity, treated?

3. Why did the Mongol Empire collapse? Provide a one or two sentence answer for each of the empires (China, Russia, Asia Minor ...ndia).

People, Places, and Things to Know

Shang
Song
technology
paper
compass
gunpowder
printing
cast iron
ancestor worship
Confucius
Buddhism
Taoism
Lao-tzu
feudalism
shogun
samurai
Bushido
hara-kiri
Shintoism
Zen Buddhism
Angkor Wat
yurts
Chinggis Khan
Great Yasa
siege warfare
pretend retreat
kamikaze
Batu Khan
Tartars
Battle of Liegnitz
Golden Horde
Tengri
shamans
Ming
Tamerlane
Mughal
Akbar
Taj Mahal

...s World

...mission trip to China. You have a lengthy ...Chinese girl your age. She asks you, "If ...e religion, why didn't it exist in China until ...uld you respond?

...ke root in Asia until the nineteenth cen-...l groups to answer this question: Why ...know about the history covered in this ...of it concerns the advance of Christian-...d 17:24–31 in your answer. After all the ...r answers to the class, discuss which

---

Chapter 3

Guiding Questions

1. How were agriculture and ironworking important for the continued development of civilization in Africa?

2. What role did extended family groups play in African society?

3. What are the indigenous religions of Africa?

Zebra and blue wildebeest migration in Serengeti National Park

■ I. African Culture
Continued Development of Civilization

Agriculture

Just like other people around the world, Africans adapted to changing conditions and lived on the natural resources around them. Some were able to blend growing crops with raising livestock to meet their dietary needs. Others learned to thrive on either crops or livestock, depending on the available resources.

Over time, the soil became less productive and the food for livestock decreased. The people often had to move in order to survive. Eventually, the depleted soil would again become able to support crops and sustain life. As the Africans found better ways to fertilize the soil, more permanent dwellings were built and groups were able to build cities.

Improved efficiency resulted in greater yields. As more food was produced than was needed, the excess provided opportunity for trade. Increased trade and permanent settlements helped the continued development of civilization.

Crops

Depending on the region, crops such as roots or various grains were harvested. In the rain forests, inhabitants gathered roots such as yams. On the **savannah** (suh VAN uh; flat grasslands), the people developed grain crops such as millet, sorghum, and maize (corn). Other crops such as cotton and watermelon began to appear in West Africa and

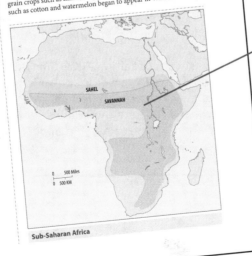

SAHEL

SAVANNAH

0   500 Miles
0   500 KM

Sub-Saharan Africa

Maps help the students visualize geographic locations.

PRONUNCIATION GUIDE

Vowels

symbol	example	symbol	example
a	cat = KAT	aw	all = AWL
a-e	cape = KAPE	o	potion = PO shun
ay	paint = PAYNT	oa	don't = DOANT
e	jet = JET	o-e	groan = GRONE
eh	spend = SPEHND	oh	own = OHN
ee	fiend = FEEND	u	some = SUM
i	swim = SWIM	uh	abet = uh BET
ih	pity = PIH tee	oo	crew = CROO
eye	icy = EYE see	oo	push = POOSH
i-e	might = MITE	ou	loud = LOUD
ah	cot = KAHT	oy	toil = TOYL
ar	car = KAR		

Consonants

symbol	example	symbol	example
k	cat = KAT	th	thin = THIN
g	get = GET	th	then = THEN
j	gentle = JEN tul	zh	fusion = FYOO zhun

The pronunciation key used in this text is designed to give the reader a self-evident, acceptable pronunciation for a word as he reads it from the page. For more accurate pronunciations, the reader should consult a good dictionary.

Stress: Syllables with primary stress appear in LARGE CAPITAL letters. Syllables with secondary stress and one-syllable words appear in SMALL CAPITAL letters. Unstressed syllables appear in lowercase letters. Where two or more words appear together, hyphens separate the syllables within each word. For example, the pronunciation of Omar Khayyam appears as (OH-mar kie-YAHM).

■ Why World Studies?

Have you ever wondered why you should study history? Historians have given many answers to this question, but for the Christian the most important answer is found in God. God created a world that works historically. God created a world in which events unfold through time. And when Adam sinned, God gave a promise of redemption that would take thousands upon thousands of years to fulfill. God didn't bring redemption immediately. Since the time of Christ, the church has spread around the world in a historical process.

Learning What God Is Doing in the World

God has planned all of human history. There is no historical happening that is out of God's control or that does not help to accomplish God's great purpose in the world (Ps. 22:28; Prov. 16:33; Acts 17:26). God's great purpose is to establish the kingdom of Christ (Dan. 4:35; Acts 28; Eph. 1:11).

When you read this book, it is right to continually ask the question "What was God doing in this event?" This is a harder question to answer than you might think. The Bible does tell us God's purpose for some events in the world. But most of the events in this book take place after the New Testament was written, and the Bible does not comment on them. Christians can look at what the Bible says God's goals are in history: redeeming sinners, establishing Christ's kingdom, and bringing glory to His name. Christians can then look at how historical events contributed to these purposes. Such answers will remain tentative, and Christian historians must present them humbly. Nonetheless, the question of what God is doing in history is important for the Christian historian to consider.

The Creation Mandate and the Development of Civilization

When God created Adam and Eve, He gave them a command: Be fruitful, multiply, and subdue the earth (Gen. 1:28). Human history is a record of the fulfillment of this command. God created mankind in His image. This bestowed on them the abilities to carry out the Creation Mandate. He also placed them in a garden with rivers that flowed out to the wider world. Those rivers were highways to places with resources that were needed to develop civilization (Gen. 2:10–14).

This original command from God is being fulfilled. The human population of the earth has grown from two people to over seven billion people. The story of civilization is the story of how people have subdued the earth. But the fulfillment of this command has been corrupted by the Fall of man into sin. The development of civilization is good. God intended it from the beginning. But sin has entwined itself deeply in the rise of every particular civilization. As you read about civilizations in this book, you will at times marvel at the artistic achievements of a civilization or the wisdom displayed in framing a government. But in those same civilizations you will be dismayed to see the presence of slavery or the evidence of widespread moral decay.

Evaluating History from a Christian Worldview

The reality of sin means that civilizations cannot simply be celebrated. Events in world history must be evaluated from a Christian worldview. You will gain a great deal of benefit from this evaluation. History allows you to look at previous generations facing the big issues of their day and deciding how to respond to them. There is much wisdom to be gained by learning from both the mistakes and successes of previous generations. To know which is which requires careful evaluation from Scripture.

In world history there are four major themes around which this book will focus its evaluation: justice, power, citizenship, and environment.

Justice

A society is just when people do right and respect each other's rights. For Christians, the rights that people have are based on the image of God that each human bears. Because humans are made in God's image, it is wrong to murder or steal or commit any number of sins against other people. Instead the Bible commands that people love others as they love themselves.

Most civilizations base their understanding of justice on something other than the Bible. Much of conflict in human history comes from conflicting views of what is just. As you read this book, we will draw your attention to issues of justice that need to be evaluated from a Christian worldview.

Power

Power is essential to any civilization. For a civilization to grow and thrive, its leaders must be able to provide order for the people who live there. In addition, civilizations need to exercise power over forces of nature that could threaten the civilization.

A Christian views the use of power as good and necessary. The command to exercise dominion over the earth is a command to exercise power in the world. But in a fallen world, power is often abused. Humans have used power to oppress others. Power that should have been used to cultivate creation has instead been used to damage it. You will notice these issues throughout this study of world history.

Citizenship

Within civilizations, some people are citizens. A citizen has a status that gives him certain rights, privileges, and duties within his civilization. Citizenship gives individuals a say in how their community is run. It also imposes duties that require significant sacrifice. Christians need to evaluate who should be granted citizenship, what rights citizens should have, and what duties should be required of a citizen.

Environment

Every civilization is placed in a particular geographical location. Each location has special features. Many civilizations grew up along great rivers. Others learned how to flourish in harsh climates. Whatever the environment, God called mankind to rule over this world in all its variety. Understanding the role the environment has played in shaping civilizations is important. Understanding how civilizations have shaped their environments in fulfillment of the Creation Mandate is also important.

Multiple Perspectives

Historians often have to evaluate different perspectives of historical events because the world is complex. Events often happen for a multitude of reasons, and untangling them all is not easy. In addition, everyone interprets the events of history from his own worldview. Throughout this book we will give you the opportunity to evaluate the perspectives of different historians. Sometimes you will be asked to judge if a historian is accurately understanding the historical evidence. In each case you will be looking to see if the historian is interpreting history from a biblical worldview.

UNIT 1

Foundations
Creation – AD 800

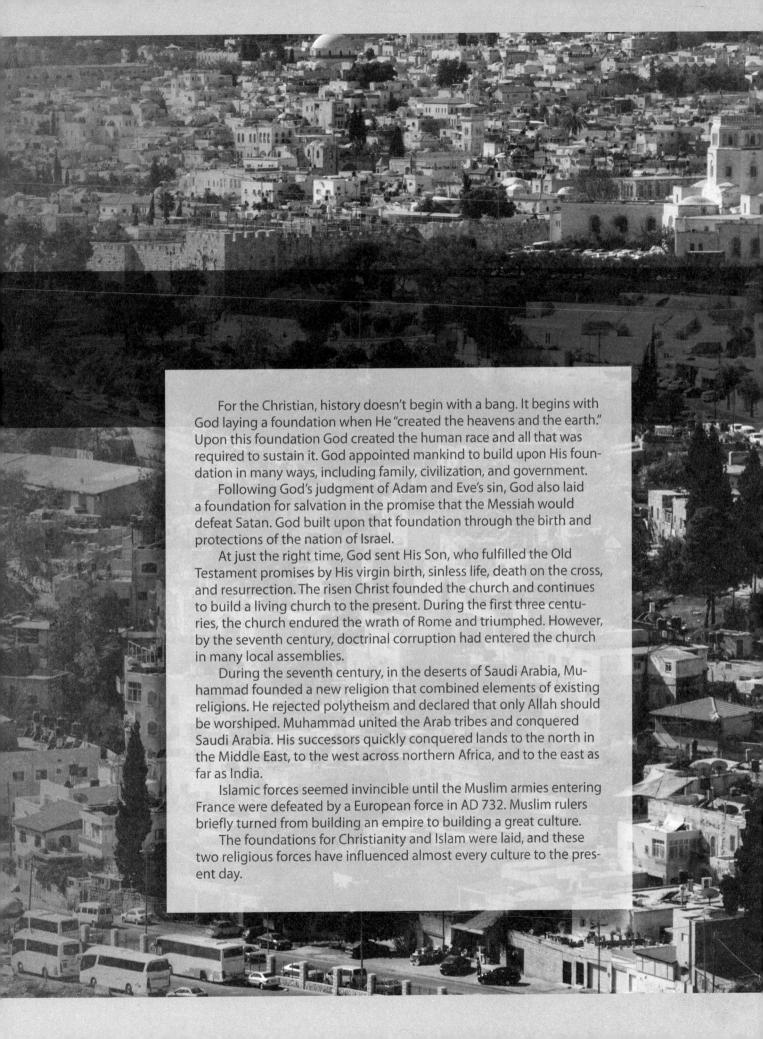

For the Christian, history doesn't begin with a bang. It begins with God laying a foundation when He "created the heavens and the earth." Upon this foundation God created the human race and all that was required to sustain it. God appointed mankind to build upon His foundation in many ways, including family, civilization, and government.

Following God's judgment of Adam and Eve's sin, God also laid a foundation for salvation in the promise that the Messiah would defeat Satan. God built upon that foundation through the birth and protections of the nation of Israel.

At just the right time, God sent His Son, who fulfilled the Old Testament promises by His virgin birth, sinless life, death on the cross, and resurrection. The risen Christ founded the church and continues to build a living church to the present. During the first three centuries, the church endured the wrath of Rome and triumphed. However, by the seventh century, doctrinal corruption had entered the church in many local assemblies.

During the seventh century, in the deserts of Saudi Arabia, Muhammad founded a new religion that combined elements of existing religions. He rejected polytheism and declared that only Allah should be worshiped. Muhammad united the Arab tribes and conquered Saudi Arabia. His successors quickly conquered lands to the north in the Middle East, to the west across northern Africa, and to the east as far as India.

Islamic forces seemed invincible until the Muslim armies entering France were defeated by a European force in AD 732. Muslim rulers briefly turned from building an empire to building a great culture.

The foundations for Christianity and Islam were laid, and these two religious forces have influenced almost every culture to the present day.

1

- The Beginnings of the Human Race
- The History of Israel
- The Coming of the Christ

Creation – AD 500

Creation

Flood

Birth of Abraham c. 2166 BC

Jacob and family travel
to Egypt c. 1876 BC

Exodus from Egypt
1446 BC

2000 BC

1500 BC

Big Ideas

1. How does the Bible's teaching about Creation, the Fall, and Redemption shape your thinking about culture and civilization?

2. Why are covenants God made with Israel important for understanding world history?

3. In what way was the incarnation of Christ the turning point of world history?

A turning point is a moment when great change happens. In world history a turning point may be the outbreak of a war, the migration of a large group of people, or the birth of a very important person. Before the turning point, things are one way. After the turning point, things are very different.

Some turning points change the lives of thousands of people. But some turning points are so great that they bring change to all people everywhere. This chapter is about turning points that have changed the entire world.

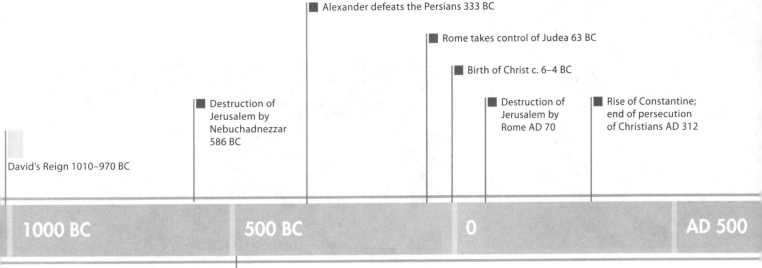

David's Reign 1010–970 BC

Destruction of Jerusalem by Nebuchadnezzar 586 BC

Alexander defeats the Persians 333 BC

Rome takes control of Judea 63 BC

Birth of Christ c. 6–4 BC

Destruction of Jerusalem by Rome AD 70

Rise of Constantine; end of persecution of Christians AD 312

1000 BC   500 BC   0   AD 500

Rome 509 BC–AD 476

Guiding Questions

1. How do the image of God in man and the Creation Mandate form the foundations for civilization?
2. How does the Fall affect the natural world and civilizations?
3. What is the thesis statement of human history?

■ I. The Beginnings of the Human Race

"In the beginning God—" The Bible's first four words make a very important point. God (or **Yahweh** as He is often called in the Hebrew Bible) existed when nothing else did, and all that has come into being was made by Him. For this reason, God owns every galaxy, every planet, and every human. All should honor and obey the one who has graciously chosen to let them exist.

The Creation of the World

God created His world simply by speaking. In six days the earth went from being a dark, water-covered planet to a beautiful place that God Himself said was "very good" (Gen. 1:31). God accomplished this amazing work with only a series of commands.

The events of this world's first week teach **divine sovereignty**, God's complete and permanent control over this world. The words of Yahweh are powerful. They determine what is and what will be. Whatever opposition He has faced in history, He has chosen to face it so that He may use it for His own purposes. Jehovah is indeed the Supreme Being, the one who "worketh all things after the counsel of his own will" (Eph. 1:11).

God's work of creation came to its climax after He made the animals on the sixth day. Up to that point, God had created by using the impersonal command, "Let there be." But just before His final creation, He said, "Let us make man" (Gen. 1:26).

Made in God's Image

The reason for this special interest was that humans were to be God's great masterpiece. Unlike the other creatures, humans would be made in God's own image (Gen. 1:27).

The **image of God** in man is a set of qualities possessed by all humans that reflect God. Because humans are made in God's image, they are like God in many important ways. Like God, they have the ability to think, love, use language, create complex structures, know right and wrong, enjoy relationships, and more. Because all humans are made in God's image, all humans are precious in God's sight. They are far more precious than the other creatures. Also, because humans are made in God's image, they are religious beings. They know that they have not made themselves, and they sense that to

know themselves, they must know their Creator. This is the reason that all human societies have been religious in some way.

Made to Rule

Yahweh created humans with a job to do. He created humans in His image so that they would "be fruitful and multiply" and exercise dominion over the earth (Gen. 1:26, 28). This command, often called the **Creation Mandate**, reveals why God made humans.

The central command of Genesis 1:28 is to "subdue" the earth by having "dominion" over it. The growth of the human population is essential to fulfilling the Creation Mandate. When people work together to subdue the earth and make it useful, **civilization** happens. The word *civilization* refers to human **culture** as it is lived in cities or under the influence of cities. Historically, a **city** is more than a place where many people live. It is a cultural institution in which humans who share certain core values work together to improve their quality of life. They work together by dividing their labor. In a city, individuals specialize in certain tasks necessary for human life. Some specialize in producing food, some in building houses, and some in making tools. The benefit of this division of labor is that individuals no longer need to do everything themselves. Also, because individuals focus on a few tasks, those tasks tend to be done with great skill. The result is progress in science, technology, language, art, and many other things. You can see now why filling the earth with people and ruling over the earth go hand in hand.

Central to the study of world history is the study of civilization. The city is not just a human idea. Civilization comes from the Creation Mandate. The foundation of world history is built on God's purpose for humans found in Genesis 1.

The Fall

The account of world history in subsequent chapters is not a story of all humans working together. It is not a story of civilizations built to benefit everybody. It is not a story of cities and nations that glorify God in all they do. In fact, many civilizations rise through bloodshed and injustice.

The reason for this is found in Genesis 3. When Adam and Eve chose to trust Satan rather than God, their sin changed the world.

Everyone is made in the image of God to reflect His glory.

Culture	
Describe the role of each of the following in creating culture.	
Image of God	*Creativity*
Be fruitful and multiply	*Humans work together*
Subdue	*Humans make creation useful*
Result	*Culture*

They did not lose the abilities they had as God's image bearers. They did not lose the drive to subdue the world. But from that moment on, sin would twist all human endeavors.

The Results of Sin

The consequences of this sin affected both the inner being of Adam and Eve as well as their physical existence. And, as the apostle Paul explained centuries later, the consequences of that choice have been passed on to all humans (Rom. 5:12).

Since God had made the man and the woman good, they originally loved God with their entire being (Mark 12:30). They also loved each other as much as themselves (v. 31). But when they sinned, their love became twisted. When God asked Adam about what he had done, Adam blamed Eve when he should have blamed himself (Gen. 3:12). And in blaming her, he blamed God too.

Love for self rather than for God and others twists all that mankind does. This is the reason that the achievements of human cities—achievements in science, art, politics, and philosophy—all bear the tragic marks of selfishness and pride. Even religion has been twisted. Humans have instead been making a god (or gods) in their own image (Rom. 1:23).

The Fall also twisted the natural world. God had made humans to subdue the earth. But when humans rebelled against God's rule, God changed the earth so that it rebelled against their rule (Gen. 3:17). Though humans were to subdue the earth, each human would in the end be subdued by it. They would return to the ground in death (v. 19).

This curse has affected the growth of human civilization. In a civilization, humans work together to improve their quality of life. To do this they work at changing their natural environment. Farmers till the ground, engineers build roads, and carpenters turn trees into houses. But in a fallen world, nature fights against mankind's attempts at dominion. The ground stops producing food, rain causes flooding, and tornadoes destroy houses. And one by one every farmer, engineer, and carpenter is taken away by death. The task of the Creation Mandate is frustrated by the Fall.

God's Plan for Redemption

In the midst of the tragic account of Adam's sin, God gave hope to the human race. While pronouncing His curse on Satan, God briefly showed His plan for redeeming this world: "I will put enmity between thee [Satan] and the woman, and between thy seed and her seed; it shall bruise thy head, and thou shalt bruise his heel" (Gen. 3:15). The human race had chosen its own destruction. But only moments after confronting the first sin, God revealed that those made in His image would have the hope of victory.

Genesis 3:15 is the thesis statement for all human history. Mankind had been called to have dominion over God's world. But now the human race would be divided into the **seed of the serpent** and the **seed of the woman**. God predicted that these two seeds would be in conflict. Each would attempt to exercise dominion according to its own core values. Through the long centuries ahead, Satan's seed (the seed of the serpent) would harm God's people (the seed of the woman) many times. But in the end, God would give victory to His people.

The Earliest Human History

The earliest history of civilization is found in Genesis 4–11. If you read these chapters carefully, you see the beginnings of civilization occurring. Cain, one of Adam and Eve's sons, moved to the land of Nod. There he became the father of a group of people who were possibly the first to live in civilization. The first city mentioned in the Bible was built by Cain (Gen. 4:17). The division of labor that is always part of city life was carried on by Cain's descendants. Jabal worked in agriculture as a herdsman. Jubal labored in the arts, making musical instruments. And Tubal-Cain worked in industry, producing tools.

Civilization was happening. But it was a civilization twisted by the Fall. Cain was a religious man, but he wanted to worship God on his own terms. In anger over God's rejection of his sacrifice, he killed his brother Abel. His civilization was built away from the presence of the Lord. It was civilization apart from God. It was the first example of the seed of the serpent harming the seed of the woman.

The seed of the woman, those loyal to God, was at first maintained in the line of Seth, another of Adam and Eve's sons. But the Sethites did not remain true to God. Even righteous people die. Therefore, a godly culture cannot remain godly unless it passes on its love for God to each new generation. At some point in their history, the Sethites allowed their children to marry Cainites (Gen. 6:2). Eventually the Sethites were no different from the Cainites (6:5).

Grieved by the great sinfulness of the human race, God determined to judge His world. He would cover the whole earth with a great flood. But God chose to show favor to one member of the Sethite line (Gen. 6:8). God instructed Noah to build a massive ark. Noah was to take his family and representatives of the animal kingdom into the ark, where they would be safe. God held back His judgment for 120 years (Gen. 6:3). But in the end Noah, his wife, his three sons, and their wives were the only people to enter the ark. Then the "fountains of the great deep" were broken up, and rain fell (7:11). Eventually the entire earth was under water. The Creator had caused the earth to return to its original state: once again it was "without form, and void" (1:2).

The Rise of Nations

After the Flood, God repeated the Creation Mandate to Noah and his descendants (Gen. 9:1-7). But instead of spreading out to fill the earth and subdue it, humans gathered to build a great tower (Babel). They were going to build a civilization on their own terms. Fallen man could use civilization-building abilities God gave him for evil. God chose to restrain mankind's ability to do evil by confusing the people's languages. Unable to communicate and work together, the people were forced to scatter and fill the earth.

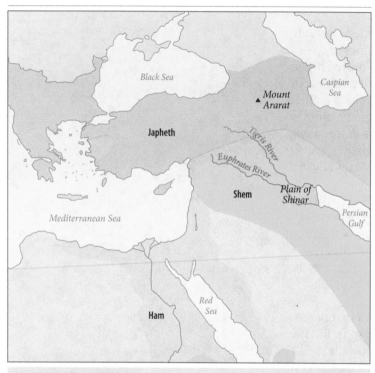

The Post-Flood World

The human race reorganized itself into groups of people who spoke the same language. It was during this period that the first nations developed. A **nation** is a very large group of people (usually including many cities) who share the same language, family history, land area, and culture.

The nations of this ancient time were different from modern nations. Only a few of them became **nation-states**, nations having their own governments, independent of other nations. Most of these early nations were composed of many **city-states**, cities that had their own governments, independent of those of other cities (even those within their own nation). Genesis 10 is often called the **Table of Nations** because it lists the descendants of Shem, Ham, and Japheth according to the nations that arose from their families. Japheth's descendants developed nations in eastern Europe and modern-day Turkey. Ham's descendants developed nations in eastern Asia and Africa. In particular, Ham's son Canaan settled along the eastern end of the Mediterranean Sea. Shem's descendants formed nations to the east and north of Ham's descendants.

Section Review Questions

1. How does God's work of creation show divine sovereignty?
2. Why is the Creation Mandate important for the study of human civilization?
3. Why is Genesis 3:15 important for the study of world history?
✶ How does the Fall affect human efforts to develop civilizations?
✶ Was God's confusing of the languages at Babel a judgment, a mercy, or both? Why?

■ II. The History of Israel

After the fall of Babel, many nations prospered in Asia, Africa, and Europe. These nations built impressive civilizations, and their accomplishments fill books about ancient history. But all these nations attempted to fulfill the Creation Mandate in a sinful way. God, however, had a plan to set the world right again. A key part of His plan was to raise up a new nation.

God's Covenant with Abraham

Abraham, born around 2166 BC, was a descendant of Shem (Gen. 11:27–32). He grew up in Mesopotamia. Like everyone else in his culture, Abraham initially practiced **polytheism** (PAHL ee thee IZ um), the belief that there are many gods (see Josh. 24:2). But when he was about seventy-five, Yahweh appeared to him and told him to leave all this behind and move to the land of Canaan. Abraham became a believer in the one true God.

Following his conversion, about 2091 BC, God made a covenant (a solemn agreement) with Abraham (Gen. 12:1–7). At the core

Guiding Questions

1. How do the Abrahamic, Mosaic, Davidic, and New Covenants restore the promises of the Creation Mandate?
2. How do the Abrahamic, Mosaic, Davidic, and New Covenants advance the promise of redemption given in Genesis 3:15?

of this covenant were promises of a seed, a land, and a universal blessing. <u>First</u>, Yahweh said He would give Abraham a group of descendants who would become a great nation. Abraham and his seed would be fruitful and multiply. <u>Second</u>, He said that this nation would possess the land of Canaan. Abraham's seed would have a part of the earth to subdue for God's glory. <u>Third</u>, Jehovah promised that Abraham's seed would bring a blessing to all the nations of the earth.

This covenant is often called the **Abrahamic Covenant**. Though very brief, it revealed God's plan to redeem humans. God intended Abraham's seed to be the seed of the woman. And God reaffirmed that humans would continue to have dominion.

Covenants	
List the provisions of each covenant.	

Covenant	Provisions
Abrahamic	
Mosaic	
Davidic	
New	

The Mosaic Covenant

God did turn Abraham's seed into a great nation. But this nation grew up as slaves in Egypt. God's promises of many descendants were coming true, but God would have to rescue the slaves from Egypt in order to fulfill the land promise as well. So God freed Israel from Egypt in 1446 BC.

But the Israelites did not go immediately to Canaan. God directed them to camp at Mount Sinai. There Yahweh established a covenant, often called the **Mosaic Covenant**. At the center of this covenant were the **Ten Commandments** (Exod. 20:1–17), ten laws showing Israel how to love God and other humans. The first of these commands demanded **monotheism** (MAHN uh thee IZ um), the belief in one God. Unlike the other nations, Israel was to worship only one God, Jehovah. From these central commands flowed many other commands about good government and proper behavior.

Mount Sinai

These commands were to guide Israel in exercising good and wise dominion over the land that God promised Israel. If Israel obeyed these commands, God would bless them in the land. Israel would also bless the other nations by keeping God's commands. The other nations of the world would see how wise God is when they saw Israel living in the land according to God's commands. The nations would be drawn to worship God.

The Mosaic Covenant was a way of moving God's promises in the Abrahamic Covenant forward. But the Mosaic Covenant was also different from the Abrahamic Covenant. The covenant with Abraham had no conditions. It was a gracious promise to bless Abraham and the whole world. But the covenant through Moses contained a huge condition: Israel must obey God's laws or be cursed and exiled from the land (Deut. 27–28).

Rise and Fall of Israel's Kingdom

Repeatedly, Israel disobeyed the covenant they had promised to obey. This disobedience began in the wilderness when Moses tried to lead the people into the land (Num. 14), and it continued through the days of the judges. There were some bright moments under the leadership of Joshua and some of the judges, but this struggle with God continued until God raised up David.

David, a descendant of Jacob through his son Judah, was Israel's greatest king. During his reign (1010–970 BC), he defeated Israel's enemies and extended his rule to the Euphrates River. In the middle of this reign, Jehovah made a covenant with David (2 Sam. 7:1–17). God promised that his dynasty (a line of rulers from one family) would last forever.

This covenant, called the **Davidic Covenant**, is very important to world history. It revealed that David's descendants would play a key role fulfilling the three promises of the Abrahamic Covenant (as well as the promise of Genesis 3:15). David himself understood this, and he wrote about this covenant in many of his psalms. In some of these psalms, David speaks of a particular descendant who would be great and rule over the entire world (see Pss. 2, 22, 45, 89, 110). The Israelites referred to this great son of David as the **Messiah** ("the anointed one").

These psalms reveal that the Davidic Messiah will not only rule Israel. He will rule over all the nations. He will bring justice to the earth (cf. Isa. 42:1-4). He will be the mighty king who leads humans to exercise dominion just as God has intended from the beginning.

The Davidic Covenant promised a glorious future for Israel (and for all the world), but it did not remove the curses of the Mosaic Covenant. Those curses were fulfilled in stages as David's descendants disobeyed the law of Moses. The final judgment came in 586 BC. In that year the Babylonians destroyed Jerusalem (the capital city) and took many people captive.

The New Covenant

Exile and judgment were not God's last words. Through Jeremiah, God promised to make a **New Covenant** with His people (Jer. 31:31–34). This covenant would be different from the Mosaic Covenant. It was God's promise to put His rules in the hearts of His people so that they would want to obey. Ezekiel told the people that it would be the gift of the Holy Spirit that would make this possible (Ezek. 36:27). Also in this covenant, Jehovah promised to forgive the sins of His people.

After Israel had spent seventy years in Babylon, God moved the heart of Cyrus, the Persian king who had conquered the Babylonians. He released the captives, and many of God's people returned and began rebuilding Jerusalem. Out of the ashes of God's judgment, a new nation began to emerge.

Section Review Questions

1. What were the three main promises in the Abrahamic Covenant?

2. What do we call the laws at the center of the Mosaic Covenant? What did these laws show?

3. What did God promise in the Davidic Covenant? Why is this promise important to human history?

4. What did God promise to do for His people in the New Covenant?

★ How do the three main promises of the Abrahamic Covenant correspond to the Creation Mandate?

■ III. The Coming of the Christ

God's people returned to their land at the end of the 500s BC. The next several centuries were filled with upheaval. In 333 BC Alexander the Great defeated the Persians and began to establish the Greek Empire. Then the Romans rose to power. In the 200s BC, they defeated the Greeks, and in 63 BC they took over Judea (one of the names for what had been Israel). The Jews (a name for Israelites living in Judea) longed to be set free.

Guiding Questions

1. How did the life and ministry of Christ fulfill Old Testament prophecies of a coming kingdom?
2. Where did Christianity spread after Pentecost?

Jesus of Nazareth

After centuries of predicting the coming of a great Savior, God raised up the Man who would prove to be the most important human who has ever lived, **Jesus of Nazareth**. When Jesus was about thirty, He began to travel throughout Judea preaching and healing people. The main point of His preaching was the bold statement, "The kingdom of God is at hand." As a result, people needed to repent and believe the good news that Jesus announced (Mark 1:15).

Bethlehem

The kingdom that Jesus announced was the one that God had promised to David's seed. In that kingdom the King would right all the wrongs in the earth. He would stamp out all injustice. He would finally set up a civilization in which the earth is ruled by image bearers of God who subdue the earth in wisdom (see Daniel 7). Jesus, as King, would bring about the world promised to Adam, Abraham, Moses, and David.

But this good news is bad news to sinners. Sinners are the ones who make things wrong in the world. They are the ones who do injustice. They are the ones who twist the Creation Mandate. And everybody is a sinner (Rom. 3:23).

For the announcement of the kingdom of God to become good news, the sin problem had to be dealt with. The seed of the woman had to crush the head of the serpent. And God's judgment for sin had to be satisfied. God's plan called for Jesus, the victorious King, to also be the suffering Savior. Around AD 30, the Jewish religious leaders brought Him before the Roman governor, Pontius Pilate. They said that since He claimed to be the **Christ**, the King of the Jews, He was opposing the Roman authorities. Pilate then sentenced Jesus to die by crucifixion.

Jesus told His disciples the night before it happened that the shedding of His blood would mark the beginning of the New Covenant (Luke 22:20). Without the death of Jesus, repenting and believing would be useless. The heel of the woman's seed had to be bruised if the serpent—along with all his evil—was to be crushed.

Three days after Jesus' death, His tomb was empty. When His followers came to the tomb on the third day, they were confronted by an angel who told them good news: "He is not here: for he is risen" (Matt. 28:6).

The death and resurrection of Jesus Christ mark the most important turning point in history. Prior to this event, the nations of the earth were descending deeper and deeper into sin. But now there was hope. God had sent His own Son to live a sinless life, die in the place of sinful humans, and rise again so that death might be

There is no way to know whether this is the tomb in which Jesus was buried. This site does, however, fit the description given in the New Testament.

Themes in World History

Citizenship was important in ancient Rome. Possession of Rome citizenship gave people special rights. Paul used his citizenship to help him spread the gospel in the Roman Empire.

defeated. This is the **gospel** in its fullness—that Jesus has died for the sins of humans and has been raised again to save them forever (see 1 Cor. 15:1, 3–4). All who repent and believe this gospel enter God's kingdom; those who reject Jesus will one day be judged by Him.

The Early Spread of Christianity

"All power is given unto me in heaven and in earth. Go ye therefore, and teach all nations" (Matt. 28:18–19). With these words, Jesus told His disciples to tell all nations about the gospel. The kingdom of God was not for Jews only. It was for all people. The Christ—the seed of the woman, Abraham's seed, David's great descendant—had conquered sin and death. It was now time to bless all the nations with this good news.

Ten days after Jesus ascended to heaven, during the Jewish Feast of Pentecost, He gave the Holy Spirit to His people, just as was promised in the New Covenant (Acts 2). Through the work of the Spirit, thousands believed the gospel. Once they believed, they too received the Holy Spirit. The Christian church was born.

As the Christian church grew, so did opposition from **Judaism** (the religion of the Jews, distinct from Christianity). An early leader of this opposition was **Saul of Tarsus**. Saul showed great zeal in attempting to wipe out the church. But one day, while traveling to persecute Christians, he was confronted by Jesus personally (Acts 9:3–6). Saul then believed the gospel and began preaching that Jesus was the Christ. Many Jews were offended by these teachings. But great numbers of Gentiles believed Paul. These Gentiles abandoned their polytheism and became Christians. Paul spread Christianity in Asia Minor, Greece, Rome, and perhaps even Spain. By the time Paul died (c. AD 67), Christianity was well established in many major cities of the Roman Empire.

Around this time, another event took place that propelled Christianity forward. In AD 66 the Jews rebelled against the Romans. Rome sent a large number of troops to stop the rebellion. In AD 70 the Roman soldiers broke through Jerusalem's defenses, destroyed the city, and burned the temple. The Jews were then expelled from Jerusalem and from their homeland.

This tragic event actually helped the spread of Christianity. First, it ended the persecution of Christians from Judaism. This religion no longer had authority to harm Christians. Second, it drove Christians out of Judea. The church at Jerusalem had become huge. Those believers were now scattered throughout the empire.

Later Growth in the Ancient World

In the years following AD 70, the Christian church experienced amazing growth in and beyond the Roman Empire. This growth occurred even though the church faced opposition.

Roman Persecutions

At first, Roman authorities were not bothered by Christianity. As it grew, however, they worried that the Christian belief that Jesus was Lord was at odds with the Roman state. Roman officials accused Christians of not being loyal to the empire.

The first official Roman persecution of Christianity began under the emperor **Nero** (NEE roh; r. AD 54–68). He blamed the Christians for a great fire that swept through Rome in AD 64. The Roman historian Tacitus recorded many of the violent ways in which Christians were killed, including dipping them in tar and using them as human torches.

From Nero until AD 250, the persecution of Christians was sporadic and limited to small areas. But beginning in 250, persecution spread empire-wide.

The last and most widespread persecution happened during the reign of **Diocletian** (dy uh KLEE shun; r. AD 284–305). In decree after decree, he dismissed Christians from the army, ordered the destruction of church buildings, and had copies of the Bible burned. Later, it was decreed that all Christians would have to offer sacrifices to pagan gods or be tortured and killed.

The Romans hoped that these persecutions would put an end to Christianity. But Jesus Christ, the Lord of the earth, was on the side of His church. He had given His followers the Holy Spirit to give them strength and wisdom. He had also promised them the same victory over death that He had experienced. Some people did leave the Christian church because of the persecution. But, with few exceptions, the true followers of Jesus remained faithful. Christianity was purified through this opposition, not destroyed.

Christianity Spreads East

The persecution in Rome pushed some Christians beyond the boundaries of the empire. It seems that some Christians, especially Jewish Christians, moved east to Edessa in Persia. The Persian Empire stretched from Rome's eastern border all the way to what is today Afghanistan. Beginning in the first century, Christians began to take the gospel to the major Persian cities. Christians did not initially face persecution in Persia. Some local rulers may have even become Christian. Sea trade in the Persian Gulf and Indian Ocean allowed Christianity to spread to the coasts of Arabia and probably to India as well.

However, the Christian church in Persia had to struggle with heresies. The heresy of Manicheanism started in Persia and then moved west into Rome. Then, from the 270s to the 290s, a Persian monarch began the first persecution of Christians in Persia.

Roman Acceptance

The situation changed dramatically when, in 312, the Roman emperor **Constantine** (KAHN stun teen; r. 306–337) converted to Christianity. The next year, in 313, he issued the **Edict of Milan**, which put an end to almost three hundred years of persecution. Many have questioned whether Constantine's conversion was sincere. What is not questioned, however, is that his acceptance of Christianity changed history. Rome now protected and helped the church. Constantine gave back property that had been taken from Christians. He made Sunday a legal holiday. He gave money for new church buildings, and he encouraged people throughout the empire to become Christians.

The emperor even became involved in controversies within the church. When a church teacher named **Arius** (EHR ee us) claimed that Jesus was not God, Constantine stepped in and organized a council of church leaders. In 325 the **Council of Nicaea** (ny SEE uh) met to consider the deity of Christ. The council concluded that Jesus was God. They also affirmed the doctrine of the Trinity—the

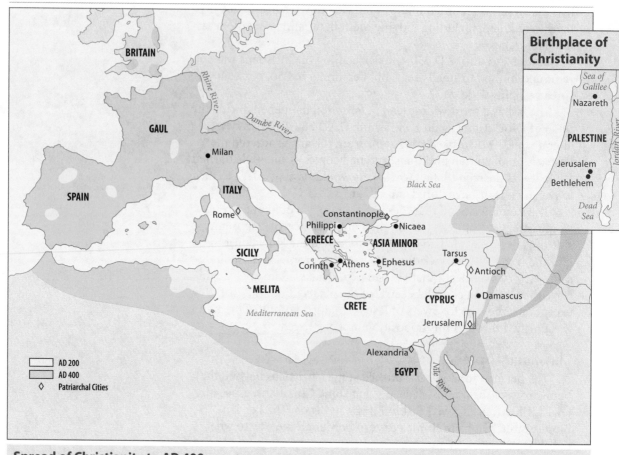

Spread of Christianity to AD 400

teaching that there is only one God, but He exists in three distinct persons: the Father, the Son, and the Holy Spirit.

As Constantine and his successors became more involved in supporting churches, Christianity gained more favor and power in the Roman world. At the end of the 300s, the emperor **Theodosius** I (THEE uh DOH shis; r. 379–395) made it the only recognized religion in the empire. All other religions were considered illegal.

As a result of the freedom and privileges granted by the Roman government, church congregations grew rapidly in numbers. But this favor also led to a swift decline in the purity of many church members. Some people truly believed the gospel. But others simply wanted to enjoy the favor that church membership granted. Such "Christians" brought with them many of their pagan beliefs and practices. For this reason, many churches soon began to look like the pagan religions that had once filled the Roman world.

STOP

Christianity Spreads East, South, and West

Constantine's support enabled Christians in the Roman Empire to practice Christianity without persecution. But Persia, an enemy of Rome, responded by increasing the persecution of Christians under Sassanid rule. They now saw Rome as Christian. So Christians were now a foreign threat. Persia did, however, accept Christians who were considered heretics in the Roman Empire. Some of these Christians taught that Jesus has divinity and humanity united into a single nature. The Coptic Church, for example, taught this. But orthodox Christians said this made Jesus not fully divine and fully human but something unique. Others, such as the **Nestorians,** taught that Jesus was both God and human but was not a single person.

Nestorians and Copts grew to be powerful in the east. By the seventh century, the Nestorians had sent missionaries into China. The Copts, who were most powerful in Egypt, sent missionaries south along the Nile River to establish churches in Nubia and Aksum (Ethiopia). The king of Aksum, Ezana, became a Coptic Christian. The Coptic church remains the official church of Ethiopia today.

In the far west, Christianity spread beyond the Roman Empire through men such as **Patrick**. Born in Britain in the late 300s, Patrick was captured by pirates and taken to Ireland as a prisoner when he was about sixteen. He later escaped back to Britain, where he became a Christian. Around 432 he returned to Ireland and served there as a missionary. Through his work, thousands were converted, and the Christian church not only thrived there but also began sending missionaries to other regions. Several Irish monks traveled to various parts of Europe during the 500s and 600s. Their goal was to spread Christianity to such groups as the Picts and Franks. Although records are scarce, it seems that Christianity continued to spread beyond the Roman Empire.

The Sassanid Persian Empire

Christianity and the Decline of the Empire

Christianity continued to grow even as the Roman Empire continued to decline. For years the empire had struggled with political turmoil, high taxes, and problems along its borders. By the time Constantine came to the throne, the empire was in a crisis. Constantine attempted to bring renewal by moving the capital from Rome to the ancient Greek city of Byzantium. He renamed the city New Rome. The people called it **Constantinople** ("Constantine's City").

The western part of the empire deteriorated as it was invaded by wave after wave of **barbarians** (a Roman name for peoples not part of Greek or Roman culture). In 395 Theodosius I declared that the empire was now two separate empires. The western portion became known as the Roman Empire, and the eastern portion became the **Byzantine Empire**.

Cut off from the stronger, more secure Byzantine Empire, the Roman Empire was easy prey for the barbarians. In 410 the city of Rome was plundered. Though the empire had been in serious decline for more than a century, its citizens—Christians included—were shocked. As the empire fell apart, many pagans blamed the rise of Christianity for the decline of Rome.

Constantinople

15

Augustine (354–430), a Christian leader in Hippo, North Africa, responded by writing *The City of God*. In this book he laid out a Christian view of history. He said that history is the story of two cities with two opposing ways of life. The earthly city is the home of sinful men. The heavenly city, however, is the city of God, filled with those who have turned away from evil. These two cities exist side by side in this world, but at the final judgment, God will separate them. Citizens of the heavenly city will enjoy eternal life, while the earthly city will perish. Augustine concluded that Christians should not fear Rome's fall. Empires come and go, but God's city is forever.

Rome's decline continued as barbarian tribes reached deep into the empire. Finally, in 476, a barbarian general claimed the emperor's throne. The Roman Empire had officially ended. But just as the destruction of Jerusalem contributed to the growth of the Christian church, so also the fall of Rome helped spread Christianity. In time, many influential barbarians converted and Christianity continued to spread throughout these new cultures. These cultures became the foundation of Medieval Europe.

Conclusion

With the coming of God's Christ, the doors to the kingdom of God were thrown open to all the peoples of the earth. Millions crowded into this kingdom by repenting of sin and believing the gospel. Nevertheless, there were many problems. Persecutions attacked the church from the outside, and insincere Christians threatened it from the inside. But God would not fail to keep His promise of giving the seed of the woman victory and eternal life.

From the time of Christ onward, Christianity began to spread to all corners of the earth. Wherever it went, it challenged the civilizations twisted by the Fall. It testified to the present and future kingdom that would see God's purposes brought to fulfillment. Empires would rise and fall, but Jesus, the King of kings, would never abandon His throne.

Section Review Questions

1. What is the gospel?

2. Name three causes of the early spread of Christianity.

3. What group sent missionaries into China by the seventh century?

★ How did Constantine's acceptance of Christianity affect Christians in Rome and Persia?

★ What did Jesus mean when He said, "The kingdom of God is at hand: repent ye, and believe the gospel" (Mark 1:15)?

Making Connections

1. Why have all human societies been religious in some way?

2. How has the Fall damaged human religion?

3. Explain how Genesis 3:15 tells the story of human history.

4. How were the Abrahamic and Mosaic Covenants similar? How were they different?

5. How did Christ fulfill the Creation Mandate in His coming?

6. Why is Jesus of Nazareth the most important human in world history?

7. How did the favor of the Roman government change the Christian church?

Developing History Skills

1. Scan through the chapter, writing on a separate piece of paper each date mentioned. Place these dates on a timeline and label the significance of each date. What does this timeline suggest about the character of Jehovah?

2. In Paul's sermon in Acts 17, he says that God has scattered the nations and set boundaries for them, boundaries of time and place. Paul then states that God has done this so that the nations might "seek the Lord" (v. 27). Review the main events of this chapter. Explain what these boundaries did that could lead people to seek the Lord.

Thinking Critically

1. Suppose the United States were invaded by another nation, and many of your friends were fearful that Christianity would be destroyed. What would you say to reassure your friends?

2. Evaluate this statement: "The Christian church poisons everything it touches. It caused the fall of the Roman Empire. Before the empire embraced Christianity (AD 313), the empire was strong. After this, however, the empire declined and fell."

Living in God's World

1. Study Genesis 6:1–7 in the light of this chapter's presentation of world history. Prepare a brief Sunday school lesson on what these verses teach a Christian about dating and marriage.

2. Go online or use an encyclopedia to study the history and culture of a particular nation. From that research, write a brief report on the core values that have held that nation together throughout its history.

People, Places, and Things to Know

Yahweh
divine sovereignty
image of God
Creation Mandate
civilization
culture
city
seed of the serpent
seed of the woman
nation
nation-states
city-states
Table of Nations
polytheism
Abrahamic Covenant
Mosaic Covenant
Ten Commandments
monotheism
Davidic Covenant
Messiah
New Covenant
Jesus of Nazareth
Christ
gospel
Judaism
Saul of Tarsus
Nero
Diocletian
Constantine
Edict of Milan
Arius
Council of Nicaea
Theodosius I
Nestorians
Patrick
Constantinople
barbarians
Byzantine Empire
Augustine

CHAPTER 2

The Rise of Islam
622 – 800

- The Origin of Islam
- The Spread of Islam
- The Culture of Islam
- The Confrontation with Islam

500 – 950

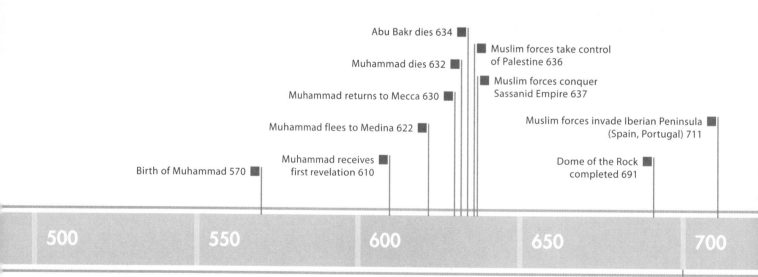

Abu Bakr dies 634

Muslim forces take control of Palestine 636

Muhammad dies 632

Muslim forces conquer Sassanid Empire 637

Muhammad returns to Mecca 630

Muhammad flees to Medina 622

Muslim forces invade Iberian Peninsula (Spain, Portugal) 711

Muhammad receives first revelation 610

Birth of Muhammad 570

Dome of the Rock completed 691

| 500 | 550 | 600 | 650 | 700 |

Golden Age of Islam

Big Ideas

1. Where did Islam originate and spread?
2. How did the Byzantine state respond to the expansion of Islam?
3. What were the major contributions of the Abbasid caliphate?
4. What were the consequences of Charles Martel's victory over the Muslim army in 732?

While the Roman Empire in the west declined and collapsed, the Eastern Roman (**Byzantine**) Empire thrived. In addition, a revived Persian (**Sassanid**) empire prospered. These kingdoms fought against each other for the next two centuries and were left severely weakened. The people living there, weary of the wars and the heavy taxes, were not loyal to either side. The potential for dramatic change was great.

The Arabian Peninsula gained importance during this time period. Because piracy and frequent wars hindered trade along the Red Sea, merchants began to transport goods by camel caravan along the western side of the peninsula. This increase in land trade brought great wealth to cities such as Mecca. It also provided a means for the rapid spread of ideas.

■ Muslim forces defeated at Battle of Tours in France 732

■ Abbasid dynasty begins 750

| 750 | 800 | 850 | 900 | 950 |

Ka'bah

The Ka'bah is a stone building in Mecca that was used for pagan rituals. The original structure existed long before Muhammad's time. The Arabs worshiped hundreds of gods prior to the rise of Islam. Many of these gods were stored in the Ka'bah. Today the Ka'bah is about forty-three feet high with sides measuring thirty-six feet by forty-two feet. A black stone is set in the eastern corner of the structure. (Some people believe this stone is a meteorite.) The outside of the Ka'bah is covered by a black curtain made of silk and embroidered with gold. Muslims are required to walk around this structure seven times (in the morning and the evening) as part of their pilgrimage to Mecca.

■ I. The Origin of Islam

Life of Muhammad

Birth and Early Life

Muhammad (moo HAHM ahd) was born in **Mecca** in 570 as a member of the Quraysh tribe. This tribe was responsible for care of the **Ka'bah** (KAH buh). Muhammad's father died before his birth, and his mother died when he was six years old. His uncle cared for him and took him on commercial trips to Syria. As a young man he became a merchant and led caravans across Arabia in behalf of a wealthy widow. They married and had several children.

His travels brought him into contact with many religions, including Judaism and forms of Christianity. Muhammad used his acquaintance with these religions to form a new faith.

Visions

At the age of 40, during the month of **Ramadan** (rahm uh DAHN), Muhammad claimed to have had a vision in which the angel Gabriel gave him revelations. He memorized the content of this and other visions. Muslim historians teach that the revelations were later written down by his followers and combined in a work known as the **Qur'an** (ku-RAHN; "recitations"). Muhammad rejected polytheism and began to teach that there was only one god (in the first chapter you learned that this practice is known as monotheism). He declared the name of this god to be **Allah** (ALL uh), which is an Arabic word meaning "the god." Muhammad began to speak out against the evils practiced by the people of Mecca. He rebuked them for their practice of polytheism and other vices. At this time the Ka'bah contained many idols and helped to bring a measure of unity to the Arab tribes. Muhammad's message threatened this unity and the prosperity that resulted from Mecca's religious importance. He gained a small following but also faced strong opposition from his own tribe (Quraysh) and was forced to flee from Mecca in 622.

Flight to Medina

Muhammad and a small group of followers traveled to an oasis called **Medina** (mih DEE nuh). This move to Medina became known as the **Hegira** (hih JIE ruh; "flight"). (This event would later mark the beginning of Islam.) Medina was north of Mecca and was occupied by a group of Arab warriors. Three clans of Jews also lived and grew profitable crops there. The Arabs soon accepted Muhammad's teachings and submitted to his leadership. The Jews initially welcomed Muhammad's teaching about monotheism. However, they soon rejected many of his other teachings that contradicted the Old Testament text. Muhammad quickly changed from being friendly toward the Jews to oppressing them. He expanded his influence and increased his following among Arab tribes by raiding passing caravans. Muhammad took the treasures from these caravans and divided them with his growing army. These attacks also served to punish the merchants of Mecca for their rejection of his teachings. During this time he began to develop the beliefs of this new religion that would be called **Islam** (is LAHM; "submission"). The Five Pillars of Islam comprised the core of these beliefs (see below).

Return to Mecca

The attacks on caravans led the people of Mecca to send a force against Muhammad. His army was outnumbered but prevailed in the **Battle of Badr**. Muhammad saw this victory as divine approval of his religious teachings. By 630 he had gathered an army of ten thousand and gained control of Mecca with little resistance. He removed the idols from the Ka'bah and established monotheism. Muhammad forced the people of Mecca to accept Islam and submit to his leadership. He continued his conquest of the Arabian Peninsula until his death in 632.

Early Successors and Divisions

When Muhammad died, some **Muslims** (followers of Islam) chose Abu Bakr, one of Muhammad's first converts, to lead the movement. He took the title of **caliph** (KAY lif; from an Arab word meaning "to succeed"). However, many of the Arab tribes decided that their loyalty to Islam ended when Muhammad died. They sought political and religious independence. This breach led to conflicts that became known as the **Wars of Apostasy**. Abu Bakr's forces defeated all who sought independence. He maintained political and religious unity by military force. Bakr and his successors also sent Arab forces to attack areas of the Sassanid Empire to distract the Muslim soldiers from possible rebellion. These attacks revealed the weakness of the Sassanids and led to a conquest of their territories.

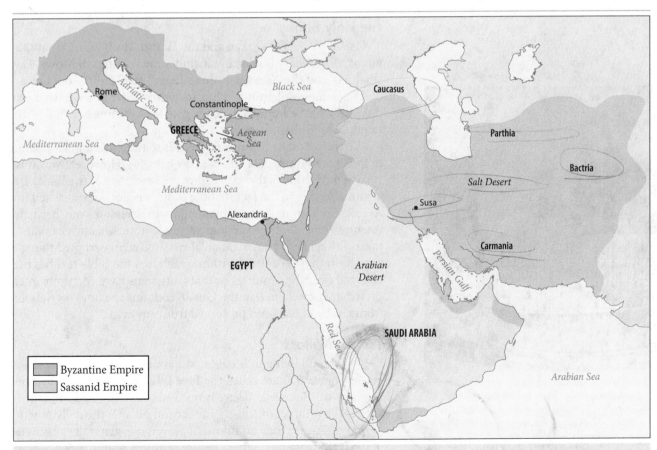

Byzantine and Sassanid Empires

Uthmann, the third caliph, was killed by his own troops in 656 during a dispute. His army chose Ali, a cousin of Muhammad, as the next caliph. This led to a split that resulted in the two major groups in Islam: **Shiite** ("follower") and **Sunni** ("adherent"). The Shiites believe that Muhammad intended Ali, his cousin (and son-in-law), to be his successor. They insist that he retained Muhammad's political and spiritual authority. The Shiites refer to their leader as **imam** (ih MAHM) rather than caliph. The Sunnis believe that Muhammad did not appoint a successor. Instead, they believe that any worthy Muslim could be selected to lead Islam. The Sunnis refer to their political leader as caliph and their spiritual leader as imam.

Teachings of Islam

The Qur'an

Muslim scholars use Sura 7:157 to prove that Muhammad could neither read nor write. They claim that his teachings had been recited and memorized by his closest supporters. Muslim historians credit Abu Bakr and other early Muslim leaders with collecting these oral teachings and composing the Qur'an. Whether these claims are accurate or not cannot be proven. However, several versions of the Qur'an did appear among the Arab tribes. Some contained significant differences. Uthmann became caliph in 644 and collected the different versions of the Qur'an. According to tradition, he then produced an edited version that would become the official text of Muhammad's recitations. All other versions were burned. Some believe that Uthmann's text excluded distinctly Shia teachings. This may have played a part in his death.

The Holy Books

Islam places the Qur'an and the **Hadith** (huh DEETH) at the top of a list of holy books that includes the writings of Moses, David (Psalms), and the "Gospel given to Jesus." The Hadith contains a description of Muhammad's life, including what he said, what he did, and what he approved. A key goal for Muslims is to follow the example of Muhammad's life.

There are many positive references to the Bible and its teachings in the Qur'an (Sura 5:44, 46, 68; 10:94; 29:46). However, Muslims believe many things that contradict the teachings of the Bible. This is probably due to the fact that the Bible was not yet translated into Arabic. Muhammad was dependent on oral versions of Christian teaching. Not all of the versions were accurate. Muslims explain these differences by saying that Christians have corrupted the revelation they received. Muslims teach that the Bible text has been changed over the centuries or that Christians have corruptly interpreted it. They claim that the Qur'an contains the final revelation from God and has been preserved from any error.

The Five Pillars

While still living in Medina, Muhammad developed the five requirements that are called the **Five Pillars** of Islam. The first pillar is repeating the creed, "There is no God but Allah, and Muhammad is the prophet of Allah." The second pillar is the daily practice of prayer. Rather than an informal prayer, it is generally a recitation of passages from the Qur'an. Before Muslims pray, they engage in a thorough ritual cleansing. The third pillar is almsgiving. Muslims

---

The "Unlettered Prophet"

He said, "My chastisement shall fall on whom I will, and my mercy embraceth all things, and I write it down for those who shall fear me, and pay the alms, and believe in our signs, [and] who shall follow the Apostle, the unlettered Prophet—whom they shall find described with them in the Law and [Gospel]." (Sura 7:156–157)

Dome of the Rock with cleansing fountain in the foreground

Muslims throw seven stones at a wall representing Satan during their pilgrimage.

are required to give a percentage of their wealth to those in need. The fourth pillar is fasting (going without food or drink) during the month of Ramadan (the holy month to Muslims). This fast extends from sunrise to sunset. After sunset, Muslims are allowed to resume normal eating and drinking. The fifth pillar is a pilgrimage or trip to Mecca at least once in a lifetime. Each Muslim must make this journey if he is able to do so. While at Mecca, Muslims are expected to perform several rituals, including throwing seven stones at the devil.

Islamic Law

Sharia (shah REE uh) law developed early in the history of Islam. It is based on four sources: the Qur'an, the Hadith, the consensus of Muslim scholars on what the Qur'an and Hadith teach, and deductions from the previous three sources. These deductions allow sharia to be applied to new situations. Four schools of sharia exist, from relatively liberal to strict. Sharia is considered divine law for Muslims, and it extends to all of life: from what food may be eaten to how marriage and divorce is conducted. It is to be enforced by Muslim states. Sharia promises that Jews and Christians are to be protected minorities under certain restrictions. But sharia demands the death penalty for Muslims who convert to another religion. This has made Christian evangelism difficult in areas controlled by Islam.

Jihad

Jihad (jih HAHD) is a controversial topic because of its current practice by radical Islamists. Some Muslims rightly say that the radicals are violating verses in the Qur'an that restrict violence. However, defining jihad as merely the mental struggle that every Muslim endures in trying to become a good Muslim is not historically accurate. In the Qur'an and other Muslim writings, jihad is clearly a holy war against non-Muslims (see especially Sura 9; Sura 47:4; Hadith 4:55, 125, 161; 9:45). In theory, the Qur'an teaches

The Five Pillars of Islam

Portion of the Saudi flag, which includes the Shahadah in Arabic

① Shahadah
Recitation of the creed

"There is no God but Allah, and Muhammad is the prophet of Allah."

② Salat
Daily practice of prayer

Muslims are called to prayer up to five times a day. Before they recite the Fatiha (Sura 1), they wash their hands, forearms, face, and feet. The also rinse their mouths and clean their nostrils. Their prayers are composed of recitations from the Qur'an.

"In the Name of God, the Compassionate, the Merciful, PRAISE be to God, Lord of the worlds! The compassionate, the merciful! King on the day of reckoning! Thee only do we worship, and to Thee do we cry for help. Guide Thou us on the straight path, The path of those to whom Thou hast been gracious;—with whom thou art not angry, and who go not astray." (Sura 1)

Muslims must pray toward Mecca.

③ Zakat
Almsgiving

Muslim pilgrims during their hajj

Feasting follows fasting during Ramadan.

❹
Sawm
Fasting during the month of Ramadan

❺
Hajj
Pilgrimage to Mecca at least once in a lifetime

Only Muslims are permitted to enter Mecca. This is the holiest city in Islam for at least two reasons. Muhammad was born there. Also, the Ka'bah is located there.

The participants in this pilgrimage perform several rituals including:

- Circling the Ka'bah seven times.
- Running seven times between the two hills of Mecca.
- Traveling to the place where Muhammad is believed to have preached his last sermon.
- Traveling to a village to throw seven stones at a wall said to represent Satan.
- Sacrificing an animal

Then they repeat the first two in reverse order.

The rituals of the Hajj actually predate Islam. They were practiced by Arabs long before the birth of Muhammad.

25

Islam and the Trinity

O ye people of the Book! overstep not bounds in your religion; and of God, speak only truth. The Messiah, Jesus, son of Mary, is only an apostle of God, and his Word which he conveyed into Mary, and a Spirit proceeding from himself. Believe therefore in God and his apostles, and say not, "Three." (there is a Trinity)—Forbear—it will be better for you. God is only one God! Far be it from His glory that He should have a son! . . . whatever is in the Heavens, and . . . the Earth [is His]! And God is a sufficient Guardian. (Sura 4:171)

Islam and Jesus

And when God shall say—"O Jesus, Son of Mary: hast thou said unto mankind—'Take me and my mother as two Gods, beside God?'" He shall say—"Glory be unto Thee! it is not for me to say that which I know to be not the truth; had I said that, verily thou wouldest have known it: Thou knowest what is in me, but I know not what is in Thee; for Thou well knowest things unseen! I spake not to them aught but that which thou didst bid me—'Worship God, my Lord and your Lord.'" (Sura 5:114)

that Muslims are only to fight those who fight against them. (In other words, they are allowed to defend themselves.) However, later developments in Islam required Muslims to fight to preserve Islam in areas where sharia was the supreme law. Muslims were permitted, but not required, to fight for lands not in submission to Islam, but they were not permitted to violate any peace treaties they had made. Jihad is historically significant because Islam spread by conquest. Only in a few areas did Islam take root by another means. This does not mean that people were always forced to convert to Islam by the sword. But once Muslims had gained enough influence in an area, they pressured people to convert to Islam. Many did.

Evaluation of Islam in Light of the Bible

The Trinity

The Qur'an denies the doctrine of the Trinity. But in rejecting this Christian teaching, it refers to the Trinity as the Father, Jesus, and Mary (Sura 5:116). The Bible nowhere teaches that Mary, the mother of Jesus, is God. And even though many through the centuries have honored—even worshiped—Mary, Christians have never claimed that she was part of the Trinity. Though Muhammad claimed to have received the Qur'an from Gabriel (who spoke for Allah), these inaccurate descriptions of Christian beliefs suggest that he received inaccurate information or misunderstood Christian teaching.

The Bible, however, teaches that God is Triune. There is only one God (Isaiah 44:6). But God exists in three Persons. The Father is called God (1 Corinthians 8:6), Jesus Christ is called God (John 1:1), and the Holy Spirit is referred to as God (Acts 5:3–4). Because God is Triune, Christians are instructed to baptize new believers in the name of the Father, the Son, and the Holy Spirit (Matthew 28:19).

Jesus Christ

Islam teaches that Jesus was a prophet and that he taught with authority. However, they deny His deity and death by crucifixion.

Muslims circling the Ka'bah in Mecca

The Qur'an (in Sura 4:171) declares that it is offensive to say that Jesus is God. However, the Bible is clear in such passages as John 10:30, Matthew 14:33, and Mark 2:5–10 that Jesus is God and has the authority to forgive sins. Muslims also deny Christ's death on the cross. They do not believe that any great prophet of God would die such a shameful death (Sura 4:157–159). Yet each of the Gospels details the crucifixion of Jesus (Matthew 27, Mark 15, Luke 23, and John 19). And the New Testament contains many references to the crucifixion of Christ as a historical event.

Cutaway of the Ka'bah

Salvation

Muslims are required to perform the Five Pillars of Islam and model their lives after that of Muhammad. Islam speaks of a day of judgment and each man's works being weighed on a great scale. Those with few good works will not have a chance to enter Paradise (Sura 7:9). However, there is no guarantee that good works will bring salvation. Muslims are taught that Allah predestines them to Paradise or Hell as he pleases. Therefore, no Muslim can have assurance of entering Paradise and escaping Hell.

The Bible teaches that one who trusts in Christ as Savior is saved by God's grace alone (Eph. 2:8–9, Titus 3:5). Those whom God saves live in a manner characterized by good works (Eph. 2:10; Titus 2:11–14; 3:8). In addition, those who trust Christ and are saved by Him have assurance of eternal life with Christ (John 6:40, 47; 10:28).

The Bible

Muslim teaching about the Bible is inconsistent and contradictory. Muhammad taught that Allah had sent many prophets (including Moses and Jesus) to remind man of Allah's teaching (Sura 5:44–48). However, he also taught that the teachings of these prophets had been lost or corrupted (Sura 2:75, 144–146; 3:65–67, 71, 78, 187). It is worth noting that Muslims do not prove that the Bible has been corrupted. They simply quote verses in the Qur'an that make this claim. Even so, the Bible declares its contents to be inspired of God in passages such as 2 Timothy 3:16 and 2 Peter 1:19–21.

Muslims believe that Muhammad was the final spokesman for God. However, the Bible reserves this unique role for Jesus Christ. Passages such as John 1:1–3 and Hebrews 1:1–5 speak of Christ as the Word of God and the ultimate revealer of God. While Islam professes to exalt Jesus as a prophet and representative of God, it rejects Him as the Son of God. Muslims refuse to acknowledge the Christ who is clearly revealed in the Bible.

Section Review Questions

1. What term describes the worship of many gods?
2. What book is based on the teachings of Muhammad and means "recitations"?
3. What does the term *Islam* mean?
★ Explain the difference between Shiite and Sunni Muslims.
★ Make a chart that compares the beliefs of Christianity and Islam on the Trinity, Jesus, salvation, and the Bible.

1. Why were Muslim forces able to conquer Byzantine and Sassanid lands?

2. How did Arab Muslims establish an empire stretching from western Europe to India?

■ II. The Spread of Islam

Conquest of the Arabian Peninsula

Following the Wars of Apostasy when Abu Bakr consolidated his control over Muhammad's followers, the Islamic armies quickly swept over the Arabian Peninsula and claimed it for Islam. This military campaign was a practical move for Bakr and his successors because it kept the various Arab tribes fighting the **infidels** (unbelievers) rather than opposing the caliph or fighting with each other. In addition, it proved to be a strategic move because the Muslim forces encountered little resistance. They were able to rapidly seize large areas and greatly expand the region under Islamic control.

Expansion of Islamic Forces

Conquest of Sassanid and Byzantine Territories

The Islamic armies advanced north and west. They quickly absorbed Egypt, Syria, Palestine, and Iraq. In 637 the Arabs defeated

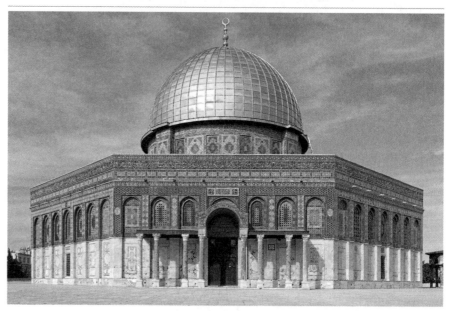

The Dome of the Rock was built in Jerusalem on or near the Jewish temple site. Construction was completed in 691.

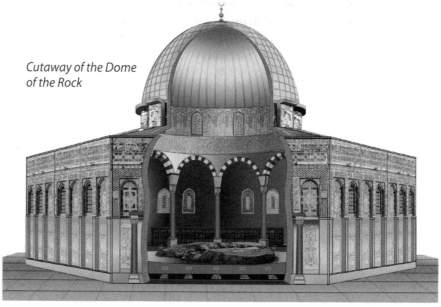

Cutaway of the Dome of the Rock

the Sassanid forces. They were able to topple the Sassanid Empire. They also took large sections of the Byzantine Empire. Muslim forces were able to do this for several reasons. The Sassanid and Byzantine empires had fought over land for almost two hundred years. This had drained both empires of financial and military resources. They also taxed the people heavily. These empires combined many ethnic groups (including Arabs) and tribes with little in common. Many of the people living in these regions were open to change. The Muslim forces appeared to many as liberators. The caliphs also quickly gained support by lowering taxes.

Spread of Islam into Asia and the Mediterranean Region

From 661 to 750 the Muslim Empire continued to gain control of territory. This expansion began after internal conflict led to a new Muslim dynasty known as the **Umayyad** (oo MYE ad) Caliphate (KAL ih fate). This dynasty moved the capital of the Muslim Empire to **Damascus** in Syria. By 732 the Muslims had expanded west across northern Africa and into Europe through modern Spain. By 750 they had conquered additional territory in Southwest Asia to the western border of India.

Islamic Conversions

During the early years, Muslim leaders were often content to allow Christians and other non-Muslims to worship freely. Non-Muslims paid a tax that became a great source of income for the Muslim rulers. Some Islamic rulers even sought to reserve Islam for Arabs. For various reasons, they discouraged others from converting to Islam.

Pressure to convert to Islam developed over time due to various causes. The Crusades provide one example. These campaigns by Europeans were intended to free the Holy Land from Muslim control. Islamic powers reacted by forcing religious groups to convert to Islam. Other threats to Islam had a similar effect.

In addition, under Islam, conversion became a one-way process. Those who converted to Islam were not allowed to return to their previous faith. Also, Muslims were not allowed to convert to Christianity or any other religion. To do so meant abandonment by family and friends, and it often meant death. According to Islamic teaching, those who reject Islam and those who convert to another religion from Islam are condemned to hell.

Early Success of Islam	
Identify causes for Islam's early success.	
Causes	**Effect**
	Islam conquers Byzantine land and Southern Persia

Section Review Questions

1. What term did the Muslims use to describe those who did not accept Islam?

2. Name the two large empires that lost territory or were destroyed by a Muslim invasion.

3. What Muslim dynasty moved the capital of the Muslim Empire to Damascus?

4. Were non-Muslims initially required to convert to Islam? What circumstances led to forced conversions?

★ Explain why the Muslim armies were able to defeat the Sassanid and Byzantine forces so quickly.

Guiding Questions

1. What contributions did the Abbasid dynasty make to mathematics, science, literature, philosophy, and technology?
2. How did Islam win converts among culturally diverse peoples?

■ III. The Culture of Islam

In 750 the Islamic Empire came under new leadership with the defeat of the Umayyads. This dynasty became known as the **Abbasid** (ah BASS id) Caliphate. The capital was moved to **Baghdad** in Iraq. This move reflected a growing influence by Persians on the Muslim Empire. The emphasis of this dynasty shifted from conquest to learning and culture.

Beginning in the eighth century, Islam achieved a golden age. Many non-Muslim scholars who lived under Islamic rule preserved knowledge from earlier civilizations, including Egypt, Rome, and Greece. In addition, they worked with Muslim scholars to develop important advances in science, math, and medicine. Much of this knowledge had been lost in Europe. Baghdad became the intellectual center, and many works of antiquity were initially translated

Historical Perspectives

Bernard Lewis and Rodney Stark are two historians who have written about the early development of Islam. Read the following summaries of their arguments and answer the questions that follow. Keep in mind that neither author is making up facts, but they are arguing for a different conclusion. (Look at the title of each book for a hint.)

Bernard Lewis points out that Islamic civilization, at a certain point in the Middle Ages, was among the most advanced cultures in the world. Islam's military power was clear as it spread east, west, north, and south. It had the most active economy of the time. It had trading relationships with Asia, Europe, and Africa. It adopted the knowledge of Greece and Persia upon conquest, and it imported knowledge from India and China and built upon this knowledge. For instance, it combined Indian numbers with knowledge of mathematics gained from other civilizations. It encouraged additional scientific experiments and added to scientific knowledge. But at some point the advance of scholarship in the Muslim world stopped while that of Europe leaped forward.

Bernard Lewis, *What Went Wrong? Western Impact and Middle Eastern Response* (New York: Oxford University Press, 2002), 3-7

Rodney Stark argues that Islamic culture never was superior to European culture. He says that Muslims learned from the people they conquered. They learned about science, math, shipbuilding, and philosophy this way. He admits that they knew more Greek philosophy than Europeans.

Stark says that Europe was not trapped in the Dark Ages. He points out that Europe had many advances in the Middle Ages. Europeans developed better harnesses. This meant they could use horses for plowing. Horses could also draw wagons. This helped their armies move equipment. They developed better plows and methods of crop rotation. This made Europeans healthier. They wore better armor than the Muslims. For this reason European armies won in the First Crusade and sustained others.

Rodney Stark, *God's Battalions: The Case for the Crusades* (New York: HarperOne, 2009), 56-76.

1. What is Lewis's point?
2. What is Stark's point?
3. How do they select facts to bolster their point of view?

Averroës—Muslim scholar who preserved Aristotle's Greek philosophy into Arabic. Muslim scholarship became a storehouse from which Western scholars would later recover vital information.

Math

Nestorian and Christian groups shared with Muslim scholars knowledge of ancient mathematical learning such as geometry (developed centuries earlier by Euclid). In addition, a Persian mathematician developed algebra during this period. Syriac Christians introduced "Arabic" numbers (1, 2, 3) to the Muslim world.

Science

Scientific Method

Alhazen (al HAY zen) developed an early scientific method based on experiments (empirical method) to prove or disprove a scientific theory. He is also regarded as the Father of Optics for his research on the theory of light. He recorded his findings in his *Book of Optics*.

Medicine

Muslim physicians took the information passed on by Nestorian scholars and made great advances in medicine during this period. Over eight hundred doctors worked in Baghdad, and they discovered important information about anatomy and diseases. One of the best-known doctors during this time was the Persian scientist Avicenna (avih SEN uh). He is regarded as the Father of Modern Medicine for works such as *The Canon of Medicine* and *The Book of Healing*.

Astronomy

Islamic scientists made corrections to the geocentric (JEE oh SEN trik) model (the earth is the center of our solar system); Copernicus later used these studies to develop his heliocentric (HEE lee oh SEN TRIK) theory (the sun is the center of our solar system). They also made improvements on a Greek invention, the astrolabe (AS troh labe; a tool used for solving problems relating to time and the position of the sun and stars). This instrument was later taken to Europe. It was used for such functions as computing the time during the day and night during naval travel.

Chemistry

Muslim scientists laid the foundation of modern chemistry with their experiments and writings. Men like Roger Bacon and Isaac Newton read the works of Arab scientists and were greatly influenced by these works. Muslim scientists discovered chemical processes that included refining of liquids and production of chemicals such as alcohol.

Literature

While Muslim writers composed much literature during this period, the work that is best remembered is *The Book of One Thousand and One Nights* or *Arabian Nights*. This work is a collection of many folk tales told over several centuries. Characters such as Aladdin, Sinbad, and Ali Baba remain popular to this day.

Among their many works, the Persians composed a poetic romance filled with tragedy and eternal love. This work is similar to Shakespeare's *Romeo and Juliet*.

Astrolabe

Philosophy

Islamic philosophy was not limited to religious issues. It was also not restricted to Muslims. Rather, it could be described as a type of philosophy that occurred in the Muslim Empire. The Muslims gained access to the teachings of Aristotle, Plato, and others from groups such as the Nestorians and Byzantines during this period. The works of these philosophers were debated and interpreted. Perhaps the key Muslim contribution to philosophy was helping to preserve the writings of these Greek philosophers and other Greek manuscripts.

Technology

Papermaking and Other Chinese Technologies

Muslims learned from the Chinese how to make paper. They improved the process by inventing mills to make the paper. Several centuries would pass before Europe would learn of this process.

Muslim contact with China also led to knowledge of gunpowder. Muslim scientists refined the mixture and developed a much more powerful form of gunpowder.

Farming

The Muslim world made great improvements in farming by effective use of irrigation. They also developed the windmill to pump water out of the ground. This invention led to the increased production of crops such as almonds, sugar cane, and citrus fruit. These goods were later exported to Europe and brought great wealth to the empire.

Engineering

Muslim engineers learned how to use water, wind, steam, and oil to produce power. They used this energy to power such devices as paper mills, saw mills, and steel mills. They also developed crankshafts and water turbines to provide power to factories.

Industry

Many industries were developed in the Muslim Empire during this period. As new discoveries were made, factories were often built to produce new products. Some examples include glass, medicines, silk, and various chemicals. Many of these processes were later taken to Europe.

Water turbine and crankshaft

Section Review Questions

1. What Muslim scholar is regarded as the Father of Modern Medicine?

2. What Greek invention that aided naval travel did the Muslims improve?

3. What farming improvement did the Muslims make to increase productivity?

4. What natural resources did the Muslims harness to produce power?

★ Contrast the Umayyad dynasty with the Abbasid dynasty.

★ Summarize the positions of Lewis and Stark about Islamic civilization.

■ IV. The Confrontation with Islam

Byzantine

Obstacle to the Spread of Islam

The expansion of Islam into Asia Minor was delayed for centuries by the stubborn resistance of the Byzantine Empire. While the Muslim armies conquered all the Byzantine lands in the Middle East, they could not overpower **Constantinople** (KON stan tih NO pul), the capital of the Byzantine Empire. This large city was located on an easily defended point. It was surrounded on two sides by water and rugged terrain. The city's walls were also thick and extensive. In addition, the Byzantines had a secret weapon known as **Greek fire**. This chemical mixture burned upon impact and spread when doused with water. The Byzantine Empire gained and lost ground over the next four centuries but effectively halted the spread of Islam in this region.

During the eleventh century, Seljuk Turks took control of the Muslim Empire. In 1071 they destroyed the Byzantine army and threatened Constantinople. However, a small remnant of the Byzantine Empire survived for another four hundred years before a final Muslim victory.

Guiding Questions

1. How did the Byzantine state withstand Muslim attacks between the 7th and 10th centuries?
2. What role did the Byzantines play in preserving and transmitting ancient Greek learning?
3. What is the significance of the expansion of Greek Orthodox Christianity into Russia?

Byzantine ships launching Greek fire to destroy enemy ships

Contributions

With the fall of the Western Roman Empire, the Byzantine Empire became the preserver of knowledge from previous generations in the West. The Greek language and important Greek manuscripts were carefully stored and copied. In addition, Greek Orthodox Christianity spread from the Byzantine Empire to the north into the Balkans and beyond. In 988 Vladimir I established Orthodox Christianity as the approved religion in Russia. The Orthodox Church had a great impact on Russia, including the development of a Slavic (SLAH vik) alphabet based on the Greek alphabet. This script made possible the translating of Greek works into the Slavic language. Russian literature prospered as a result. In addition, the Russians copied the Byzantine style of construction for their cathedrals.

European

Under the Umayyad dynasty, Islam rapidly spread across northern Africa. Soon Muslim forces were within striking distance of Europe. They crossed a narrow strait from western Africa into Europe and quickly conquered the Germanic tribes on the Iberian Peninsula. Charles, ruler of the Franks (French), led an army to stop the advance of the Muslim forces in Europe. At the Battle of Tours in 732, Charles decisively defeated the Muslim army. He effectively

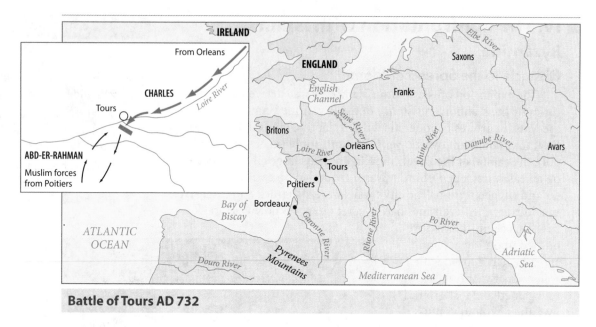

Battle of Tours AD 732

used heavy cavalry and wise military tactics to stop the Muslim advance. This victory earned him the name **Charles Martel** ("the Hammer") and ended the Muslim threat.

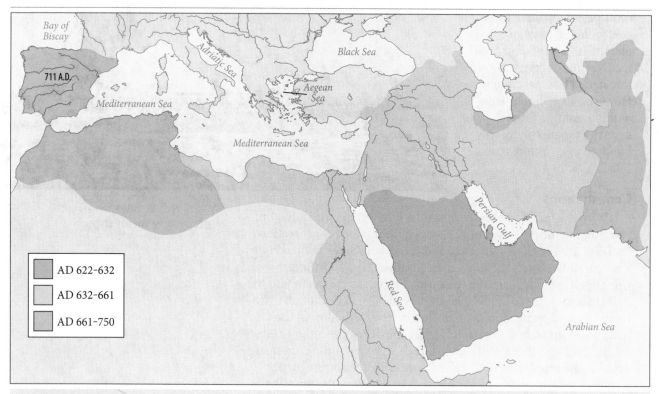

AD 622–632

AD 632–661

AD 661–750

The Spread of Islam

Section Review Questions

1. What empire delayed the Muslim advance into Asia Minor?

2. What title did Charles, ruler of the Franks, receive after defeating the Muslim forces? What does this title mean?

★ Why was the Byzantine Empire able to withstand Muslim conquest from the seventh through the tenth centuries?

■ Making Connections

1. How did Muhammad and his followers gain wealth while in Medina?

2. How did Uthmann resolve the problem of various versions of the Qur'an?

3–5. What technological contributions did the Muslim world make that you use today? List three.

6. How did Constantinople impede the advance of Islam into Asia Minor?

7. What was the significance of the Battle of Tours?

■ Developing History Skills

1. Based on the information in this chapter, construct a timeline for Islam.

2. While the Muslim world was experiencing a golden age, what was occurring in Europe during this same time period?

■ Thinking Critically

1. Look at the Historical Perspectives feature box contrasting Lewis and Stark. Both authors select the facts that strengthen their case. What lesson should a Christian learn about how to read history from looking at how Lewis and Stark write their histories?

2. What reason do Muslims give for claiming that the Bible cannot be trusted? What evidence do they provide to support this claim?

■ Living in God's World

1. With several of your classmates, write a tract that shows the differences between Islam and Christianity. Use verses mentioned in this chapter to support your work.

2. Using your graphic organizer, identify which characteristics of Byzantine and Persian societies contributed to their collapse. Write a brief paragraph describing how a Christian living in such a society should respond to those weaknesses.

People, Places, and Things to Know

Byzantine
Sassanid
Mecca
Ka'bah
Ramadan
Qur'an
Allah
Medina
Hegira
Islam
Battle of Badr
Muslims
caliph
Wars of Apostasy
Shiite
Sunni
imam
Hadith
Five Pillars
sharia
jihad
infidels
Umayyad
Damascus
Abbasid
Baghdad
Constantinople
Greek fire
Charles Martel

UNIT

Changes and Development in the Cultures of the World

1000 – 1650

2

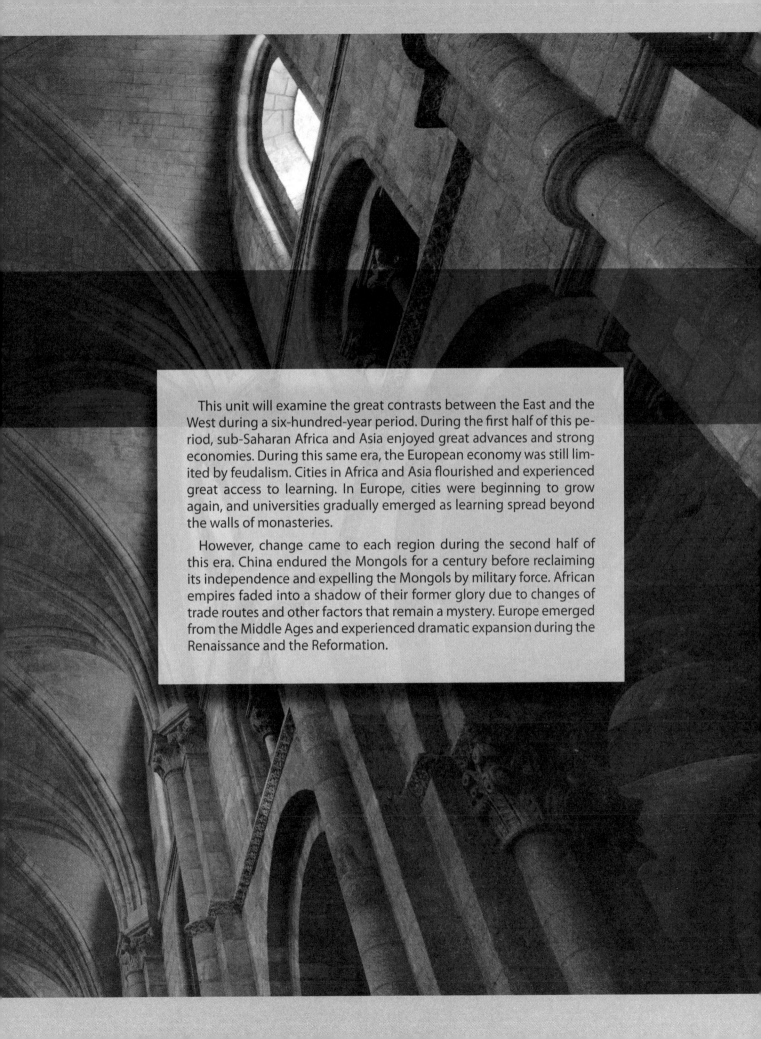

This unit will examine the great contrasts between the East and the West during a six-hundred-year period. During the first half of this period, sub-Saharan Africa and Asia enjoyed great advances and strong economies. During this same era, the European economy was still limited by feudalism. Cities in Africa and Asia flourished and experienced great access to learning. In Europe, cities were beginning to grow again, and universities gradually emerged as learning spread beyond the walls of monasteries.

However, change came to each region during the second half of this era. China endured the Mongols for a century before reclaiming its independence and expelling the Mongols by military force. African empires faded into a shadow of their former glory due to changes of trade routes and other factors that remain a mystery. Europe emerged from the Middle Ages and experienced dramatic expansion during the Renaissance and the Reformation.

CHAPTER

Transition in Sub-Saharan Africa
0 – AD 1600

3

- African Culture
- Early African Empires
- Centers of Civilization in East Africa

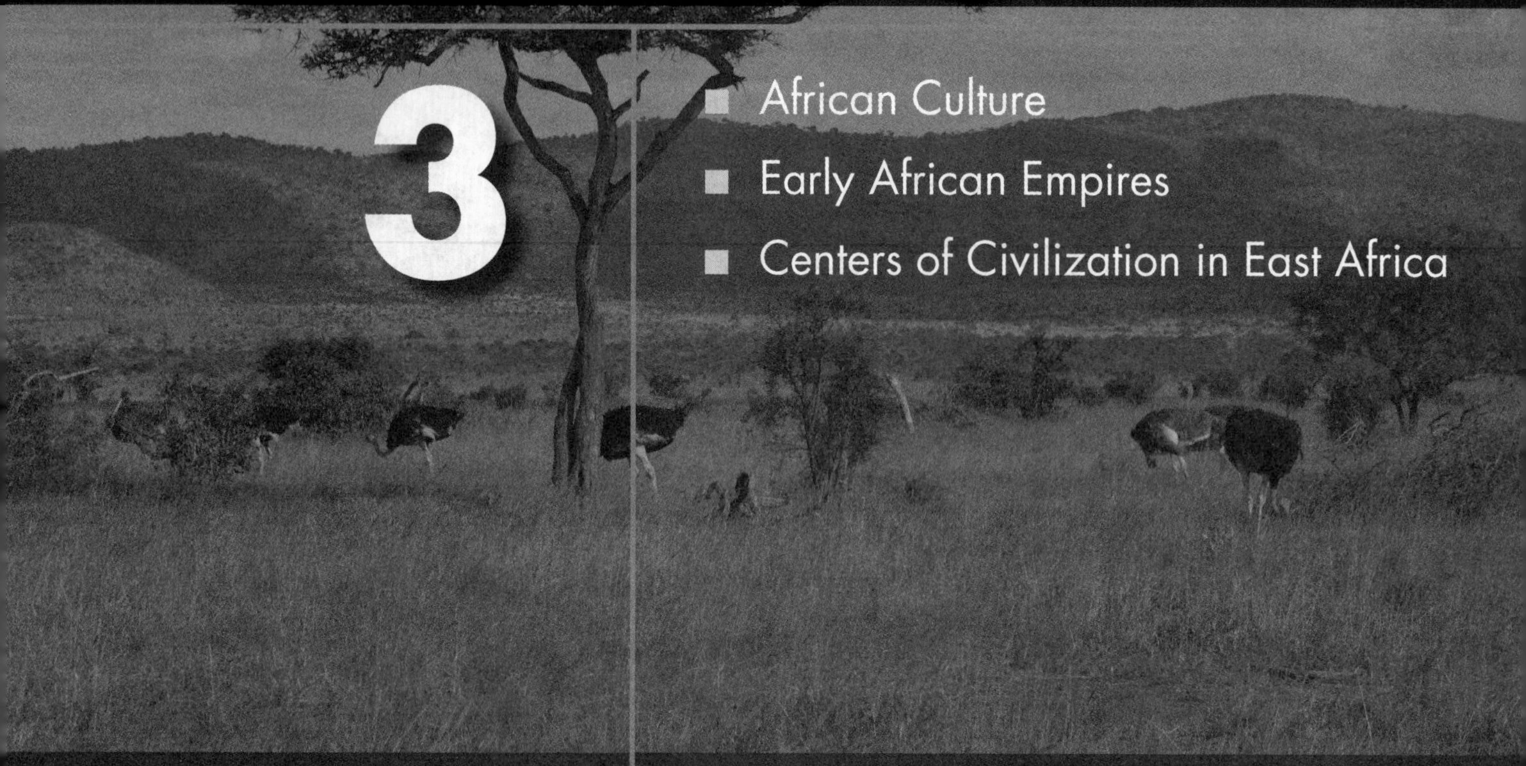

0 – AD 1600

	Greeks trade with Aksum (Ethiopia) 1st century AD		Frumentius introduces Coptic Christianity to Ethiopia 4th century		Rise of kingdom of Ghana in West Africa c. 500		Muslim traders begin to spread Islam to sub-Saharan Africa c. 700
0	**100**	**200**	**300**	**400**	**500**	**600**	**700**

Golden Age in West Africa 500–1500

Big Ideas

1. What are the key elements of African culture?
2. Why were the states in Ethiopia and West Africa important in early African history?
3. What was the significance of the rise of towns and the development of a maritime trade in East and South Africa?

In the last chapter we discussed the spread of Islam across northern Africa. Arabic, the language of Islam, became the dominant language of this region. Muslim culture also replaced or mingled with the cultures of these African countries. This Muslim influence spread from Egypt to Morocco. However, change occurred more gradually in the lower half of the continent of Africa. This region lies south of the vast desert known as the **Sahara** (suh HAR uh). Thus it is called sub-Saharan Africa. While Western Europe slowly awakened through the Middle Ages (particularly between 1000 and 1600), much of sub-Saharan Africa blossomed with the growth of cities, the expansion of empires, and an explosion of trade.

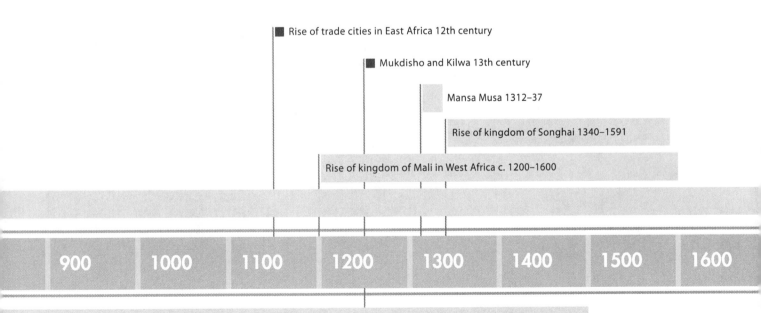

Rise of trade cities in East Africa 12th century

Mukdisho and Kilwa 13th century

Mansa Musa 1312–37

Rise of kingdom of Songhai 1340–1591

Rise of kingdom of Mali in West Africa c. 1200–1600

| 900 | 1000 | 1100 | 1200 | 1300 | 1400 | 1500 | 1600 |

Great Zimbabwe established 1200s
(abandoned around 1450)

1. How were agriculture and ironworking important for the continued development of civilization in Africa?

2. What role did extended family groups play in African society?

3. What are the indigenous religions of Africa?

Zebra and blue wildebeest migration in Serengeti National Park

■ I. African Culture
Continued Development of Civilization

Agriculture

Just like other people around the world, Africans adapted to changing conditions and lived on the natural resources around them. Some were able to blend growing crops with raising livestock to meet their dietary needs. Others learned to thrive on either crops or livestock, depending on the available resources.

Over time, the soil became less productive and the food for livestock decreased. The people often had to move in order to survive. Eventually, the depleted soil would again become able to support crops and sustain life. As the Africans found better ways to fertilize the soil, more permanent dwellings were built and groups were able to build cities.

Improved efficiency resulted in greater yields. As more food was produced than was needed, the excess provided opportunity for trade. Increased trade and permanent settlements helped the continued development of civilization.

Crops

Depending on the region, crops such as roots or various grains were harvested. In the rain forests, inhabitants gathered roots such as yams. On the **savannah** (suh VAN uh; flat grasslands), the people developed grain crops such as millet, sorghum, and maize (corn). Other crops such as cotton and watermelon began to appear in West Africa and

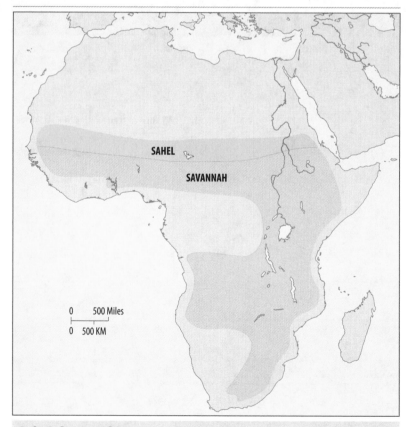

Sub-Saharan Africa

Sahel

Flaxseed (left) *and millet* (right) *that will be ground into flour*

in the **Sahel** (sah HEL; a narrow strip of land between the Sahara and the savannah). Crops such as finger millet, peas, and flax took hold in Ethiopia.

Livestock

Africans raised a variety of animals, including sheep, goats, and cattle. However, they prized these animals and seldom killed them. The animals provided milk and other benefits (such as wool) for their masters. Cattle especially were considered a sign of wealth.

Ankole Watusi cattle in the plains of Uganda

41

Therefore, to kill an animal meant the loss of one's wealth. Rather than kill their livestock, the Africans added to their diets by hunting or fishing.

Ironworking

No one can say with certainty where the processing of iron ore began. There is evidence that iron was hammered into useful items from the earliest human civilization. Many think that smelting of iron was first developed in modern Turkey or the Middle East around 1400 BC. However, processing of iron may have developed separately in sub-Saharan Africa as early as 1000 BC. Even though few details are known, processing of iron seems to have appeared very early across this region. Iron proved to be valuable because it is more durable than stone, wood, or bone. In addition, it can be bent into various shapes when heated. African craftsmen forged the iron into tools, weapons, and other devices. Items made from iron also could be traded for food or other commodities. Bars of iron even served as a form of money in countries such as Ethiopia.

Importance of Extended Families

The family was the most important element of traditional African culture. An African's family affected every area of his life. The family provided a person not only with a history and traditions but also with guidance throughout his life. The family leader decided where members lived and how they earned their living. Family leaders also told them how to behave and what to believe. Often, Africans evaluated a person according to his position in a family rather than as an individual.

Africans believed that children were important. A man would often have several wives to rear many children. As was true in many ancient cultures, love was rarely the motivation for marriage. The parents of the children arranged the marriage for money and political benefit. In these cultures, love was expected to follow marriage rather than precede it. In addition, one of the primary reasons for marriage was the rearing of children. This would make possible the survival of family traditions. Marriage and large families also led to increased family honor and wealth.

A man with several wives had children who were either brothers and sisters or half brothers and half sisters. Sometimes rivalry to gain the father's favor occurred among the wives and their children. Keeping peace at home was a difficult job for the husband. Usually each wife had a dwelling in the family compound. Daughters and sons lived in separate dwellings as well. This arrangement helped to prevent many quarrels.

The typical African family had other members besides parents and children. African families often included grandparents, uncles, aunts, and cousins. When a young woman married, she left her family group to join her husband's family group. These extended family groups tended to live together. Sometimes a whole community consisted of people belonging to the same family.

The extended family was very important to the African culture for several reasons. It provided security for the family members. The extended family also provided a pool of wisdom and skills. Older members of the family could pass on life experience and provide a connection to the past. The extended family was a building block for African civilization.

The Family

In the Bible, family is a fundamental building block of society (Gen. 1:27–28; 2:18, 22–24). Children are also valued highly (Gen. 1:28; Ps. 127:3). But marriage is restricted to one man and one woman for life (Gen. 2:24; Rom. 7:2). In the Bible, love is an important part of the marriage (Song. 8:6–7; Eph. 5:25), and it seems that it could either precede or follow the marriage (Gen. 24:67; 29:18).

The largest family group in Africa was the **clan**. A clan included everyone who could trace his ancestry to a common relative. The clan gave the individual his history and culture. In Africa, single families belonged to clans and lived under the authority of the clan elder or chief. The clan, not families and individuals, often owned and controlled the land used by the clan members. The chief decided where the clan lived, divided the land, and determined its use. A small clan might live together in a single community, while larger clans lived in several communities. On important occasions, the whole clan met together to celebrate.

African society continued one level beyond families and clans: tribes. A **tribe** consisted of two or more clans that shared the same language, beliefs, and customs. Some tribes were small, while others had thousands of members. Africa's traditional clans and tribes formed the basis for later African states and kingdoms.

Indigenous Religions

Almost all Africans believed in a Supreme Being or High God. In addition, some African accounts of Creation often bore an amazing resemblance to the biblical account in Genesis. Some believed that the High God was a spiritual being who walked with man until something caused him to separate himself from the people. The Dinka tribe of Ghana told the story that the High God walked with man until a selfish woman made him angry and he left man's company. The Sudanese told the story that a woman was so noisy that the High God went into heaven to get away from her. Africans saw the High God as kind but generally unconcerned with the affairs of humanity.

In addition to a Supreme Being, many Africans also believed in lesser gods who had certain areas of authority. In many ways, African deities loosely resembled the gods of the Greeks and Romans. However, African clans like the **Kikuyu** did not worship many gods, but believed in one god, Ngai.

The family also played a key role in traditional African religion. Knowing that the High God was a spirit, Africans also believed that those who left this life continued to live in spirit. Thus, the family included not only living members but also those dead and unborn. Like the Chinese, Africans believed that their dead ancestors influenced their present lives. They also believed that their actions affected their yet unborn children.

Many Africans believed that when the High God left, he left both spirits and humans in the world to run its affairs. This belief resulted in most Africans living in fear of vengeful spirits. These many spirits, not the Creator God, became the object of African worship. Many Africans believed that some spirits lived in trees, rocks, rivers, or mountains, while others simply lived in the air. This belief is called **animism**. By praying and sacrificing to these spirits, the Africans hoped to receive blessings. They treated the spirits of ancestors the same as spirits in nature. They believed that all spirits had power to affect a person's life.

Islam

In Chapter 2 you saw the origins and spread of Islam across northern Africa. Less than a century after the death of Muhammad, Islam controlled this region north of the Sahara. The spread of Islam to regions of sub-Saharan Africa was more gradual. Islamic

Tribes

The use of the term "tribe" may cause the reader to picture people living in a primitive culture. However, in reference to Africa, the term is simply meant to describe groups that are united by a common language and belief system.

Creation Stories

The Kikuyu story of creation includes the creation of a male (Kikuyu) by the god Ngai. Kikuyu was given a wife (Mumbi), and they had nine daughters. When the daughters were old enough to marry, they met nine young men from a distant land. Their descendants became the Kikuyu clan in modern Kenya.

Great Mosque at Djenne, Mali, the largest mud building in the world

Dwellings

What materials were used to build the house where you live? Africans used the materials that were available to them to house their families. Existing materials varied from region to region. Where stone was plentiful, they built their houses of stone. In other areas wood was available in sufficient supply to construct their houses. Some regions had a plentiful supply of clay, and the people baked bricks to use in building. Where no other resources were available, the inhabitants used a combination of sticks, leaves, grass, and clay to build their homes.

Guiding Questions

1. How did the growth of the Christian Ethiopian kingdom impact the expansion of Islam?

2. What was the importance of agriculture, gold production, and the caravan trade in the growth of the Ghana, Mali, and Songhai empires?

3. How did Islam expand in West Africa?

merchants crossed the Sahara to the savannah of West Africa in trade caravans. Islamic merchants also traveled to East Africa from Arabia and Persia. Islam came to South Africa in yet another way—with slaves brought in from Indonesia and Southeast Asia. These Muslims brought their religion with them. Over time, some of the Muslim merchants settled in West and East Africa and established communities. Initially, Islam and Coptic Christianity coexisted peacefully. However, Islam eventually became dominant and, to varying degrees, imposed its beliefs on the people.

Section Review Questions

1. What types of food were grown in sub-Saharan Africa?

2. Why did the Africans avoid killing their livestock?

3. What religious belief caused many Africans to live in fear of vengeful spirits?

4. What term refers to the belief that spirits live in rivers, trees, rocks, and mountains?

★ How did traditional African views of the family depart from scriptural teaching? In what ways are traditional African views of the family closer to Scripture than contemporary American views?

■ II. Early African Empires

East—Ethiopia

As the Egyptian kingdom expanded south along the Nile, it encountered Kush. In the eighth century BC, a Kushite king conquered Egypt and established the capital of Upper Egypt in the Kushite city of Napata. Napata maintained its power for one hundred years until the Assyrians took over upper Egypt. The kingdom of Kush was not directly affected by these power changes.

Below Kush was another ancient kingdom known as Aksum. In the first century AD, Aksum and the nearby Red Sea port city of Adulis were important trading centers for the Greeks. The Greeks gave Aksum (and all the territory below it) the name **Ethiopia**.

Ethiopian legend states that the queen of Sheba and King Solomon had a child, Menelik, from whom all Ethiopian rulers are descended. The Ethiopians even use the imperial title "The Conquering Lion of the Tribe of Judah." Legend also said that the Tabot, a wooden box on the altar in the cathedral at Aksum, contained the original ark of the covenant.

In the mid-fourth century AD, in the court at Aksum, a slave named **Frumentius** rose in favor with the king and introduced Coptic Christianity to the people. When King Ezana accepted Christianity, the head of the Coptic Church in Egypt ordained Frumentius as bishop of the Ethiopian church. Over the next two hundred years, a great number of the population were converted to Coptic Christianity.

When Islam began to spread across North Africa in the seventh century, Nubia (the region formerly known as Kush) blocked its spread to the south. After defeating Muslim invaders, the Nubians negotiated a peace that lasted 600 years. At times Nubia was strong enough to send its troops as far north as Alexandria to protect Christian interests in Egypt. (In the twelfth century, Ethiopian Christians built unique structures for worship in **Lalibela**.)

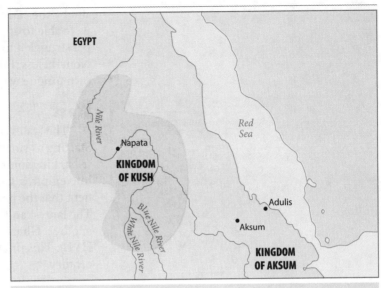

Early Ethiopian Kingdoms

Lalibela

In Chapter 2 you learned that Muslims make a pilgrimage to Mecca, which is their holy city. The Coptic Church also has a holy city which they regard as a New Jerusalem and to which they make pilgrimages. It is the city of Lalibela. In the early thirteenth century, King Lalibela led the Coptic Church to build eleven churches. These churches are unique because they were carved out of rock. In fact, they were carved out of solid bedrock below ground level. So, standing on ground level, one can look down on these remarkable structures. The churches have windows and have been sculpted inside and out. St. George's Church, the most famous of these churches, is shaped like a cross.

But by the early fourteenth century, the Mamluks who ruled Egypt were able to appoint a Muslim king over Nubia. After this, Ethiopia struggled to defend itself from the onslaught of Islamic armies. Nonetheless, Ethiopian Christianity persisted. It had developed its own unique way of worship.

West

The states of western Africa developed around the year 500. Starting as small city-states headed by a clan or tribal chief, these tribal kingdoms conquered other city-states and clans, thus growing into empires. Gold production in these nations became so prominent that the period between 500 and 1500 is called the Golden Age. The largest and most important empires of the region followed one another: **Ghana** (GAH nuh), **Mali** (MAH lee), and **Songhai** (SONG HYE). This final kingdom survived until the end of the sixteenth century.

Ghana

This ancient African empire developed from the extensive trade passing through western Africa around the eighth century. Ghana was strategically located between two rivers and the Sahel and savannah regions of Africa. Traders bearing salt came from the north, and traders bearing gold came from the south. The ruler of the Soninke, the main tribe in the region, demanded gold nuggets as a form of taxation for the traders to pass through Ghana. With the expansion of Islam after the seventh century, Ghanaians (GAH nians) began to trade with Muslim merchants. By the eleventh century, Ghana's rulers had converted to Islam.

By the beginning of the thirteenth century, Ghana's military might had faded. Leaders of another kingdom absorbed this territory into what became known as Mali.

Mali

During the early thirteenth century, a new power arose in western Africa. Under the leadership of Sundiata Keita, the forces of Mali defeated the current rulers. Sundiata then built a much

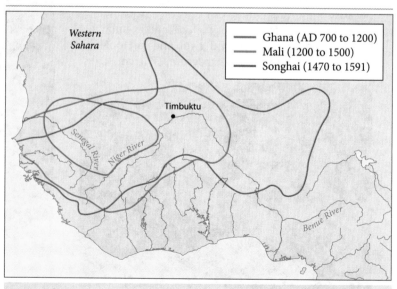

West Africa

larger empire and absorbed territories south and west to the Atlantic Ocean. In addition, the empire controlled land east across the savannah. Mali retained influence over this great region because of its ability to raise a large army and control trade, especially gold. Since the rulers were able to provide a secure environment, trade flourished and great wealth poured into this empire.

Eventually, the rulers of Mali converted to Islam. The most famous *mansa* (MAHN sa), "ruler", was **Musa** (MOO sa). In 1324, Mansa Musa made a pilgrimage to Mecca. He brought along a great number of slaves, camels, and much gold. His trip and great display of wealth brought Mali to the attention of the medieval world. According to tradition, Musa gave away so much gold that he reduced the value of gold in that region for several years.

Songhai

As Mali's influence declined, a new empire developed that replaced Mali's former power. The Songhai Empire lay farther to the east toward the Niger River. It was founded by Sunni Ali. He ruled during the last half of the fifteenth century. Ali conquered land along the Niger River and westward to the remnants of the Mali Empire. He struggled to maintain a smooth relationship with the general population and key Muslim merchants in newly conquered cities, especially **Timbuktu** (tim buk TOO). This empire collapsed in 1591 when overrun by Moroccan forces with muzzle-loading firearms.

Commerce

Agriculture

West Africa is located on the savannah and Sahel regions that lie between the Sahara and tropical forests. As previously mentioned, crops ranged from grains and roots to cotton. However, this region became one of the first to combine a farm-based economy with a trade-based economy. West Africans developed iron production and turned this ore into many useful products. They also learned to work with **camels** and soon became involved in trade across the Sahara. In addition to cultivating food, the West Africans produced valuable trading items such as iron, cotton cloth, and gold.

Gold Production

Following the decline of Mali and Songhai, some of the West Africans (known as the Akan) thrived through a combination of farming and mining for gold. They traded with tribes from the Sahel and the Ivory Coast. Their diligent labor produced wealth and power as they gained control of trade. The Akan also exchanged gold for products from distant lands through the Portuguese traders at coastal settlements. The abundance of gold mined in this region led Europeans to refer to it as the **Gold Coast.**

Trans-Saharan Caravan Trade

Caravans traveled from oasis to oasis in order to survive the hazardous journey across the Sahara. Often the distance between oases took several days to travel. As was previously mentioned, West Africans were among the first to use camels to travel across the Sahara. Camels were one of the few animals that could survive these journeys.

Timbuktu

This city is located in western Africa near the Niger River at the southern edge of the great Sahara. (See map on p. 46.) Around the year 1100, Timbuktu became a leading city of the African kingdom of Mali. Trade caravans crossed the desert to buy and sell goods in Timbuktu. Merchants from as far away as Egypt and Italy traded fabrics, salt, ivory, spices, ostrich feathers, and, most importantly, gold and slaves.

The great Mali ruler Mansa Musa (1312–37) transformed the city into a center for the arts and learning as well. He built a great Islamic mosque and encouraged the founding of schools and libraries. So many scholars came to Timbuktu that books soon became an item of trade almost as important as gold and slaves. At its height, Timbuktu had over twenty-five thousand inhabitants, a large number for medieval times. (By comparison, Rome at that time had a population of seventeen thousand.) A merchant from Florence, Italy, named Benedetto Dei visited in 1470 and found a prosperous city with ornate mosques and the rich and the poor dwelling together. In the sixteenth century, Leo Africanus, a Moor (a Muslim of North African and Berber descent), told of a splendid city with many scholars and a dazzling court life. Such prosperity did not last, however. Warfare disrupted trade and stopped the flow of wealth into the city. By 1828, French explorers found the city in ruins.

One-ounce gold nugget

Ships of the Desert

Many people believe that camels store water in their humps. However, they store water in their body fluids. This enables them to go for days without having access to water. Camels can also lose up to 30 percent of the water in their bodies with no ill effect (most mammals would die after losing 15 percent). When they do drink, camels can take in twenty-six to forty gallons in about ten minutes! They also draw moisture from green plants that they eat to meet some of their moisture needs.

The camel is able to eat plants that most other animals could not. Its lips and mouth are tough enough to allow it to eat thorns and branches. Its teeth are sharp and enable the camel to feed on many things, including skin and bones. In addition, the camel swallows food after brief chewing, like a cow, and regurgitates and chews the food as a cud later.

God designed camels in such a way that men could use them to travel across deserts. This

creature is one example of how God has enabled man to carry out the Creation Mandate to subdue the earth, even in the hostile environment of the Sahara.

Environment

God created a world with many different environmental conditions and natural resources. God placed Eden in a location in which a river watered the land rather than rain (Gen. 2:5–6, 10). That river divided into four rivers as it flowed from the garden, and those rivers flowed to different regions with different resources (Gen. 2:10–14). Mankind is to use earth's resources to carry out the Creation Mandate. Note the interaction with the environment and the use of resources in West Africa.

Camels are uniquely suited for this harsh, sand-covered terrain for many reasons. They are able to store energy-rich fat in their humps, which provides nourishment as needed. In addition, camels can store enough liquid to survive five to seven days without water. They also have long eyelashes and nostrils that can be closed during sandstorms. Finally, these animals are able to withstand the extreme temperature changes found in the desert.

Camels were used to carry many goods on trade routes through this desolate and arid region since they are able to carry loads over long distances where water is very scarce. This made them a vital tool in hauling goods. Trade across the Sahara would have been greatly reduced, if not impossible, without the use of camels.

Expansion of Islam

The expansion of Islam to western Africa by way of Muslim traders led to an increased Islamic influence on African culture. Over time, the number of Muslims in this region increased to the point that Islam became the most influential religion. There would often be a great effort to convert rulers to Islam. Their conversion would ensure the security and influence of this religion. However, the conversion of a ruler seldom led to the conversion of average citizens. The people were generally free to practice whatever religion they desired. Some blended Islam and a traditional religion, praying to Allah and offering sacrifices to their gods.

In addition to their beliefs, the Muslims brought a written language. Islamic scholars traveling in Africa taught the people to read and write Arabic. The same scholars recorded what they saw in Africa and gave us the first written history of the continent. Slowly, the ability to read and write changed the culture of Africa, which previously had known only oral recording of history and tradition.

Section Review Questions

1. What name did the Greeks give to Aksum and all territories below it?

2. What was the name of the slave who introduced Coptic Christianity to Ethiopia?

3. List the three early empires of West Africa in chronological order.

4. What famous city was located near the Niger River?

5. The abundance of gold in West Africa led Europeans to refer to this region as the _____.

★ Why was the camel essential for trans-Saharan trade?

★ How did Nubia play a role in checking the advance of Islam?

■ III. Growth of Trade in East Africa

Trading cities grew up along the coast, where Africans from the interior brought gold, ivory, and precious stones. Many of these goods arrived at the coastal cities on the heads of porters who had walked hundreds of miles across the continent. Merchants from Arabia, India, and even China sailed to these cities to trade. Eventually, these goods from Africa went to markets throughout Asia. The language of these cities reflects the meeting of many cultures. The people spoke a common trade language known as Swahili (see below).

East African Cities

Rise of Commercial Cities

Around the twelfth century, the earliest trade cities appeared along the coast of East Africa. Cities such as Mapungubwe, Manda, and Shanga thrived on the trade of products such as gold, slaves, and ivory. However, within a century, these cities declined in importance as other cities arose to take their place. Cities like Mukdisho (modern Mogadishu on the Somali coast) and Kilwa rose in prominence during the thirteenth century. (More about the city of Kilwa will be discussed later.)

Traders came to cities along the East African coast by July to have their goods loaded on ships bound for Asia. The summer monsoon winds carried the ships east. Then the goods would be exchanged for Asian products. In October the winds reversed direction and carried the ships back to the ports in Africa. As long as this trade was protected, commercial prosperity was ensured. Empires developed, in part, to protect this profitable trade.

Significance of Swahili

Swahili is a trade language built upon the Bantu language. This language has served as the native tongue of various groups living along the southeast African coastline. About 35 percent of the Swahili words are Arabic in origin. This Arab influence resulted from centuries of contact between Arab traders and many different Bantu-speaking peoples living along Africa's Indian Ocean coast. Swahili also uses words from many other languages, including English. This foreign influence was caused by the migration of many nationalities to this region and by contact through trade with different groups of people.

Guiding Questions

1. Why did commercial towns on the East African coast develop, and what was the significance of Swahili as a language of trade?

2. What impact did Islam, Arab settlement, and maritime trade have in the economic and cultural life of Kilwa and other East African coastal cities?

3. What role did Great Zimbabwe play as a state and commercial center with links to the Indian Ocean trade?

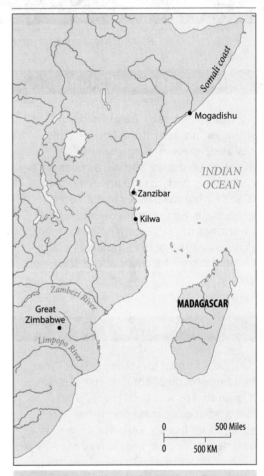

East Africa

African Civilizations

List the effects of the development of trade in Africa.

Cause	Effects
Development of trade	

Ruins of the Great Enclosure

Great House of Stone

Zimbabwe means "great house of stone" or "place of stone houses." This city-state grew into a great empire over two centuries. The ruins cover 1,800 acres and include an area more than one hundred miles in diameter. In addition, bone fragments show that thousands of cattle were killed for meat. The vast eating of beef indicates a large wealthy class who could afford such luxury.

Kilwa

Kilwa is known for its impressive buildings made of coral. In the 1200s, a large palace was built there. "The Kilwa palace occupies about two acres along a cliff overlooking the sea and is a complex of courtyards surrounded by rooms, sometimes with barrel vaulting, sometimes in double stories. The building material was coral rag set in lime mortar, but cut stone was used for roofing, decorative slabs, and architectural features such as doorways and stairs." Kilwa, with its coral buildings, was considered by some to be one of the most beautiful cities in the world at that time.

Robert W. July, *A History of the African People*, 5th ed., 83–84.

This common language enabled many tribes and nationalities to carry on trade. It made large-scale trade possible and resulted in goods traveling from Africa to places as far away as Cathay (China) and Cambay (a city in India). In addition, goods from distant countries made their way to East Africa.

Zimbabwe

In the mid-1200s, Mapungubwe was abandoned, and the city of Great **Zimbabwe** (zim BAHB weh) was established on the Zimbabwe Plateau near the Sabi River. This city grew to a population of 15,000 to 20,000 citizens in the 1300s. The empire that developed was located in southeastern Africa between the Limpopo and Zambezi Rivers. Zimbabwe thrived on raising cattle and exporting gold, slaves, and ivory to the coast. Trade from India and China also passed through this empire.

For at least two hundred years, Zimbabwe expanded and built massive stone buildings and enclosures. The most famous structure is the Great Enclosure, which still stands thirty-five feet high with a base about fifteen feet thick. Perhaps even more impressive is that these great buildings were built without mortar. The stones were carefully cut and fitted together with precision. Many of the structures have survived for over seven hundred years.

This empire lay about two hundred miles from the East African coast. Therefore, it relied on coastal cities to receive and transport goods. **Kilwa** became a key port through which Zimbabwe's gold was transported north.

For reasons unknown, this empire fell into rapid decline during the early fifteenth century. By the 1450s, Great Zimbabwe was abandoned by most of its occupants.

Section Review Questions

1. List three products traded in East Africa.

2. What trade language developed from the Bantu dialect?

3. Goods traveled from East Africa to what distant lands?

4. What was the name of the city where the Great Enclosure was built?

5. What do the remains of thousands of cattle bones indicate about the city of Great Zimbabwe?

6. What city became a key coastal port for the empire of Zimbabwe?

★ What does the development of trade reveal about the level of East African civilization?

★ Why should Genesis 1:28 lead us to expect to find advanced and beautiful cities like Kilwa in East Africa?

■ Making Connections

1. Why did early African tribes need to migrate?
2. How did Islam spread to sub-Saharan Africa?
3. How did Ghana grow into an empire?
4. What led to the decline of Timbuktu?
5. Why was the west coast of Africa referred to as the Gold Coast?
6. Why was the camel called the "ship of the desert"?
7. How did the development of Swahili enhance trade?
8. Why did Zimbabwe's empire decline?

■ Developing History Skills

1. Talk with your parents and grandparents and construct a family tree based on what you can learn from them. This is a form of oral history that was used in many cultures, including Africa. Graph your findings on a sheet of paper and share them with your class.

2. Contrast the level of trade and learning in Europe and in sub-Saharan Africa during this period. You may need to refer to a world history textbook or other sources to learn more about Europe during the Middle Ages in order to complete this assignment.

■ Thinking Critically

1. Empires are formed when one country takes control of other countries. What are the benefits of an empire? What are the problems with an empire?

2. When Europeans discovered Great Zimbabwe, they said Africans could not have built this structure. Evaluate this position biblically. (Use verses such as Genesis 4:17 and 11:1–4 for ideas.)

■ Living in God's World

1. Write an editorial on why maintaining strong trade relations with others nations in the world is important for your country. Use the history of Ghana, Mali, and Songhai as evidence to develop your argument.

2. Read the Eskimo creation myth (available in the Student Activities Manual in Chapter 3, Activity 1) and write a brief paragraph explaining why there are similarities to the Genesis account. Then write a brief paragraph explaining why there are differences from the Genesis account. Why should this comparison give you confidence in the accuracy of the Genesis Creation account?

People, Places, and Things to Know
Sahara
savannah
Sahel
clan
tribe
Kikuyu
animism
Ethiopia
Frumentius
Lalibela
Ghana
Mali
Songhai
Musa
Timbuktu
camel
Gold Coast
Swahili
Zimbabwe
Kilwa

4

- Growth of Cities and Commerce in China

- Developments in Japan and Southeast Asia

- Rise of the Mongol Empire

1000 – 1700

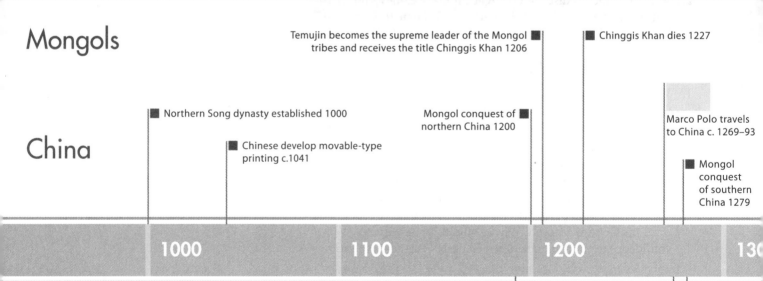

Mongols

Temujin becomes the supreme leader of the Mongol tribes and receives the title Chinggis Khan 1206

Chinggis Khan dies 1227

China

Northern Song dynasty established 1000

Chinese develop movable-type printing c.1041

Mongol conquest of northern China 1200

Marco Polo travels to China c. 1269–93

Mongol conquest of southern China 1279

| 1000 | 1100 | 1200 | 130 |

Japan

Yoritomo becomes the first shogun of Japan 1192

Mongol invasion repelled 1274

Second Mongol invasion repelled 1281

Big Ideas

1. Why did China experience growth in cities and commerce during the 11th through the 16th centuries?
2. How did Japanese and Southeast Asian civilizations develop during the 9th through the 16th centuries?
3. What were the consequences of the Mongol invasions and the Mongols' demise?

Many of the civilizations in Asia had vibrant cultures between 1000 and 1600. As in parts of Africa and Asia Minor, learning and trade thrived in China and other Asian countries. Populations increased and civilizations advanced. This period was also marked by wars and conquest. Japan proved to be the exception in some ways, mainly by experiencing an extended period of feudalism and isolation. But prior to this isolation, Japan borrowed much from China that became essential to its culture and development. The tribesmen of Mongolia rushed onto the scene and overwhelmed much of Asia for a brief period of time. Their short-term impact was dramatic.

Mongol rulers expelled
from China 1368

1400　　1500　　1600　　1700

Japanese feudalism late 12th century until the mid-19th century

Ashikaga clan becomes
dominant 1336

Tokugawa clan becomes dominant (moves
the capital to Tokyo) 1600

I. Growth of Cities and Commerce in China

Transitions in Leadership

China's history can be traced back to a very early period. In fact, China's first dynasty began about the same time that Moses was commanded to lead Israel out of Egyptian captivity. For the first two thousand years of China's dynastic history, five dynasties ruled in China, beginning with the **Shang** around 1500 BC and ending with the T'ang in the seventh century AD. After the fall of the T'ang dynasty, strong central power did not exist for three centuries. By the tenth century, China remained divided into northern and southern kingdoms. By 1000 the northern kingdom became known as the **Song** or Northern Song dynasty. This kingdom experienced strong economic growth. During the early 1200s, this region fell to the invading Mongols. The southern kingdom, or Southern Song dynasty, came under the control of the Mongols in 1279.

For nearly a century, the Mongol Empire, known as the Yuan dynasty, ruled China. However, by 1368 the Mongol rulers had been driven out of China and pushed back into Mongolia. A new Chinese dynasty was established that sought to restore Chinese influence and prestige.

Expansion

Improvements in Agriculture

China is a land of great geographical diversity. Its landscape varies from mountains to hills and from plains to river basins. China also has a variety of climates. Crops grown on the plains often differ from those grown in the hills or mountains. River basins provide growing options that vary from the plateau regions. Crops include rice, barley, sorghum, millet, soybeans, and wheat.

The Chinese developed ways to irrigate their crops and used iron farm implements to make farming more effective and to make more land available for farming. They produced larger har-

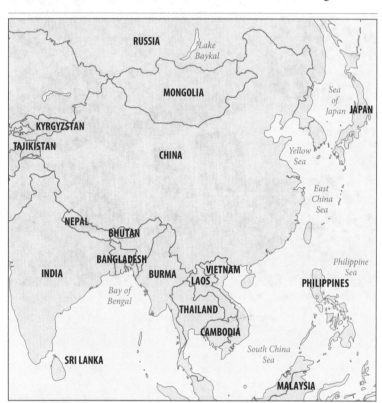

Asia and Surrounding Countries

Samples of sorghum grain

vests and made it possible to support a growing population. Chinese merchants also turned excess food into increased trade.

Increase of Population

Providing accurate population numbers in early China is difficult, if not impossible. The earliest count considered reliable by some historians was made in 2 BC. The numbers ranged from 57 to 59 million. In AD 754 the count showed a population of 52.8 million. However, by the beginning of the twelfth century, the population is believed to have risen to about 100 million. This doubling of the population occurred just prior to and during the Song dynasty in northern China. The great increase in population was sustained by increased production of rice, wheat, and other crops in central and southern China.

Growth of Cities

Another development in China during the twelfth century was the growth of large cities. Several cities in China increased to populations of over one million people. Movement of the people to the cities reflected a change from employment on farms to labor in cities. As in many cultures, population growth and an increasing food supply combined with the growth of industry resulted in growing cities.

In addition to at least ten large cities, towns developed where people met for trade. These smaller cities developed as centers of commerce where a variety of products were exchanged. The growth of trade led to the development of an urban society in China.

Sustained Development of Commerce

From the earliest days of civilization in China, the people carried on trade with their neighbors. During the Shang period, tin was imported from the southwest regions of China to make bronze. Cowry and turtle shells came from the coast of the South China Sea. Since China had an abundance of iron ore, the sale of iron products developed into a major commercial enterprise by the fifth century BC. Silk was also a major product developed by the Chinese and became a major item for export (see p. 62).

Early Chinese merchants used a variety of items as money, including bolts of silk, jade, pearls, pieces of metal, and leather. Even dogs and horses could be used as a form of money. Over time, the Chinese looked for more portable and standardized items to serve as money. By 500 BC they were casting bronze into various shapes to serve as money. Bronze coins in the shape of tiny spades or knives appeared early in China. During the Ch'in dynasty, the Chinese used small, round bronze or copper coins with a square hole in the

(see p. 62)

Shaping the Environment in China

God's first commands to mankind were to fill the earth and subdue it. These commands work together. No single person can subdue and rule the earth. This is why God said humans ought to be fruitful and multiply. As the human population grows, advances in farming and other technology enable the earth to support more people. Cities are a way for more people to live together and to specialize in different aspects of living out the Creation Mandate.

Early Chinese paper money

Early Chinese coins

Cowry shells were valued by the Chinese and other cultures.

Silk

Fabric created from silk moth cocoons was first developed in ancient China. It was initially reserved for Chinese rulers but soon spread throughout China. Chinese emperors tried to keep the knowledge of how to develop silk a secret, but the technique was eventually smuggled into other lands.

Spinning silk into thread (above)

Silk moth cocoon (left)

middle as currency. These coins would be strung together, and a certain number of them would equal a bushel of grain or a bolt of silk. The Chinese even developed the first known paper money as a form of currency.

Innovations

Scientific

The Chinese made many scientific discoveries. For example, they discovered how to process iron ore and how to make such things as paper, gunpowder, and the compass. They also invented methods for printing. These and many more discoveries, such as the development of silk fabric, became the basis for a long list of technological developments. We will briefly examine a few of these discoveries.

Technological

Technology, simply defined, is putting knowledge to effective use. Technology can be a concept (idea) or a technique (process). For example, when the proper ingredients were mixed to form paper, a recipe (concept) was developed. Over time, factories were built to make quantities of paper, and the procedure was used over and over as the paper was produced.

Technology contributes to culture. The development of culture is a natural outgrowth of the Creation Mandate that you read about in Chapter 1. God created mankind to "subdue" the earth and to "have dominion" over it. As the Chinese discovered new uses for God's creation, they were maximizing the usefulness of their resources. Even though the Chinese did not worship the Creator, they were demonstrating the truth of God's Word (Genesis 1:28).

Paper

China developed the earliest known **paper**, perhaps as early as a few years before the birth of Christ. They formed paper by combin-

Citizenship in China

In chapter 1 you learned that civilizations arise when people live out the Creation Mandate given in Genesis 1:28. You might wonder how unsaved people are able to live out this command from God. In answering this question it is important to remember that God gave this Mandate to all humans, not just to His own people. He also repeated it after the Flood to fallen people (Gen. 9:1-7). The Fall does not cancel the Mandate. But it does affect it. Now humans do not rule the world in submission to God. They rule the world in opposition to God (Ps. 2:1-3). This means that you will see some good things develop in world civilizations, but you will also see them twisted to evil purposes.

ing fibers and rags with water. The mixture was pressed and then allowed to dry. The Chinese used paper for wrapping, padding, and writing. By the sixth century, the Chinese had developed toilet paper. Later they folded and sewed paper into bags to protect the flavor of tea. During the Song dynasty, the Chinese issued the first known paper money for general use.

Compass

Lodestone, a magnetic mineral, aligns itself with the earth's magnetic field. The Chinese were among the first people to discover this. However, the Chinese probably first used the **compass** as a novelty, or possibly to determine the will of their gods. Records indicate that during the Song dynasty the Chinese learned to use compasses for finding direction.

Gunpowder

For centuries the Chinese mixed ingredients with saltpeter to make items such as medicines. In the ninth century the Chinese discovered **gunpowder** by accident. They were trying to create a substance that would give them eternal life. The Chinese quickly developed many weapons with gunpowder, including flame-throwers, rockets, and crude bombs. They developed guns or firearms around the time of the Ming dynasty in the fourteenth century.

Printing

During the third century, the Chinese became the first to develop woodblock **printing**. They carved images into a block of wood and then applied ink or paint. The woodblock was then pressed against paper or cloth. A reversed image of the carving would be imprinted on the material.

The Chinese also developed a method of printing that uses movable characters. This method, known as movable-type printing, was first developed in China around 1041. The characters were made out of ceramic. Although the Chinese invented this technology, they made little use of it. The Chinese language is very complicated, and printing with this method involved a great amount of labor. Johannes Gutenberg, around 1450, was the first known person to use movable type with great success. However, he was German, not Chinese.

Iron

Iron smelting industries developed, and these industries employed many workers. The Chinese were also among the first to develop **cast iron**. This process would not be used in Europe for another thousand years. The sale of iron products brought great wealth to the rising merchant class in China.

Trade with Southeast Asia and Other Lands

In Chapter 3 you learned that merchants brought gold, ivory, and other products from Africa to China as early as 500 BC. Camel caravans also carried silk across Central Asia from China to Europe. In addition, ships carried goods between nations in Southeast Asia and along the Indian Ocean. These ships worked out of ports in southern China. Chinese merchants served as an important link to foreign markets for several centuries.

Saltpeter

This is another name for a mixture of sulfur, charcoal, and potassium nitrate. It is commonly referred to as gunpowder. It burns rapidly and produces hot solids and gases. These gases can be used to propel a bullet or to launch and create beautiful fireworks displays.

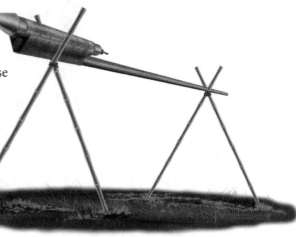

Early Chinese rocket

Cast Iron

Cast iron is formed when iron ore and a small amount of carbon and silicon are heated to about 1200°C. At this temperature the iron becomes a liquid and can be poured into a mold. Iron in this form has several advantages, including increased hardness, durability, a lower melting point (about 300°C lower than pure iron), and the ability to be cast into almost any shape. Cast iron has been used to make bridges, columns for buildings, machine parts, weapons, cooking utensils, and many other products. Archaeologists have found hundreds of molds for casting iron in China.

Growth of the Merchant Class

Various groups served as the elite members of Chinese society, including rulers and scholars. However, merchants were regarded as the lowest members of society for over two thousand years. No "honorable family" would even engage in trade. In addition, Confucianism condemned the practice of making a profit. Merchants were considered undesirable, in part because they were mobile and wealthy. These traits were thought to be dangerous. Therefore, merchants were not allowed to own property or serve in government.

Circumstances for the merchant class improved when the Song dynasty came to power in the eleventh century. The merchant class quickly took advantage of new freedoms. Members of their families took examinations to enter civil service. The merchants now had friends in government to help protect their business interests. They worked to become respected and influential members of Chinese society.

The growth of the merchant class provided many benefits to the Chinese people. As merchants bought and sold goods, they produced wealth. Factories were built to produce goods made from materials such as iron, paper, and silk. Many Chinese were employed to produce these goods. Some areas concentrated on making weapons, while others produced various products that merchants sold at home and abroad. Towns arose around trading centers, and cities multiplied to meet the needs of the growing population. Products previously reserved for the Chinese rulers became available to many of the people. Their standard of living improved, and many new products were available for them to purchase.

Chinese Religions

A great variety of religions developed in China or were brought to China. The family is very important in Chinese culture, so it is not surprising that the cult of **ancestor worship** became the leading religion early in Chinese history. Almost every home in China contained an altar where the Chinese burned incense to honor their dead. They hoped this would cause their ancestors to bless and guide them. In the fifth century BC, the teachings of the Chinese teacher **Confucius** began as a philosophy based on relationships. Later it was combined with Buddhism, which developed in India and became an influential religion in China. At the core of Confucius's teaching is ethical behavior within the five human relationships: father and son, elder and younger brothers, husband and wife, friend and friend, and ruler and subjects. What society considers fitting is the standard by which ethical behavior is judged. Confucius did not teach an absolute law of right and wrong. **Buddhism** is founded on Four Noble Truths: (1) Suffering is part of all existence. (2) Suffering has a cause—selfish desires. (3) Suffering can be overcome by destroying selfish desires. (4) If man follows the Eightfold Path, he will destroy selfish desires and end suffering. (The Eightfold Path includes right beliefs, intentions, speech, conduct, labor, effort, thoughts, and meditations.) **Taoism** (DOU iz um) developed in China from the teachings of **Lao-tzu** (LOU dzuh). He encouraged people to live in harmony with nature. This religion promoted the mystical and superstitious elements found in Chinese society.

The earliest Christian missionaries to China were Nestorians who arrived in 635. They were well received by the T'ang emperor,

Asian Religions and Christianity		
Write the main belief for each religion as well as the Christian belief that counters it.		
Religion	Main Belief	Christian Belief
Ancestor worship		
Confucianism		
Buddhism		
Taoism		

and they translated parts of the Bible into Chinese. As a witness to their Christian faith, the Nestorians erected a monument in 781. Rediscovered in 1623, part of this monument reads as follows:

> One Person of our Trinity, the Messiah, who is the Luminous Lord of the Universe, folding up Himself and concealing His true Majesty, appeared upon earth as a man. Angels proclaimed the Glad Tidings. A virgin gave birth to the Holy One. . . . A bright star announced the blessed event. Persians saw the splendour and came forth with their tribute.

Nestorian Christians were influential for several centuries and established many churches in China. But when the T'ang dynasty fell, religious liberty ended and Christians were slaughtered. By the end of the tenth century, Christianity had been pushed underground or out of China.

Section Review Questions

1. What was the name of the first Chinese dynasty?
2. Under which Chinese dynasty did the population double?
3. What product developed by the Chinese became a major item for export?
4. List four of the most important discoveries/inventions made by the Chinese.
★ What are the major beliefs of each Chinese religion, as noted in the text? What should the Christian think of each belief?
★ What contributions did merchants make that led to the development of cities?

■ II. Developments in Japan and Southeast Asia

Japan

Japan borrowed much from China. Chinese contributions included a written language, concepts of a central government, and various forms of Buddhism. However, the Japanese did more than just imitate China. The Japanese modified all of these contributions until they became thoroughly Japanese in nature.

Government

Japan's earliest known history reveals government by clans or extended families. During the eighth century, the Fujiwara (fu jee WAR ah) clan became dominant in Japan. In AD 794 Kyoto became Japan's capital, and a Chinese-style government was formed. This transition was known as the Taika (tie EE kuh; "Great Change") Reform. In theory, Japan became a centralized government led by the emperor. However, authority resided in the powerful families. They continued to control important government offices.

Over time, the Fujiwara rulers neglected the needs of the people. The decline of a central government caused Japan to pass into an extended period of **feudalism**. Japan's period of feudalism lasted from late in the twelfth century until the middle of the nineteenth century.

Guiding Questions

1. What form of government developed in early Japanese history, and how did feudalism develop in Japan?
2. What led to the rise of the warrior class, and what role did it play in feudalism?
3. How did Shintoism develop, and what distinctive forms of Buddhism did the Japanese practice?

Feudalism

Feudalism resulted when local rulers replaced a central power and the loyalties of the people were confined to that local ruler. Land formed the basis of wealth and power. Those lands were controlled by lords or warriors (the samurai in Japan). The families who worked the land owed their allegiance to the lord. They paid the lord with labor or produce in order to live on the land. Some, such as blacksmiths, were skilled craftsmen and had a measure of independence. However, most were bound to the lord and had little or no freedom. Contact with areas beyond their local region was limited, and change occurred very gradually if at all.

Japan

In 1192 the Fujiwara clan lost power and Yoritomo (yor ih TOH moh), a leader of another clan, took control. He received the title of **shogun** (SHO gun; "great general") and began to change Japan into a warrior state. Yoritomo ruled from Kamakura; therefore, this period of Japanese feudalism is called the Kamakura period.

The fighting among the clans ceased for a time during the thirteenth century while Japan fought off foreign invaders. (Later in this chapter you will read about these invaders, the Mongols.) Once the foreign threat had ended, struggle for control of Japan continued under various clans. The Ashikaga clan became dominant in 1336, and the second period of Japanese feudalism is named after them.

By 1600 the Tokugawa clan became dominant and moved the capital to Edo (Tokyo) in 1603. The final period of Japanese feudalism is called the Tokugawa period. Strife between the clans continued until the nineteenth century.

Rise of the Warrior Class

With the rise of the office of shogun, warriors became the leaders of Japanese society. The Japanese warrior was called a **samurai** (SAM uh reye) or bushi. Almost from birth, the samurai were trained in all methods of fighting, on foot and on horseback.

The samurai were also trained in history, literature, and writing. They needed to know about history in order to appreciate the culture they were fighting to protect and to understand how previous wars were won or lost. The samurai were taught literature to help them appreciate the less tangible aspects of culture and to broaden their understanding of abstract thought. Writing was an essential tool for communication. At the very least, writing instructions for battle plans or important information about troop movements could mean the difference between victory and defeat for the samurai.

The samurai lived by an unwritten military code known as the **Bushido** (BOOSH ih doh; "the way of the warrior"). This code required the warrior to display traits such as loyalty, honor, duty, and courage. It also required the warrior to commit suicide, known as *hara-kiri* (HAR ih KEER ee), rather than be captured or prove disloyal to his master. The loyalty of these warriors to their masters led to the endurance of feudalism until the 1870s.

Religion in Japan

Shintoism is an ancient form of Japanese religion. It was originally a form of nature worship. The Japanese believed that everything in nature that was unusual, such as fire, a waterfall, or a high mountain, possessed deity. Shintoism also viewed the sun as a goddess and the emperor as a descendant of the sun goddess. Shintoism inspires devotion to the homeland and worship of the emperor as a god. It became Japan's national religion and was used to further promote patriotism and loyalty to the emperor.

Zen Buddhism came to Japan from China near the end of the twelfth century. As you have already read, Buddhism emphasized suffering and meditation. Remarkably, this version of Buddhism had a great impact on the military class of Japan. Zen required its followers to develop intense mental concentration. This enabled the samurai to endure the hardships of battle. Zen also stressed self-control and concentration of energy. These qualities made the difference between success or failure on the battlefield.

Southeast Asia

Vietnam

Lying south of China and forming the western border of the South China Sea is the land of Vietnam. Much of its early history is unknown. However, there is evidence of two kingdoms living in this region during this period. The kingdom to the north was called Dai Viet. The kingdom called Champa occupied the central and southern regions of modern Vietnam. Champa traded with and was influenced by India and China.

By the ninth and tenth centuries, the kingdom of Champa had developed into a thriving civilization. However, during the next five centuries, the Dai Viet exerted increasing pressure on Champa. In 1471 troops from Dai Viet invaded and destroyed the capital of Champa. The Dai Viet came to be known as the Vietnamese. They gained complete control of remaining Champa territories in 1832.

Angkor (Cambodia)

Cambodia has a long history that may be traced back as far as 1000 BC. During the third century AD and beyond, Cambodia was influenced by India and China. An empire known as the Khmer (kuh MEHR) developed in this region between the ninth and the thirteenth centuries. Angkor served as the Khmer's center of power. Many capitals were constructed in this area during the empire's peak. In addition, over one thousand temples, including **Angkor Wat**, were built in this area.

Over time, the Khmer engaged in a failed series of wars with its neighbors and steadily declined in power. In 1432 Angkor was pillaged by the Thai and later abandoned. Over the next four centuries, the Cambodians were ruled by the Thai and Vietnamese.

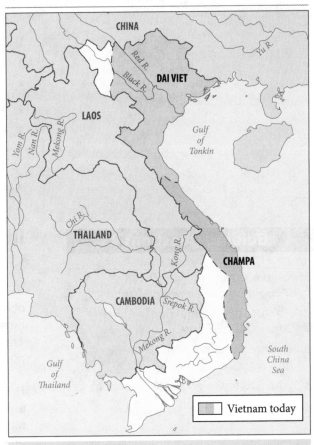

Vietnam Prior to 1471

Find It!

Angkor Wat
13.413° N, 103.867° E
A ground view is available!

Angkor Wat

Section Review Questions

1. Japan borrowed its written language from what country?
2. Yoritomo was the first Japanese leader to receive what title?
3. Vietnam developed from what two kingdoms?
4. What modern country developed from Angkor?
* Certain characteristics of Zen Buddhism easily applied to the military class in Japan. Explain what those characteristics were and how they applied.
* How is the Christian view of nature different from the Shinto view (see Rom. 1:19–23)?

III. Rise of the Mongol Empire

The Mongols were nomads who lived in tribes on the Mongolian plateau north of China. As nomads, the Mongols traveled across the plains of Mongolia in search of grazing land for their large herds of horses. Their lifestyle demanded homes that could be moved with them. The Mongols built **yurts** to provide shelter and a place to live. The yurts were designed so that they could be packed up and transported when the Mongols moved.

These tribes often fought among themselves over grazing lands. However, two factors led these tribes to combine and become a great empire. First, the climate cooled over a vast region. This cooling included Mongolia and resulted in less food for the vast herds of Mongol horses. The Mongols began to look for better grazing lands in northern China. The second factor was the birth of a gifted

Guiding Questions

1. What was the significance of the Mongol Empire on world history?
2. How did the Mongol rule in China impact this country?
3. What forms of religion did the Mongols practice?
4. What led to the end of Mongol domination?

Yurts

The Mongols were called the "People of the Felt Tents" because they lived in round tents called yurts. The round shape kept the yurt standing in the strong winds of the open plains. The Mongols made their yurts with frames of light wood covered with layers of heavy felt. The Mongols used the fur and wool of their animals to make the heavy felt, which they waterproofed by greasing. The outer layer of felt on the yurt was whitened with a coat of lime. This helped to reflect the hot summer sun and keep the tents cool inside.

The doorway of the yurt was draped with heavy felt. The women painted or embroidered designs of birds, animals, vines, and trees across the felt. These designs made each tent unique.

Regardless of their size, all the yurts were movable. When it was time to move, the Mongols took down the smaller tents and transported them on carts. The larger yurts (up to thirty feet wide) were not taken apart but were put directly on carts. Sometimes as many as twenty oxen were needed to pull these carts.

Mongol boy during the twelfth century. He proved to be one of the world's greatest military commanders.

Founding of the Mongol Empire

Chinggis Khan

Temujin (TEM yuh jihn), the son of a Mongolian tribal chieftain, was born around 1162. When he was a boy, his father was killed and he had to flee for his life. After wandering for a few years, he returned to his tribe and avenged his father's murder. He then spent several years gaining power and influence and forming alliances with other tribes. In 1206 he became the supreme leader over all the Mongol tribes. All the tribes acknowledged his position and gave him the title of **Chinggis Khan** (CHING-gihs KAHN; "Great Ruler").

Mongol Unification

Chinggis unified the Mongols using several means. Some of these means included developing a government, common law, and an organized military.

Chinggis organized Mongol government by dividing the people into groups of tens, hundreds, thousands, and ten thousands. He also chose trusted followers to lead these groups. Working through these leaders, he led the people in times of battle and peace. In this form of government, a person's loyalty to his leader was supreme. Chinggis placed great value on loyalty. He believed it was one of the greatest character qualities a person could have.

Chinggis also saw the importance of law. He wrote a law code called the **Great Yasa**, which dealt with every area of life. This law provided military rules, criminal punishments, tax regulations, court procedures, and moral standards. The punishment for many crimes was death. Less severe punishments included beatings and fines. Every Mongol, including the khan, was subject to the law. Chinggis used this code to govern his people and prepare them for military conquest.

Mongol Conquest

The Mongols were trained to be warriors from an early age. Warfare was the Mongol way of life. Chinggis used this lifestyle to organize his men into a strong, disciplined army.

The success of the Mongol army demonstrated the military genius of Chinggis Khan. He took full advantage of the Mongols' horsemanship skills in building a well-trained army. Taught to be the ultimate fighting cavalry, the Mongols quickly overran northern China and then turned west to conquer all of Central Asia.

Fast, ruthless, and deadly, the Mongol forces overwhelmed city after city. All who resisted were killed or used as human shields in future battles. The Mongol archer was skilled in battle. Trained to ride at a very young age, the archer learned to string his bow while riding and shoot his arrows when all the horse's hooves were off the ground. This ensured that his arrows would strike their target. The Mongols attacked their enemies with great speed on their horses and used arrows, lances, and swords.

Chinggis had to develop new fighting methods when his armies began to attack towns instead of other nomads. Many towns were

Citizenship Among the Mongols

The methods of organization used by Chinggis Khan show the importance of specialization and organization in the development of culture. His methods also show the importance of law in binding a society together. However, Chinggis Khan also shows how the blessings of the Creation Mandate can be twisted when separated from love for one's neighbor. Subduing the earth for the benefit of others is far different from subduing it for the benefit of self.

Mongol Army

The army was organized into units of tens, hundreds, and thousands. Ten thousand elite soldiers formed the core of the Mongol army. The entire Mongol army numbered up to 130,000. An additional 130,000 non-Mongols could be used. These forces were made up of various groups who decided to join the Mongols rather than fight them.

The Mongol army was a splendid fighting force. The soldiers lived in the saddle and even slept while riding on a march to the next battle. They endured all types of hardships in their quest to build an empire.

The Mongol horse was well suited for conquest and the extremes of the climate. Soldiers would often change horses several times a day, so vast numbers of them were needed for conquest.

Mongol Armor

To protect themselves, Mongol horsemen wore stiff armor made from animal hides. Chinggis also ordered his soldiers to wear a shirt made of raw silk because arrows could not easily penetrate the silk. Of course, if a man was shot, he was still hurt. But then his fellow soldiers gently pulled the shirt to remove the arrow from the wound. Protected from the arrow tip by the silk, the wound stayed cleaner and usually healed quickly.

Division of the Mongol Empire

Chinggis Khan had four sons: Jochi, Chaghatai, Ögödei, and Tolui. Chinggis warned them against dividing the empire and counseled them to hold the Mongol Empire together. Then he assigned the richest part of his empire to his third son, Ögödei.

This decision ran counter to Mongol tradition, which gave the major portion of an estate to the youngest son. However, Chinggis believed that Ögödei had a better grasp of human nature. Therefore, Chinggis thought Ögödei would prove to be the best one to rule.

surrounded by moats (trenches filled with water) and thick stone walls. These seemed to be unconquerable barriers at first. However, Chinggis used several methods to overcome these barriers. One effective method was **siege warfare**, in which Mongol soldiers fired arrows and flaming objects into the cities for weeks. They also kept food from going into the city until the people were starving. The Mongols borrowed rocket technology from the Chinese and fired gunpowder-filled bamboo rockets into the towns. These were not accurate but must have terrified those inside the towns.

Another effective tactic used by Chinggis and his forces was known as the **pretend retreat**. The Mongol soldiers would pretend to be beaten and appear to leave their camp empty. When the townspeople came out to plunder the Mongol camp, the Mongols would suddenly reappear. The startled people were unprepared to defend themselves, and the Mongol forces would destroy them. When everything of value had been removed from the town, it too would be destroyed.

The Mongols were ruthless. They killed and destroyed wherever they went. As stories of Mongol cruelty spread, the very name Mongol struck fear in the hearts of their enemies. The Mongols took advantage of this fear and captured towns without a fight as people chose to surrender rather than face certain destruction. Many men who were captured in this manner were used to increase the size of the Mongol forces. Women and children often became slaves.

Chinggis died in 1227. He had established a Mongol empire that spanned Central Asia from Beijing in northern China to Russia. Upon his death, his empire was divided among his sons. However, the Mongol conquests continued as before. Mongol forces marched into Korea in 1231. From Korea they renewed their advance into northern China. In 1252 the Mongols invaded the Dali kingdom. The Mongols seemed invincible.

Mongol Rule in Asia

In the west, Mongol forces took control of Kiev, Russia, in 1240. By 1258 they had overrun Baghdad in Iraq. However, Mongol forces made no attempt to invade western Europe. Some believe it was because there were not enough open plains to supply food for their horses. Whatever the reason, western Europe was spared from conquest.

In 1260 Kublai Khan, one of Chinggis's grandsons, came to power. His first priority was to become the ruler of all China. Overcoming strong resistance, Kublai gained control of the Southern Song empire in 1279. This fulfilled his grandfather's dream of conquering China. Kublai established a new dynasty that he named the Yuan (YOO ahn; "The Origin") dynasty. The Yuan was China's first foreign dynasty. However, Kublai was not content to stop with China. In 1274 he attempted to invade Japan but failed. In 1281 he assembled a larger force and attacked Japan from China and Korea. This attempt also failed. Despite great efforts, Kublai was unable to expand his empire beyond China.

Kublai tolerated the Chinese but staffed the government mostly with Mongols and other non-Chinese. The Mongols placed their subjects in four categories, with Mongols at the top and most of the Chinese at the bottom. Nevertheless, the Yuan dynasty promoted Chinese culture without trying to change it. In the end, the Mongols

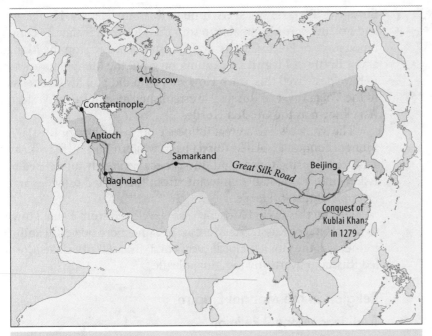

Mongol Empire 1279

brought very little change to China. By 1368 Mongol rule of China had ended.

Japanese Success at Defeating Mongol Invaders

As you have already read, the Japanese endured two invasion attempts by Mongol forces during the thirteenth century. The Japanese had been forged into a military state just prior to these invasions. This arrangement prepared the tiny country for an attack by the undefeated Mongols.

In 1274 Kublai sent a force of up to thirty thousand men from Korean ports to invade Japan. However, a storm destroyed the Mongol fleet, and the Japanese drove back those who were able to land.

In 1281 Kublai sent a much greater force, numbering 140,000 men, to invade Japan. However, the Japanese had built defenses and were prepared for another attack. Every resource was used to protect Japan against the Mongol invasion. Another storm sank the Mongol fleet during the second invasion, and Japanese monks gave credit to a **kamikaze** ("divine wind") for protecting Japan. Over time, these victories led to a myth that the Japanese could not be defeated. Not until World War II would this myth be destroyed.

Southeast Asian Resistance to Mongol Rule

Kublai Khan also sent forces to conquer Vietnam, Burma, and Java. The people of these countries resisted conquest by the Mongols. As a concession, they agreed to a ritual submission. During this time Kublai Khan also had to contend with another Mongol ruler for control of Mongolia. Kublai was forced to divert his soldiers to ensure his continued rule there. This diversion preserved Southeast Asia from Mongol domination.

The Golden Horde

Batu Khan, another grandson of Chinggis, led Mongol forces into Europe. Between 1237 and 1240, the Mongol forces (known in

The Golden Horde

The word *horde* comes from the Mongol word *ordu* which means "camp." The Russians called the Mongols the "Golden Horde" because their greased huts (yurts) shone in the sun.

Europe as **Tartars**) smashed through Russian defenses. Hungary and Poland were also unable to stop the Mongol advance. A combined force of Poles, Czechs, and Germans tried to stop the Mongols at the **Battle of Liegnitz**. Accounts vary, but the Mongol forces seem to have destroyed this army. However, Batu did pull his forces back to the Volga River in Russia. He established an empire in Western Asia known as the **Golden Horde**.

The Mongols had a great influence on the history of Russia. Mongol conquest isolated Russia from western Europe for over two centuries. During this period Russia became greatly influenced by Asian culture. Russian architecture from this period provides an example of this influence.

During this period Moscow also developed from a small town to the capital of Russia. As Moscow became more powerful and influential, the Golden Horde weakened. By 1480 cities like Moscow led Russia in overthrowing Mongol rule.

Religion in the Mongol Empire

Traditional Mongol Religion

You learned in Chapter 1 about the error of polytheism. The Mongols worshiped many gods and believed that good and evil spirits controlled the world. They also believed in a supreme god who ruled all the spirits. They called him **Tengri** (TEN gree), meaning "the great god of heaven." The Mongols lived in fear of the spirits and hoped for blessings from them.

Every yurt had small idols made of felt. The women made these idols at sewing parties. The Mongols believed that these idols protected their families and their animals. Before every meal they spread food and drink on the lips of the idols. They also prayed to them. They believed that these idols had power to bless them.

The Mongols also believed that certain men, called **shamans** (SHAH muhnz), had power over the spirits. The shamans were the priests of the traditional Mongol religion, which is called shamanism (SHAH muh NIZ um). The shamans were medicine men and witch doctors who used a special language when performing their magical rituals. The Mongols often consulted their shamans before making important decisions.

Spread of Nestorian Christianity

Under Kublai Khan, the Mongol emperor of China, Christianity once again had access to China. Kublai Khan's mother claimed to be a Christian. Kublai Khan was not a Christian himself, but he was welcoming to Christians. When the Italian explorers Niccolo and Matteo first traveled to China in the 1260s, Kublai Khan actually asked them to send additional Christian missionaries. When Marco Polo accompanied his father and uncle on a second trip, he reported Nestorian churches along the Old Silk Road and in major cities. Even some Mongol rulers professed Christianity.

Religious Tolerance

The later empire of the Mongols included people of many religions, including Christians and Jews. Some members of Chinggis Khan's family even married Nestorian Christians. However, this liberty would prove to be short-lived.

Rise of Islam

Islam also spread throughout the Mongol Empire. Once Islam became dominant, the Muslims often persecuted other religious groups. Christians and Jews were pressured to convert to Islam.

Muslim rulers made Nestorians wear distinctive clothes, such as a yellow patch, marking them as Christians. They required Christians to wear special haircuts and even ride horses sidesaddle so Muslims could easily identify them.

The final blow to Christianity under Mongol rule came during the brutal reign of Tamerlane. He persecuted the Nestorians without restraint. Following his vicious assault, Christianity disappeared from China for a time.

Trading in the Mongol Empire

The Mongols manufactured nothing beyond what they needed for daily living, such as felt, harnesses, and carts. Because they did not stay in one place for a full growing season, they rarely grew crops. The Mongols resorted to trade to obtain other goods. Even before Chinggis Khan built his empire, the wealthier Mongols traded fur and hides for Chinese silk and cotton.

As the empire grew, trade grew also. When the Mongols conquered all of China in 1279, their empire reached from the Caspian Sea to the Pacific Ocean. They reopened trade along the ancient silk routes, which had been closed for centuries. After nearly a thousand years, the West finally had direct contact with the cultures of the Far East. Between 1100 and the 1200s, the crusaders were traveling from western Europe to fight the Muslims in the Middle East. During this same period, Mongol traders brought exotic goods from the Far East into Middle Eastern markets. Western merchants and crusaders carried these goods back to western Europe.

The Mongols quickly developed a desire for the goods they saw. In time, the Mongols settled into towns and gave up their nomadic ways. Once settled, the Mongols found that their zeal for conquest faded. For example, Kublai Khan stopped living in a yurt, built a palace, and settled in northern China.

After a century of peaceful trade, the Muslims in the Middle East closed the East-West trade routes and renewed their attacks on what remained of the Byzantine Empire. Europeans, now familiar with the goods of the Far East, still wanted them. With the closing of the land routes, Europeans sought to find other ways to the East. As they searched for new routes, the Age of Exploration began.

Decline and Collapse of the Mongol Empire

Collapse of Mongol Rule in China

Over time, the Mongols' control of China weakened as the Mongol tribes returned to fighting one another. The Chinese encouraged this fighting and viewed it as a way to break free from Mongol rule. By 1368 the Chinese were able to expel the Mongols from China. The **Ming** ("brilliant") dynasty was established, and the Chinese sought to remove all traces of Mongol rule.

Timur (Tamerlane)

During the second half of the fourteenth century, another Mongol leader came to power in central Asia. Timur suffered from an accident during his youth and was lame. He was called Timur the Lame or **Tamerlane** (TAM ur LANE). Despite his physical limitation, Tamerlane became a powerful conqueror. He demonstrated unusual cruelty as he extended his empire from Turkey to India. Tamerlane's forces captured Baghdad and Damascus and defeated the Ottoman Turks. He even invaded southern Russia and weakened the Golden Horde. However, rather than building a well-ruled empire, Tamerlane concentrated on collecting treasures taken in battle. As a result, his empire collapsed shortly after his death.

The last Mongol empire was the small **Mughal** (MOO gul) dynasty in India (1526–1857). The Mughals brought an era of peace and artistic achievement to India. The most famous Mughal ruler was **Akbar** (AHK bar), a wise and generous leader. He extended his empire over most of India. The Mughals were a peaceful people, far different from their Mongol ancestors. Under the Mughals, some of India's greatest architecture was built, including the **Taj Mahal** (TAHZH muh-HAHL). After Akbar's death, the Mughals had few strong leaders. Their empire slowly declined until the British finally took over India in the nineteenth century.

Find It!

Taj Mahal
27.175° N, 78.042° E
A ground view is available!

Taj Mahal

Section Review Questions

1–3. Name the three Mongol leaders who achieved the following: first united the Mongol tribes, invaded Russia, and extended the empire from Turkey to India.

4. What was the name of the Mongol empire in western Asia?

5. What Chinese dynasty followed the expulsion of the Mongols from China?

★ What attitude among the early Mongols allowed Nestorian Christianity to spread in China for a time?

★ Why did the Japanese conclude that they were invincible?

★ How might Tamerlane have built a more lasting empire?

Making Connections

1. What impact did the invention of the compass from lodestone have on China?

2. Why were merchants prevented from serving in government in China prior to the Song dynasty?

3. Why did Japan descend into feudalism?

4. How did the rise of the warrior class in Japan affect Japanese culture?

5. Why were Japanese warriors trained in history, literature, and writing?

6. How did silk shirts minimize the damage to a Mongol soldier from an arrow strike?

Developing History Skills

1. Go to your local library or go on the Internet to discover the various raw materials that have been used to record written information. Organize them in chronological order. Compare your list with lists of others in the class.

2. Construct a timeline that includes early Chinese history through the time of the Mongol invasions and that includes the rise of the Ming Dynasty. (This assignment may require outside reading or Internet research.)

Thinking Critically

1. Evaluate traditional Mongol religion in light of God's Word (using passages such as Exodus 20:4–5 and Romans 1:23).

2. When Islam becomes dominant, as it did in the Mongol empire, how are other religions, especially Christianity, treated?

3. Why did the Mongol Empire collapse? Provide a one or two sentence answer for each of the empires (China, Russia, Asia Minor [Tamerlane], and India).

Living in God's World

1. You go on a summer mission trip to China. You have a lengthy conversation with a Chinese girl your age. She asks you, "If Christianity is the true religion, why didn't it exist in China until just recently?" How could you respond?

2. Christianity did not take root in Asia until the nineteenth century. Gather into several groups to answer this question: Why does a Christian need to know about the history covered in this chapter since very little of it concerns the advance of Christianity? Use Acts 14:15–18 and 17:24–31 in your answer. After all the groups have reported their answers to the class, discuss which answers are best.

People, Places, and Things to Know

Shang
Song
technology
paper
compass
gunpowder
printing
cast iron
ancestor worship
Confucius
Buddhism
Taoism
Lao-tzu
feudalism
shogun
samurai
Bushido
hara-kiri
Shintoism
Zen Buddhism
Angkor Wat
yurts
Chinggis Khan
Great Yasa
siege warfare
pretend retreat
kamikaze
Batu Khan
Tartars
Battle of Liegnitz
Golden Horde
Tengri
shamans
Ming
Tamerlane
Mughal
Akbar
Taj Mahal

CHAPTER 5

Emergence of European Culture

500 – 1300

- Interval Between the Fall of Rome and the Rise of Feudalism
- Decline of Feudalism and Development of States in Europe
- Expansion of Europe
- Development of Culture in Europe
- Calamities in Europe

700 – 1600

Pope Urban II calls for the first crusade against Muslim control of the Holy Land 1095

Pope Gregory VII forces a German ruler to submit to the papacy or lose his crown 1077

Pepin the Short is crowned king of the Franks and founds the Carolingian Dynasty 751

William of Normandy successfully invades England 1066

The pope crowns and proclaims Charlemagne Roman Emperor December 25, 800

700	800	900	1000	1100

Hugh Capet, Count of Paris, founds the Capetian Dynasty 987

Big Ideas

1. How did the papacy and feudalism replace a declining Rome?

2. Why did feudalism decline, and what replaced it?

3. How did Europe expand after 1000?

4. How did European culture develop?

In Chapter 1 you learned about the Roman Empire and the ultimate victory of Christianity despite persecution. While Rome could boast a history that endured for one thousand years, no human empire lasts forever. For a number of reasons, including the continued decline of morality, a series of weak leaders, and the use of Germanic mercenaries to fill the ranks of the Roman armies, Rome continued to decline. Following Rome's collapse, there was a period of confusion that was briefly interrupted by the reign of a Frankish king. Following his death, Europe declined into a number of feudal estates.

Great Famine 1315–22

Hundred Years' War between England and France 1337–1453

Roman Church achieves its political height under Pope Innocent III (r. 1198–1216)

Execution of Joan of Arc by the English 1431

Ferdinand and Isabella of Spain expel the last Muslims and complete the Spanish Reconquista 1492

Black Death 1347–50

Rise of modern universities 12th century

| 1200 | 1300 | 1400 | 1500 | 1600 |

Writers begin to write in the vernacular languages 12th century

I. Interval Between the Fall of Rome and the Rise of Feudalism

Rise of European Kingdoms

During the fifth century, German tribes began to migrate onto land governed by the Roman Empire, often fleeing more aggressive tribes. As the Roman Empire weakened, German tribes increased in power. By 476 the Western Roman Empire had fallen.

While the Roman government collapsed, Christianity thrived and spread throughout the German tribes. These tribes became the foundation of medieval Europe. For example, the Franks settled in the region of Gaul (France) and formed several powerful kingdoms.

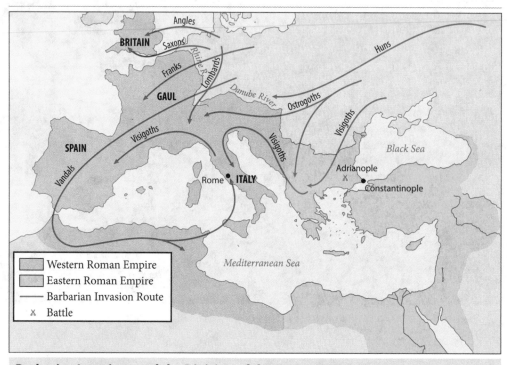

Western Roman Empire
Eastern Roman Empire
— Barbarian Invasion Route
x Battle

Barbarian Invasions and the Division of the Roman Empire

Merovingian House

Clovis became the leader of one of these Frankish kingdoms in 481. He used military force and other means to combine several kingdoms. During an important battle, he cried out to God for victory and promised to be baptized. He won the battle and fulfilled his promise. Clovis also ordered three thousand of his soldiers to be baptized into the Roman Church. The embracing of this form of Christianity won Clovis the support of the Roman Church. This alliance between the Frankish rulers and the Church of Rome endured for centuries.

When Clovis died, the kingdom was divided among his four sons. This royal line became known as the Merovingians. By the seventh century, the family had lost influence due to careless and immoral living. The **mayor of the palace** (the leading palace official) became the real power in the kingdom.

Carolingian House

Near the end of the seventh century, Pepin II became the mayor of the palace in a strong Frankish territory. He conquered neighboring

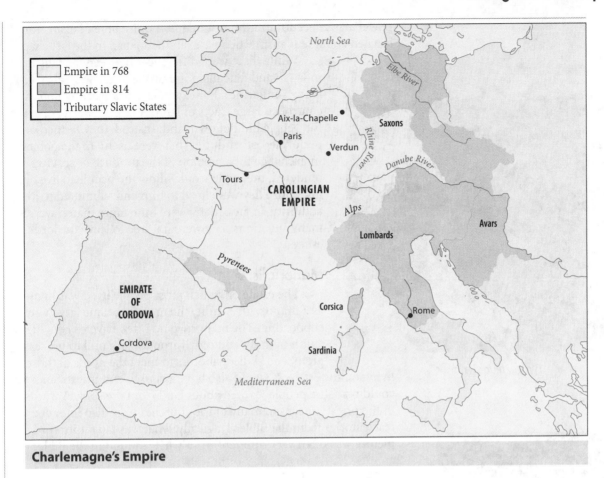

Charlemagne's Empire

territories and united them under one rule. Charles Martel (see Chapter 2), Pepin's son, expanded the kingdom. Charles's son, Pepin the Short, received permission from the pope to take the title of king in 751. A new family now ruled the Franks. It would be named after its most famous member, Charlemagne.

After Pepin the Short died, his sons Carloman and Charles ruled together. Carloman soon died, and Charles became the sole ruler of the Frankish kingdom. His influence over Europe resulted in his title **Charlemagne** (SHAR luh mane), or "Charles the Great."

Charlemagne demonstrated strong leadership in many ways. He led his army and defeated many other tribes in Europe, including the Lombards and the Saxons. Charlemagne also organized his empire into districts. His government worked to ensure justice and maintain peace throughout his kingdom. (Charlemagne's contribution to education will be discussed later.)

On Christmas Day in 800, another important event occurred. The pope placed a crown on Charlemagne's head and proclaimed him Roman emperor. While this did not increase Charlemagne's power, it did raise an important question: who is supreme—the state or the church? Later popes would point to this event and claim authority over kings.

Feudal Lordship

Following Charlemagne's death, Europe was divided among his sons. The division of Europe and lack of strong leadership led to the decline of central

The exterior of the cathedral in Aachen, where the pope crowned Charlemagne

73

Typical feudal manor

Twelfth-century mosaic of Roger II being crowned by Christ rather than a pope. His attire is Byzantine, and the work visualizes his ambition. It also implies the church is subordinate to the state.

power. This decentralization resulted in the rise of feudalism. You learned about feudalism when we examined Japan in the last chapter.

While there were differences between feudalism in Japan and feudalism in Europe, there were also many similarities. For example, a few wealthy nobles controlled large tracts of land. A large majority of the people did not own land. Instead, they farmed or performed other duties that were useful to the nobles. In exchange for a portion of the produce or services rendered, the noble would allow the people to live on his land. They were loyal to him and submitted to his authority. In fact, many were little more than slaves. In many situations they were not free to leave the lord's estate.

Manorialism

The estate on which most people lived was known as a **manor**. Over time, the manor became largely self-supporting. The manor would often have its own blacksmith to make and repair iron tools, a mill to process grain, and skilled laborers to meet the needs of those living on the estate. It would also have a church and priest. Since few could read, the people learned about God from the spoken words of the priest. Images in many of the churches were also intended to teach stories from the Bible. Tragically, what was taught in word and picture was often very different from what is found in the Bible.

European Monarchies

Even though Europe descended into a feudal society, there were men who retained the title of king. During this period they often had little real power. The king needed the support of the nobles. He depended on them for financial and military support. Several generations of monarchs worked to strengthen their office and increase their authority, often using wars and marriage alliances to expand their influence.

Preservation of Learning

You may be surprised that learning survived after the fall of Rome. The Roman Church, through monasteries, preserved much of the Greco-Roman knowledge.

Charlemagne also became a strong supporter of education during his reign. He encouraged the education of the clergy and children of nobility. His reforms stirred an interest in the Bible and the writings of classical authors. Charlemagne also encouraged the discovery and copying of many ancient works. His royal court became a place of learning and scholarship.

Under Charlemagne's influence, monasteries became centers of Western knowledge. Monks taught others to read and write. They also preserved Christian learning by storing and copying documents. Long after Charlemagne's death, monasteries continued to educate and preserve written works. European culture and civilization would be built upon this preserved knowledge.

Growth of Papal Power

As you have already learned, the Roman Empire declined and collapsed. During this same time, the Roman Church began to develop. Gradually, the Church of Rome became a powerful member of medieval society. A brief examination of key popes will help to show this growth of power.

Leo I, bishop of the city of Rome, became the first to receive the title of **pope** ("papa") in the fifth century after he convinced a violent barbarian tribe (the Huns) not to destroy the city of Rome. Gregory I (6th century) was one of the first bishops of Rome to claim supremacy over all other Christians. **Papal** (PAY pul) power increased during the ninth century when Pope Nicholas I claimed that the pope was supreme over the church and state. Gregory VII also confirmed the power of the papacy during his reign. In 1077 Gregory forced a German ruler to submit to him or lose his crown.

The power of the papacy peaked during the beginning of the thirteenth century under Pope **Innocent III**. He took the title "vicar of Christ" and claimed to have supreme authority over the church and state. While others had claimed an increasing level of authority for the papacy, Innocent III succeeded in enforcing absolute authority over clergy and kings. He sent armies and issued papal decrees to force rulers and nation-states to submit to his will.

In addition to the growth of the power of the bishop of Rome, other changes slowly took place in the church. For example, pastors (clergy) were forbidden in 1074 to marry. This decree led to a class of men who were loyal to the pope. However, it also created a terrible problem since it violated the Creation Mandate in Genesis 1–2. God made humans to marry, have children, and exercise dominion over His creation. Forbidding the clergy to marry minimized the marriage bond created by God. In addition, the Roman Church determined that the bread and wine in the Lord's Supper changed into the body and blood of Christ during mass. A church council led by Innocent III decreed this to be official church doctrine in 1215. To believe otherwise was considered heresy (false teaching). Heresy was punishable by torture or death.

The Christianizing of Europe

As we have noted, Christianity spread throughout Europe through missionaries and believers who lived among the German tribes. The bishop of Rome sent monks to areas such as Gaul (France), Spain, and Britain to introduce them to a form of Christianity. He also appointed church leaders who were loyal to him.

Rulers found an alliance with Rome useful. Men such as Clovis and Pepin the Short encouraged or required their people to submit to the Church of Rome. There were certainly genuine conversions throughout this period. However, many people were baptized into a form of Christianity that imitated their pagan worship.

These rising nation-states were considered Christian if the king accepted Christianity as the official religion of his realm. Sadly, however, many of the people in these realms remained ignorant of the Bible's most basic teachings. As a result, medieval European Christianity was very different from biblical Christianity.

Nevertheless, the Bible was accepted by most Europeans as God's Word. Medieval Europeans did not divide their world into the religious and political spheres as later Europeans would. Christianity was understood to have something to say about every aspect of life. The influence of Christianity in the culture paved the way for the Reformation, in which the fullness of the gospel was once again widely proclaimed.

The Sacraments

Over several hundred years the Roman Church developed several sacraments or ways to earn grace necessary for salvation. Eventually the Church of Rome established seven:

1. Baptism (to remove original sin)
2. Confirmation (to receive the Holy Spirit)
3. Confession/penance (to receive forgiveness from a priest)
4. Communion/Eucharist (This is the primary sacrament to receive redemption from sin.)
5. Matrimony (Marriage is controlled by the church, and children are to be educated by the church.)
6. Holy orders (The priest is considered another Christ; the nun is considered the bride of Christ.)
7. Last rites (Anointing of the sick brings forgiveness of sin and prepares one for death.)

Justice in Medieval Europe

In theory, the church did not have the power to impose secular penalties like execution. Likewise, the state's laws were not designed to direct people in spiritual matters. Human law was to be based on natural law rather than Scripture. Based on this understanding, heresy should not have been punishable by physical punishments.

But since most Europeans were baptized into the church as infants, the Roman Church could ask the state to punish people for breaking the vows repeated by their parents when they were baptized as infants. Breaking a vow or a contract was considered a crime that the state could punish.

Guiding Questions

1. How did long-term climate change contribute to Europe's economic and population growth beginning in the eleventh century?

2. How did European monarchies expand their power? Were there limits to this power?

3. What were some of the Jewish contributions to Europe's development?

4. How did the political relationship between the Roman Church and nation-states change?

Population and Productivity

It is hard to say which came first, population growth or increased productivity. However, each depended on the other. (This is reflected in the twin commands of the Creation Mandate to multiply and subdue the earth.) A larger population required additional food. Greater productivity required more laborers. Several factors during the period between the eleventh and fourteenth centuries led to the increase of population and productivity.

Early in the eleventh century, people in Europe began to carve additional farmland out of forests and marshes. (The heavy wheeled plow made it possible to farm this rich, dense soil.) As the people plowed more land, more crops were grown. With increased production came larger families. Farmers needed big families to help run their farms. The increase of food also enabled others to sustain larger families.

Farmers also learned to increase yield by rotating crops and allowing some fields to lie fallow (to rest) for a season. These methods renewed the soil and enabled the fields to produce crops for many years.

Also, beginning in the eleventh century, there was a warming of the climate in Europe known as the **Medieval Warm Period**. This provided a longer growing season and further enabled the farmers to grow more crops.

Section Review Questions

1. What leading palace official held the true power in the Merovingian dynasty?

2. Who granted Pepin the Short the right to take the title of king?

3. What ruler supported a revival of learning and made monasteries the centers of Western knowledge?

4. Under what pope did the papacy reach its peak?

5. The Roman Church taught that sacraments were means of earning _____.

★ Evaluate the Roman Church's sacrament of Communion/Eucharist in light of 1 Corinthians 11:23–26 and Hebrews 10:11–14.

■ II. Decline of Feudalism and Development of States in Europe

Decline of Feudalism

Castles had dominated Europe's landscape during the early Middle Ages, but from the beginning of the Crusades to about 1500, a change occurred. Although many people continued to live on lands controlled by nobles, more and more people moved to towns. These new townspeople came from many places for many reasons and started new towns or settled in old ones. Towns began to dominate the land.

One reason for the growth of towns was Europe's population growth. Improved farming methods meant that farmers could produce more and better crops to feed more people. Better methods in crop production meant that the nobles needed fewer people to run the castle lands. Many people, no longer needed by their lord, bought their freedom and moved to towns. Younger children of nobles also moved to the towns, since only the firstborn son would inherit the land.

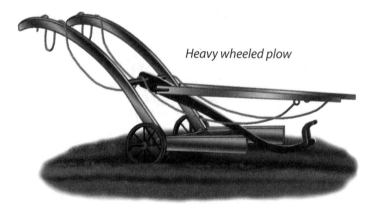

Heavy wheeled plow

Another reason for the growth of towns was the growth of trade. Along the trade routes reopened by the Crusades came exotic, desirable goods from the East. Places where trade routes or roads intersected became logical locations to build settlements. These settlements grew into towns and became centers of trade for all types of goods.

Towns became places of opportunity. Poor farmers, butchers, bakers, carpenters, and other craftsmen moved to towns and prospered. In time, they would challenge the power of the nobles to govern their lives.

Nobles often owned or controlled the land on which towns developed. Over time, the leading citizens of towns convinced nobles to give their town a charter. The **town charter** was a legal document listing the privileges of the townspeople. This freed the people from many feudal duties. The people still paid taxes to the lord, but they were now allowed to govern themselves. Kings also expanded their power by granting town charters. This redirected the loyalty of the people to the king and the taxes to his coffers. These were significant advances and contributed to the decline of feudalism.

Development of States in Europe

Rise of Strong Monarchies

England

The conquest of England by **William the Conqueror** in 1066 laid the foundations for a strong monarchy in England. He established a new royal dynasty, the Normans. This line was soon replaced by another dynasty through William's great-grandson, **Henry II**. Henry strengthened English royal authority by expanding the use of royal courts. He developed **circuit courts**, with judges who heard cases in a particular province (circuit) of England. This strengthened the power of the king and captured the loyalty of the people.

France

France began as a fragmented piece of Charlemagne's empire. However, by the end of the tenth century, **Hugh Capet** (HYOO KA-pit), the count of Paris, founded a new royal line in France. The Capetian (kuh PEE shun) rulers gained territory by conquest and marriage alliances. They also developed an efficient centralized government. The Capetians supported the claims of the Roman Church

Citizenship

A citizen is a person who has legal protections and rights within a region or nation.

Citizenship in England

The move toward limiting royal power and giving citizens a greater voice is consistent with two Scriptural principles.

First, the reality of the Fall means that it is unwise to give unchecked power to anyone. Such power will be abused.

Second, God gave all humans the responsibility of ruling over the world. Though this is not inconsistent with an order of authority (Rom. 13:1–7), it is an argument for a democratic element in government.

Jewish Contributions and Tribulations

Rulers such as Charlemagne and Louis the Pious valued the skills and contributions of their Jewish subjects. Since many Jews had connections to the Middle East and Asia, they became vital to trade. Jewish merchants were able to travel freely in Muslim-controlled areas where others were not. They traded in slaves, fur, and other items from the Near East. From China they bought spices and silk.

In some countries, they served as ambassadors, physicians, or tax collectors. Many Jews developed great skills in manufacturing glass, making jewelry, and processing gold. Others farmed the land, served as merchants, or built ships. Wherever Jews were allowed to live in peace, those countries prospered in a variety of ways.

However, the Crusades drastically changed the way many Europeans viewed Jews. Many who answered the call to expel the infidels from the Holy

Land also viewed Jews with suspicion. Because the Jews often refused to convert and be baptized, they were viewed as the enemies of "Christian" Europe. Under the banner of the cross, crusaders slaughtered helpless Jews by the thousands.

The hard-working Jews often had great wealth. This made them become even more despised by many in Europe. Rumors about the Jews were spread, and often whole villages of them were murdered. Some Europeans killed Jews simply to take their land and wealth. Perhaps the worst lie told about the Jews was that they poisoned wells and rivers. As the plague known as the Black Death spread across Europe, the Jews were often blamed and whole Jewish populations were slaughtered.

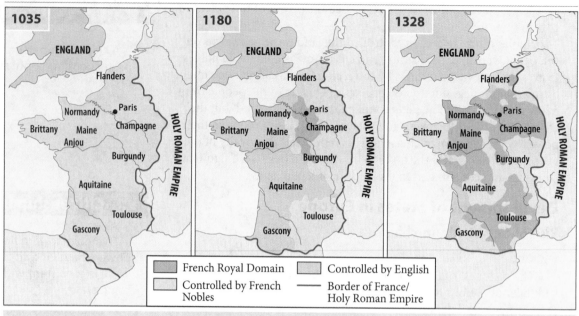

1035	1180	1328

■ French Royal Domain	■ Controlled by English
■ Controlled by French Nobles	— Border of France/ Holy Roman Empire

Growth of France from the 11th to the 14th Century

and granted rights to towns in exchange for their support. These strategies increased royal power.

Philip II continued the thrust to develop a strong monarchy in France. At this time the English controlled large areas of French land. Philip responded by seizing much of the English-controlled land in France during the reign of King John of England. In addition, he improved the effectiveness of the royal government by sending out royal officials called **baillis** (bah YEE), or bailiffs. These men collected taxes for the king and ensured justice in carrying out laws.

The Capetian family ruled France for over three centuries. During this time each ruler was able to pass the crown to a son. Thus France was spared from revolts and major struggles for power. The resulting stability made possible a strong and powerful monarchy in France.

Developments in English Legal and Constitutional Practices

Before a circuit judge would travel to his province in England, a **jury** (group of local citizens) would make up a list of accusations known as **indictments**. This list was a record of the crimes committed and the people suspected of committing the crimes. The modern grand jury developed out of this procedure. (A grand jury decides if there is enough evidence to bring an accused person to trial.)

Trial by jury had its beginnings in this system of dealing with crime. However, in early English practice, the jury provided evidence to the judge to determine guilt. In modern practice, the jury hears the evidence and renders a verdict of guilty or not guilty.

The justices that Henry II sent out across England developed uniform laws for all of England. These laws overruled local laws that varied from region to region. This **common law** was intended to guarantee justice, and it helped to unify England.

England differed from other countries such as France by setting limits on royal power. The abuses of King John (1199–1216), including demanding excessive taxes and ignoring the will of the nobles, led to a revolt. The victorious nobles forced John to sign the

Magna Carta ("Great Charter"). Originally, this document only assured rights for the nobility. However, over time, the English people viewed this document as declaring the principle that the king's power over all citizens was limited.

During the reign of Edward I, **Parliament** developed. It began as a group of advisors to the king. By the fourteenth century, Parliament was composed of two groups. The leading vassals were represented in the prominent group (House of Lords), and the knights and leading citizens were represented in the less prominent group (House of Commons). Over time, Parliament gained more power by granting or withholding its approval of new taxes. Through this "**power of the purse**," Parliament could limit the king's power.

Changing Political Relationships

The Decline of Political Power of the Roman Catholic Church

You have learned that the political power of the Roman Church grew during the Middle Ages and peaked during the rule of Pope Innocent III (1198–1216). However, within a century, the political influence of Rome had almost disappeared. There were many reasons for this decline, including weak popes and frustration over the abuses by the Roman Church. Kings were quick to take advantage of Rome's loss of political power to increase their own power during this period.

The Rise of Political Power in the Nation-States

At least two obstacles stood in the way of the rise of a central power in the emerging nation-states: feudal lords and the Roman Church. Nobles were naturally reluctant to submit to a king and accept a reduction of their power. The Roman Church had made great claims about its authority over religious and political affairs. Thus Rome opposed the growth of political power in the nation-states. Monarchs used various means, including granting town charters, expanding royal courts, and arranging marriage alliances, to bring the nobles under control. They also struggled with the Roman Church to limit its control in their land.

City-States Versus Centralized Monarchies

Another form of government that developed during this period was the city-state. Venice was the most successful and prominent of these city-states. Located on the Adriatic Sea, this city traded extensively with the Byzantine Empire and the Muslim world. To carry out its trade, Venice developed a vast navy of over three thousand ships. These ships could be used to promote trade and defend trade routes against pirates.

The form of government practiced in Venice was similar to the republican form of government in ancient Rome. Power was shared by a senate made up of nobles and a lower body composed of a large number of wealthy citizens. Through the lower body, the citizens had the power to accept or reject the newly elected leader of the ruling council.

Venice, like rising nations, struggled with the demands of the Roman Church. Venetians remained loyal Catholics but refused to persecute their citizens for religious "heresy." Rome responded by placing Venice under the **interdict** (the people were denied access to most of the sacraments) on at least two occasions.

Grand Canal and Basilica Santa Maria della Salute in Venice

Bridge of Sighs (Ponte dei Sospiri) in Venice

A Representative Government

The city of Venice was governed by the Great Council, which was made up of members of the wealthy families in Venice. Around two hundred members of the Great Council were selected to form the Senate. From the Senate, the Council of Ten made the day-to-day decisions of government. One member of the Council of Ten was chosen to be the *Doge* (duke) and often held this ceremonial position until death.

Venice retained its independence until Napoleon conquered the city in 1797.

Guiding Questions

1. What steps did Christian states take in overthrowing Muslim powers, and what were the consequences of the Crusades?

2. How were population growth, increased agricultural production, and technological innovation connected?

3. How did urban growth, expansion of trade, and the development of a money economy impact Europe?

Providence

Christians cannot approve of the idea that fighting a holy war will merit forgiveness of sins. Nor does the Bible mandate that Christians maintain holy sites for pilgrimages. Nonetheless, God in His providence often turns evil to good. The recovery of Greek and Hebrew in Western Europe laid the groundwork for the Reformation.

Section Review Questions

1. After 1500 many people moved from the manor to _____.

2–3. List two things that contributed to the decline of feudalism.

4. What nobleman conquered England in 1066?

☆ Why did Philip II take land from an English king?

☆ How was the government of Venice similar to the government of ancient Rome?

■ III. Expansion of Europe

The Crusades

When Islam spread over the Middle East and North Africa, it pushed the Byzantine Empire out of the Holy Land. Nevertheless, Christians were permitted to travel to the Holy Land to visit Christian sites. During the eleventh century, however, the Seljuk Turks cut off this access. The Byzantine Empire also found itself increasingly under attack by Muslim forces. Byzantine emperors began to appeal to popes to send military aid to Constantinople. In response to the first plea for help, Pope Urban II called for a **crusade** to liberate

Crac des Chevaliers, a crusader castle in Syria

Grandmasters Palace in Greece

Historical Perspectives

Popular View

During the eighteenth century, European writers began to describe the Crusades in negative terms. Well-known men, including Voltaire, Edward Gibbon, and Sir Walter Scott, portrayed the crusaders as uniformly greedy, ignorant, and bigoted. In contrast, they pictured the Muslims as peaceful, advanced, and moderate. This view continues to be popular in film portrayals. In some portayals, the priests are foolish and violent. Crusaders are clearly the "bad guys" who work to prevent any peaceful solution. Muslims, such as Saladin, are presented as thoughtful, tolerant, and wise.

Historian's View

Some modern writers are working to correct this bias. For example, Crusade historian Jonathan Riley-Smith has sought to restore a balanced view of the Crusades. Riley-Smith notes that the Crusades were reactive rather than wars of conversion. The Muslims had cut off pilgrimages to the Holy Land. As a result, the goal of the First Crusade was to recapture Jerusalem and allow renewed access. For many, the Crusades were a means of doing penance and avoiding purgatory. Thus, the Crusades were driven by religion, not conquest. The journey was long, the hazards were many, and the lack of vehicles made transport of wealth nearly impossible. The dangers of a crusade, including high mortality rates, suggests that only the bravest of people would choose to go on a crusade. Since the cost of a crusade could bankrupt most knights, the trip was made at great sacrifice.

There is no doubt that abuses did occur on both sides during the Crusades. However, the popular view found in many historical works and novels is one-sided and often based on faulty information.

1. What inaccuracies do you find in popular versions of the Crusades when compared with a leading historian's research?

2. Why might these inaccuracies persist?

the Holy Land and defeat the infidels. This call was issued in 1095, and several armies traveled to the Middle East over the next two centuries. Only the First Crusade enjoyed a measure of success and gained control of a narrow strip of land for a brief period. Other crusades failed, and the effort to free the Holy Land ended by the late thirteenth century.

When efforts to free the Holy Land ended, the Roman Church redirected the Crusades and began to target Muslims on the Iberian Peninsula. Other groups in Europe that taught doctrines that differed from those approved by the Church of Rome were killed by crusading armies as well.

Motives

Motives for the Crusades differed. For many, the idea of a crusade was exciting and provided opportunity for an adventure. For the Roman Church, the Crusades created an opportunity to expand its influence. Religious fervor motivated many as well. The Crusades were seen as an act of penance. It was expensive for a lord or knight to go on a crusade. It was also dangerous. Many who went would not return. It meant leaving family behind. But the popes promised great reward for those who went. By fighting in a holy war, the crusader believed he could earn forgiveness of sins.

Results

The Crusades resulted in the deaths of many thousands of fighters and civilians. Yet, after all of the violence and bloodshed, the Europeans were unable to maintain their hold on the Holy Land. Numerous historians have called these religious wars a mistake and a failure. However, many positive results emerged from the Crusades.

The Crusades and the Protestant Reformation

Important documents traveled back to Europe with the crusaders. Manuscripts of ancient Greek works and other documents were reintroduced to European scholars. However, none were more important than copies of the New Testament. These were compared with the Latin texts that had been used in Europe for centuries. For the first time, the accuracy of the Latin Vulgate was questioned. In addition, enterprising men such as Erasmus prepared Greek New Testaments for printing on the newly invented movable-type printing press. Access to these Greek texts played a role in the Protestant Reformation during the sixteenth century.

For example, much of the knowledge that had been preserved by the Muslims and the Byzantine Empire found its way back to Europe. Knowledge about science, diseases, astronomy, math, and many other subjects was recovered. Greek and Arabic documents brought to Europe played an important role in the revival of education and the rise of universities in Europe.

Merchants filled their ships with spices, muslin, silk, and furs as they returned from taking crusading forces to the Middle East. These goods found a ready market in Europe and resulted in a great increase in trade. Merchants became very wealthy and formed part of a new economic class, a **middle class**. The middle class was composed of those who lived in towns and included merchants, bankers, craftsmen, and other skilled laborers.

In addition, manufacturing methods used by the Muslims were copied and taken back to be developed in Europe. New factories provided work for many poor Europeans and contributed to the growth of towns. New products and goods became available, and opportunities to make wealth abounded.

The Development of Cities

God made humans to work together in exercising dominion over the earth (Gen. 1:28). For this reason, cities have always been important to human existence. In almost every period of human history, as culture develops in a region, cities emerge to help the development of that culture. As a people group grows, it becomes highly centralized, its members begin to specialize in particular tasks, and thus a city begins to flourish. Tragically, as time progresses, another nation often invades, and the city is destroyed or goes into decline. Then, eventually, the cycle is repeated.

Following the decline of Rome, the empire splintered and cities fell into decay. Populations declined for various reasons, including war and famine. However, over time, the population began to increase again. Then, once again, cities began to emerge in Europe.

Population Growth

In the eleventh century, the population began to grow rapidly and continued to grow for three hundred years. Towns grew into cities as more and more people moved from the feudal estates and as the birth rate continued to rise.

Food was plentiful, and workers were needed to produce goods in newly built factories. Trade and the growth of a money economy also created many jobs and great wealth. Cities symbolized the prosperity and liberty that were not available on the feudal estates.

Cities such as Paris and Venice had large populations. It is estimated that the population of Paris may have reached two hundred thousand during this period. The population of Europe may have grown to one hundred million people.

Technological Innovation

Medieval Europeans were skilled in finding new ways to use technology. For example, Europeans used ancient Roman inventions and recently acquired knowledge of Muslim devices to improve their lives. Use of such discoveries as the horse collar, water mills, Arabic numerals, and windmills enabled European civilization to develop. Wind and water were also harnessed to power industry and

Medieval weapons: longbow, crossbow, and trebuchet

Convex and concave lenses

enable mass production. Use of the compass and stern-mounted rudders made it possible to navigate the oceans. And instruments of war such as the cannon, crossbow, and armor changed the ways wars were waged.

While the Europeans improved many existing devices, they also invented several things themselves. For example, mechanical clocks are believed to have been invented in Europe around the thirteenth century. In addition, spectacles (or glasses) were developed in Florence, Italy, near the end of the thirteenth century. The first spectacles used convex lenses, which improves the vision of the farsighted. Concave lenses (for the nearsighted) were probably not developed until the fifteenth century.

Continued Growth of Trade

The increase of trade was tremendous. The wealthy had their gold and silver turned into coins in order to buy many of the items that became available. Farmers and others sold their excess produce and other goods for money. Over time, they bought their freedom from the nobles and moved to the towns. The growing towns promised greater opportunity and freedom.

Money Economy

With the increase of trade, a money economy developed. Problems arose, however, because every town had its own kind of money. Merchants traveling from town to town had to use many different kinds of money. To handle this problem, some men became moneychangers. They knew the value of different kinds of coins. At the market they exchanged money from other towns for local coins.

Banks developed as a result of the use of money. The word **bank** comes from the Italian word *banca* (BAHNG kuh), meaning "bench." Moneychangers and early bankers sat on benches, and people referred to doing banking business as "going to the bench."

Banks soon became more than just places of exchanging money. As banking grew, bankers began to lend money to merchants for business and trading ventures. With this extra money, a merchant could expand his business. Banks also issued letters of credit to wealthy merchants. To obtain a **letter of credit**, a merchant first left an amount of money with the banker, who gave him a letter that credited the merchant for that amount. Thus, the merchant could travel without having to carry large sums of money. When he arrived at his destination, the banker in that town accepted the other bank's letter of credit and gave the merchant his money.

The Expulsion of Muslim Powers from Iberia

Driving out foreign powers became another way to expand European culture and influence. In Chapter 2 you learned about the Islamic conquest of the Iberian Peninsula (modern Spain and Portugal) in the eighth century. The reconquest (**Reconquista**) of this peninsula began almost immediately. Christian and Muslim forces struggled for control of sections of this peninsula over the next five centuries. By the end of the thirteenth century, non-Muslim forces had regained control of most of this region. Only the Muslim kingdom of Granada remained. In 1492, Ferdinand II of Aragon and Isabella I of Castile took control of Granada, and Muslim rule came to an end.

Letters of Credit and the Crusades

The Knights Templar, a monastic order of knights, formed around 1120 to protect pilgrims who traveled to the Holy Land. Over time, they developed a banking system to aid wealthy pilgrims. A noble would deposit his funds with the Templars in Europe to be managed and protected during his journey. In exchange he would receive a letter of credit stating the value of his deposit. Upon arriving in the Holy Land, he would submit his letter of credit to the Templars and receive his funds. This arrangement made travel much safer for pilgrims. The fees charged added to the Templars' wealth.

This concept became common practice in the growing banking industry. The modern version would be a checking account and the writing of checks.

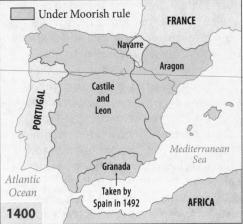

Iberian Peninsula

Medieval knights at the Metropolitan Museum of Art in New York

The University of Bologna

Most students at the University of Bologna (buh LOAN yuh) came from outside Italy. They were forced to organize in order to protect themselves from local citizens, robbers, and teachers who might otherwise fail to give the students a quality education. They elected officials to perform such duties as making sure the bells rang on time, presiding over examinations and graduation, and assembling student committees to report on faculty abuses. If town officials refused to resolve a student's complaint, the students had the right to carry out a university strike to demand justice. Powerful leaders such as Pope Honorius III protected this university and intervened on students' behalf.

Section Review Questions

1–3. List three motives for the Crusades.

4–5. List two devices invented by Europeans in the Middle Ages.

★ What is wrong with the belief that one can have his sins forgiven by going on a crusade (or pilgrimage)?

★ How did the growth of cities play an important role in the expansion of Europe? Was this growth a good thing for Europe?

■ IV. Development of Culture in Europe

In Chapter 1 you learned that culture is the physical and mental environment developed through human thought and labor. The concept of culture and its development began in the Garden of Eden. Although sin forced Adam and Eve from the garden, it did not nullify the Creation Mandate. Even the unbeliever tends to fulfill aspects of this mandate in one way or another. We will find more and more examples after AD 1000 of men exercising dominion over God's creation through thought and labor.

Chivalry

Knights were trained to live by a strict set of rules called the "code of chivalry." **Chivalry** comes from a French word meaning "horseman." It is also similar to the English word *cavalry*. Knights were expected to be brave in battle and limit their fighting to other armed knights. A group of knights could not attack a single knight. Instead, they were expected to fight him one at a time.

The Roman Church also sought to influence the behavior of knights. They worked to improve the conduct of the knights and to limit the destruction of warfare. The church decree known as the **Peace of God** placed church property out of bounds for fighting. This decree was also intended to protect those not directly involved in the fighting. The **Truce of God** restricted fighting to certain days of the week. For example, combat was not allowed from Wednesday evening until Monday morning. While these decrees were not always followed, an effort was made to improve conditions when fighting occurred.

Rise of Universities

During the Middle Ages education was not available to most Europeans. However, as previously mentioned, education was preserved in monastic and cathedral schools (eleventh century) for a privileged few. Students were trained in the **liberal arts**. These studies were reserved for "free" (*liberei*) men (nobility) rather than "common" men. All subjects were taught in Latin.

The concept of a university became one of the unique contributions of European culture. Universities began to develop in the twelfth century. During the formative years, students would travel to places where well-known teachers instructed, and a university would later develop. Newly acquired Muslim and Byzantine documents about medicine, science, and other subjects also provided a wealth of information for instruction in these universities.

Italy boasted two early universities, and Paris developed one soon thereafter. Over time, the universities became known for particular areas of study. Students traveled to Salerno in Italy to study medicine. Those interested in studying law traveled to Bologna. The university in Paris concentrated on the study of theology.

From the universities of Bologna and Paris, two types of universities developed. The university in Paris was made up of teachers who had earned masters of arts degrees. They regulated the university. The university in Bologna was made up of groups of students who regulated the university and hired their teachers. Nations in Northern Europe tended to follow the Parisian pattern as they established universities. Nations in Southern Europe tended to follow the Bologna pattern.

Students attending these universities often met in rented buildings, and some sat on straw as they listened to their teachers. Since paper was expensive and hard to find, the students often spent hours each day memorizing their lessons. The typical day for a student began at 4 a.m. and ended at bedtime around 9 p.m.

While Italy and France were the first countries to develop universities, schools began to appear in England, Spain, and Portugal by the end of the twelfth century. Warfare often made travel difficult or impossible, and countries started their own universities to meet the needs of their students. By the fourteenth century, Germany, Bohemia, and other countries were establishing their own universities as well. More subjects were offered, and universities began to meet in permanent buildings.

Universities served a vital role in increasing literacy and scientific advancement. They produced medical doctors, lawyers, theologians, and many other professionals. This system enriched European culture and spread knowledge throughout Europe. Kings and popes supported universities because they valued the services of graduates to promote their causes.

Works of Art, Architecture, and Literature

Christian religion played a central role in European culture and society. Christian themes were found at the center of European culture during the Middle Ages. These themes are evident in art, architecture, and literature from this period.

Art

During the Middle Ages, Christian themes and subjects dominated most art. Bible characters such as John the Baptist, Mary, Christ, and various saints appeared in most of the artwork. Halos were often added to emphasize holiness. John the Baptist was typically shown wearing an animal skin (to represent camel's hair). Art served to visually teach stories from the Bible and the Roman Church.

Architecture

During this period in Europe, architecture often centered on the construction of **cathedrals**. Growing towns and cities displayed their wealth and prosperity by building these large and impressive churches.

Citizenship at the University

Knowledge is important to keep a civilization running. The university therefore has an important role in furthering the Creation Mandate.

It was no accident that the university developed in Christianized Europe. Philosophers disagreed for centuries about the substance of the world. Some said it was one element (such as water or fire). But this led to a meaningless label to describe everything. Others focused on the complexity of the world, but this approach failed to show how everything holds together.

The Christian answer to this problem comes in part through reflection on the Trinity. God is both one and many. The Christian can see that God also created a world that is both one and three. The university became a way of unifying the study of the many parts of God's world.

Jesus and the raising of Lazarus

Notre Dame Cathedral serves as an example of Gothic architecture.

During the early Middle Ages, the architectural style was called **Romanesque** (ROH muh NESK) because it used many elements of Roman style. This style used rounded vaults (made from putting several arches together) for roofs. Thick stone walls were needed to support these heavy roofs. These buildings were dark inside because only small windows could be used. Candles and torches provided some light, but Romanesque churches were generally dark and cold.

A new style of construction, called **Gothic**, developed during the thirteenth century. Using external supports known as **flying buttresses**, the cathedrals could have higher ceilings and thinner walls. This construction allowed for larger windows and doors. Gothic cathedrals were warmer and brighter. Stained-glass windows added beauty and color to the interior of the churches. These windows often used arranged pieces of colorful glass to picture Bible stories.

Literature

Latin was the language of the Roman Empire. It remained the language used for writing, government, and instruction during the Middle Ages. However, it was not the language spoken by most of the people in Europe. Languages varied by region and included French, German, Italian, Spanish, and English.

During the twelfth century, writers began to compose their work in the **vernacular** (vur NAK yuh lur; common spoken languages). Writing in the languages of the people helped to develop and preserve those languages. Use of the vernacular also contributed to the growth of nationalism.

Two of the best known writers from this period are **Dante** and **Chaucer**. Dante, an Italian, wrote the *Divine Comedy*, a poem about an imaginary journey through hell, purgatory, and paradise. His work sheds light on the unrest and skepticism of the late Middle Ages. Chaucer, an English poet, wrote *The Canterbury Tales*, which is about a group of pilgrims traveling to visit the tomb of a famous religious leader in England. He gives the reader a glimpse of English life during this period.

Divine Comedy

It may seem odd to name a 14,000-line poem about hell, purgatory, and heaven a comedy. However, in its historical context, this name makes sense. During the medieval period, writing that had a sad ending was called a tragedy. A work that had a happy ending was called a comedy. A comedy had to be written in the vernacular so the common individual could read it or understand it when it was read to him.

Guiding Questions

1. How did famine, plague, and warfare decimate Europe?
2. How did the Hundred Years' War lead to the development of modern France and England?

Section Review Questions

1. Knights were trained to live by what code?
2. Which church decree limited the days on which fighting could occur?
3. During the Middle Ages, students were taught in what language?
★ Why did students at the University of Bologna hire their teachers?
★ What was the significance of writing in the vernacular?

■ V. Calamities in Europe

A calamity can be defined as an event that causes dreadful loss, enduring suffering, or great misery. Famine, war, and plague are examples of calamities. Beginning in the fourteenth century, Europe was decimated (great loss of population) by all of these.

Great Famine

The **Great Famine of 1315** was the first calamity to strike large areas of Europe during this period. It began with heavy and frequent rain over much of Europe starting in 1315. The spring and summer remained cool, and the crops rotted in the fields. Food for people and animals became very scarce. Also, salt to preserve meat became scarce. The producers of salt needed dry weather to extract it from salt water through evaporation. So meat spoiled. As a result, the price for food and salt became too high for the vast majority of the people.

To survive, people slaughtered their farm animals for food and ate seed grain. Some parents abandoned their children because they could no longer feed them. This calamity even resembled scenes from the Old Testament (2 Kings 6) as some resorted to cannibalism to survive. The frequent rain continued until 1317, and people were reduced to eating roots, grasses, and even tree bark to survive.

Many of those who survived the two years of rain and famine had been weakened by pneumonia and other illnesses. In addition, with the destruction of livestock and lack of seed for planting, the recovery was slow. Somewhere between 10 and 25 percent of the people died of starvation or illness between 1315 and 1322. While other calamities would take more lives, this one lingered for years and caused slow and agonizing deaths.

Hundred Years' War

Between 1337 and 1453, England and France fought a series of battles to settle the issue of English control of land in France. This became known as the **Hundred Years' War**. The French had steadily taken land away from the English for many years. However, the death of the last Capetian king without a male heir led to a crisis.

The English king, **Edward III**, was related to the French royal line through his mother and claimed the right to the French throne. However, the French nobles rejected this claim and selected Philip VI of the house of Valois (val WAH) as king. War was to be expected. This series of battles began as a contest between feudal nobles and ended as a rivalry between two emerging nations.

English forces started the war by crossing the English Channel. Although they were outnumbered, the English quickly won several key battles. They defeated the French by using new tactics and weapons. English longbows destroyed French forces from a safe distance. Thousands of French soldiers were slaughtered in these battles.

Although the English won most of the battles, the drain on English forces and England was great. Over time, the people of England tired of the cost of war, and political unrest resulted. Also, a plague killed many in England. There were simply not enough soldiers to take advantage of English victories.

The French finally rallied to victory under the leadership of a peasant girl named **Joan of Arc**. She believed that she was being directed from heaven to drive out the English. Desperate for a leader, the French followed her and defeated the English. The English were able to capture her and burned her at the stake. However, her example strengthened the French to emerge as victors.

Black Death

Historians differ on how the plague known as the **Black Death** originated and was spread. However, there is no doubt that something similar to the bubonic plague killed millions of people throughout the world. Europe suffered a great loss of people as this plague spread from city to city and engulfed whole countries.

The plague may have begun in China and spread by trade ships to Europe by 1347. Rats and their fleas have been blamed for the spread of the fatal bacteria, although opinions vary, and we cannot be certain. What is certain is that millions of people were killed by this disease. Some estimate that up to twenty-five million people in Europe died from the Black Death.

Cities in Europe were especially vulnerable to the spread of the plague for several reasons. Open sewers and improper disposal of trash made the cities unsanitary. Rats and fleas thrived in the cities. Houses were also often close together, and the people lived in crowded settings. These unhealthy conditions provided a breeding ground for disease and its spread.

Besides the obvious reduction of the population in Europe, there were several other consequences. The people quickly turned to the Roman Church for deliverance. Many made trips to Rome and made donations to the church in hopes of rescue from the plague.

However, the Roman Church proved to be unable to stop the plague. When people saw the priests and nuns dying as quickly as others, they lost faith in the claims of the Roman Church. In addition, many concluded that the plague was sent by God to punish the people for their sins. The Roman Church lost much of the authority that church leaders had built up over the years. People began to look in other places for answers.

The wealthy left the cities and lived on secluded estates in order to avoid contact with the plague. Others gave themselves over to sinful living since they decided that death was imminent anyway. Crime also became a serious problem. As previously mentioned, many blamed Jews for the plague, and thousands of Jews died as the people slaughtered whole Jewish communities for their imagined crime.

By 1350 the Black Death had run its course, but it took many years for Europe to recover. The Church of Rome had lost much of its credibility during this time. On the other hand, the movement toward nationalism continued to gain momentum. The Hundred Years' War, interrupted by the Black Death, resumed and concluded with France and England emerging as nation states.

Section Review Questions

1. Which of the three calamities mentioned in this chapter caused the slowest and most agonizing deaths?

2. What English king triggered the start of the Hundred Years' War?

3. What animals have been blamed for spreading the Black Death?

✶ Why were the French ultimately able to defeat the English during the Hundred Years' War?

✶ Why did the Church of Rome lose influence during the Black Death? What did this do to the faith of the common people in Europe?

■ Making Connections

1. What tribes moved into Roman territory and eventually took over the Roman Empire?

2. After whom was the Carolingian house named?

3. How did monarchs develop centralized power during this period?

4. Why did Pope Urban II call for the First Crusade?

5. What were some positive results of the Crusades?

6. Why were Gothic cathedrals considered warmer and brighter than Romanesque cathedrals?

7. What chain of events resulted in the Great Famine of 1315?

8. Why did the English win most of the battles during the Hundred Years' War and yet lose the war?

■ Developing History Skills

1. Using this chapter and information found in Chapter 2, compile a list of the kinds of documents that crusaders would have brought back to Europe. Based on this list, what kinds of cultural changes would have resulted?

2. Construct a timeline by centuries that includes the significant events of political development in France.

■ Thinking Critically

1. What developments in England limited royal power? Why?

2. How would you respond to the following statement: "An important lesson we learn from the Black Death is that the Christian religion is unable to live up to its claims. It claims that God will take care of those who follow Him. But many Christians in Europe died from this plague." (Make use of Job 2:3–10, 1 Thess. 3:2–3, and 1 Peter 1:6–7.)

■ Living in God's World

1. Divide the class into two groups, one group favoring the Crusades and one opposing them. Have each side discuss its reasons for its position and then choose a spokesman to present its reasons. After both sides have spoken, the groups should again discuss among themselves how to respond to the opposing side. Then different spokesmen should give each side's responses.

2. Pretend that you are a preacher in England in 1210. The king is claiming a divine right to rule England; that is, he believes he has complete authority because God has made him king. Using Scripture, write a speech that disputes the claim of the divine right of kings.

People, Places, and Things to Know

Clovis
mayor of the palace
Charlemagne
manor
pope
papal
Innocent III
Medieval Warm Period
town charter
William the Conqueror
Henry II
circuit courts
Hugh Capet
Philip II
baillis
jury
indictments
common law
Magna Carta
Parliament
power of the purse
interdict
crusade
middle class
bank
letter of credit
Reconquista
chivalry
Peace of God
Truce of God
liberal arts
cathedrals
Romanesque
Gothic
flying buttresses
vernacular
Dante
Chaucer
Great Famine of 1315
Hundred Years' War
Edward III
Joan of Arc
Black Death

CHAPTER

Renaissance and Reformation
1300 – 1650

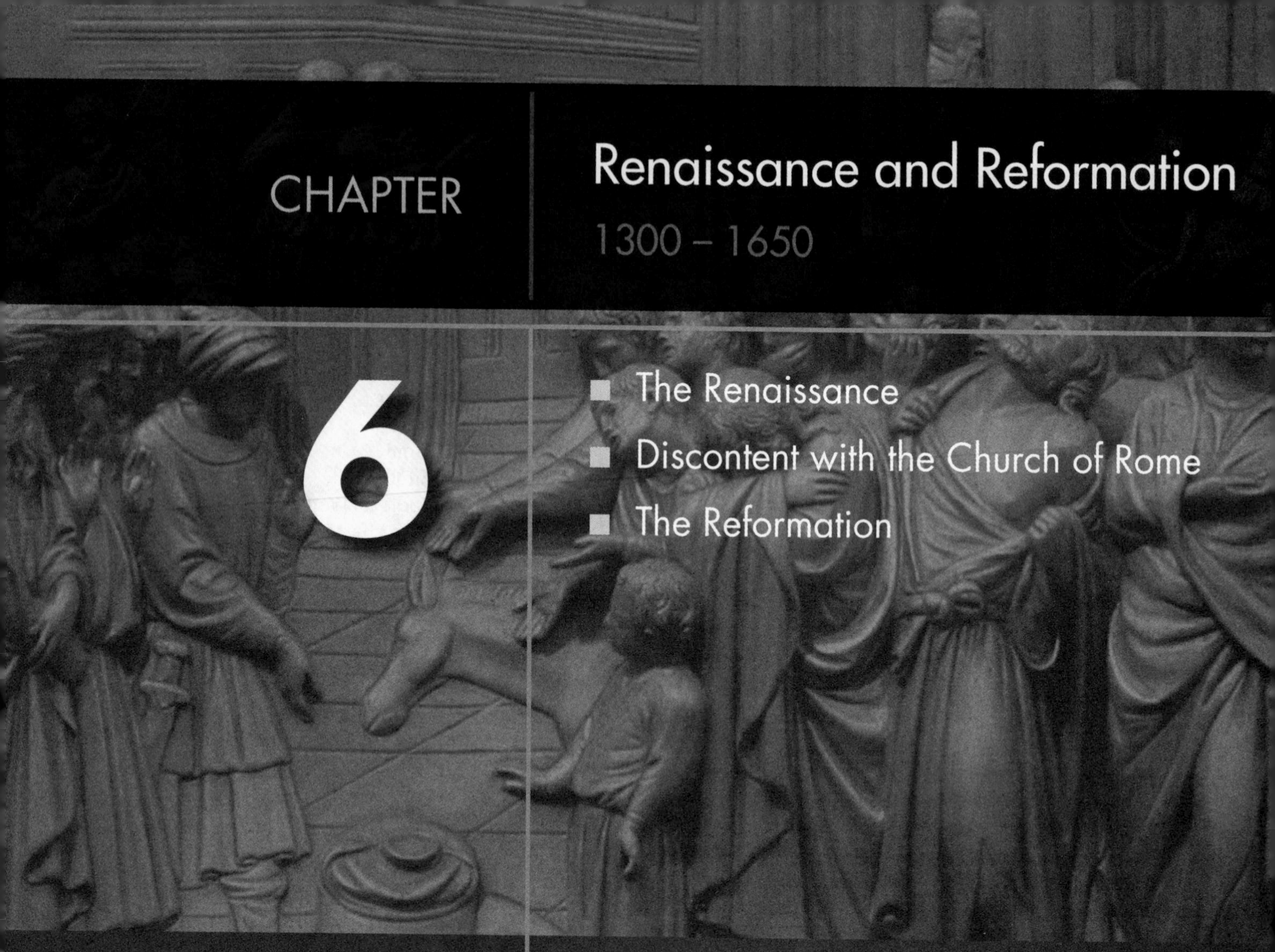

6

- The Renaissance
- Discontent with the Church of Rome
- The Reformation

1200 – 1700

Fall of Constantinople 1453

Johannes Gutenberg invents the movable-type printing press c. 1450

Fourth Lateran Council 1215

John Huss burned at the stake (during the Council of Constance) 1415

Brief and failed papacy of Boniface VIII 1294–1303

Life and ministry of John Wycliffe c. 1320–84

1200	1300	1400

Inquisition by the Roman Catholic Church 13th through 17th century

Council of Constance ends the controversy over multiple popes 1414–18

Big Ideas

1. What were the major causes of the Renaissance?
2. Why were many Europeans disillusioned with the late medieval church?
3. What were the three key principles of the Reformation?
4. How was the Protestant Reformation different from the Counter Reformation?

There was a definite change in people's attitudes and actions beginning in the fourteenth century. With the growth of towns and trade and the discovery of lost Greek and Roman writings, people had much to be excited about. A revival of learning known as the Renaissance resulted.

The rebirth of learning shed more light on the problems in the Roman Church. This resulted in intense criticism and skepticism regarding Rome's teachings. The renewed study of Hebrew and Greek exposed important weaknesses in the Latin Vulgate. Many began to openly challenge the Roman Church's claims.

Martin Luther posts 95 Theses in Wittenberg, Germany
October 31, 1517

The Roman Church excommunicates Luther 1520

Birth of Anabaptist movements 1525

Council of Trent meets periodically
during this period 1545–63

Thirty Years' War
1618–48

Pope Leo X authorizes sale
of indulgences 1513–21

1500

1600

1700

Life and ministry of John Calvin
1509–64

Catholic massacre of Huguenots in Paris 1572

Guiding Questions

1. What impact did the rediscovery of classical learning have on European thought and culture?
2. What were some of the positive and negative consequences of the Renaissance?

Lorenzo de Medici of Florence, Italy, was an early and generous patron (financial supporter) of the Renaissance. He was also an accomplished poet. His poetry is considered to be some of the finest written during the Italian Renaissance. A careful look at his statue reveals a broken nose. He considered this a blessing because it prevented him from smelling unpleasant odors.

The Printing Press

Europe began to produce paper during the thirteenth century. However, an efficient method of printing was needed in order to turn out a large volume of work at a low cost. You may recall that the Chinese first developed the movable-type press centuries earlier. However, Gutenberg appears to have developed this process on his own in the fifteenth century. While the Chinese did not find much use for a printing press, Europeans found this invention to be revolutionary. The printing press would prove to be an essential tool in spreading Renaissance writings. It would become even more vital for the spread of the Reformation.

I. The Renaissance

The **Renaissance** (REN ih sahns; rebirth, revival) began in Italy and spread north into other European countries. The change was gradual, but the results were profound. The Renaissance affected many areas of life, including art, architecture, and literature.

Transition

In the last chapter you learned about the rise of universities. In addition, you found that there was a rediscovery of classical Greek and Roman learning. Crusaders had brought many documents to Europe from Constantinople that provided scholars with much information. Also, the fall of Constantinople in 1453 caused many scholars from that city to travel to Europe. This flood of information led to a revival of learning.

During the Middle Ages, life was difficult, and opportunities for education were very limited. However, with the growth of a middle class and wealth, funds were now available to support this revival of learning. Wealthy merchants and the wealth of the Roman Church paid for paintings, sculptures, and architecture that reflected the new spirit of the Renaissance. Talented writers produced enduring works in the vernacular.

Profound Changes

Tools

As we learned in the last chapter, writers had already begun to write in the vernacular. During the Renaissance, this practice continued and expanded. Works produced in the language of the people allowed Renaissance ideas to spread to many more people. As citizens became more prosperous, they found time to read and discuss these new ideas. The often tedious life of the Middle Ages was being replaced by a period of hope and optimism.

The invention of the movable-type printing press by **Johannes Gutenberg** in the mid-fifteenth century made literary works available to the public at a very low cost. Prior to his invention, books had to be copied by hand. This made them very expensive and available only to the very wealthy. The printing press now made books available quickly and at a cost that many more people could afford.

Art and Architecture

Art

The two paintings at the top of page 93 show the same subject: the Madonna and Child (Mary and Jesus). The first one comes from a medieval Gothic church. The second was painted during the Renaissance. You can see that they differ, but you may not be able to tell why. By taking a closer look, we will find out how the Renaissance artists made their paintings look different.

Perhaps the first thing you notice is that the people in the Renaissance painting look real, whereas the people in the other painting look flat. Renaissance artists had begun to study how bones and muscles work together. The artists learned about **anatomy**—the structure of humans, animals, and plants. Using this information, they could make their subjects appear more real. The change toward realism reflected a change in thinking. During the Middle Ages, people stressed heavenly things. By the Renaissance, people began

Two Madonna with Christ child paintings; the first painting was done in the 13th century; the second painting was by Raphael during the Renaissance.

to realize that nature and humans were important too because they were creations of God. Instead of painting flat people who were only symbols of the saints, Renaissance painters painted real people.

The Renaissance artist also added dimension to his figures by **shading**. You can see that some parts of the faces, bodies, and clothes are darker. This shading makes these areas seem farther away. The Renaissance artist painted nearer areas lighter and farther areas darker to make objects and figures appear rounded. The gradually changing colors in the folds of cloth show this technique especially well.

In the Renaissance painting, the background seems to be far away. The Renaissance artist gave depth to his background by painting far-away objects smaller than nearby objects. The ability to give depth to paintings was the result of the new study of **perspective**. The artist could figure out mathematically what size objects should be and at what angle they should be placed to give the appearance of reality. A Renaissance artist had to be a good mathematician as well as a painter.

Two men stand out as Renaissance artists, both from Italy. **Leonardo da Vinci** (LEE-uh-NAR-doh duh VIN-chee) was truly a Renaissance man in that he developed many skills. His best known paintings are *The Last Supper* and the *Mona Lisa*. The second man,

Mona Lisa, da Vinci's famous painting

Da Vinci's Last Supper

The Sistine Chapel

Michelangelo's David, *perhaps the most impressive example of Renaissance sculpture, represents the exalted ideal of man as the measure and center of all things.*

Michelangelo (MY kul AN juh loh), is best known for his painting on the ceiling of the **Sistine** (SIS teen) **Chapel** in Rome. He worked on this project for four years while lying on scaffolding.

Sculpture

The sculptures of the Renaissance resemble the sculptures of the Greeks and Romans. The statues are lifelike, powerful, and stunning. The new knowledge of anatomy helped sculptors in forming human figures. Working with stone or bronze, they tried to make their figures as realistic as possible.

Much medieval sculpture was relief sculpture. That is, it was attached to a flat surface such as the wall of a cathedral or castle. This type of sculpture could not be viewed from all sides. Many Renaissance sculptors preferred to make freestanding statues. They followed the principles of classical art: balance, harmony, and realism. Yet, even in relief sculpture, Renaissance works differed from medieval sculpture. By rounding the figures, showing anatomy, and following the rules of perspective, the artist brought flat sculpture to life. One of the greatest examples of Renaissance relief sculpture is the doors sculpted by **Ghiberti** for the baptistery of Florence.

Architecture

Renaissance architecture rejected most of the Gothic style. Architects came to believe that pointed arches, tall towers, and flying buttresses were neither graceful nor beautiful. Instead, they wanted to return to the architectural style of the Greeks and Romans. Rounded arches, columns, and domes characterized Renaissance structures. The soaring towers and ornate decoration of the Gothic cathedrals were considered old-fashioned. In contrast, Renaissance churches and palaces sat solidly balanced on the ground.

Ghiberti's self portrait in one of the doors

Scenes from Ghiberti's doors to the baptistery in Florence

Brunelleschi and the Dome

In 1419 a competition was held to design the dome for the Cathedral of Florence. Two men were leading competitors: Brunelleschi and Ghiberti (who won the competition to create the baptistery doors). This time, Brunelleschi won and designed a unique dome that was double-walled and constructed from over four million bricks. This dome weighs about thirty-seven thousand tons. He had to design special machines to lift the heavier stones. Brunelleschi even had to develop new methods of laying the bricks to make construction possible.

The Cathedral of Florence, pictured to the left, is a stunning example of Renaissance architecture. **Brunelleschi** (broo nuh LES key) designed the dome for this huge structure. He solved several architectural problems in order to construct this eight-sided dome. The structure demonstrates Brunelleschi's keen understanding of mathematics. This dome even exceeded the one atop the Roman Pantheon. Men like Brunelleschi demonstrated that the Renaissance man had surpassed the ancient Romans, whose knowledge they had used.

Learning

Knowledge about science, medicine, and many other fields improved at an ever increasing pace. The recovery of ancient knowledge led to more study and new discoveries. An education became more and more important.

To study the world around him, the Renaissance man needed to know how to read, write, and reason. With increased prosperity, students could afford to hire private teachers. In addition, many towns started academies where boys could learn Latin and Greek. Girls often had tutors at home. Students spent hours reading classical works. Wealthy men collected and read large libraries of manuscripts.

The subjects taught in the Renaissance differed from those of the Middle Ages. Known as the **humanities**, these subjects covered human interests and experiences. Literature, philosophy, art, history, grammar, and speech were all taught. Renaissance teachers encouraged their students to invent, explore, and discover. They also expected students to appreciate and create beauty through art. The goal of Renaissance education was to make the student a well-rounded person, one who was educated and interested in many fields.

As previously mentioned, Leonardo da Vinci was an excellent example of the Renaissance man. He excelled in sculpture, architecture, painting, music, and poetry. Leonardo also studied anatomy, botany, engineering, and mathematics. His notebooks were filled with sketches of inventions, including early versions of a tank, a submarine, a helicopter, and a machine gun.

Variations

An examination of the writings from Italy and Northern Europe reveals two distinct themes.

Italy

Italian writers patterned their writing after the works of ancient Greece and Rome. They studied the ancient writings and imitated their style. They were also concerned with advancing human knowledge and acceptable behavior. Three Italian authors will be briefly examined.

Petrarch was a pioneer of Renaissance humanism and a central figure in Italian literature. He sought out ancient manuscripts and studied them. He also composed poetry in Latin and followed the style of ancient Roman poets. Petrarch spread the ideas of the Renaissance and became known as the **Father of Humanism**.

Castiglione (cah stil YOH nay) was another Italian author. He wrote a famous book on etiquette (social behavior). Good manners were considered essential to the growing middle class, who were eager to behave properly. His book, *The Courtier*, described proper conduct for the Renaissance man.

Machiavelli (mahk ee uh VEL ee) worked for the government in Florence, Italy, and observed political events in Europe. From his observations he wrote a book called *The Prince*. In previous works on politics, the Greeks held up the virtues that a good prince should possess. These writings, along with the Bible, were very influential during the Middle Ages. But Machiavelli taught that those who lived by the classical and biblical virtues would not be able to gain or keep power. If a virtue helped a ruler gain power, Machiavelli wrote that the ruler should use it. If not, the ruler should disregard it. In this way Machiavelli represented the Renaissance trend of freeing people from religious tradition. This would allow man to be the measure of all things.

Northern Europe

The writers of Northern Europe tended to emphasize religious issues. They often gave more attention to Christian rather than classical sources. Two authors will be briefly examined.

Erasmus of Rotterdam was one of the most highly regarded and influential scholars of the Renaissance. He mastered Latin and Greek. In the last chapter we learned that he was the first to publish a Greek New Testament that was printed on a movable-type press. This work became an essential tool for the Reformation. Reformers like Luther and Calvin used Erasmus's text to help prepare their own translations of the Bible. Despite having made this contribution to the Reformation, Erasmus refused to leave the Church of Rome.

Sir **Thomas More** was a close friend of Erasmus and served in the court of King Henry VIII in England. His work *Utopia* (which means "nowhere") is a story about an imaginary country based on Christian principles and the philosophy of Plato. In this work More presented his view of an ideal state.

While More was a man of personal piety, he vigorously rejected the principles set forth in the Reformation. More supported the supremacy of the pope and wrote in defense of Rome's teaching on subjects including purgatory and the seven sacraments.

Consequences

Positive

The Renaissance was an age in which many placed their faith in human ability. Yet the Renaissance also led men to inquire and seek the truth. People were no longer content to accept the teachings of Rome without question. For many, this scrutiny led to a return to the clear teachings of Scripture and a Christianity that was free of unbiblical rituals.

The Renaissance also led to a renewed interest in the manuscripts and languages of the Old Testament and first-century Christianity. Copies of the Old and New Testament Scriptures were recovered and studied. Access to these documents resulted in an interest in the study of Greek and Hebrew.

The individual was emphasized in the Renaissance. A brief look at portraits from this period demonstrates this new attitude of the

---

Proper Conduct

Another book of etiquette, *The Book of Manners*, written by Giovanni Della Casa, provides some useful advice for the Renaissance man.

"When you have blown your nose, you should not open your handkerchief and inspect it, as if pearls or rubies had dropped out of your skull."

"It is bad manners to clean your teeth with your napkin, and still worse to do it with your finger. . . ."

Power in Machiavelli's *The Prince*

Some people have argued that Machiavelli was talking only about politics in this book, not religion. But Machiavelli's argument that wickedness rather than virtue is the true means to power only works if there is no God who will judge all men after this life. Machiavelli would have known this. Thus, one possible message of his book is that power should be achieved by any means possible because there is either no God or no future judgment.

In Praise of Folly

Erasmus wrote this satire to expose many of the abuses in the Roman Church. However, even though he was critical of the failures of the church, he supported reform of the Roman Church, not separation from it.

Consequences of the Renaissance

List the positive and negative consequences of the Renaissance.

Positive	Negative

Prospero Alessandri

Sir Thomas More

Guiding Questions

1. Why did political and religious authorities struggle to limit the power of the papacy?

2. How did the Inquisition encourage discontent with the Roman Church?

3. How did the behavior of clergy and popes impact the reputation of the Roman Church during the Renaissance?

importance of the individual. It was also found in Renaissance education, where the student was encouraged to discover and develop his abilities.

Finally, the development of movable-type printing and widespread education provided lasting benefits to Europe and far beyond. Literature became more available and education became accessible to many more people. Europe began to experience an intellectual renewal.

Negative

The emphasis of the Renaissance was on man rather than God. This emphasis led to the weakening of moral restraints. Instead of setting a righteous example, many of the Renaissance clergy and popes openly lived in great wealth and immorality. They spent church funds on such luxuries as expensive architecture. To bring in additional funds, they sold church offices to the wealthy and empty promises of forgiveness to the poor. Many noted the failures of the Roman Church and looked elsewhere for the truth.

Section Review Questions

1. What does the term *Renaissance* mean?

2–4. List three techniques that resulted in differences between medieval and Renaissance art.

★ What did the change in art reveal about the shift in thinking from the medieval to the Renaissance periods?

★ Evaluate the consequences of the Renaissance.

■ II. Discontent with the Church of Rome

We have discussed the growing dissatisfaction with some of the practices and doctrines of the Roman Church. We will briefly examine four doctrines with which many disagreed. When men argued against these doctrines, the Roman Church often resorted to persecution. In addition to disagreement over doctrines, an embarrassing period of scandals connected to the papacy further eroded faith in the Roman Church.

Doctrine

In the last chapter you learned that the Church of Rome declared that the bread and wine of the Lord's Supper were transformed into the body and blood of Christ. This teaching was made official church doctrine at the Fourth Lateran Council in 1215 and is known as **transubstantiation** (TRAN sub STAN shee AY shun; the transforming of the substance). According to this teaching, the wine and bread change into the very blood and body of Christ each time the priest recites the Latin phrase *hoc est corpus meum* (this is my body). Those who rejected this dogma (doctrine) were charged with heresy.

Another teaching that had become accepted in the Church of Rome was the necessity of works in addition to faith for salvation. Works varied from being mildly inconvenient to extreme and health threatening. However, no amount of self-inflicted suffering could guarantee anyone acceptance before God. Not even the greatest saint or most pious pope could be sure of going to heaven upon death.

Over the centuries many writings and practices came to be placed on an equal basis with the Scripture. The writings of the early church fathers, anonymous works, and traditions became authoritative in the Roman Church. Even though a careful study reveals that these works often contradicted the Scriptures, the Church of Rome preserved this error.

A fourth error taught by Rome was that believers had to confess their sins to a priest. The Church of Rome taught that the priest was empowered to forgive sin. This kept the repentant sinner from seeking direct access to God and also forced him to endure sensitive and probing questions from the priest. Many instances of priests abusing their power resulted.

Persecution

By the thirteenth century, more and more people questioned the teachings of Rome. The Roman Church responded by authorizing the **Inquisition** (in kwi ZISH un). The Inquisition was a church court set up to find and punish heretics. New monastic orders such as the Dominicans demonstrated their zeal by leading in the search for heretics. Many people were tried and tortured to confess their heresy. The suspect had no right to counsel, and his accusers could remain unnamed. Suspects were considered guilty and had to prove their innocence, often without even knowing the charge against them. However, what was intended to purge the Roman Church of false doctrine led many to reject the Church of Rome entirely.

Corruption

Beginning in the fourteenth century, several scandals further weakened the influence of the Church of Rome. In the last chapter you learned that the Roman Church lost credibility during the plague known as the Black Death. The behavior of many of the clergy and popes during the Renaissance further reduced respect for the Roman Church. Two events in particular, the Great Schism and the sale of indulgences, brought the Church's reputation to a new low.

Pope Boniface VIII (1294–1303) tried to strengthen the power of the Roman Church by issuing a decree that everyone, including kings, had to submit to the pope in order to be saved. This was a bold statement, but Boniface did not have the power to enforce this decree. Instead, he was removed from office by an invading French force.

For the next seventy years, the French and Italians struggled for control of the papacy. Beginning in 1378 there was a French pope and an Italian pope at the same time, a division that became known as the Great Schism. In a failed effort to resolve this embarrassing problem, a third man was chosen to become pope, but that only resulted in there being three popes. This problem was finally solved at the Council of Constance (1414–18). All three men were convinced to step down, and Martin V became the next pope. However, this struggle left many in the Church shaken and doubting. Faith in the authority of the pope and in the claims of the Church of Rome was further diminished.

In an effort to repair some of the damage, church officials decided to have church councils meet and resolve future issues. This

Avignon palace, where the kings of France kept a watchful eye on French popes

Interior of St. Peter's Basilica

Pope Leo X

would limit the power of the pope and seek to restore confidence in the Roman Church. However, this movement was short-lived because popes resisted this limitation of their authority.

The second event that created a major controversy was the sale of **indulgences** (in DUL jens ez; a paper that granted pardon from the punishment of sins). Indulgences had been granted for centuries to people in the Roman Church who performed good works and prayers. However, Pope Leo X (1513–21) needed money to finish building St. Peter's Basilica in Rome. So he sent out agents to sell indulgences and raise the needed funds. One monk in particular, Johann Tetzel, sold indulgences near Wittenberg, Germany, where Martin Luther pastored. Many people opposed the sale of indulgences, but Luther wrote his views on paper and offered to debate church officials about the practice. The resulting controversy over the sale of indulgences played an important role in the birth of the Reformation.

Dissatisfaction of the People

Individuals often had to express their dissatisfaction with the corruptions of the Roman Church behind closed doors. To speak out publicly might lead to a hearing before an inquisitor. However, broad discontent often found expression in the works of popular writers such as Erasmus. The following is an excerpt from Erasmus's writings in which Pope Julius II finds himself excluded from heaven by St. Peter:

JULIUS: Hey in there, open this door at once!

ST. PETER: It's a good thing we have adamantine doors; otherwise this man would have broken in. . . . Who are you and what do you want?

JULIUS: As if you could not see for yourself!

ST. PETER: Indeed I see a key silvered all over although it is only one and very different from those keys which Christ as the true pastor of the church once gave over to me. And how should I recognize this proud crown? No barbarian tyrant ever wore such a one, still less anyone who demanded to be admitted here. Nor does this pallium in the least move me who have always despised gold and gems as rubbish.

JULIUS: I am Julius the Ligurian and you will surely recognize the two letters P.M.

ST. PETER: I believe they stand for "Pestis Maxima" [Supreme Plague].

JULIUS: No, "Pontifex Maximus" [Supreme Pontiff].

ST. PETER: If you were three times "Maximus" . . . you would not come in here unless you were also "optimus," this is, holy. . . . What kind of monster are you who, although you wear outside the garments of a priest, underneath bristle and clink with a covering of bloody armor? . . . how savage are your eyes, how stubborn your mouth, how threatening your brow and how haughty and arrogant your glance! It is shameful . . . that you always belch and smell of [drunkenness] and seem to me to have just vomited. . . . I suspect that you are that most pestilential heathen Julius returned from hell to [make fun of] me.

Section Review Questions

1. What Roman Church doctrine declares that the bread and wine are changed into the body and blood of Christ?

2. What is the name of the Church court that was established to discover heresy?

3–4. List two practices in the Roman Church that led to discontent among many in Europe.

★ Why was the papal decree requiring submission by all not successful?

★ Why was the effort to have church councils meet and resolve church issues doomed to fail?

■ III. The Reformation

Forerunners

John Wycliffe (c. 1320–84) was a pastor, teacher, and theologian in England. He rejected the authority of the papacy and much of the authority claimed by the Church of Rome. Wycliffe taught that an individual became part of the church of Jesus Christ through an invisible, miraculous work of the Holy Spirit. Once made a part of the body of Christ, a believer could not be excluded by anyone—pope, council, or bishop. He also produced the first Bible in the English language. This translation played a key role in a later English Bible known as the King James Version.

Guiding Questions

1. How did the Protestant Reformation develop in Germany, Switzerland, and France?

2. How did the Counter Reformation develop as a response to the Protestant Reformation?

3. How did the Protestant Reformation influence European cultural values?

English reformer and scholar, John Wycliffe

Bohemian reformer, John Huss

Excerpts from Luther's Theses

81. This unbridled preaching of pardons [indulgences] makes it difficult, even for learned men, to rescue the reverence due to the pope from slander, or even from the shrewd [clever] questions of the laity. [At first, Luther was willing to give the pope the benefit of the doubt. Later he would learn that the pope played a key role in the sale of indulgences.]

82. [They ask] such questions as the following: Why does the pope not empty purgatory, for the sake of holy love and for the sake of desperate souls that are there, if he redeems an infinite number of souls for the sake of miserable money with which to build a church?

Martin Luther burning a copy of the papal bull
Exsurge Domine *at a student gathering*

John Huss (c. 1372–1415) was a pastor in Bohemia who was influenced by Wycliffe's teachings. Huss also spoke out against the claims of the papacy and the corruption of the Church of Rome. He was called to defend himself at the Council of Constance and given a promise of safe conduct. Instead, the Roman Church tried Huss and burned him at the stake for his teachings.

Reformers

Martin Luther (1483–1546)

Martin Luther lived in Germany and became a monk after a frightening experience during a thunderstorm. He studied the writings of the church fathers and prepared to be a priest. As he continued his studies, he began to read the Scriptures. Luther studied Greek and Hebrew in order to study the Scriptures in their original languages. He struggled with the fact that he was a sinner and often went to his superior in order to make confession. The head of Luther's monastery pointed him to the Scriptures. Soon Luther was appointed to preach at the church in Wittenberg.

When Luther learned of Tetzel and the sale of indulgences to his congregation, he became angry. Luther wanted to debate the value of indulgences and so followed the custom of the day, writing his arguments on a sheet of paper and posting it for debate (October 31, 1517). These ninety-five points of disagreement are commonly called Luther's **Ninety-five Theses**. Although he wrote them in Latin, they were quickly printed in German and read by many citizens.

The Roman Church ignored Luther for a time but finally threatened to dismiss him from the Roman Church in 1520. This action, known as **excommunication** (EKS kah myoo ni KAY shun), denied him the possibility of salvation. By this time Luther had discovered the truth found in Romans 1:17—"The just shall live by faith." He realized that salvation is a gift of God that cannot be earned. (A gift is by nature free, or else it is not truly a gift). Luther was transformed by this truth as he trusted in Christ's work on the cross rather than his own works for salvation.

At first Luther believed that he could reform the Church of Rome from within by debate. However, he soon learned that church councils and popes were not free from error. When he was ordered to recant (take back what he had written) in 1521 he told the assembly:

> Unless I am convinced by the testimony of the Scriptures or by clear reason . . . I am bound by the Scriptures I have quoted and my conscience is captive to the Word of God. I cannot and I will not retract anything, since it is neither safe nor right to go against conscience. I cannot do otherwise; here I stand, may God help me. Amen.

Luther went on to translate the New Testament and then the whole Bible into German. This work was printed many times, and copies spread throughout Germany. He also wrote many commentaries and an official statement of Lutheran beliefs called the Augsburg Confession.

Luther married a former nun in 1525, and they had six children. (We will look at Luther's family life later in the chapter.) Despite his status as a wanted man, Luther traveled freely through much of Germany and ministered until his death in 1546.

Ulrich Zwingli (1484–1531)

Ulrich Zwingli was born in the German-speaking area of Switzerland. He became acquainted with Erasmus, who encouraged him to study the Bible. Zwingli became a priest in the Roman Church but was displeased with the corruption he found there. In 1519 he became the preacher at the largest church in Zurich, an important town in the Swiss city-states.

Zwingli read some of Luther's writings, and he too realized that salvation comes by grace through faith. He began to preach and teach from the Bible and made important changes in his church. Just as Luther had penned his Ninety-Five Theses, Zwingli wrote a document known as his Sixty-Seven Conclusions. Like Luther, Zwingli rejected Roman doctrines such as the mass (bread and wine turned into the body and blood of Christ), celibacy (being forbidden to marry) of the clergy, purgatory, and the exalted claims of the pope.

Civil war broke out in Switzerland between the city-states still loyal to Rome and those who embraced the Reformation. Zwingli accompanied his companions in 1531 and served as their chaplain. He was killed in battle as he attempted to help a wounded soldier. However, Zwingli's work was carried on by his followers in Zurich.

Ulrich Zwingli

Anabaptists

There was another group in Switzerland who followed Zwingli in the early days of the Reformation. However, by 1525 they had become impatient with Zwingli's slow reforms that were subject to approval by the magistrates (city rulers). They called themselves the Swiss Brethren, but their rejection of infant baptism soon earned them the name **Anabaptists** (those who baptize again). While many groups received this label, a core group of the Brethren continued to promote their views about a genuine reformation. The Anabaptists spread throughout Switzerland, Germany, and the Netherlands. They fled from country to country and endured suffering and death. Even though they were often persecuted, some of their teachings contributed to the completion of the Reformation.

For example, Anabaptists rejected the idea of Luther, Zwingli, and other reformers that everyone who lived under a Lutheran or Reformed prince should be a member of the state church. Many congregations of state churches included godly and ungodly members. Most Anabaptists refused to attend a state church. Instead, they insisted that true believers should be members of local churches that were free of state control.

Most Anabaptists also concluded that Christians should not serve in government but should follow Christ. One Anabaptist writer noted that since Christ did not judge in worldly disputes, neither should Christians (Luke 12:14). The writer pointed out that Christ refused to be made king (John 6:15) and forbade his disciples from ruling like Gentiles (Matt. 20:25–28). Thus Christians should not be magistrates or princes. (Anabaptists were frequently persecuted by magistrates and princes.) The Anabaptists also did not want the state to interfere in the affairs of the church.

John Calvin (1509–1564)

John Calvin was born in France and became a leading figure in the Reformation. However, he ministered from Geneva, Switzerland, due to the hostility of the French government toward Protestant

John Calvin

believers. Shortly after leaving France, Calvin wrote the first edition of his *Institutes of the Christian Religion*. He addressed the king of France in the preface. He wanted the king of France to understand that Protestants simply believed what the Bible taught. But his main purpose for writing the *Institutes* was to teach the basics of Christianity so that people, especially his own French people, would live godly lives. In the opening line of the *Institutes*, Calvin wrote that all knowledge is either knowledge of ourselves or knowledge of God. And if we are to know ourselves rightly, we must know God. As a pastor in Geneva, Calvin pursued this goal, the knowledge of God, in the sermons he preached and in the many commentaries he wrote.

For Calvin, knowing God meant living a life of godliness. When certain citizens of Geneva acted wickedly, Calvin would not give them the Lord's Supper. This angered the leaders of Geneva. For a time they exiled Calvin from the city. Eventually, however, he was invited back.

Calvin's teaching was not free from controversy. His name is often associated with the doctrine of **predestination** (pree des tih NAY shun). Calvin taught that no sinner would come to God on his own. Therefore God chose to give grace to people of His choosing so that they would repent and believe. This doctrine was controversial then and continues to be so today.

Nonetheless, many persecuted Protestants found refuge in Geneva. Calvin saw the city as a missionary training center and founded a school there. John Knox called it "the most perfect school of Christ that ever was in the earth since the days of the apostles." Persecuted Christians would come to Geneva, receive training, and then return to evangelize their own people. Calvin especially wanted to see the gospel take root in his own France. He sent hundreds of missionaries into France where they planted churches—and many died as martyrs. In addition, his written works were smuggled into France to educate and encourage the Christians who remained despite persecution.

Central Doctrines

While there were doctrinal and practical differences between Luther, Zwingli, Calvin, and other reformers, there were also central doctrines upon which all agreed. We will briefly examine three of them:

Scripture alone—The reformers pointed out that Scripture and tradition often conflicted. However, God's Word is inspired, while man's traditions are not. Therefore, Scripture is the only reliable authority on anything it speaks of (2 Tim. 3:16).

Faith alone—As each of the reformers read the Bible, he discovered that salvation cannot be earned but is a gift received by faith. The sacraments of the Roman Church had no power to save. The reformers taught that a person is saved by faith in Christ's shed blood alone (Titus 3:5; Eph. 2:8–9).

Priesthood of the believer—The Renaissance emphasis on the individual prepared people to accept this doctrine. The reformers emphasized that people had to come to God as individuals. Upon receiving salvation through Christ, each person is made a priest (1 Pet. 2:9; Rev. 1:6). In other words, each believer has direct access to the saving benefits of Christ without the need of priests and sacraments. The Roman Church had taught that priests stood between individuals and God. However, the reformers pointed to passages such as 1 Timothy 2:5—"For there is one God, and one mediator between God and men, the man Christ Jesus."

Section Review Questions

1. Name a forerunner of the Reformation.
2. What action by the Roman Church denies an individual access to salvation?
3. What does the term *Anabaptist* mean?
★ How did the Anabaptists differ from other Protestant reformers?

Results

The Reformation spread throughout Europe, including countries such as Germany, Switzerland, France, and England. The printing press made possible the rapid publication and spread of Reformation writings and Bibles in the vernacular. Protestants who were persecuted in one region fled to other regions and helped to spread the scriptural truths rediscovered during the Reformation. Despite political and religious opposition, the Reformation could not be contained.

Freedom

The reformers opposed spiritual oppression. This prepared the way for a greater emphasis on freedom in many areas of European life. Limited religious freedom was given to those who lived under a prince who shared their religion. However, the Anabaptists sought full religious freedom—the right to worship according to one's own conscience no matter where one lived.

Citizenship

The reformers emphasized the role of Christians in society. They taught their followers that God desired servants who worked not for their own glory but for God's glory (1 Cor. 10:31). Christians are responsible to God for how they use their talents and abilities. Unlike the Renaissance humanists, the reformers said that a person should dedicate his talents to God, not to himself.

They also encouraged Christians to work hard at their occupations. Any faithful Christian worker, whether shoemaker, carpenter, or farmer, is serving God just as much as a pastor or missionary is serving God. The reformers taught that everything a believer does is to honor God. They encouraged their followers to be a testimony of God's grace as they performed their daily tasks.

Family Life

Besides emphasizing right doctrine, the reformers also emphasized right family relationships. They knew families were a gift from God. For example, while Luther remained single for several years after breaking with Rome, he encouraged other former monks and nuns to marry. In 1525, he was convinced to marry when a former nun, Katherine von Bora, refused to marry any other man but him. They had six children and also took in several orphans.

From the Scripture the reformers formed definite ideas about families. A faithful, loving, and obedient wife was a blessing second only to the Word of God for the Christian man. The husband was also to love his wife as Christ loved the church (Eph. 5:25). Parents

Technology and Reformers

It was no accident that the Reformation began with Luther rather than Wycliffe or Huss. In God's providence a number of factors put Luther in a different position than either of his predecessors. Gutenberg's printing press made it possible for Luther's writings to spread widely and quickly around Europe. (In Wycliffe's time writings had to be copied by hand.) The printing press also made it possible for the Bible to be more readily accessible. The spread of Erasmus's Greek New Testament meant that others in Europe could read the New Testament in the original language. Many who did so became convinced that Luther's teaching was correct. Finally, Luther and reformers who followed were often protected by their princes rather than tried and executed as Huss was.

Luther's Example

Luther's family set an example for other Christian families. The Luther home was a happy, busy place. Mealtimes with children and students were usually times of talking. The students so admired their teacher that they often brought paper and pens to the table to take notes. On special occasions, Luther wrote pageants and songs for his household. His children especially enjoyed the Christmas carols he wrote for them.

The Importance of Literacy

The reformers placed a high value on teaching everyone, from the prince to the peasant, to read. They realized that since every believer is a priest, every person needs to be able to read in order to have access to God's Word. The principle of Scripture alone also commits Christians to work toward universal literacy.

were to love and discipline their children to teach them to obey authority—whether it be God's, a parent's, or the government's. Bringing up children to honor and serve the Lord is a Christian parent's God-given responsibility. The reformers knew that what a child learned at home greatly influenced his moral and spiritual life.

Education

Many of the reformers were well educated. They often knew Latin, Greek, and Hebrew, and some had read many ancient manuscripts. Therefore, the reformers placed a high priority on teaching everyone to read and to study diligently. Luther, Calvin, Zwingli, and many other reformers established schools and made education a priority.

Following Luther's example, many reformers also translated the Bible into the vernacular. This enabled the people to read God's word in their own language. In addition, books and pamphlets were printed in the common languages, and the people learned about many subjects related to the Reformation.

Reaction

The Church of Rome was slow to react to the initial development of the Reformation. However, as the church leaders realized how quickly the Protestant movement was spreading, the reaction quickened and intensified. Through existing monastic orders and the introduction of new orders, the Roman Church launched an extensive campaign to stop and reverse the spread of the Protestant movement. In addition, the Church of Rome used a revived Inquisition and other means to counteract this challenge to Roman Catholic doctrine.

Catholic Counter Reformation

Sometimes known as the Catholic Reformation, the Counter Reformation differed greatly from the Protestant Reformation. The Protestants had opposed the false doctrine that had slipped into the Church of Rome. However, the Catholic Reformers worked to give the Roman Church a new image by dealing with some of the more obvious moral problems. For the Catholic reformers, doctrinal change was not an option. Four aspects of the Counter Reformation will be briefly discussed.

Society of Jesus

In previous centuries, monasteries had been established for various reasons that included escaping the influences of the world, helping the poor, or practicing self-denial in an attempt to satisfy God. However, as the Reformation developed, new monastic orders, such as the Society of Jesus, or **Jesuits**, were founded to stop the spread of the Reformation. This order ruthlessly sought to suppress heresy (Protestantism) and zealously promoted Roman Catholic education. The Jesuits used any means necessary to gain converts for Rome and reverse the gains of the Protestants.

Inquisition

The Inquisition was reorganized by Pope Paul III to root out heresy. These church courts assumed that anyone who was accused of heresy was guilty. Many were arrested at night, taken before an inquisitor, and told to confess their errors. The accused weren't even allowed to know the charges or who had brought the accusation. Failure to confess led to torture and being burned at the stake. Other members of one's family could also be arrested and property taken.

Index

When the Roman Church realized the impact that printed materials were having on the spread of the Reformation, the Church of Rome established the *Index of Prohibited Books.* Most versions of the Bible and all Protestant literature were declared heretical. The Roman Church forbad Catholics from reading anything that appeared on this list.

Council of Trent

As the Reformation spread throughout Europe, the supporters of the Roman Church grew more dissatisfied with their church. Many members of the Roman clergy were corrupt and lazy. The Roman Catholics began to demand change. In response to these demands, a meeting of high church officials was called. Known as the **Council of Trent**, it met several times over a twenty-year period.

The council wrote a statement of Roman Catholic beliefs and practices. This was the first written statement that contained all Catholic doctrines. The council members confirmed the authority of both Scripture and tradition. They insisted that faith *and* works were necessary to receive justification. They also preserved the doctrine of a human priesthood that stood between God and the individual. Essentially, the Roman Church made no changes in its doctrines. Instead, the council ordered some of the corrupt practices to stop, removed many of the corrupt clergy, and set stricter standards of discipline. While the visible corruption was reduced, the doctrinal errors remained.

Council of Trent

Wars of Religion

Wars erupted in several regions, including France. These wars were motivated by a desire for territory and other typical reasons for war. However, these wars were also fought over religion.

Even though rulers in France vigorously supported the Church of Rome, the number of Protestants continued to increase. Known as **Huguenots** (HYOO geh nahts), these French Protestants endured fierce persecution and broken promises of peace. In 1572 twenty thousand Huguenots in Paris were massacred in their homes during a carefully planned attack. Seventeen years of fighting between Catholic and Protestant forces followed. In 1589 the French Protestants received a temporary reprieve (relief) when Henry of Navarre became king of France (see margin box).

The **Thirty Years' War** (1618–48) began as a revolt by the Bohemians against loss of religious liberty. However, it soon became a major conflict between Catholic and Protestant forces in Europe. While most of the fighting occurred on German soil, many nations joined the battle for one side or the other. Germany was destroyed by these battling forces. Eventually, Catholic France supported the Protestant forces in order to end the war. This move by the French prevented their political enemies in Spain and the Holy Roman

"Paris Is Well Worth a Mass"

Henry of Navarre is said to have spoken these words when he agreed to convert to Roman Catholicism in order to become king of France. While he did abandon his Huguenot supporters, Henry also guaranteed them limited religious toleration in the **Edict of Nantes** (1598). However, even with this written guarantee, the toleration was gradually reduced. Under a future French king, this edict would be revoked, and the Huguenots would be forced to flee France.

Historical Perspectives

J. H. Merle d'Aubigné

Merle says that in 1300 Pope Gregory VII made a proclamation that those who came to Rome on a pilgrimage could have their sins forgiven. Many pilgrims came to Rome bringing gifts, and as a result such pilgrimages became a regular occurrence to raise money for Rome. Eventually, Rome sent emissaries out to sell indulgences. For a price, sins could be forgiven. It was Luther's disgust at people being deceived into purchasing forgiveness without a true reformation of life that lay at the root of the Reformation.

J. H. Merle d'Aubigné, *History of the Reformation in the Sixteenth Century* (New York: Hurst, 1835), 1:56–57.

Brad Gregory

Gregory argues that the problem with medieval Christianity was not what the Roman Church taught. The problem was falling short of that teaching. It was "a failure to practice what was preached." The solution, according to Gregory, was not to abandon Roman Catholic teaching. It was to work harder at practicing church teaching. Gregory says by changing church teaching, the Reformation unintentionally led to the problems of secular modern culture.

Brad S. Gregory, *The Unintended Reformation: How a Religious Revolution Secularized Society* (Cambridge, MA: Belknap, 2012), 366–69.

Are Merle's and Gregory's explanations for what was wrong with the medieval church compatible?

1. Given your reading in this chapter, which historian is most correct? Why?

2. Is it fair for Gregory to blame Protestantism for secular modern culture when orthodox Protestant teaching is opposed to secularism?

Empire from becoming too powerful. This became the last great religious war fought in Europe.

The people of Europe emerged from the medieval period to experience the beauty and wealth of knowledge made available to them in the Renaissance. While the Renaissance failed to address the spiritual needs of men, it did prepare the way for the Reformation by stressing the importance of the individual and providing access to the Bible in the vernacular.

Men like Wycliffe and Huss prepared the way for a break with the Roman Church. Luther and many others built upon their work, and the Reformation brought to light the scriptural principles by which men are saved (by faith alone) and led by God (through Scripture alone).

The Thirty Years' War demonstrated the futility of fighting over religion. Following this three-decade-long struggle, nations became nominally (in name only) either Catholic or Protestant. Nations turned to building empires, and religion became more of a personal matter. Religious competition continued, but it was generally characterized by nonviolent efforts to convert others, including the populations encountered in the Age of Exploration.

Section Review Questions

1–2. What were two results of the Reformation?

3–4. List two ways the Roman Church responded to the Reformation.

✦ Why were Anabaptists persecuted by the Roman Church and some Protestant groups?

✦ Distinguish the Reformation doctrine of Scripture alone and the teaching of Rome regarding Scripture. Provide a scriptural reference to support the position that most closely reflects your personal view.

Making Connections

1. What things contributed to the revival of learning known as the Renaissance?
2. How did Gutenberg's invention contribute to the Renaissance and Reformation?
3. How was Renaissance art different from medieval art?
4. How did the subjects taught in the Renaissance differ from subjects taught in the Middle Ages?
5. Why was Petrarch called the Father of Humanism?
6. Briefly describe the subject of Thomas More's book *Utopia*.
7. What rights did a suspect have when standing before the inquisitor during an inquisition?

Developing History Skills

1. Using the information found in this chapter, compile a list of books that would have been included on the *Index of Prohibited Books*.
2. Construct a timeline that includes the significant events of the Reformation.

Thinking Critically

1. What changes were made to the Roman Church at the Council of Trent? What was the importance of these changes? What was the end result?
2. What impact did the Reformation have on family life?

Living in God's World

1. Pretend that you are a French believer who has had to flee to Geneva. In a letter to your family, state what you believe, why you believe it, and how your beliefs differ from Catholic teaching. Be sure to base your defense in Scripture.
2. Choose a significant person from the Renaissance or the Reformation and research that person. Tell his or her life story in first person. Talk about personal history as well as significant achievements. If you have time, decorate the room and use costumes. A list of people to choose from might include the following: Leonardo da Vinci, Michelangelo, Machiavelli, Erasmus, Thomas More, Henry VIII, John Wycliffe, John Huss, Martin Luther, Ulrich Zwingli, Balthasar Hubmaier, John Calvin, Catherine de Medici.

People, Places, and Things to Know

Renaissance
Johannes Gutenberg
anatomy
shading
perspective
Leonardo da Vinci
The Last Supper
Mona Lisa
Michelangelo
Sistine Chapel
Ghiberti
Brunelleschi
humanities
Petrarch
Father of Humanism
Castiglione
Machiavelli
Erasmus
Thomas More
transubstantiation
Inquisition
indulgences
John Wycliffe
John Huss
Martin Luther
Ninety-Five Theses
excommunication
Ulrich Zwingli
Anabaptists
John Calvin
Protestants
predestination
Jesuits
Index of Prohibited Books
Council of Trent
Huguenots
Edict of Nantes
Thirty Years' War

UNIT

Dominant Powers in Europe and Asia

1450 – 1750

3

European states, beginning with Portugal and Spain, began to search for new trade opportunities and routes to the Orient. Soon other nations joined in this exploration. Some established routes by sailing around Africa, while others traveled west in search of other avenues to access vast wealth. Anyone who could bring spices and other sought-after treasures to Europe would gain an immense profit.

Quite by accident, some of these explorers discovered many lands not previously known to Europeans. The explorers mapped and settled the Americas, Australia, and other remote lands during this period. The raw materials they discovered would soon fuel an accelerated period of industrial growth. In addition, Europe experienced a period of rapid scientific discovery that produced the Scientific Revolution.

1200 – 1700

Marco Polo travels to
the Far East 1271–95

Aztecs build the city
of Tenochtitlán 1347

Ottoman Turks capture
Constantinople 1453

| 1200 | 1300 | 1400 |

Big Ideas

1. How did complex societies develop in North America and Mesoamerica?
2. What initiated European overseas exploration?
3. Whom did the European explorers encounter in their explorations?
4. What were the consequences of the introduction of new plants, animals, and diseases to the Americas?

European explorers sailed west in search of trade routes to the Orient. However, they discovered a vast landmass that we now refer to as the Americas. The Europeans quickly learned that this New World was populated by many tribes and civilizations with long histories. Once the news spread about this new land, European nations scrambled to get in on the colonization and the search for wealth. While the discovery of this New World was providential, it was not without tragedy. Without realizing it, Europeans carried with them diseases, including smallpox and measles. The Indian populations had no previous contact with these diseases (and therefore no resistance), and the death toll among the Indians was staggering.

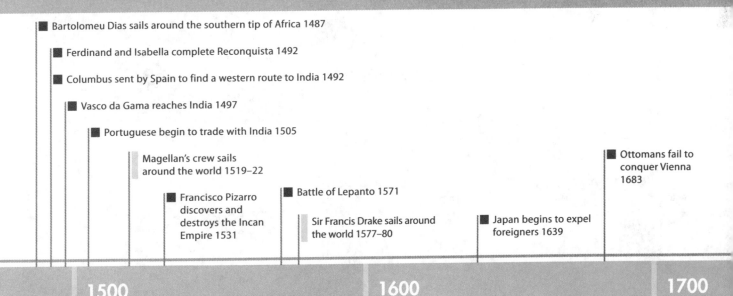

- Bartolomeu Dias sails around the southern tip of Africa 1487
- Ferdinand and Isabella complete Reconquista 1492
- Columbus sent by Spain to find a western route to India 1492
- Vasco da Gama reaches India 1497
- Portuguese begin to trade with India 1505
- Magellan's crew sails around the world 1519–22
- Francisco Pizarro discovers and destroys the Incan Empire 1531
- Battle of Lepanto 1571
- Sir Francis Drake sails around the world 1577–80
- Japan begins to expel foreigners 1639
- Ottomans fail to conquer Vienna 1683

1500   **1600**   **1700**

- Portuguese begin to trade with Japan c. 1550
- Hernando Cortés discovers and destroys the Aztec Empire 1519–22

Guiding Questions

1. What Indian groups lived in North America, and how did they adapt to their environment?
2. What were some societal, religious, and cultural distinctives of the Mayas, Aztecs, and Incas?

Complex Indian Societies

The Europeans were startled to find highly developed Indian societies with towns and political structure. However, Christians should remember that man was created in the image of God and given dominion over the earth (Genesis 1:26–28). God enabled man to develop complex cultures. Rather than be startled to find complex cultures, we should expect to discover them all over the world.

■ I. Native American Civilizations

At some point in early history following the Flood, the ancestors of the American Indians came to the American continent. Theories vary about how and when they came. Those explorers fanned out across the continent, moving in all directions. Some settled in the East and some in the West, and others migrated into Central and South America. Most lived in settled villages and cultivated the land. They also developed societies of great complexity. Corn, squash, and beans were common crops among most of the tribes. While few details are available, we will briefly examine some of the civilizations that developed.

North America

Pueblos

Many of the Indians who lived in the Southwest region of North America were known as the **Pueblos**. *Pueblo* means "town." These Indians lived in small villages composed of several family groups or clans. Some of the Pueblo Indians made their homes in caves and became known as cliff dwellers. Others made homes out of adobe (uh DO bee; dried clay). Each Indian town was independent, and population growth was restricted by limited food and water supplies due to the desert climate in which they lived. Some of the tribes among the Pueblos included the Hopi, Ute, Paiute, Navajo, and Apache.

Plains Indians

These Indians migrated over the grasslands of the Great Plains and lived in tepees. They hunted buffalo, elk, and antelope. Before the Spanish brought horses to this continent, the Plains Indians

A Pueblo village

Tepees used by the Plains Indians

traveled and hunted on foot. The Plains Indians included such tribes as the Sioux, Cheyenne, Crow, Blackfeet, and Comanche.

The Plains Indians had no single religion. However, most, if not all, practiced animism—the belief that all things possess spirits. Many worshiped the Great Spirit. In addition, they believed in good spirits as well as evil spirits. Plains Indians often expressed their worship in prayer, song, and dance. Many tribes also had shamans (people who claimed to have the power to heal, seek spiritual direction, and look into the future).

Eastern

Many of the Indians who settled in eastern America built villages and developed structured societies. They farmed, hunted, and fished to provide food for their families. We will look at three of the Indian cultures found in the East: the Mound Builders, the Iroquois, and the Five Civilized Tribes.

Mound Builders

Hundreds of mounds have been found throughout the eastern half of North America. Indians who built these earthen mounds are called the **Mound Builders**. These mounds varied in size from three feet high to eighteen feet high. Some of them are a hundred feet across. Some were grouped together and formed the first cities in America–cities that in their time were larger than some European cities. Some mounds were built as grave sites, while others served as temple mounds. The Indians also built another kind of mound called an **effigy mound** (a mound in the shape of an animal or object), such as the Serpent Mound located in southern Ohio.

Often the animal shape is only seen when viewed from the sky. Despite the fact that Indians would never have viewed the mounds from this perspective, they put in a great amount of work to create these sites.

These Indians probably lived in wooden structures made from bent saplings that were covered with animal skins or tree bark. While little is known about them, archaeologists have discovered that the Mound Builders obtained copper from the Great Lakes area, seashells and shark teeth from the Atlantic and Gulf coasts, and quartz and grizzly bear teeth from the Rocky Mountains. This means the Mound Builders had developed extensive trade networks. By the time the Europeans began to explore North America, the mound-building Indians were dying out.

Indian Religions in the Americas

Identify the religious beliefs of each group.

Group	Beliefs
Plains Indians	
Aztecs	
Incas	

Alligator Mound located in central Ohio

Serpent Mound located in southern Ohio

Iroquois Confederacy

Between 1400 and 1450, an Indian leader convinced several Iroquois tribes to establish a peace treaty known as the Great Law of Peace. Five nations initially joined. By 1570 the confederacy was composed of six Indian nations: Mohawk, Oneida, Seneca, Cayuga, Onondaga, and Tuscarora.

Although the tribes of this confederacy were able to develop complex cultures, they were also capable of great savagery. They often tortured captured enemies to death. The Iroquois were also known to eat parts of their enemies in order to gain some of the fallen warriors' courage. The combination of complex culture and cruelty illustrates how the abilities God gave humans in the Creation Mandate continued to exist after the Fall but were twisted by the Fall.

Mayan Civilization

The Mayas fulfilled aspects of the Creation Mandate by developing an advanced civilization that included mathematical and astronomical discoveries. However, they also revealed the tragic consequences of the Fall through their idol worship and human sacrifice. How is the Mayan civilization reflected in Romans 1?

Iroquois longhouse

Eastern Woodlands Indians

Six tribes who spoke the common language of Iroquois formed a league in the early fifteenth century known as the Iroquois Confederacy. These tribes lived in what is today northern New York and became one of the most powerful groups in eastern North America. British and French colonists as well as other Indian tribes needed the cooperation of the Iroquois in order to accomplish anything.

In the Southeast, five tribes formed an alliance similar to the Iroquois Confederacy. The Cherokees, Chickasaws, Choctaws, Creeks, and Seminoles formed what came to be known as the Five Civilized Tribes. These tribes were given this name because they maintained peaceful relationships with neighboring tribes and adopted many colonial customs.

Central and South America

The Mayas

The Mayas (MAH yuz) lived in what is today a portion of Central America that includes Guatemala and the Yucatán Peninsula. Unlike the Aztecs and Incas, the Mayas did not have one strong

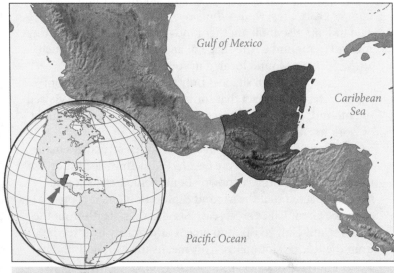

Mayan Civilization

central government. Mayan civilization, like that of the ancient Greeks, consisted of many independent city-states. Each city-state had its own ruler and government.

The height of Mayan culture lasted from AD 300 to 800. They developed a calendar as accurate as the one we use today. The Mayas also had a form of writing far superior to any other system found in the New World. They were accomplished mathematicians and astronomers as well. For example, they predicted eclipses of the sun and moon with impressive accuracy. For easier numbering and counting, the Mayas also understood and used the concept of zero.

Maya Codex

The Mayas built large pyramids similar to the ones in Egypt in the middle of many of their cities. The Mayan pyramids, however, were not always burial places for kings. Usually they served as temples. Mayan religion was cruel and involved human sacrifice. Archaeologists have found large graves containing the remains of men and women whom the Mayas slaughtered to please their gods.

The different Mayan city-states often fought against one another. As a result, they proved unable to unite in resistance against other enemies, especially the Aztecs, who took many Mayan cities. The Mayas grew weaker and weaker. The Spanish came in 1450, and the remaining Mayas came under Spanish control in the early 1500s, despite strong Mayan resistance.

The Aztecs

Around 1345 the **Aztecs** built their capital, **Tenochtitlán** (te noch tee TLAHN), on an island in the middle of a lake in central Mexico. To build the city there, the Aztecs first made floating islands from mounds of water plants and put them in the middle of the lake. When these had rooted, the Aztecs filled the roots with soil and built on them. The finished city had many islands that the Aztecs accessed by boats and bridges. Several long causeways connected the islands of Tenochtitlán to each other and to the mainland.

Aztec society was characterized by war and warriors. Every Aztec man who was able to fight had to serve in the army. Aztec warriors used ferocity and military skill to conquer many tribes around them. Over time, the Aztecs conquered a large area with five million people who were required to pay them tribute (taxes).

They worshiped many gods and built large temples to honor these gods. Part of their worship included human sacrifice, during which they cut out the hearts from living people and offered them to the gods. Many of those captured in war were sacrificed to appease (satisfy) these gods.

The Aztecs believed that one of their gods, Quetzalcoatl (ket sahl ko AH tul), once lived on the earth and brought prosperity to the people. He was forced to leave but promised to return in the future. The Aztecs anticipated his return, and this belief made them open to deception by the Spanish conquerors.

The Environment in Tenochtitlán

Ruling over the earth and subduing (Gen. 1:28) involves reshaping the environment. Take note of the complex process by which the Aztecs built an island city in a lake.

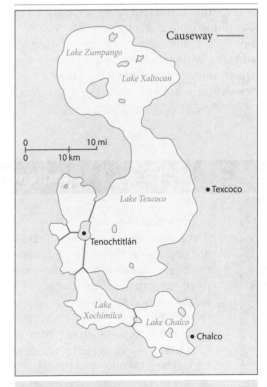

Valley of Mexico

Human Sacrifice

Cortés wrote about the Aztec practice of sacrificing humans and described it as "the most terrible and frightful thing they [had] ever witnessed." (Anthony Pagden, tr. and ed., *Hernan Cortes: Letters from Mexico*, p. 35)

However, Europeans could be cruel too. The Spanish often burned heretics to death during the infamous Spanish Inquisition. In fact, the Spanish conquistadors burned Indians at the stake because they would not accept the teachings of the Church of Rome.

The human sacrifices of the Aztecs and the burning of heretics in the Spanish Inquisition both reflected cultural values. The Aztecs believed that pleasing the gods was so valuable that humans could be sacrificed. Roman Catholics believed that heresy was so dangerous that heretics should be burned to stamp it out.

Justice Among the Aztecs

The penalties that cultures attach to certain behaviors reveal the values of a culture. In ancient Israel, adultery was punishable by death (Lev. 20:10). Several U.S. states have laws prohibiting adultery, with penalties ranging from prison sentences to fines. These laws, however, are not enforced.

Aztec Sun Stone

The Aztec people were governed by an elected monarchy. The nobles selected four noblemen who chose the monarch from the brothers or nephews of the deceased monarch. Once elected, the monarch lived in great splendor.

The Aztecs also developed a judicial system with a chief judge for each of the major cities. Aztec law was recorded in picture writing. The crimes considered most serious were punishable by death. For example, the punishment for adultery was death by stoning because marriage was recognized as a vital part of Aztec culture.

The Incas

The **Incas** developed their civilization very early and built upon earlier cultures. At the empire's peak, the territory under Incan rule

Indians: The First Environmentalists

According to some historians, Indians are "the first American environmentalists." These historians argue that even though American Indians did change their environment, they recognized "the need to restrain human impact."

Roderick Frazer Nash, ed., *American Environmentalism: Readings in Conservation History*, 3rd ed. (New York: McGraw-Hill, 1990), 13.

"As the historian Richard White remarked, the idea that the Indians left no trace of themselves on the land 'demeans Indians. It makes them seem simply like an animal species, and thus deprives them of culture.' . . . 'Like most anthropologists

today, I would assert that to be human is fundamentally to be a cultural being.' "

Shepherd Krech III, *The Ecological Indian: Myth and History*. (New York: Norton, 1999), 26-27.

1. Which view of the American Indian fits best with the data provided in this chapter? Provide details.

2. Which view fits best with the Bible's teaching about the image of God in man and the Creation Mandate? Explain why.

extended three thousand miles in length and up to three hundred fifty miles in breadth. Located along the western coast of South America, the Incan empire developed in the Andes (AN deez) Mountains. In order to make travel, communication, and trade possible, the people constructed two major highways that ran the length of the empire. They built long bridges to cross the steep valleys and ravines.

The capital of the Incan empire was **Cuzco** (KOOS ko). Here the Incas built large buildings out of stone with great precision. Without the use of mortar, they constructed buildings with such accuracy that a knife blade cannot fit between the stones. This city served as both the political and religious capital of the empire. The buildings were said to be covered with sheets of gold to reflect the sun and remind the Incas of their sun god. Tribute poured into the capital city in the form of food, copper, gold, silver, and alpaca wool. Since the Incas did not have a money economy, gold was used to make such items as ornaments, vases, and temple vessels.

Ruins of Machu Picchu, an Inca city built around the year 1450 high in the mountains of Peru

Alpaca

While the religion of the Incas was polytheistic, the ruler retained the title of "Inca" and served as the empire's living god. He owned the land, and authority resided in him. The people sacrificed animals during the four great festivals, but there is no record of human sacrifice. The Inca and his officials made all significant decisions for the people. This control produced a society of passive followers. Conquest by a foreign power would be easy in the event that the Inca were captured or killed.

Section Review Questions

1. Which group of North American Indians migrated?

2–3. List two reasons why Indians built mounds.

4. Which Indian civilization punished adultery by stoning?

★ Why do humans, wherever they live and whatever their environment, develop cultures?

★ How did the Iroquois Confederacy influence other Indian tribes and European explorers?

Guiding Questions

1. What were major social, economic, political, and cultural features of European society that stimulated exploration and conquest overseas?
2. What major developments in ship-building, navigation, and naval warfare made exploration and conquest possible?
3. What were the religious motivations for Spanish and Portuguese expeditions?

Reasons for Exploration and Conquest

Identify the various reasons for exploration and conquest.

Category	Reasons
Economic	
Social	
Political	
Religious	

■ II. Origins of European Exploration

Between the years 1271 and 1295, Italian explorer Marco Polo journeyed to the Far East, a land of mystery to thirteenth-century Europe. His descriptions of the vast wealth of China were recounted in a book. Europeans were amazed by what they read. Polo spoke of a land of gold, silks, and spices. He referred to the burning of black stones (coal) instead of wood to provide heat. With this expanded knowledge of foreign lands, Europeans spent the next several centuries finding ways to get there. This period is known as the Age of European Exploration.

Motives

Exploration was driven by many motives. These motives ranged from practical to noble.

Economic

While trade with the East continued after the Crusades, the goods passed through many agents, and the final cost was very high. Therefore, Europeans began to search for new trade routes that bypassed Muslims, local leaders, and Italian merchants. Many believed that a water route to the East could be discovered.

Adventurers sailed south and west with the confidence that they could find another route to the wealth of the East. Motivated by dreams of shiploads of gold, silver, and spices, explorers risked their lives by sailing into uncharted waters.

Social

Others explored to experience the thrill of adventure and receive the praise of men. Some were driven by curiosity and others by the quest for glory. Explorers often wrote journals of their exploits, and some sent detailed letters back to their monarchs to document their activities.

Political

In addition to potential wealth, the prospect of political gains motivated European monarchs. As news of initial discoveries reached Europe, some rulers authorized exploration in order to lay claim to foreign lands. When empire building became popular, explorers were sent to establish colonies and discover raw materials needed by the home country.

Religious

The continuing threat of Muslim invasions gave Europeans great concern. With the fall of Constantinople in 1453, the Ottoman Turks swept into what remained of the Byzantine Empire. Muslim forces also posed a serious threat to Italy because the Muslims had made several attempts to invade nearby Austria. Explorers sailed in search of a mythical king in Africa, **Prester John**, who was thought to be a Christian. Europeans hoped to get his help to defeat the Muslims and preserve Christianity.

Some explorers went out with the goal of spreading the gospel to heathen cultures. Since most of the early explorers were followers of the Roman Church, the converts were often won to the Church of Rome and its teachings.

Technology

Technological advances made exploration possible. Newer and better ships that could cross the open seas and tools to navigate those voyages were essential. With each returning ship, mapmakers learned more and produced more accurate maps. As more and more countries built navies and explored, they depended on improved weapons to protect trade routes.

Shipbuilding

Ships that were built to sail along the coastlines of the continents were not capable of traveling on long journeys on the open sea. Advances in shipbuilding resulted in the **caravel**. Utilizing a combination of previous designs, the caravel could travel on the open sea and also sail upriver in the shallow coastal waters. This ship had three or four masts and used triangular sails combined with one or more square sails. The triangular sails enabled the caravel to maneuver in port and travel swiftly over shallow water. The square sail allowed the ship to catch more wind and travel quickly on the open sea.

Ships played a central role in exploration, trade, and defense. Since the Muslims had cut off the land routes to the Orient, water routes were the only other option. The caravel and other ships carried spices, silk, and other treasures back to Europe. Eventually, nations would realize the importance of a navy both to defend trade routes and to enable the establishment of colonies. Ships would also play a key role in wars between nations.

Replica of a 15th century Portuguese caravel

Navigation

As Renaissance scholars learned more about their world, they provided explorers with new inventions. Other navigational information came to Europe through contact with the Islamic world.

Maps

Maps of the areas familiar to Europeans became more and more accurate by the fifteenth century. Italians excelled at making maps and improved them with input from traders and fishermen. However, for areas beyond the Mediterranean Sea or the coast of Europe, little or no information was available. Those who sailed west in search of trade routes to the Orient traveled in uncharted seas. As they returned from their journeys with new information, existing maps were updated and improved. The invention of the printing press made rapid reproduction of maps possible and reduced the cost of making them.

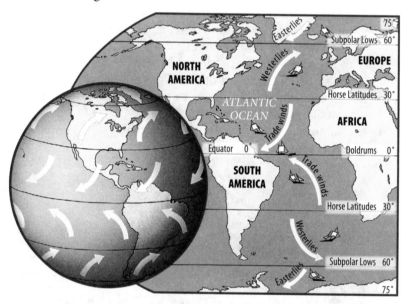

Over time, these maps would include valuable information about wind patterns. Winds that were especially important to the early explorers were the **trade winds**, belts of consistent winds that blow from east to west. These fast-moving, favorable winds blew the explorers across the Atlantic Ocean.

Instruments

The sailor's most useful instrument was the **compass**, which allowed him to set a course and follow its direction faithfully. As you learned in Chapter 4, the Chinese developed the first crude compass from a magnetic mineral called lodestone. The European sailors found the compass to be essential for navigating the open sea with no landmarks. By the fifteenth century, an improved compass was composed of a needle spinning on a pin over a base. Several points of direction were marked on this base, making it possible to set and maintain an accurate course.

The **astrolabe** proved to be another helpful instrument. Sailors used it to measure the angle between the sun or a star and the horizon at a specific time of day or night. From this measure the sailor could determine his latitude. However, the astrolabe had serious limitations. For example, measuring the angle on a tossing ship was difficult or impossible. In addition, time was measured by an hourglass, so the captain rarely knew the exact time of his reading. Eventually, the astrolabe was replaced by more accurate measuring devices.

Most early seamen navigated by **dead reckoning**. They decided what they thought their location was, estimated their speed, looked at the map, and aimed for a compass heading that they believed would get them to their goal. With the aid of the astrolabe, the sailors were able to improve their accuracy by traveling north or south to get to the desired latitude. Then they would sail east or west on that latitude until they came to land.

Naval Warfare

Naval warfare is ancient and can be traced back to battles such as those between the Greeks and the Persians in the fifth century BC. During the Age of European Exploration, a new weapon was attached to ships: the cannon. The Venetians were among the first to use cannons onboard their ships. They used their fleet both to carry on trade and to defend against piracy. Later, the Portuguese developed fighting vessels to escort their ships along their many trade routes. Soon the use of cannons on ships became common as Europeans discovered how to use them effectively at sea and in coastal attacks on their enemies.

Initiation of Exploration

It is remarkable that Columbus sailed in search of a western route to the East in the same year (1492) that the Iberian Peninsula was freed from the last trace of Muslim influence (see margin text box). From this peninsula Portugal and Spain began to explore Africa, Asia, and the Americas. These two nations had several advantages that enabled them to take the lead in European exploration.

Spain and Portugal were bordered by the Atlantic Ocean and the Mediterranean Sea. Therefore, they had a long history of shipbuilding and navigating these bodies of water. With access to the Atlantic Ocean, Spain sent explorers west and Portuguese sailors traveled south to find a new water route to the East. These experienced sailors also had the advantage of navigational and mapmaking skills that they had acquired from the Moors (Spanish Muslims).

Finally, Spain and Portugal were motivated by a strong crusading spirit that had enabled them to forcibly remove the remnants of Muslim influence in their region. They went out to spread the doctrine of the Roman Church and to continue the struggle against Muslims in other lands. Everywhere they explored and every colony they established had a strong Roman Catholic presence. Every effort was made to convert the Indians to Catholicism.

1492—A Remarkable Year

Two important events occurred during the year 1492. The nation of Spain had been formed in 1469 when Ferdinand II of Aragon married Isabella of Castile. Together they used their forces to push the remaining Muslim powers out of the Iberian Peninsula. This struggle ended in 1492 with the victory of the Spanish. With all the important decisions to be made, it is significant that one of those decisions involved sending Columbus on a voyage to discover a route to the East. Given the great financial cost and risk of this voyage, it was a remarkable choice.

Section Review Questions

1–3. List and briefly describe three motives for European exploration.

4–5. List and briefly describe two navigational improvements that made exploration possible.

✶ Why were Spain and Portugal among the first European nations to send explorers?

✶ Which motives for exploration were inconsistent with a Christian worldview and why?

Guiding Questions

1. How did the Portuguese expand to India and Southeast Asia, and how did they interact with the people of these regions?

2. How successful were the Ottoman, Indian, Chinese, Japanese, and Siamese powers in restricting European incursion?

3. What impact did Spanish conquest have on the Aztec and Incan empires?

■ III. Growth of European Exploration

New Regions and New Routes

To compete with Arab and Italian traders (who controlled the land routes to India and China), countries needed to find a sea route to those lands. Portugal and Spain eagerly set off to accomplish that goal.

Portuguese Exploration

Prince Henry of Portugal sent out sailors and ships to explore the coast of Africa in the fifteenth century. For these explorers the sea contained many unknown dangers. They heard stories of sea monsters, deadly heat at the equator, and violent storms. Despite these dangers, some men, supported by their kings, set out to find and explore distant lands.

To prepare his sailors for these dangerous voyages, Prince Henry set up a school for navigation. Portuguese sea captains learned how to use new methods and instruments. For his emphasis on training, Henry became known as Prince Henry the Navigator.

The Portuguese gradually sailed farther and farther south along the western coast of Africa in search of a route to the East. In 1487 the Portuguese explorer **Bartolomeu Dias** (DEE us) finally turned the corner that would open sea trade with India. Caught in a bad storm, Dias's ships rounded the tip of Africa without his realizing it. When Dias did become aware of where he was, he turned back and saw land. He wanted to continue to explore, but his frightened crew insisted on returning to Portugal. The Portuguese had proved that they could reach the East by sailing south around Africa.

Ten years later, in 1497, the first Portuguese ship landed in India. After rounding the **Cape of Good Hope** (southern tip of Africa), **Vasco da Gama** (VAHS-ko duh GAHM-uh) and his crew

The Monument to the Discoveries in Belém, Portugal (left).
Prince Henry the Navigator (right).

sailed up the east coast of Africa, stopping at trading cities where they met both African and Arab traders. Landing on the southwest coast of India, da Gama and his men were surprised to find an advanced people.

When they tried to trade, the Portuguese were surprised that the Indians rejected the items they had brought. The Indians were not impressed by the Portuguese goods of cloth, honey, and oil. In addition, Muslim merchants opposed da Gama's efforts to trade with the Indians. Eventually, the Portuguese sold enough to buy spices and return to Portugal. The spices that were bought in India were sold to pay for the voyage, and enough money was left over to finance sixty more voyages. This insured that the Portuguese would make many more trips and extend their exploration even farther east.

Portuguese sailors soon made regular voyages to the port cities of East Africa and India. Muslim efforts to block Portuguese trade were easily defeated by the heavily armed Portuguese ships. The Portuguese sent a fleet of twenty-two ships to India in 1505 to establish settlements and to protect their growing trade there.

Early in the sixteenth century, the Portuguese became the first Europeans (after Marco Polo) to make contact with China. Portuguese traders quickly moved to establish trade directly with the Chinese. This further weakened the Muslim and Italian monopolies on goods from the East and resulted in great wealth for Portugal.

In the mid-sixteenth century, the Portuguese were among the first Europeans to land in Japan. A few years later, the Jesuit missionary **Francis Xavier** arrived in Japan and sought to convert the people to Roman Catholicism.

Early Spanish Exploration

While the Portuguese monarchs sent their ships to the East by sailing south, an Italian explorer believed he could get to the East by sailing west. When his ideas were rejected by the Portuguese and others, **Christopher Columbus** met with **King Ferdinand and Queen Isabella** of Spain. He convinced them to finance his exploration. By sailing west, Columbus hoped to discover a shorter route to China and the Indies (the islands near China, now known as Indonesia). In August 1492 he set sail with three ships. In October he landed on an island in what he thought were the Indies.

Although Columbus was right about sailing west to get east, he did not sail far enough. Thinking he had landed in the Indies, he called the natives "Indians." However, he had actually landed in the Caribbean. The nearby

Vasco da Gama

Vasco da Gama

Da Gama led a fleet of four ships on a one-year journey to India. Instead of following the African coast as others had done in the past, he sailed west and then south in a broad sweep. This maneuver allowed him to take advantage of favorable winds and currents. By the time his ships reached the southern tip of Africa, he had sailed out of sight of land for fourteen weeks. In future explorations, wind-driven ships would often use this maneuver.

One of the men who accompanied da Gama on this voyage was Dias, the explorer who had first discovered the passage around Africa ten years earlier.

Christopher Columbus

Ferdinand Magellan

Pacific Ocean

When Magellan rounded the tip of South America, he left the Atlantic and entered a new ocean. This ocean was so calm and peaceful that he named it the *Pacific*, from the Latin word for "peace." Unfortunately for Sir Francis Drake, he did not find this ocean peaceful at all when he encountered it on his voyage.

Power and the Spanish Conquest

The Spanish were able to make conquests in Central and South America because of the power their technology gave them. The use of this power was defended in a document called the *Requerimiento* which said that God made Saint Peter and his heirs, the popes, rulers over all the earth. Therefore, if the Indians did not convert, the Spanish had the right to conquer their lands and make them slaves.

mainland was not China but the Americas. Neither the Caribbean islands nor North America yielded the gold and spices sought by the explorers. Yet Columbus did discover a new continent that would influence the course of Western civilization in years to come.

In 1519 **Ferdinand Magellan** (FUR-duh-nand muh-JEL-un) sailed west from Spain in an effort to sail around the world. His ships rounded the tip of South America and crossed the Pacific Ocean. Tragically, Magellan was killed in the Philippines. The surviving members of his crew continued the voyage and returned to Spain. This journey lasted three years, but it proved that Columbus's theory was correct: it was possible to reach the East by sailing west.

Early English Exploration

Not to be outdone by the Spanish and Portuguese, Queen Elizabeth of England sent **Sir Francis Drake** to sail around the world in 1577. On returning from his three-year journey, Drake published a report of his voyage. He told of seeing new lands and peoples and enjoying God's gifts in nature. He also described times of hardship on this expedition. For example, winds, storms, heat, and lack of fresh water plagued the voyage.

Sir Francis Drake

Spanish Conquest

Columbus always believed that America was China, a land of gold. America was not China, but later explorers continued to believe that America was a land of gold. Spain sent out several men to find this gold, conquer the people, and convert them to Roman Catholicism. Called **conquistadors** (kon KEES tuh dorz), Spanish for "conquerors," these men discovered and brutally destroyed Indian civilizations in Central and South America in search of gold.

Central America

In the region of modern Mexico, the conquistador **Hernando Cortés** (er-NAHN-do kor-TEZ) encountered the Aztecs. In 1519 he arrived in the Aztec capital, Tenochtitlán (modern Mexico City). The Aztec ruler, **Montezuma**, greeted Cortés and gladly showed him samples of the Aztec's great wealth. Cortés convinced Montezuma that the king of Spain was the Aztec god Quetzalcoatl and demanded that the Aztecs submit to Cortés as the king's representative. Montezuma submitted to Cortés's demands and urged his people to cooperate.

Despite the honor and gifts he received, Cortés eventually massacred (MAS uh kurd; killed a large number of) most of the Aztecs. As the Aztec people began to realize that the Spanish appetite for gold and power knew no bounds, they refused Cortés's leadership. When Montezuma again urged his people to submit to the Spanish, they stoned him to death. However, with guns, armor, and horses, the Spanish had a great advantage over the Aztecs. In 1521, during a four-month siege, Cortés destroyed Tenochtitlán. In its place he built Mexico City. Over the temple of the Aztecs, Cortés built a Roman Catholic cathedral. The Spanish compelled the Indians to outwardly submit to the Church of Rome while allowing them to retain many aspects of their pagan worship.

South America

Francisco Pizarro (pih ZAHR oh) proved to be even more brutal than Cortés. He traveled to the New World to find gold, and he used violent methods to seize it at every opportunity. Pizarro heard of an Indian nation in South America—the Incas—that had much wealth. He led a small group of men and sailed from Panama to Peru in 1531. Pizarro and his men worked their way through jungles for six months and attacked villages along the way. When they reached the Inca Empire, they took the Inca, **Atahualpa** (ah tuh WAHL puh), captive. The Inca offered to fill the room in which the Spanish held him prisoner with gold and silver in exchange for his release. Over the next few weeks, the Incas delivered about thirteen thousand pounds of gold and almost twenty-six thousand pounds of silver. However, Pizarro brutally murdered Atahualpa anyway and made himself ruler of the Inca Empire.

Pizarro destroyed Cuzco and founded the city of Lima along the coast. However, he did not live to enjoy the treasures he had violently taken from the Incas. In 1541 a group of Spaniards stormed Pizarro's palace and killed him.

Efforts to Limit European Access

As the Europeans explored other continents, they interacted and sometimes collided with other civilizations. Responses to European exploration varied from one area to another. We will briefly examine some of these responses.

Ottoman

While Europe ventured out on the seas to explore new lands, the Ottoman Empire continued its expansion. Having conquered Constantinople in 1453, the Ottomans continued to capture land and expand their Muslim empire. A collision with Europe was unavoidable. Clashes between Europe and the Ottomans occurred in several battles. In 1571 an alliance of Roman Catholic nations, led by Phillip II of Spain,

Francisco Pizarro

Inca Empire

defeated the Ottoman naval fleet at the Battle of Lepanto. However, the Ottoman Empire quickly rebuilt its fleet and forced Venice to sign a peace treaty. By 1683 the Ottoman Empire found itself unable to maintain the two armies needed to fight the Austrians in Vienna and a rival Muslim kingdom in Persia. After this time the Ottomans fell behind the Europeans in the areas of military technology and strategy. The Ottoman Empire faded as a threat to Europe and its continued expansion.

Indian

During this period of European exploration, India struggled with internal conflicts and was unable to resist European efforts to establish colonies. Many countries, including Portugal, the Netherlands, France, and Great Britain, set up trading posts that were followed by colonies in India. Soon much of India was under the control of Europeans.

Chinese

The Chinese allowed limited trade with Europeans during the early period of European exploration. Portuguese traders had only restricted access to China by way of coastal cities such as Canton. As long as the Chinese government remained strong, European trade remained limited. However, Europeans continued to pressure China to open its borders for more trade and on terms that were favorable to the Europeans.

Japanese

As noted earlier, Jesuit missionaries traveled to Japan during the sixteenth century. For a brief period, commerce and cultural exchange occurred between Japan and Europe. However, by 1639 the Japanese began to expel foreigners and isolate themselves from continued foreign influence. This isolation continued for the next two and a half centuries.

Siamese

Siam (Thailand) traded with Europeans beginning with the arrival of the Portuguese in the sixteenth century. However, this country stood alone in Southeast Asia in its ability to resist European efforts to establish colonies on its soil. Strong leaders and skillful diplomacy protected Siam from European pressures to allow the development of European colonies. The Siamese leaders quickly recognized a tension between French and British powers and used this situation to their advantage.

Section Review Questions

1. What Portuguese prince prepared his sailors for exploration?

2. Name the first Portuguese explorer to land in India.

3. What European country was the first to establish trade with Japan and China?

4. Who was the ruler of the Aztecs when the Spanish conquistadors arrived?

★ In contrast to the *Requerimiento*, what does Romans 13:1–7 say about whom God appointed to rule over nations?

★ Why were the Siamese able to avoid European colonization?

IV. Consequences of European Exploration

Spread of Roman Catholicism in Latin America

As previously mentioned, Spanish explorers were sent to the Americas to find gold, to conquer territory, and to convert the natives to Roman Catholicism. History demonstrates that they had great zeal for the first two. However, most of the work of converting the surviving Indians was left to the Catholic clergy. In 1502 a Roman Catholic friar named **Bartolomé de Las Casas** came to the Americas to serve as a missionary to the Indians. Las Casas and others like him spoke out against the cruel treatment of the Indians by their fellow Spaniards. Las Casas spent the rest of his life seeking the passage of laws to protect the Indians from slavery and forced conversion to the Roman Church. He played a key role in improving the treatment of the Indians.

Since the Roman Church became the protector of the Indians, many converted to Roman Catholicism. The Indians developed a strong loyalty to the priests and the Catholic Church. The Roman Church took advantage of this loyalty and brought most of Central and South America under its influence.

Introduction of Plants, Animals, and Diseases

While the Americas were not barren of food-producing plants before the arrival of the Europeans, the explorers did bring several new crops to the New World. These included fruit trees and grapevines from Europe. However, the plant that had the greatest impact was tobacco. While the Indians already grew tobacco, the English brought tobacco from the West Indies and planted it in America. This variety of tobacco proved to be very profitable, and colonists planted large areas with this plant. Tobacco brought wealth to the settlers, but it also depleted the soil rapidly. Soon more and more land was needed to maintain production and meet the growing demand. Forests were cleared in order to plant more tobacco, and depleted soil was used for grazing growing herds of livestock.

In addition to plants, the explorers also introduced several animals, including cattle, horses, and pigs, to the Americas. The horse proved to be the most beneficial animal to the Indians. Previous to the arrival of horses, all hunting and travel by the Indians was on foot. The horses were a welcome addition for their speed and strength. Horses made it possible for the Indians to hunt bison herds more effectively. In addition, horses made carrying loads and traveling much easier.

Some scholars believe that pigs were the most destructive of the animals brought with the explorers. The pigs often ran wild and tended to eat many of the plants used by Indians for food, including the corn planted by the Indians. Pigs also carried various diseases that may have spread throughout the wildlife and into the food supply of the Indians. Opinions vary about what caused the spread of disease among the Indians and killed many of them, but pigs brought from Europe may have played a role in this tragic loss of life.

Various human-borne diseases also killed large numbers of Indians. Smallpox is now believed to have killed many Incas beginning around 1525. It spread rapidly throughout the empire. This plague

Guiding Questions

1. How did the influence of the Roman Catholic Church spread across Latin America?

2. How did the exchange of plants, animals, and diseases affect European and American Indian societies?

Bartolomé de Las Casas

Environmental Changes in the New World

Humans were given the responsibility to manage creation before the Fall (Gen. 1:28). This means that human efforts to reshape the environment are not wrong. But notice how the Fall complicates that task. Tobacco is not good for food, and it depletes the soil, but because it was profitable, more and more land was cleared to plant it. Pigs are good for food, but after the Fall they began to carry diseases that kill. And because they were not managed as they ought to have been, they destroyed the Indians' food rather than providing food.

How Many Indians Were There?

Estimates vary greatly regarding the number of Indians living in the Americas when the Europeans arrived. Las Casas, an eyewitness of Spanish atrocities, referred to the death of about fifteen million Indians at the hands of the Spaniards (although he provided no documentation). It has become popular in the last few years to speculate that the Indian populations could have totaled over one hundred million. However, others point out that there is no evidence for such inflated numbers. Historians know that many Indians died around the time of European colonization, but no one knows with certainty what killed the Indians and how many died. The truth is that we don't have any evidence that enables us to answer the question of how many Indians there were.

destroyed many of the Inca leaders about six years before Pizarro and his men arrived. No satisfactory source for this outbreak has been determined, although there are several theories. Other diseases such as typhus and measles were possibly brought with the explorers and settlers. Without realizing it, those who survived the plagues that had reduced populations in Europe may have brought these diseases to the Indians. Since the Indians had no previous exposure to these diseases, they had not developed immunity to them. For reasons that are not entirely known, the death toll among the Indian populations was great.

Results of Interaction with Other Cultures

European explorers struggled to understand many of the cultures they encountered in foreign lands. Some were surprised to find complex cultures in India, China, and the Americas. Others were horrified at the sight of human sacrifice among the Aztecs in Central America. Europeans were also appalled by the violent methods of defeating enemies, such as beheading and cannibalism.

While most Europeans looked down on other cultures as being less civilized, some of these cultures challenged the Europeans to consider their own barbarities. Yet many of the European explorers displayed a disregard for the lives of native populations. Conquistadors like Cortés and Pizarro slaughtered Indians by the thousands and destroyed whole villages. Spanish forces in general were especially brutal in conquering the Indian civilizations and then enslaving the survivors to labor in the mines and fields. Some of the Spanish invaders were even willing to kill their own countrymen in order to attain these goals. If the Europeans and Indians were both barbaric, who could say that one culture was better than the other? This kind of thinking would later prove to be a challenge to Christianity when it confronted pagan religions.

Section Review Questions

1. What Roman Catholic friar traveled to the Americas as a missionary to the Indians?

2. Why did many Indians convert to the Roman Catholic Church?

3–4. Describe the impact of the introduction of horses and pigs to the Americas.

★ Why did human-borne diseases brought by Europeans devastate Indian populations?

★ Compare the typical European response to Indian civilizations with the conduct of the conquistadors.

■ Making Connections

1. What did the relationship between Europeans and the Iroquois Confederacy reveal about these tribes?

2. How did the Mayan civilization respond when the Spanish conquistadors arrived?

3. How was the city of Tenochtitlán built in the middle of a lake?

4. Why were the Aztecs open to deception by the Spanish conquerors?

5. Why did the Incas cover their buildings with sheets of gold?

6. Why was the caravel better suited for exploration?

7. How did Prince Henry of Portugal contribute to Portuguese exploration?

8. Why were Portuguese sailors willing to endure the risks and difficulties to sail to India?

■ Developing History Skills

1. Using the information found in this chapter, create a timeline of European exploration.

2. Draw a basic map of Central and South America and label the locations of the empires of the Aztecs, Incas, and Mayas.

■ Thinking Critically

1. In what ways are the views that Indians were savages without civilization and the views that Indians had little to no environmental impact similar? How are such views demeaning to the Indians and contrary to Scripture?

2. Evaluate the religions of the civilizations in the Americas in light of Romans 1.

■ Living in God's World

1. Find online and read an excerpt from Michel de Montaigne's essay "Of Cannibals." Compose an essay in response from a Christian perspective. Note both what is correct and what is incorrect with Montaigne's essay.

2. Divide into groups representing counselors to the monarch of an exploring nation. Each group will write a document giving the reasons for an upcoming exploration of the Americas along with guidelines for how to interact with the Indian peoples. Write as Christian counselors of a Christian king. Upon completion, each group will present its document to the class.

People, Places, and Things to Know

Pueblos
Mound Builders
effigy mound
Iroquois Confederacy
Five Civilized Tribes
Mayas
Aztecs
Tenochtitlán
Quetzalcoatl
Incas
Cuzco
Prester John
caravel
trade winds
compass
astrolabe
dead reckoning
Prince Henry
Bartolomeu Dias
Cape of Good Hope
Vasco da Gama
Francis Xavier
Christopher Columbus
King Ferdinand
Queen Isabella
Ferdinand Magellan
Sir Francis Drake
conquistadors
Hernando Cortés
Montezuma
Francisco Pizarro
Atahualpa
Battle of Lepanto
Bartolomé de Las Casas

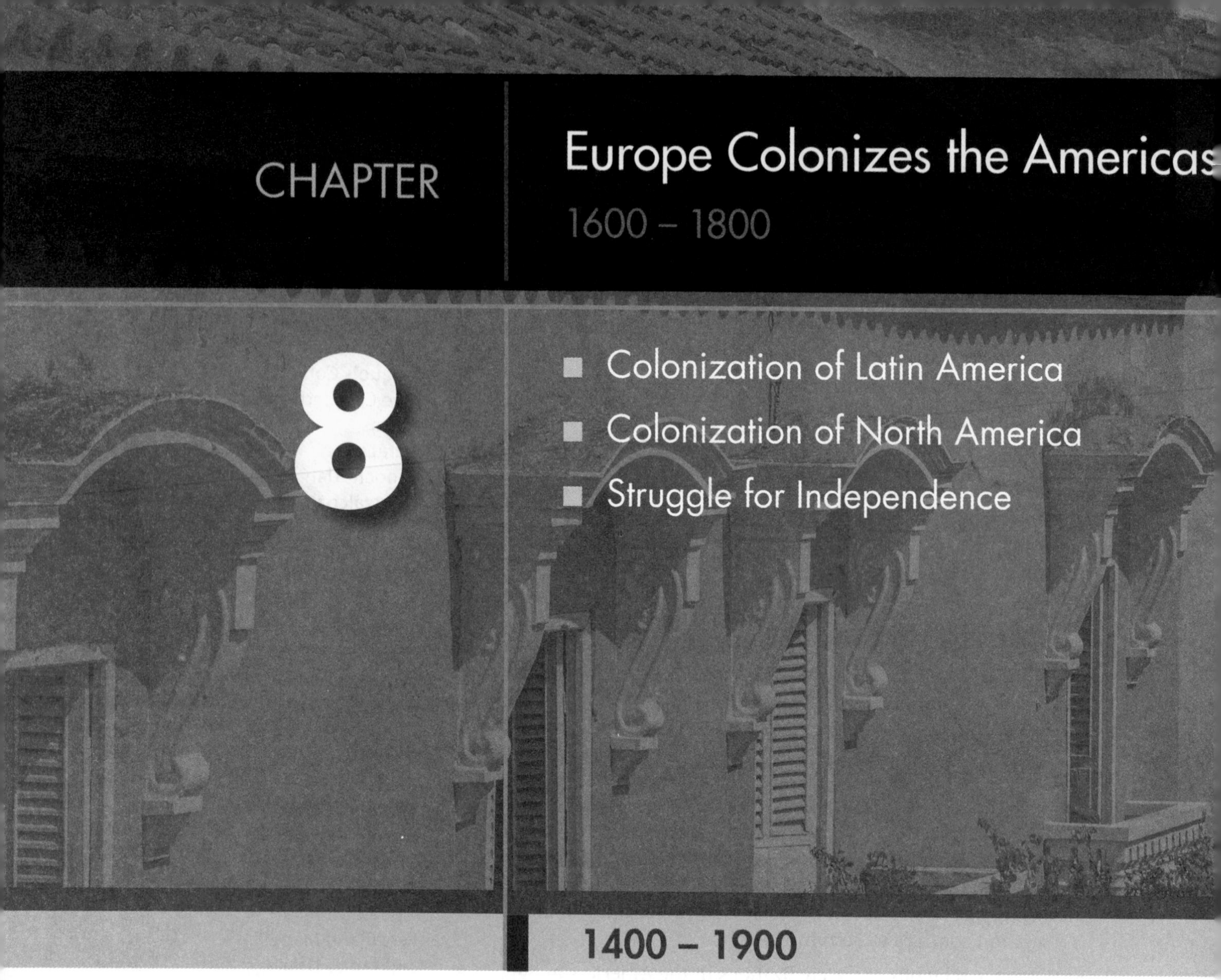

CHAPTER 8

Europe Colonizes the Americas

1600 – 1800

- Colonization of Latin America
- Colonization of North America
- Struggle for Independence

1400 – 1900

- Portuguese begin to buy slaves and transport them to Europe c. 1441
- Treaty of Tordesillas 1494
- Portugal accidentally discovers Brazil 1500
- Spain establishes Council of the Indies to oversee its colonies 1524
- Jacques Cartier explores America for France 1534
- New Laws of 1542 passed to protect Indians and Mestizos 1542
- Jamestown founded 1607
- Massachusetts Bay Colony founded 1630

1400 | 1500 | 1600

Big Ideas

1. How did Latin America become colonized, and why was it difficult to rule the colonies from Europe?

2. How did the colonization of North America differ among the French, Spanish, and English?

3. How did the struggles for independence differ between North America and Latin America?

When Columbus discovered a new world, he set off a chain of events that led to the migration of multiplied millions of people from Europe and beyond. What began as colonies that were established to benefit European countries grew into two continents with many nations. The process was often turbulent, and the results were mixed.

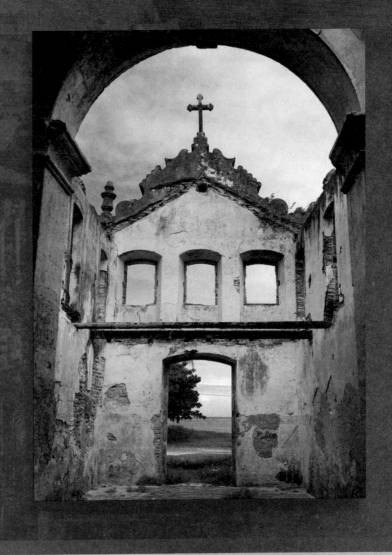

■ American colonies win their war for independence 1783

Spanish colonies break from Spain 1813–22

1700

1800

1900

Birth of Simón
■ Bolívar 1783

Brazil declares freedom and ends
■ Portuguese rule 1822

Latin America

South America is often referred to as **Latin America**. The term *Latin* refers to the fact that Spanish and Portuguese are classified as Romance (or Romanic) languages. In other words, they developed out of the Latin language used by their Roman conquerors during the time of the Roman Empire.

South America

■ I. Colonization of Latin America

South America was settled by people from the Iberian Peninsula in Europe—that is, from Spain and Portugal. Once the boundaries dividing their holdings were set, the Spanish and Portuguese rarely conflicted. Their similar cultures enabled them to establish a single Latin American culture. This development was often accomplished by abusing the native peoples through forced labor and requiring them to adopt European customs.

European Settlement in South America

Settlement

In the previous chapter, you learned that the Portuguese led in the race to find a sea route to China. Prince Henry the Navigator had trained his sailors to navigate, and they were charting new waters. Once the Portuguese had traveled around Africa, they quickly established a monopoly (exclusive control) on trade to the East along this route. This monopoly forced the Spanish to seek another route to China. However, instead of finding a way to China, Spanish explorers discovered what they called the New World.

Spanish architecture in the New World

The Spanish rushed to establish a monopoly over the New World just as the Portuguese had over the Eastern trade route. Spain laid claim to lands in North, Central, and South America. To support their claims, the Spanish established colonies as they continued their search for riches. Over time, the Spanish established settlements in Peru, Ecuador, Bolivia, Chile, Argentina, and Venezuela, all along the western coast of South America. A logical question to ask would be why the Spanish didn't settle all of South America. The answer lies in a line drawn by a pope on a map in 1493 and a treaty between Spain and Portugal.

The Line of Demarcation

To establish their early claims, Queen Isabella and King Ferdinand of Spain called on Pope Alexander VI, a Spaniard, to decide which country (Spain or Portugal) could explore and lay claim to certain areas. The line the pope decided on was called the **Line of**

Demarcation. Everything to the east of the line could be claimed by Portugal; everything to the west, by Spain. The Portuguese were not pleased with this arbitrary division. The route they followed to catch favorable winds for their voyages around Africa often took them into Spanish waters and put them at risk for conflict.

In a final agreement between Spain and Portugal, the line was moved in 1494 by the **Treaty of Tordesillas** (tor deh SEE yuhs). The new line was moved west about 10° longitude, or about 600 miles west of the original line. If the Spanish had understood what they were giving up, they probably wouldn't have signed this treaty. Without realizing it at the time, the Portuguese gained a vast territory now known as Brazil. The "island of Brazil," as the Portuguese referred to it, was accidentally discovered by the Portuguese in 1500 when one of their ships was blown off course on its way to Africa. Several years later, the Portuguese took advantage of this discovery and colonized this region of South America. Hence, Portuguese became the spoken language of Brazil on a continent where Spanish is spoken in most of the countries.

Conflicts over Settlements

Although conflict between Spain and Portugal was unusual, it did erupt at times as their claims to territories overlapped. A major conflict occurred in present-day Uruguay. The Portuguese had claimed the land down to the Uruguay River, but Spanish settlements were established on the Portuguese side of the river. The Spanish agreed to give up these settlements but then established other Spanish settlements in disputed lands. The conflict continued until a treaty was signed in 1777.

Other European nations were not willing to stand back and allow the New World to be divided between Spain and Portugal. The French, Dutch, and English wanted to make their own claims. The French explored the Brazilian coast from 1503 to 1509. Their explorations made the Portuguese nervous enough to send a fleet of ships to protect Portuguese claims. However, the Portuguese soon gave up this effort, and in 1604 the French established a settlement in the northern region of South America. This territory later became known as French Guiana.

Guiana seems to have been a popular name for settlements in South America. The Dutch and English also established settlements by this name in the northern region of South America. Oddly enough, in 1581 the Dutch settled what later became British Guiana, and the British settled the area that later became Dutch Guiana. The Dutch lost their original territory to the English after several battles, and the English traded their Guiana to the Dutch for New York. Later, the names of both areas changed. British Guiana became Guyana, and Dutch Guiana became Suriname.

While the Spanish were certainly the most brutal in their treatment of the native populations, other European explorers also tended to take advantage of the natives. Even with the best of intentions, Europeans tended to look down on the Indians and to pressure them to become more civilized, or European. The Europeans often claimed the right to control the land and the development of natural resources without the consent of the natives. At best, the natives were second-class citizens who were expected to perform whatever menial tasks the Europeans were unwilling to do.

Settlement Areas

The Power of the Roman Church

Spain and Portugal were the leaders in early exploration. They were also both Roman Catholic nations. It was a belief of some influential Roman Catholics that the pope, as the Vicar (representative) of Christ, was given the right to rule the whole world. It seemed logical, therefore, to appeal to the pope to decide who could settle where. Of course, the Reformation emerged shortly after the Treaty of Tordesillas was made. The pope's power was weakened by the refusal of Protestant nations to recognize the authority he claimed.

Early Missionary Efforts in South America

The Reformer John Calvin sent missionaries from Geneva to take advantage of French explorations in South America. This was one of the earliest attempts at Protestant foreign missions.

The ocean often proved to be tempestuous for travelers.

Creoles and Citizenship

God ordained a world in which there are orders or authority. God ordains rulers and commands Christians to obey their rulers (Rom. 13:1–7). But God also gave all humans the mandate to rule over His world. This latter truth indicates the injustice of arbitrarily excluding certain classes of people from participation in government. Persistent injustice of this kind typically leads to revolutions, which themselves often lead to additional injustices.

Ruling Distant Settlements

The problems Spain and Portugal faced when they tried to rule distant settlements directly were enormous and similar to the dilemmas faced by the Roman and Mongol Empires. The Romans and Mongols made traveling easier with well-planned roads and routes. However, the Spanish and Portuguese were separated from their colonies by hundreds of miles of ocean. To add to the difficulty, the ocean was an ever-changing and often dangerous route for travel.

Attempts at Direct Rule

Early Spanish and Portuguese rule in Latin America was strict. Since the rulers of Spain and Portugal had absolute power in their own countries, they exercised the same level of authority in the new settlements. At first, this method of governing was acceptable, but as the settlement populations increased, more problems needed to be resolved quickly. Waiting for orders from the Spanish or Portuguese ruler proved to be impractical.

The Spanish and Portuguese also made other decisions that doomed their long-term control of these colonies. For example, they ignored the **Creoles** (KREE olz; people of pure Spanish or Portuguese descent born in the Americas). The kings of Spain and Portugal gave all the governing duties to those born in the **mother country** (European country) and did not grant the Creoles any rights to rule even though they were direct descendants of noble families from the mother country. This disregard eventually led to revolt.

European management of the production of goods in the colonies also created difficulties. Spain and Portugal determined the price, quantity, and types of goods that could be produced and sold in the colonies. The mother country also placed a high tax on goods being **exported** (taken out of the colonies) and charged high prices on goods being **imported** (brought into the colonies). This practice severely restricted personal as well as colonial economic growth. The unrest that arose in response to these policies eventually led to revolt against the mother country.

Portuguese Rule in the New World

The system of government initially used by the Portuguese proved to be very ineffective. Instead of retaining most of the power for itself, Portugal granted great authority to twelve nobles. These nobles received the title of **donatario** (doh nah TAH ree oh), and their rule was to be hereditary (passed on to their children). The Portuguese government gave the donatarios total control of the land, and the donatarios determined how the land would be divided among colonists. They were responsible to colonize, defend, and tax their territory and to send excess funds to Portugal.

The Roman Church provided some checks to the power of the donatarios. Church officials brought the complaints of the colonists before the donatarios. If these complaints were ignored, the officials would send word of the complaints on to authorities in Portugal. This resulted in many bitter disputes between the colonial governors and the Roman Church.

In 1549, King John of Portugal began a process that eventually enabled Portugal to regain control of the colonies in Brazil. Conditions in Brazil improved for a time, but the Portuguese officials also proved unable to govern well. Despite these problems, the tiny country of Portugal was able to maintain control of a colony eighty times its size for three hundred years.

Spanish Authority in the New World

As was stated earlier, all laws and policies for the Spanish colonies came directly from Spain. This included all religious and economic policies. For example, the Roman Church became the official church in all Spanish colonies. No other forms of worship, such as Protestantism, were allowed. In addition, Spain took advantage of the economic resources by taking 20 percent of the mined gold and silver from the colonies.

In 1524, Spain established the Council of the Indies to oversee its colonies. The king appointed a **viceroy** (*vice*=in place of; *roy*=king) to rule each colony. Early viceroys appeared to be very powerful when dealing with the problems that affected the colonies; however, the viceroys ultimately had to answer to the council. This supervision limited their options when making decisions.

The Council of the Indies tried to direct colonial affairs from Spain. Since the viceroys lived in Mexico, the distance and expanse of land over which the authorities ruled proved too great to allow for effective rule. To solve this problem, the territories were subdivided into several lesser levels, and more government officials were appointed so that there was an official for each village or city. The Spanish allowed only Spaniards born in Spain, *peninsulares*, to hold most government positions. Creoles played only a minor role in government even though some had great wealth and owned much land. Over time, the Creoles and the native peoples would repeatedly rebel against Spanish authority.

Developing the Colonies

At the beginning of exploration, possessing and controlling an area was the goal. The Spanish rulers saw the New World as a vast supply of resources for the mother country. The Portuguese, with their attention directed toward their African and Indian trade routes, at first paid little attention to Brazil other than to ensure its possession. However, the Spanish were driven by the desire for riches. The discovery of gold and silver motivated them to explore farther and farther south along the western region of South America. In the last chapter you read about the discoveries of Cortés and Pizarro. Long-term settlement and development of the colonies proceeded after these early, dramatic discoveries.

Treatment of the Indian Population

Officially, the Spanish government never approved of enslaving the native South Americans. They sent the explorers as ambassadors from the Spanish ruler to the Indian empires. The explorers and settlers were given permission to enslave only those Indians who were cannibals or who attacked the Spanish. Given these instructions, it was not long before the explorers sent reports back to Spain that most Indian groups were cannibalistic and hostile. Thus, virtually all of them could be enslaved.

The Roman Church gained great influence as the clergy worked with the Indian population. The Church sent friars and priests to the colonies to convert the Indians to Catholicism. While they evangelized, many of the priests also promoted European culture. Thus,

Justice for the Indian Population

European countries had long been under the influence of Christian teaching. That teaching was often combined with error, and many European Christians were Christian in name rather than in heart. But the knowledge that Indian peoples were being enslaved and mistreated was evident. This is why the protests of Las Casas and others led to the New Laws of 1542. Nonetheless, greed is a strong motivator for people to find their way around laws that seek to establish justice.

Expulsion of the Jesuits

Some Jesuits with their Indian helpers eventually controlled large tracts of land and the agricultural production on the land. They operated sugar mills and slaughter houses. Because the Roman Church did not have to pay taxes and also received additional income from tithes, the Church was often able to monopolize an industry. The tradesmen who did not have these advantages could not compete. Jealousy over profits and power led to the expulsion (forced removal) of the Jesuit order from the New World. The Jesuits were expelled by the Portuguese in 1759 and by the Spanish in 1767.

the clergy played a key role in pressuring the native peoples to adapt quickly as the colonies grew.

When the Spanish wanted to reward a conquistador, they awarded him an estate or property that often included an Indian labor force. With this ready-made group of virtual slaves, the former conquistadors were able to farm, mine, or manufacture goods for trade or sale. Unfortunately, many conquistadors were brutal in their treatment of the Indians. Mistreatment, exposure to European illnesses, and harsh responses to Indian uprisings all drastically reduced the Indian population.

The Roman Church often represented the Indians during labor disputes and defended them against ill-treatment. As you learned in the last chapter, Dominican friar Bartolomé de Las Casas spoke out against the terrible treatment of the Indians. Through his efforts, the **New Laws of 1542** were passed. Those laws set up a government system in which courts were established to protect the Indians and **Mestizos** (mes TEE zohz; people with Indian and Spanish parents) from some of the abuses they suffered. The laws also prohibited the enslaving of the Indians and outlawed the passing on of government-awarded estates to later generations. Sadly, the landowners used their political influence to overturn many of these reforms.

STOP

Limiting the Control of the Roman Church

The Roman Church had an increasing influence on and control over the Spanish and Indian population of South America. Because of its protecting power, the Church received more loyalty from the Indians than the Indians gave to the Spanish and Portuguese.

The Jesuits, a powerful arm of the Roman Church, especially fell into disfavor with the Spanish and Portuguese governments. The disfavor resulted largely from the Jesuits' control over trade and their influence over the Indians.

The Jesuits established missions soon after initial settlement in the New World. In those missions the priests worked toward converting the Indians. They learned the Indians' language and taught them to read and write. Over time, Jesuit control over the Indians resembled that of Spanish and Portuguese control over the Indians. While the Jesuits spoke out against abuse of the Indians and supported Indian rights, they often used them as workers at the mission facilities. This apparent contradiction angered the other landowners. Eventually, the Portuguese and Spanish governments acted to correct this problem.

Bringing African Slaves into Latin America

The Portuguese began buying slaves in Africa and taking them to Europe as early as 1441. The number of slaves purchased was small at first but increased with demand. Slaves were common in Portugal and Spain, and some conquistadors even brought their slaves with them when they traveled to the New World.

In Brazil and the Caribbean Islands, the Indian population declined to the point where more workers were needed. Tragically, large numbers of African slaves were brought in to work on the plantations and in the mines. At least nine million Africans were enslaved and brought to the New World–over three million of them to Brazil alone and millions more to other Latin American colonies. Between six and seven hundred thousand black people were taken as slaves to the colonies in North America.

Developing Natural Resources

Refined silver and sugar were the two major exports of colonial Latin America. Slaves were most often used in mines in Peru and on sugar plantations in Brazil and the Caribbean. In the mines, Indians often worked as free laborers. Over time, the Indians were elevated to serve as skilled laborers and to provide supervision. Black slaves performed the general hard labor of digging and loading.

One of the most important resources of South America was the land itself. Development of the land occurred as the immigrant population increased. Overcrowding and lack of available land in Europe made people willing to move to the colonies, where they could make a new life for themselves and their children.

One of the most profitable exports in South America today is coffee. But coffee is not native to South America. Coffee originated in Arabia, and coffee plants were later taken to Indonesia. Eventually, a coffee plant was brought to the Caribbean island of Martinique. Coffee plants flourished in South America and became a major crop.

Coffee plants (left) and coffee beans (above)

Living in the Colonies

The people who came from Spain and Portugal to the New World faced many changes in lifestyle. Although the European world at the time was not extremely advanced by today's standards, the colonists still faced many surprises when they came to a world where there were unusual animals, strange foods, foreign people, and few roads. Even so, those who came adapted quickly to this new situation. Since many of the early settlers came from Spain and Portugal, they brought their Iberian culture and architecture to the New World.

Living in the City

Much of South America's colonial redevelopment took place around cities. The center of the city became the hub of trade and society. The wealthy built their homes and businesses nearby to have ready access to this center of trade.

Upper-class homes were easily distinguished from those of the lower classes. Often two-story in design, the houses of the wealthy were set up for business on the first floor while the second floor was reserved for the family. The whole house opened onto an interior courtyard. The kitchen was often a separate building at the back of the house. Not only was the house itself a beautiful structure with

If You Can't Stand the Heat . . .

Why would the kitchen be separated from the house? Remember that the climate in Central and South America is often hot and humid. If you add the heat produced by cooking and baking, then it makes the temperature in the house unbearable. The colonists quickly learned to move the kitchen away from the main house to prevent unwanted heating of the home. It may also have been a practical measure to prevent a kitchen fire from burning down the house.

Homes of wealthy South Americans

Barrios where the poor live

decorative moldings and carved shutters, but the furnishings inside were elegant as well. Imported Spanish goods were often intermingled with oriental silk draperies and items made from New World silver.

Beyond the wealth of the central city were the **barrios**, or neighborhoods, of the poor. These were the homes of the free blacks, Indians, and mestizos. Here apartments provided most of the housing. A family often lived in a one-room apartment divided into two rooms by a blanket. While simple and small, these apartments were better than the shacks where the very poor people lived.

Social or economic status played a part in the poor *barrios* just as it did in the wealthy area of the central city. New immigrants from Spain, poorer Spanish people, and Indian craftsmen formed the highest level. On the next level were gardeners, laborers, porters, and merchants. Unskilled or temporary Indian laborers and others often occupied the bottom level.

City life held more opportunity for entertainment than rural life did. In the city, the rich could attend plays, banquets, and concerts. They entertained with lavish parties to display their wealth or show off the latest imports.

The poor in the city also had several diversions. Cock fights, where roosters were made to fight to the death while crowds bet on the outcome, were common. Religious holidays with parades and religious ceremonies also provided a break from work. The poor even enjoyed watching the wealthy parading in their fancy clothes and fine carriages.

Living in the Country

The settlement of the Latin American countryside took a different course from that of North America. Most Latin Americans did not settle on individual family farms because the government did not generally allow immigrants to own land. Instead, a few wealthy men owned most of the land, from which they made large country estates called **haciendas** (hah see EN duhz). Most of the people remained poor and worked on these estates for low wages. They had little hope of ever owning their own land.

Home on a Latin American hacienda

Many of these landowners cared little for developing their own land or those forced to work it. As long as landowners gained wealth from the crops grown on their estates, they were content. This attitude prevented the workers from improving their lives and the land from being developed.

Section Review Questions

1. What line divided the world between Spain and Portugal?

2. People of pure Spanish or Portuguese descent who were born in the Americas were called _____.

3. Spaniards born in Spain who held government positions in the American colonies were called ____.

4. What institution first spoke out against the unjust treatment of the native population but later participated in oppressive practices?

★ What role did the donatarios play in Brazilian society?

★ How do Genesis 1:27 and Mark 12:30–31 condemn the European treatment of Creoles and native peoples?

■ II. Colonization of North America

If the Americas were the New World for many Europeans, then Europe had become the **Old World**. To many Europeans, the New World was more attractive than the Old. Many of these Europeans became so attracted to the New World that they left Europe for the growing settlements in America. From the early period of American settlement up to 1780, the greatest number of Europeans came from England, France, and Spain.

Patterns of Immigration

Because Spanish exploration began in the Caribbean and Gulf of Mexico, the Spanish tended to establish their settlements in southern North America. Explorers did travel farther north, but the difficulties that they faced there caused them to give up further exploration or settlement inland.

With reports of Spanish successes in the New World, the French and English soon began to send out explorers and establish colonies. They concentrated their efforts in the north. The winters there were treacherous, but the rewards were great.

You learned in Chapter 7 that Europeans left the Old World for the New for several reasons. Some came to discover wealth and become rich. Religion was another motivation for coming to the Americas. Many came to escape the religious persecution they had experienced in Europe.

The French in the Far North

In 1534 the French king sent explorer **Jacques Cartier** (kar TYAY) to find riches in the New World and a water route to China. While he did not find riches or a route to China, Cartier made several trips and discovered the St. Lawrence River. He also made contacts with several Indian tribes with whom the French would later establish trade. Cartier traveled farther into modern Canada and built a settlement in modern Montreal.

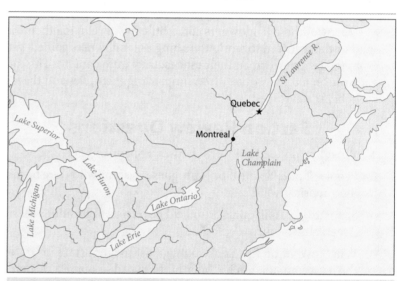

Early French Exploration

Samuel de Champlain was another major French explorer. He discovered two of the Great Lakes (Ontario and Huron) and Lake Champlain, but Champlain's greatest legacy may have been his love for the French frontier. He was given the title Father of New France.

A New World for the English

The English began to settle the New World after the Spanish and French had already claimed regions of it. English nobles and private companies sponsored settlements from the Carolinas to Massachusetts. Early efforts often met with failure, but ships continued to bring colonists to the New World and settlements began to survive. Many of the early settlers were not properly equipped to carve out settlements from the wilderness, and others were not willing to work and help make the venture a success. Strong leadership by men such as **John Smith** and **Sir Thomas Dale** turned the **Jamestown** settlement into a thriving colony.

In addition to fishing and farming, the colonists developed **cash crops** (crops which could be sold for cash or supplies) with the introduction of tobacco in 1614 and indigo, a plant used to make blue

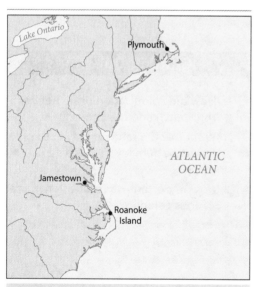

English Settlements

Pilgrims going to church

dye, in 1744. These crops enabled settlers to pay off their debts in England and develop a thriving economy in the New World.

Another group sailed to the New World in 1620 and landed near modern Plymouth, Massachusetts. Several of those who arrived on this ship came to escape persecution, to establish a place to bring up their children, and to advance missions. They were the **Pilgrims**. Since they landed in a region unclaimed by the Virginia Company in England, they were free to establish the colony according to their religious convictions. They set up a legal system that included trial by jury as well as a free market system where prices were set by individuals, not the government.

The Pilgrims had less difficulty with the local Indians than some of the other colonies for two reasons. Just prior to the arrival of the Pilgrims, the Indian tribes had been decimated by a plague. The surviving Indians were too weak to pose a serious threat. In addition, the Pilgrims treated the Indians with respect and shared the gospel with them. When the Indians were willing to do so, the Pilgrims made alliances with them in order to maintain peace.

The English settlements differed from French and Spanish settlements in three important ways. Most of the English colonists came under private investors, not government sponsorship. The English colonists brought their families with them, and most English colonists who came were Protestants. However, the English settlements were similar to the French and Spanish in that they found, instead of Eden, a hostile and unfamiliar environment filled with dangers, challenges, and adventures.

Religion and Education

When Columbus made his voyage to the New World, he asked King Ferdinand and Queen Isabella to set it aside for Roman Catholics alone. But God ordained that people of other faiths would come to the New World. Their religious convictions would affect every area of life in this new land.

Religion in North America

Many people traveled to the New World for religious reasons. A group of English settlers came in order to establish a society based

Pilgrims

These English believers had separated from the Church of England because of the worldliness and unscriptural practices in the state church. They were persecuted and forced to flee to the Netherlands, where they were allowed to worship according to their understanding of the Scripture. However, they began to worry that their children might cease to be English and might also adopt the culture and morals of the Dutch. A group of these believers traveled to the New World in 1620 and established the Plymouth colony. William Bradford served as their first governor and wrote a detailed history of the colony.

Bradford wrote of the missionary motivation of the Pilgrims:

"Last and not least, they cherished a great hope and inward zeal of laying good foundations, or at least of making some way towards it, for the propagation and advance of the gospel of the kingdom of Christ in the remote parts of the world, even though they should be but stepping stones to others in the performance of so great a work."
(*Of Plymouth Plantation*, Vision, 1999, p. 21.)

John Cotton was an early leader in the Massachusetts Bay Colony.

Typical one-room school

Characteristics of English and French Education

List characteristics of English and French education in the New World

English	French

on biblical principles rather than remain in a society that retained some false practices of the Roman Catholic Church. In addition to the Pilgrims in Plymouth, the **Puritans** settled the **Massachusetts Bay Colony** (1630).

Initially, each English colony had its own **established church**, a church recognized and supported by the colony's government. Because the Puritans had a vision for creating a pure church in a pure society, they wanted every aspect of life to be lived in conformity to God's Word. They believed that they, like Israel, were a nation in covenant with God. Their nation was therefore bound to obey His will. As a result the colonists were expected to attend church and live by its teachings. Those who openly refused were often expelled from the colony. This approach suffered from two problems. First, when the children did not follow the faith of the parents, the church began to be populated with unbelievers. Second, Christians who held different beliefs about issues such as baptism or church government were often treated harshly.

Roger Williams was expelled from the Massachusetts Bay Colony for his opposition to the established church there. He established the colony of Rhode Island and refused to allow an established church there. Soon other colonies were set up that encouraged religious pluralism, which allowed many different religions to be freely practiced in a colony. Pennsylvania was the largest of these colonies. In the parts of Canada ruled by France and in the Spanish colonies, there was no religious freedom. The Roman Church controlled the religious life of these settlements and did not allow Protestantism in their lands. The concept of separation of church and state was rejected in Catholic-controlled French and Spanish colonies.

Education in the New World

In the English North American colonies, education was considered important. The settlers in Massachusetts believed that education was necessary for reading Scripture, learning about God, and understanding His will. Initially, parents taught their children at home. Many parents recognized their God-given responsibility to teach their children (Deut. 6:7; Prov. 22:6). As villages and towns developed, one of the first buildings the settlers constructed was a one-room school. The local pastor often taught the students in early colonies. In time, a teacher was hired, and the students learned the basics of reading, writing, speaking, and mathematics. Colleges were founded to promote biblical learning and to train preachers to minister to the people. Harvard and Yale were founded during these early years to prepare men for the ministry.

In the colonies where the Roman Church was strong, the colonists placed less emphasis on education. In French Canada, for example, only the wealthy pursued an education. The sons of wealthy families received a basic education in these colonies and often traveled to Europe to study in the universities. Because the Roman Church strongly discouraged Bible reading, there was little motivation to teach the poorer people to read or write. Although the Church established some schools, few people had the time or money to attend.

Section Review Questions

1. What region was regarded as the Old World?
2. What man was sent by the French king to find riches in the New World?
3. What type of crop could be sold or traded for supplies?
4. What group settled Plymouth, Massachusetts?
5. What colony was settled by the Puritans?
★ How did religion motivate the English to colonize North America?
★ What are the benefits of permitting many religions in a country? What are the problems?

■ III. Struggles for Independence

Given the great distance between the mother countries and the colonies and the desire for self-rule, independence was inevitable. However, the differences between independence in North America and South America were immense.

Despite Britain's military and naval advantages, the British colonists were enabled by God to obtain their independence. The stable nation that emerged resulted in large part from a strong religious influence among its people.

In South America, independence came through a series of revolutions. However, the religious tyranny of the Roman Church had not prepared the people for self-rule, and instability became common for many years to come.

North America

By the mid-1700s, the English colonies between the Atlantic coast and the Appalachian Mountains contained over one million people. In contrast, only about seventy thousand settlers lived in the French territory stretching from Canada down along the Mississippi River to Louisiana. Fewer than eight thousand Europeans called the Spanish territories in the West and in Florida home.

Ruling the Colonies

In their new lands, European nations established colonies, which they controlled. The level of control differed from colony to colony. In general, France kept a tighter hold on its colonies, while England gave its colonies more freedom for self-rule. This freedom allowed the English colonies to prosper and grow at a greater rate.

Each English colony in the New World had some control over its own government. Every colony had a governor. Some were appointed by the king, but most were elected by the colonists. The governor ruled with the help of the legislature. The citizens of the colony had the right to elect members of the legislature, although citizenship was limited to free, white men who owned some property or paid taxes. The king and governor reluctantly granted more rights and privileges when the colonial legislatures withheld money. The English colonists' heritage of self-rule helped to prepare them for independence.

In contrast to the English colonists, the French colonists had little say in their government. The French king believed he should have absolute rule over his Canadian colonies just as he had over

Providence in New England

The Pilgrims and the Puritans often looked for God's providence in their lives. For instance, the preservation of their lives in voyages across the ocean, the direction of their way to a part of America not then inhabited, and help from Indians who spoke English were all evidences of God's providential care. When disaster struck, the Puritans were careful to examine their hearts and communities to see if there was any cause for judgment that they needed to repent of. They did not believe that all disasters were judgments, but they did not ignore the possibility that some might be.

Guiding Questions

1. How did colonial participation in government differ between French and English colonies?
2. Why was there discontentment in Latin American colonies?
3. What roles did Simón Bolívar and José de San Martin play in bringing independence to Latin America?

William Penn was an early supporter of religious liberty.

France. He appointed governors who ruled Canada without a legislature. The French Canadians had no opportunity to develop a heritage of self-rule. The king also controlled the colonies' trade and taxation. Canada's wealth supported the king's court in France rather than developing the colonies in Canada.

Independence in the Colonies

Between 1776 and 1867, most of the colonies of North America gained independence from their mother countries. The story of how the thirteen English colonies in North America became the **United States of America** is probably familiar to you. The colonists' success in the **War for Independence** finally delivered them from English rule in 1783. Following a brief period of trial and error, a constitutional convention produced the **Constitution**. When the states ratified (voted to accept) the Constitution, it became the working document outlining the pattern of government. The Constitution sets down limits of power on both the government and the citizens and guarantees certain rights for the citizens.

The type of government set up by the United States recognized a biblical view of man and attempted to restrain his sinful nature. Both the government and the people are meant to be kept in check by this form of government. No single part of the government— whether it be president, legislature, or court—should have too much power. Each branch of government is designed to check the power of the others. The government then protects the people by passing and enforcing laws. Most important, the people are able to limit government by electing those who run it.

Latin America

Independence came to Latin America through numerous revolutions in the nineteenth century. The Creoles had grown to resent their lack of power in the government. They saw an opportunity to gain independence while the Iberian nations fought in Europe.

Discontentment in the Spanish Colonies

Part of the colonies' dissatisfaction with Spanish rule was the control exerted by the mother country. Until the 1700s, the Spanish colonies were allowed to trade only with Spain. They could not even trade with each other. The Spanish did not limit their control to physical goods. They also tried to limit the sharing of new ideas among the colonies. The Spanish government had no desire for their subjects to accept the teachings of English and French philosophers. These teachings eventually helped revolutionary ideas take hold in America and France. The Spanish wanted to keep their colonies isolated from European influence. But that tight control only made the colonists want more information and freedom. European philosophies were smuggled in, and discontentment spread from person to person. This quiet network of information spread seeds of revolution.

Leaders of the Movement for Independence

The desire for independence grew stronger in Latin America. The only missing element was effective leaders to unite the various classes and defeat the Spanish. Two men are best known for their role in leading the Spanish colonies in their struggle for independence: **Simón Bolívar** (boh LEE vahr) and **José de San Martín**

Replica of the U.S. Constitution

(ho-ZAY day san mahr-TEEN). They are still regarded as great heroes in Latin America today.

Born in 1783 in Caracas, Venezuela, Simón Bolívar was the fourth child of Juan Vicente and Doña María Bolívar. Both his parents had died by the time Bolívar was nine. Bolívar and his brother and sisters were left in the care of an uncle.

As a boy, Bolívar learned Latin, Greek, Spanish, and French from a tutor. His tutor introduced him to the teachings of several eighteenth-century philosophers. Bolívar came to believe that freedom was the source of men's happiness. This conviction stirred the spirit of independence in his heart.

In 1810 Bolívar was sent to England as an ambassador. Despite his objections to being sent to this country, he gained valuable insight that would help him later when he wrote constitutions for the emerging Latin American nations.

Beginning in 1813, Bolívar led his troops to push the Spaniards out of Venezuela from the south, east, and west. Bolívar's men followed him through plains, deserts, swamps, and rivers. On several occasions Bolívar led his men through the Cordillera Mérida in the Andes, which rises to sixteen thousand feet in some places.

In 1816, the final move toward independence began with Venezuela and then spread to Colombia. Bolívar determined that the only way to free Venezuela was to free the entire continent of foreign rule. His greatest victories came in 1819 at the battle in Boyacá, Colombia, and in 1821 at the battle for Carabobo, Venezuela, with the support of his faithful general **Antonio José de Sucre** (SOO cray). In 1822, Sucre went on to free Ecuador from Spanish dominion.

While Bolívar was fighting for independence in the north, Buenos Aires, Argentina, declared its independence from Spanish control in 1810. That independence quickly spread across the country. The Argentine government then chose José de San Martín to take independence to Peru.

San Martín was born to a prominent Argentine family in 1778. At age nine he crossed the ocean to study in Spain and went on to

Cordillera Mérida

Gaucho

Independent but Not Free

After obtaining independence, the Spanish colonies faced many problems in governing themselves. The wealthy landowners took over the governments and continued many Spanish policies. The only difference in their rule was that the wealth went to them rather than to Spain. The common people still had no say in government. They were no better off under these leaders than they had been under the Spanish. These weak governments were often overthrown by other strong men, called *caudillos* (kaw DEE yohs). Most of these men ruled as dictators. Civil wars and revolts became a way of life in many of these new nations.

serve in the Spanish army. In 1812, San Martín resigned from the army to help in the independence movement in South America.

San Martín chose as his troops the **gauchos** (cowboys in Argentina). Although they were not disciplined, they proved to be faithful fighting companions and fought fiercely for independence. Prior to following San Martín, the gauchos had been little more than outlaws. However, their role in the fight for independence caused the people to respect them. Many of them began herding cattle for the wealthy landowners.

Unlike Bolívar, who tended to rush into battle, San Martín studied the strategies of great European generals as he made decisions about the best methods to defeat the Spanish. San Martín decided that instead of attacking the Spanish in Peru as ordered, he would cross the Andes Mountains and free Chile first. In 1817, his troops crossed the Andes and forced the Spanish from one city after another. With Chile free, San Martín turned to liberating Peru.

In August of 1820, San Martín packed troops onto ships and set sail for Pisco, Peru. It was there that San Martín received a letter from Bolívar offering his assistance in Peru's struggle for independence. San Martín's forces moved up from the south and Bolívar's troops came down from the north. Through these combined assaults, Peru was liberated from Spanish control.

Independence in Brazil

Brazil gained its independence at the same time as the other Latin American nations, but without violence. There were early stirrings of revolution supported by the upper class. However, the plans were discovered in the early stages, and the leaders were executed.

Oddly, independence came as a result of Portugal's capture by Napoleon of France. In 1807 the Portuguese royalty fled to Brazil and declared it the center of the Portuguese empire. King João (John) then adopted economic reforms to make Brazil a proper environment for the monarchy. He repealed an earlier ban on factories, introduced a trade treaty with England, established a printing press, and declared Brazil to be equal to, instead of a colony of, Portugal. All these things pushed Brazil toward independence.

In 1820 Portugal demanded that King João return. He left his son Pedro as regent of Brazil. In 1822, when Pedro was to return to Portugal, he refused. On September 7, 1822, Pedro shouted "Independence or death!" and tore the symbol of Portugal from his military uniform. He was crowned emperor of an independent Brazil as **Pedro I**.

Section Review Questions

1. Which European country had the most colonists in North America by the mid-1700s?

2. What document outlines the pattern of government for the United States?

3. What man liberated Venezuela?

4. What liberator freed Chile from Spanish rule?

5. Who became the first emperor of an independent Brazil?

★ Why did many people in Latin American countries fail to get freedom when they became independent of Spain?

■ Making Connections

1. Why did Spain and Portugal ask the pope to decide where they could explore?

2. When did the Spanish and Portuguese argue over settlements?

3. Why was it difficult for Spain and Portugal to rule their American settlements?

4. How did the Roman Church limit the power of the donatarios?

5. How did landowners respond to reforms that were designed to protect the Indians and Mestizos?

6. Why was Samuel de Champlain given the title Father of New France?

7. What did John Smith and Sir Thomas Dale provide to turn Jamestown into a thriving colony?

8. Why did the Puritans establish the Massachusetts Bay Colony?

■ Developing History Skills

1. Based on the information in this chapter, briefly describe the role of the Constitution of the United States.

■ Thinking Critically

1. Contrast the approaches to education in the English colonies with those found in French colonies. Explain what accounted for these differences.

2. Based on his reading of philosophers, Simón Bolívar came to believe that freedom was the source of man's happiness. Is this a biblical conclusion? Why or why not?

■ Living in God's World

1. If you as a Christian had the authority to change the colonial systems set up by the Spanish and Portuguese, how would you change them in light of Genesis 1:27?

2. Some people claim that modern missions is just as bad as the mistreatment of the Native Americans by the European powers because Christians are encouraging people to abandon their own cultures to adopt a European religion. Pretend that you have been asked to defend the Christian position on a nightly news program. Write a two- to five-minute dialogue between you and a news anchor. These can then be performed in class. Be sure to deal with the following potential objections:

- Christianity is a European religion.

- Evangelism implies that you think you are better than those of another religion.

- Converting people from other cultures to Christianity destroys cultures that Christians should learn to appreciate.

- Missionaries are intolerant of other viewpoints.

People, Places, and Things to Know
Latin America
Line of Demarcation
Treaty of Tordesillas
Creoles
mother country
exported
imported
donatario
viceroy
peninsulares
New Laws of 1542
Mestizos
barrios
haciendas
Old World
Jacques Cartier
Samuel de Champlain
John Smith
Sir Thomas Dale
Jamestown
cash crops
Pilgrims
Puritans
Massachusetts Bay Colony
established church
United States of America
War for Independence
Constitution
Simón Bolívar
José de San Martín
Antonio José de Sucre
gauchos
Pedro I
caudillos

9

- The Rising Power of European States
- The Scientific Revolution
- The Enlightenment

1500 – 1800

Charles I tries to arrest opponents in Parliament ■
and starts England's Civil War 1642

■ Copernicus states that the earth
revolves around the sun 1543

Charles I rules England
1625–49

1500	1550	1600

James I rules England
1603–25

Big Ideas

1. Why did military and bureaucratic power increase in some European countries, and how were the Netherlands and England exceptions to this trend?

2. What major advances were made during the Scientific Revolution?

3. What is the significance of the Enlightenment?

The seventeenth and eighteenth centuries proved to be a time of great change in European society. Nations were expanding politically and economically. The field of science experienced tremendous advances not seen since the Renaissance. Philosophy and religion were influenced by these changes, and Europe entered a period that came to be known as the Enlightenment. Many changes improved the lives of the people of Europe. Other changes threatened to destroy the Christian heritage that had emerged from the Reformation. During this period European culture was transformed in a way that had long-term consequences.

First noted sighting of Halley's comet 1682

England's Glorious Revolution 1688

English Bill of Rights 1688

Oliver Cromwell governs England and establishes the Protectorate 1653–58

Charles II rules England 1660–85

George II rules England 1727–60

Reign of Catherine the Great over Russia 1762–96

1700

1750

1800

Reign of Louis XIV over France 1643–1715

Maria Theresa rules Austria at Vienna 1740–80

James II briefly rules England 1685–88

William Herschel builds telescope 1787–89

Guiding Questions

1. Why was the development of strong monarchies significant in the sixteenth century?

2. How did the English Civil War and the Revolution of 1688 affect government, religion, and society in England?

3. How did the English Revolution impact attitudes in the North American colonies?

Louis XIV

■ I. The Rising Power of European States

Countries throughout Europe profited from the growth of trade and the influence of the Renaissance and the Reformation. States such as Spain and Portugal took the lead in exploring and expanding their empires. Other nations followed their example, and European nations extended their influence around the world.

Monarchs continued to strengthen their power and increase their authority over their subjects. During the seventeenth century, rulers began to claim and exercise absolute power. Absolute monarchs sought to make all decisions for their people. This absolutism resulted in less freedom and economic opportunity for many of their citizens. Other nations chose another path and became powerful through economic and representative means. These later nations provided their citizens with greater freedom to build wealth and prosperity.

Growing Wealth and Royal Power

European countries rushed to establish colonies and take advantage of unclaimed lands to enhance the wealth and prestige of the mother country. Trade in such products as furs, fish, precious metals, and tobacco brought great wealth to these countries. At the same time, many European governments were growing in influence and power. Royal control of the colonies and taxation of the wealth from the colonies enhanced royal power.

Of all the rulers who sought to become absolute monarchs in this period, the French king **Louis XIV** (r. 1643–1715) was one of the most successful. As an absolute ruler, he had unlimited power over his people. Louis directed all of the activities in his kingdom, from major state decisions down to everyday details. In return, every activity of his subjects was designed to glorify the king. Other rulers followed Louis's example and tried to establish absolute rule

Powerful Women in Europe

In 1740 **Maria Theresa** (r. 1740–80) became monarch of Austria. During her reign she turned Vienna into an important center for the arts, especially music. She sought absolute power by tightening her hold on the government and by improving conditions for the peasants. Her foreign affairs policies included sending troops to fight in the wars of Europe and taking territory from Poland.

Catherine the Great (r. 1762–96) reigned in Russia and increased the power of the Russian monarchy. She also increased Russian territory, adding land in the west and south, including part of Poland. During Catherine's reign, Russia became a strong power in Europe.

Empress Maria Theresa of Austria (far left); Catherine the Great (left)

over their people. Sadly, the financial and social cost of absolute monarchies was great. While these kingdoms seemed to thrive in the short term, the people suffered, and ultimately these nations declined in power and prosperity.

Growing Wealth Without Royal Power

During the seventeenth century, the Dutch Republic of the United Provinces stunned everyone by building a vast economic empire. This nation had no centralized monarchy to forge a political or economic plan. Instead, Dutch merchants played a major role in world trade. They sent out a huge fleet of ships to establish a large colonial empire and bring great wealth to the Dutch Republic. For example, their powerful navy enabled the Dutch to end the Portuguese monopoly on trade with India and China. In a spirit of free trade, the Dutch also established a modern stock market to raise funds and finance trade. The Dutch developed a banking system to manage the wealth and enable financial business. Other countries, such as England, were quick to adopt the Dutch banking system, and English economic productivity expanded as a result.

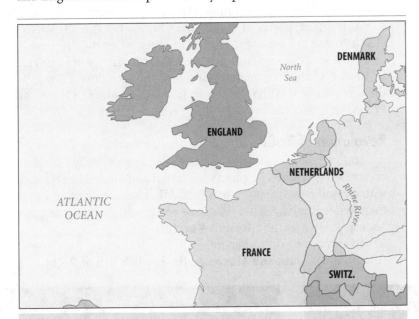

Western Europe, 1648

Growing Wealth with Limited Royal Power

While nations such as France, Austria, and Russia were developing governments that gave the ruler more and more power, the English struggled to limit the power of their monarchy. In Chapter 5 you learned that Parliament gained the power to approve taxes. This power of the purse forced the king to work with Parliament in order to raise funds. However, King James I (r. 1603–25) refused to work with Parliament and built up a strong resentment between the king and Parliament.

James's son **Charles I** (r. 1625–49) followed in his father's footsteps. Charles continued to assert the divine right of kings and struggled to defeat Parliament's efforts to deny him absolute power. He also secretly supported the Church of Rome and sought to bring Scotland and England into submission to Rome. The Scots defeated Charles's forces when the English invaded Scotland, trying to force

Power in the European States

The idea of absolute monarchs who had the divine right to rule however they willed was a new idea at this time. During the Middle Ages it was believed that kings had to rule in submission to the natural law that God had placed in His world. Though medieval scholars believed that monarchy was the best form of government, they also believed that monarchs had obligations to others. These were spelled out in the feudal system.

The divine right of kings sounds superficially biblical. Romans 13:1–2 says that God ordains the governmental authority. But Deuteronomy 17 also provides laws that the king must live under. A king limited by God's law and accountable to his subjects is actually a more biblical approach to government.

Charles I

Cromwell and the Protectorate

Following the capture and execution of Charles I, England experimented with new forms of government. When Parliament refused to cooperate with Cromwell, he dismissed its members in 1653 and ruled the country until his death in 1658. He called himself the Lord Protector and established the **Protectorate**. To provide some guidelines, he wrote a constitution, *Instruments of Government*. Despite his efforts to introduce a constitutional government to England, the people soon longed for a king and the restoration of the English monarchy.

Providence

Consider how history might have been different had England reverted to Roman Catholicism under the heirs of James II. How would that have affected the modern missions movement or even the religious make-up of the United States?

the Scottish church to use the English prayer book, which had a strong Catholic emphasis.

English Civil War

In January 1642, Charles entered the House of Commons with several hundred soldiers and tried to arrest his opponents. They had already escaped, but this move caused both the king and Parliament to hire soldiers and prepare for battle. The **English Civil War** resulted. After the king's forces won the first battles, Parliament reorganized its forces and appointed **Oliver Cromwell** to lead its army. Cromwell defeated the king's forces and eventually took Charles into custody. Charles was tried and executed in 1649. Cromwell filled the resulting power vacuum and ruled until his death in 1658.

Shortly after Cromwell's death, the English invited **Charles II** (r. 1660–85), son of Charles I, to take the throne. Charles II continued the policies of his father and grandfather. However, he was often able to ignore Parliament by raising funds from the French king Louis XIV. In exchange for French support, Charles promised to promote French foreign policy and become a Roman Catholic. When Charles died in 1685, his brother **James II** (r. 1685–88) became king. James was a strong supporter of the Roman Church, but the English tolerated him due to his advanced age. However, when his wife gave birth to a son, the English feared that their country would be ruled by Roman Catholic monarchs for many years to come. They solved the problem by inviting the son-in-law and daughter of James, both Protestants, to come to England and receive the throne.

Revolution of 1688

In June 1688, William of Orange and his wife Mary (daughter of James II) accepted England's invitation and landed in England with a small Dutch army. James found that he had no other option than to flee England. This change of power without resorting to war became known as the **Glorious Revolution**.

In exchange for this generous offer of the throne, Parliament insisted that **William and Mary** sign the **English Bill of Rights**. This

Oliver Cromwell

William and Mary

document set limits on royal power, provided the English people with basic civil liberties, and prevented future rulers from being Roman Catholics.

Effect on England

In addition to basic civil liberties and limits on royal power, the English moved toward a more representative government. During the reign of George II (r. 1727–60), a **cabinet** system of government developed. The men who formed the cabinet gradually answered less to the king and more to Parliament. This transferred additional power to Parliament, which had more contact with the people. Eventually, the leader of the cabinet, the prime minister, was elected by the people. These changes made the government more directly answerable to the people and more responsive to their needs.

Influence on American Colonies

The American colonists took note of the Glorious Revolution and the granting of rights to the people. They saw that the king did not have absolute power and that abuses by the king could be resisted. When the king and some members of Parliament decided to impose a number of taxes on the American colonies, the colonists resisted. Most taxes had been collected by colonial legislatures for many years. This intrusion by the king and Parliament threatened the independence of the Americans. The king responded by sending troops to force the colonists into submission and by suspending their freedom. However, the English had declared a standing army during time of peace to be illegal. The quartering of troops in the homes of the colonists was also illegal according to the English Bill of Rights. The colonists responded by insisting on having the same civil liberties as those found in the English Bill of Rights. When British forces invaded the colonies, the colonists fought to preserve their liberty.

Section Review

1. Who was the most successful of the absolute monarchs?

2. What nation built an economic empire without a centralized monarchy?

3. Who led Parliament's forces during the English Civil War?

4. What event resulted in the Revolution of 1688 in England?

✶ How did the cabinet system of government benefit the English people?

✶ How did the English Bill of Rights influence the American colonies?

◼ II. The Scientific Revolution

The seventeenth and eighteenth centuries in Europe are often called the **Age of Reason**. The implication is that people before this time were guided not by reason but by superstition and religion. Many believe that before the Age of Reason people relied on traditions and old writings, but with the arrival of the Age of Reason people began to use reason to learn about the world. This is a popular view, but it is not accurate. Scholars in the Middle Ages observed the world around them. They also read the observations of others. They

English Bill of Rights

This document prohibited the king from

"assuming and exercising a power of dispensing with and suspending of laws";

"raising and keeping a standing army within [his] kingdom in time of peace . . . and quartering soldiers contrary to law";

"causing several good subjects being Protestants to be disarmed at the same time when papists [are] both armed and employed contrary to law."

Cabinet Government

George of Hanover (Germany), a descendant of James I, became king of England in 1714. He could speak no English and relied on English advisors to conduct most of the tasks of government. These advisors or ministers later developed into a cabinet (committee) headed by a prime minister. Gradually, many of the powers of the king shifted to the cabinet.

Guiding Questions

1. What is the connection between the Scientific Revolution and previous civilizations and movements?

2. What is the significance of the discoveries in medicine, mathematics, and chemistry?

3. How did the Scientific Revolution diminish the reputation of Christianity in the public square?

then reasoned from these observations to general principles about the way they believed the world worked. During this process they drew some incorrect conclusions. But given the knowledge they had, some of their assumptions and conclusions seemed to make good sense at the time. In fact, some medieval scholars translated ancient scientific texts, started universities, and trained men to study the natural world. Thus they laid the foundation for the great advances made during the Scientific Revolution.

Contributions from the Past

Man has demonstrated an interest in the world about him since the beginning. One of the descendants of Cain, Tubalcain, is mentioned in Genesis 4 as working with brass and iron. So the process of extracting and purifying ore to produce metals preceded the Flood. This demonstrates man's God-given ability to take parts of God's creation and press them toward the ideal. In the example from Genesis, Tubalcain took the raw ore that God had created and processed it into useful metals. Man's instinct to fulfill the Creation Mandate appears again and again in civilization. In this section we will review a few examples of this impulse.

Greeks

The Father of Medicine was a Greek physician who lived around 400 BC. **Hippocrates** (hih PAHK ruh teez) rejected the popular notion that disease was a supernatural punishment by the gods. Instead, he taught that every illness has a natural cause. Rejecting magic and superstitious cures, he prescribed rest and a healthy diet as part of a treatment. The oath taken by many modern physicians is named after Hippocrates, although many changes have been made to his original oath.

Euclid (YOO klid) earned the title Father of Geometry. He founded a school of mathematics in Alexandria, Egypt, during the fourth century BC. Euclid also developed a system of mathematic principles that is known as Euclidean (yoo KLID ee uhn) geometry.

Hippocratic Oath (Original)

I will prescribe regimens for the good of my patients according to my ability and my judgment and never do harm to anyone.

I will not give a lethal drug to anyone if I am asked, nor will I advise such a plan; and similarly I will not give a woman a pessary [device] to cause an abortion.

In every house where I come I will enter only for the good of my patients.

If I keep this oath faithfully, may I enjoy my life and practice my art . . . but if I swerve from it or violate it, may the reverse be my lot.

Christians and Science

It is popularly thought that the Roman Church opposed Copernicus and Galileo because they removed mankind from the central place in the universe that Christianity had given him. Another popular thought is that Roman Church leaders thought that Copernicus and Galileo must be wrong since the Bible speaks of the sun, not the earth, moving (e.g. Gen. 15:12). Often skeptics will use these stories in an attempt to demonstrate that Christianity is hostile to science and reason.

In fact, no one accused Copernicus or Galileo of removing mankind from his central place in the universe. People understood then, as they do today, that the importance of humans does not depend on their location. Humans are important because they were created in the image of God.

Although there were some who thought Galileo was wrong both for scientific reasons and because of Bible passages that speak about the sun's movement, others pointed out that there is a difference between the Bible's speaking about the way things appear and scientific descriptions. For instance, when we speak of the sun rising or the sun going down, we are not denying that the earth moves around the sun. It is simply a natural way of speaking about how things appear from our vantage point on earth.

His textbook, *Elements*, formed the basis for future geometry textbooks, including those used today.

The early Greek astronomer and geographer **Eratosthenes** (er uh TAHS thuh neez) determined the distance around the earth (circumference) with great accuracy. He used Euclid's geometry to make this calculation. Eratosthenes also devised the lines of latitude and longitude found on maps today.

Muslim Science

In Chapter 2 you learned that Muslims preserved Greek and Roman scientific discoveries. In addition, they expanded knowledge in areas including medicine, optics, and chemistry. This information was passed to the Europeans through various means, including the Byzantine Empire, the Crusades, and a growing trade in Arab documents.

Medieval Science

Much of the knowledge that led to the development of science in Europe resulted from access to Muslim documents. **Albert the Great**, a Dominican friar, played an important role in introducing the documents to medieval universities. Robert Grosseteste, Bishop of London, also proved to be a central character in advancing medieval science. Grosseteste influenced one of his students, **Roger Bacon**, in the areas of optics and astronomy. Bacon made significant contributions in the areas of physics, geography, and optics.

The scientific thinking of medieval scholars was shaped by the writings of Aristotle. But these scholars knew that Aristotle was not right about everything. For instance, Aristotle taught that the world was eternal. Medieval scholars, however, believed the Bible's teaching that God created the world from nothing. In this and other areas, these scholars modified Aristotle's thought. Some of their work prepared the way for the Scientific Revolution. However, the most important preparation was the development of the university as a place where people learned and wrote about nature.

Renaissance Humanism

You learned in Chapter 6 that knowledge expanded rapidly during the Renaissance. Science enjoyed a renewal during this period as well. Positively, the Renaissance led to the translation of even more ancient texts that carried scientific knowledge. It also brought advances in mathematics, which would be necessary for the Scientific Revolution. Negatively, the Renaissance led people to overlook the real advances in science made during the Middle Ages. The discoveries of many, including Copernicus, Galileo Galilei, and William Harvey, will be discussed in the next sections. These men and others made major contributions to the fields of astronomy, medicine, mathematics, and chemistry. Some made contributions in multiple fields.

Astronomical Discoveries and Innovations

The discoveries in astronomy that occurred during this period changed people's understanding of nature as well as the way people thought about themselves and the world. In 1543 **Copernicus** (koh PUR nuh kus) presented his view that the earth revolved around the sun, not the sun around the earth. He relied on mathematics

Roger Bacon

Copernicus

Andreas Cellarius portrayed Copernicus's theory of the universe on a two-dimensional chart.

Galileo Galilei

to develop his theory. Another astronomer, **Galileo Galilei** (gal-uh-LAY-oh gal-uh-LAY), used the newly invented telescope for his observations. His results supported Copernicus's ideas.

By the time Galileo made his observations in the early 1600s, a great controversy had arisen over these ideas. Neither the Roman Church nor the Bible was committed to a geocentric view of the universe. Some people within the church supported Galileo's views, and others opposed him. Nor was the opposition unreasonable at the time. Galileo pointed to the tides as one of the main pieces of evidence that the earth moves. In fact, the tides are not caused by the earth's motion. So Galileo was right about the earth moving, but not all his reasons were right. The pope was said to have given Galileo permission to publish only if he acknowledged in his book that some of his evidences for the movement of the earth could have other explanations. Galileo did this, but he put these words in the mouth of a character that the rest of the book revealed to be a fool. This was one of several missteps on Galileo's part that led the Roman Church to investigate him.

Sir Isaac Newton (1643–1727) discovered concepts that have become known as the **laws of gravity and motion**. According to these laws, gravity keeps the planets in their orbits. Among his many other accomplishments, Newton developed an advanced form of calculus (method of calculating) and invented the reflecting telescope. These contributions enabled an improved use of mathematics

Replica of Newton's reflecting telescope

and more detailed observation of the universe.

English astronomer **Edmond Halley** (1656–1742) recorded the position and motion of hundreds of stars. He also developed a theory about the orbit of comets. Halley accurately predicted that a comet which appeared in 1682 would return to our solar system seventy-six years later. This comet was later named Halley's comet.

Sir William Herschel (1738–1822) spent much of his life contributing to the field of astronomy. He made many discoveries, including the planet now known as Uranus. In 1784 he began to build telescopes to sell, and many wealthy men purchased them. His large telescopes enabled men to look farther out into the universe and view sights that previously could not be seen. Between 1787 and 1789, Herschel built a massive forty-foot-long telescope. With this telescope he could see several of the moons around Saturn.

Discoveries in Other Fields

While some were looking to the heavens to find new worlds, others were looking through newly invented microscopes or expanding ancient knowledge. Advances were made in many areas, including medicine, mathematics, and chemistry.

Medicine

Rejecting superstitious remedies, scientists began to investigate the body and treat its diseases. One scientist, **Paracelsus** (pehr uh SEL sus), stated that the body is mostly chemicals and should be treated with chemicals. Other scientists studied anatomy. By learning the positions of bones, muscles, and organs, they were able to give better diagnoses and treatment. For example, **Andreas Vesalius** (vi SAY lee us; 1514–64) developed his work on human anatomy by dissecting human bodies. The Englishman **William Harvey** also made important contributions to medicine by discovering that blood is pumped by the heart, travels through the body in blood vessels, and returns to the heart in the circulatory system. Another Englishman, **Edward Jenner** (1749–1823), discovered a way to prevent people from getting a disease known as **smallpox**. This disease killed or terribly scarred many until Jenner found a way to protect against it by developing a **vaccine**, or weakened form of a similar disease known as cowpox. Jenner's research led to the practical elimination of this disease.

Mathematics

The interest in business and science encouraged improvements in mathematics. Three improvements that occurred around the time of the Renaissance were the more common use of Arabic numerals, the decimal point, and mathematical notation. Prior to this time, mathematic equations were written in standard form (every number word written out), making equations enormous and difficult to read.

Herschel's telescope

Edward Jenner administering a smallpox vaccination (Detail from "Jenner: Smallpox is Stemmed" from "A History of Medicine")

Title page of Robert Boyle's work The Sceptical Chymist *(right); Robert Boyle (below)*

During this period great advances were made in the theoretical understanding and practical application of mathematics. For example, it was vital to understand mathematics in order to explain the orbit of planets or to predict when asteroids would return to our solar system. As we noted, Sir Isaac Newton used mathematics to develop his theory of gravity.

Chemistry

You learned in Chapter 2 that Muslim scholars laid the foundation of modern chemistry. They introduced careful observation and controlled experimentation. Over time, these scholars discovered many chemicals. Chemistry became important in Europe as a result of repeated plagues. Men labored with various substances to develop medicines that would prevent or cure diseases.

Robert Boyle (1627–91) contributed to chemistry with his work on gases that produced **Boyle's law**. His book *The Sceptical Chymist* was foundational for modern chemistry. Boyle was also a Christian who lectured in defense of Christianity. He actively opposed the enemies of Christianity who arose during the Enlightenment.

Antoine Lavoisier (luh VWAH zee ay; 1743–94) is known as the Father of Modern Chemistry. His many contributions include naming oxygen and hydrogen and working to develop the metric system. Lavoisier formulated the law of conservation of matter. This law states that matter cannot be created or destroyed. Rather, it can only change form. Lavoisier also assembled the first-known list of elements.

Antoine Lavoisier and his wife (above); Lavoisier's laboratory (right)

Scientific Methodology

The scientific method refers to a pattern of steps that scientists use to answer questions about the physical world. These steps may vary, and their order may differ depending on the circumstance. However, they are designed to produce accurate and provable answers to the questions that scientists encounter. The steps may include the formation of an initial theory, experimentation to test the theory, collection of information, revision of the theory, and repetition of the experiments to prove the accuracy of the theory.

Historical Perspectives

Popular View

In the Middle Ages, the Bible and the writings of Aristotle and other Greek philosophers "were the most trusted guides to the natural world." But these "unquestioned traditions and superstitions" were challenged by the "careful observations and mathematical calculations" which brought about the Scientific Revolution. In this way, "the Scientific Revolution demonstrated that natural causes could explain the workings of the universe." By showing that "the Aristotelians and the biblical writers held ideas about the natural world that were untrue," the Scientific Revolution showed how reason could be used to challenge even more "unquestioned traditions and superstitions."

Richard W. Bulliet, et al., *The Earth and Its Peoples*, 5th ed. (Boston: Wadsworth, 2011), 465-67.

Scholarly View

Too often medieval scholars are "dismissed as irrational or superstitious. But this harsh judgment is faulty." They did hold some incorrect ideas. For instance, when they saw that sunflowers faced the sun as it moved across the sky, that magnets are attracted to iron, or that the moon has effects on the sea, they concluded that there were invisible "sympathies" that connected various parts of the natural world. The medieval people observed their world, formulated the principle of sympathies from their observations, and "then the rest of the system builds upon it rationally." We can say, based on knowledge that we have gained since, that the medieval ideas about science contained errors. "But that does not permit us to say that their methods or conclusions were irrational, or that the beliefs and practices that came from them were 'superstitious.'"

Lawrence Principe, *The Scientific Revolution: A Very Short Introduction* (New York: Oxford University Press, 2011) 35.

1. What did the popular view omit in its telling of the story? What is the significance of this omission?

2. What might motivate some people to tell the history of the Scientific Revolution as the triumph of science and reason over religion and superstition?

Development

In Chapter 2 you learned about the Muslim scientist known as Alhazen. He was one of the first to develop a scientific methodology in his research on light. He demonstrated this process in his *Book of Optics*. Many of the people already mentioned in this chapter developed their own procedures to answer questions and prove their theories through observation and experimentation.

Significance

The Scientific Revolution is often told as a story of how Europeans finally cast off the shackles of religion and tradition and instead embraced reason and science. In doing so, they made the modern world the wonderful place it is today. However, this story is not entirely accurate. Though myth and superstition did have some influence (particularly in medicine), not all medieval scholars were bound by tradition and superstition. In addition, many of the scientists of the Scientific Revolution claimed to be Christians. They did not think they needed to be freed from religion in order to practice science. Many of them believed scientific investigation brought glory to God. Their religion motivated them to pursue science.

The Scientific Revolution did have some negative effects. Before this time, reason was seen as a tool. It was a tool that could be used to understand the Bible. It was also a tool that could be used to understand the world. But with the Scientific Revolution, reason came to be seen as an authority and not just as a tool. Instead of seeking to understand Scripture as God's authoritative Word, some people began to decide which parts of Scripture they would accept and which parts they would reject based on what seemed reasonable to them.

Section Review

1. What early example of pressing creation toward the ideal is found in Genesis 4?
2. Who was the Father of Medicine, and what did he reject?
3. Who determined the circumference of the earth?
4. Who first declared that the earth revolves around the sun?
★ What is the significance of Jenner's discovery for you personally?
★ Why did the theory of a sun-centered solar system create such alarm?

■ III. The Enlightenment

The very name *Enlightenment* shows how the philosophers and scientists of this period viewed the previous eras. To them, earlier periods were covered in darkness and urgently needed the new ideas of this new era. Those ideas came from the belief that human reason and careful observation were the only sure ways to know the truth. Freed from devotion to the past, Enlightenment thinkers re-examined the values and religious beliefs of Europe. This period introduced many political and social changes that were important to democratic societies, but it also undermined the central role of Christianity in the culture of Europe. Europe would never be the same.

Leading Ideas of the Enlightenment

While a student, **René Descartes** (day KART; 1596–1650) read many of the classics recovered by the Renaissance, but he found them to be as weak as structures built on sand. Descartes noted that philosophy settled nothing. Instead, every philosophical point was debated. And though Descartes professed to be a good Catholic, he realized that the Reformation showed that even theology was a matter of great dispute. Descartes also concluded that man can even be deceived by what he observes through his senses and through experiments. To demonstrate this, Descartes pointed to the foolishness of alchemy and astrology. He decided that only mathematics led to certainty. This belief motivated Descartes to develop a method for knowing truth that was based on mathematics. He proposed doubting everything except basic axioms (statements about which there can be no doubt). Working from the axiom, a person should then reason through all the issues until truth is established.

Because Descartes did not trust any path to truth except human reason, his approach is a form of **rationalism.** This approach to truth was very different from the previous thousand years of European history. During most of this time, reason had been a servant to Scripture and theology. In Reformation churches, reason retained its position as a servant under the supreme authority of Scripture. Reason played an important role because it was necessary for understanding both Scripture and the world. But reason was not the authority that decided what was true and false.

Descartes insisted that he was not trying to undermine Christianity. But the Dutch philosopher Benedict de Spinoza applied Descartes's approach to the foundation of the Christian faith, the Bible. **Spinoza** said the Bible was written by humans at particular times in history. He said a person seeking to interpret the Bible should try to

Guiding Questions

1. What were the principal ideas of the Enlightenment?
2. What impact did Enlightenment ideas have on modern institutions?

René Descartes

Views of Religious Freedom

Describe the following views of religious freedom.

View	Description
Traditional View	
Spinoza	
Locke	

understand what each part of the Bible meant in the time at which it was written. Since different people wrote portions of the Bible at different times, readers of the Bible should expect to find disagreements among the authors. The careful reader, Spinoza said, would use reason to distinguish what was true in the Bible from what was false. But the point of reading the Bible was not to learn how to live—reason taught that. It was simply a historical investigation. Spinoza read the Bible as a historical artifact rather than as revelation from God.

Unlike Descartes, **John Locke** (1632–1704) insisted that the ideas Descartes found axiomatic (obvious) were not implanted by God in the human mind (as Descartes had claimed) but were developed through careful observation of the world. Locke argued in favor of **empiricism**, the belief that the best way to find true knowledge was through experience rather than through human reason. Instead of arriving at truth through a sequence of careful reasoning, the empiricist observes the world around him to determine truth. The scientific revolution seemed to strengthen the case for empiricism. For example, close observation of nature resulted in important discoveries like Newton's formulation of the concept of gravity.

Spinoza

Influence of the Enlightenment

No single Enlightenment philosophy gained prominence over another. Other philosophers disputed Locke's arguments for empiricism. Various people responded to Spinoza's atheism and skepticism. The debates raised in the Enlightenment have not, even to this day, been resolved with one side clearly victorious over the other. However, key ideas that are commonly accepted today find their origins in the Enlightenment.

Democratic Thought and Institutions

Despite disagreements about various philosophies, Enlightenment thinkers shared a democratic urge. Before the Enlightenment, people accepted that God had given them rulers and overseers in both the state and the church. Because wrong ideas could condemn souls to eternal punishment, rulers worked with ministers to prohibit books that promoted heretical teaching.

Enlightenment ideas challenged not only Christian orthodoxy but also the very idea that anyone should attempt to regulate the ideas of a nation. Descartes taught that all people have the same reasoning capacity (though some use it better than others). If this is true, then why should some men decide what others may or may not read?

Spinoza critiqued the Bible for the purpose of promoting the toleration of all ideas. He labored to demonstrate that the Bible was a historical book with no modern relevance. (If the Bible was irrelevant, then it could not set a limit on what ideas were tolerated.) Spinoza believed that religion limits liberty and does not tolerate contrary views. As a result, he argued it was the responsibility of the state to limit the influence of the church for the sake of liberty. Spinoza especially wanted the state to lessen the influence of Christianity in education. What Spinoza really desired was **secularism**, that is, a society free from religion.

Many Christians were suspicious of secularism. They feared that a government without religious influence would be unjust and evil. Those who cried the loudest for freedom rejected a biblical basis

John Locke

163

for morality and rejected the Bible's teaching about the sinfulness of man. These same philosophers rejected the core biblical principle of salvation through Jesus Christ. Some were even atheists, denying the existence of God.

On the other hand, there were some Christians who had been persecuted by other Christians for their beliefs. These Christians did not want to see Christian morality rejected, nor did they want a government without religious influence. Rather they wanted their religious view to be tolerated. For these Christians, the ideas of John Locke were attractive. Locke did not reject God or the Scripture. Instead, he pointed out that Roman Catholics, Lutherans, Anglicans, and Puritans all shared the same basic morality. Agreement about what was moral would allow people from different religions to live together in peace. Locke's ideas were most readily accepted and put into practice in Great Britain's North American colonies.

Corruption of Christianity in Culture

As Enlightenment thought became increasingly accepted, it threatened the dominant place of Christianity in Europe. Rationalists questioned whether miracles were reasonable. Empiricists wondered why miracles were not observed today if they had happened before. Also, science seemed to be able to explain in natural terms events that people had long considered supernatural. By Enlightenment standards, the Bible's claims about a God who providentially works His will in all things were unreasonable.

Scholars influenced by the Enlightenment—including ministers and professors—began to study the Bible not as Scripture but as any other religious book. They compared it with other religions in the Middle East and looked for evidence of contradictions. These theologians claimed the Bible had been stitched together by men long after the period when the biblical books themselves claimed to have been written. Spinoza pioneered this approach to Scripture. His goal was to convince philosophers to abandon the use of Scripture in philosophy.

Those who wished to defend Christianity often failed to attack the false theories at the root of Enlightenment thought. Instead of rejecting the idea that reason or sensory experience is sufficient to determine truth and asserting the necessity of revelation, these defenders tried to reveal the truth of Christianity on the terms set by the Enlightenment. What often resulted was not true Christianity but some form of deism that fell far short of Christianity as revealed in Scripture.

Section Review

1. What did Descartes conclude about the philosophy he had studied as a student?

2. According to Descartes, what leads to certainty?

3. Rationalism teaches that _____ _____ provides a path to truth.

4. John Locke rejected rationalism in favor of _____.

★ Why did Spinoza reject the Bible?

★ Why were Christians suspicious of secular pleas for government that was not influenced by religion?

Making Connections

1. What was the long-term effect on a nation ruled by an absolute monarch?

2. How did Parliament respond to threats of arrest by Charles I?

3. How did Edward Jenner's observations and experiments result in the saving of many lives?

4. How did men use science to challenge the authority of Scripture?

5. How did Descartes's approach to truth differ from that of the previous thousand years?

6. According to John Locke, how is truth discovered?

7. Why, according to Enlightenment reasoning, should the ideas of a nation not be regulated?

8. Why did Enlightenment thought threaten the dominant place of Christianity in Europe?

Developing History Skills

1. Using the information provided in this chapter, develop a timeline of English rulers.

2. Historians are divided in their appraisal of Cromwell. How should a historian work through this debate?

Thinking Critically

1. Read the excerpts from the Hippocratic oath on page 156 and write down several issues that Hippocrates addressed. Are any of these issues currently being debated in our society?

2. Does the Bible support the divine right of kings? Provide references to support your answer.

3. Why are reason and experience not sufficient to judge the truthfulness of Scripture?

Living in God's World

1. Imagine that you are sharing the gospel with someone who protests that the Bible is full of errors. The person notes specifically that Joshua 10:12–13 speaks of the sun's stopping in the sky, which implies that the sun, rather than the earth, is moving. How would you respond? Include Psalm 50:1 in your answer.

2. Individually, or as small groups, research an Enlightenment figure (Descartes, Spinoza, Locke, Newton, Hume, Rousseau, Voltaire, Leibniz). Present a brief report to the class that explains the philosopher's belief along with a Christian response.

People, Places, and Things to Know

Louis XIV
Maria Theresa
Catherine the Great
Charles I
English Civil War
Oliver Cromwell
Protectorate
Charles II
James II
Glorious Revolution
William and Mary
English Bill of Rights
cabinet
Age of Reason
Hippocrates
Euclid
Eratosthenes
Albert the Great
Roger Bacon
Copernicus
Galileo Galilei
Sir Isaac Newton
laws of gravity and motion
Edmond Halley
Sir William Herschel
Paracelsus
Andreas Vesalius
William Harvey
Edward Jenner
smallpox
vaccine
Robert Boyle
Boyle's law
Antoine Lavoisier
René Descartes
rationalism
Spinoza
John Locke
empiricism
secularism

10

- The Islands of Oceania
- Early European Exploration
- European Exploration in the 1700s
- European Settlement in Australia

1550 – 1900

■ Alvaro de Mendaña discovers
the Solomon Islands 1567

■ Mendaña and Pedro Fernández de Quirós
discover the Marquesas Islands 1595

■ Abel Tasman begins exploration trip
for the Dutch 1642

1550	1600	1650	1700

Tasman charts and maps out sections
■ of Australia's western coastline 1644

Big Ideas

1. What are the islands of Oceania, and who discovered and colonized them?
2. How did European contact with the island peoples impact these peoples?
3. How did English settlements take root in Australia?

This vast body of water dotted with islands became one of the last inhabitable regions to be discovered on the earth. Early travelers had navigated hundreds of miles across oceans to discover and settle these scattered lands formed by volcanoes. Civilizations developed and generations of people traveled between these islands before European ships stumbled upon them. The Europeans found a wide variety of cultures and peoples. They also found plant and animal life that was unique to these islands.

Louis Antoine de Bougainville begins his trip to the Falkland Islands 1763

Cook is killed on the Hawaiian Islands 1779

The First Fleet arrives at Australia 1787

John Paton begins missionary work in the South Pacific 1858

Gregory Blaxland finds a passage to the western plains and outback 1813

James Chalmers arrives in Papua New Guinea 1877

| 1750 | 1800 | 1850 | 1900 |

Arthur Phillip leads English colonists to Sydney Cove January 26, 1788, Australia Day

James Cook lands in Botany Bay 1770

Guiding Questions

1. What are the characteristics of high and low islands?
2. What are the three groups of Pacific islands?
3. How did John Paton and James Chalmers impact the Pacific Islands?

High island (above); *low island* (below)

◼ I. The Islands of Oceania

During the exploration of the Pacific in the 1700s and 1800s, many of the Pacific islands were discovered and claimed by Europeans. The island people of the Pacific had developed interisland trade and navigation many years before the Europeans arrived. The people of these islands saw no need for European discovery and did not want to be claimed by other nations. However, the Europeans used many of these islands to supply their trade ships sailing from the Orient.

Defining the Islands

The islands of Oceania lie east of the Philippines and south of Japan. If all the islands were combined, they would be about the size of the state of Texas. The largest island is New Guinea, and half of it is claimed by Indonesia. Some of the islands have achieved independence, while others are still territories of other countries.

There are two types of islands in the Pacific—**high islands** and **low islands**. The high islands are composed of volcanic mountains and volcanic debris; the low islands are composed of coral remains that developed on submerged volcanoes. The resources of each type of island greatly affect the lifestyle of the inhabitants.

High islands tend to be better for people and agriculture. The high altitude of volcanic mountains allows the islands to capture moisture from the warm ocean breezes. As the air travels across the island, it rises over the mountains, cools, and then releases its moisture in rain or snow. Consistent moisture makes it easier to grow crops, and mountain streams provide plentiful drinking water. High island soil is fertile volcanic soil that makes plants more productive. This steady agricultural supply provides a stable economy for the

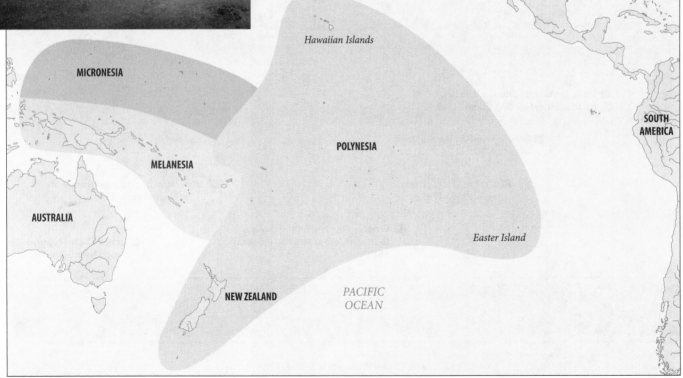

The Islands of Oceania

people. When explorers were sailing around the Pacific, they were much more likely to find needed supplies on high islands.

Low islands, on the other hand, tend to be drier. The low profile of these islands results in much less rainfall. Coral sand lacks the nutrients needed to grow most crops. Therefore, people living on these islands are more dependent on fishing as a food supply. Low islands also tend to suffer greater damage from tropical storms and high waves.

Another way of defining the Pacific islands is by the geographic groups of **Melanesia**, **Micronesia**, and **Polynesia**. Melanesia is named after the dark-skinned people who live in the region. It includes Papua New Guinea, the Solomon Islands, and Fiji. Micronesia ("small islands") is north of Melanesia and east of the Philippines. Most of Micronesia's more than two thousand islands are small and low. Some are less than one square mile in size. Polynesia ("many islands") lies within the great triangle formed by the Hawaiian Islands, Easter Island, and New Zealand.

Original Discovery and Colonization

Some scientists have theorized that the islands of the Pacific were first colonized from the west. They believe that Indonesians and Asians first made their way to New Guinea and then "island hopped" across the Pacific.

Scientists who support this theory offer at least three observations about these islands. First, the archaeological record (remains of buildings) of New Guinea shows earlier civilizations than the other Pacific islands. Second, the languages of the island people are similar to Indonesian and Asian languages. Third, many of the plants and animals on the islands are also found in Indonesia and Asia.

At first, Europeans and others doubted that the islanders could navigate miles of open water. Then scholars found evidence of islanders trading with far-off islands. These modern islanders were able to cross as much as five hundred miles of open ocean. This evidence forced the scientists to agree that the Pacific islanders could have traveled as far as Easter Island, which is near South America—a distance of two thousand miles.

Offering a different theory, Norwegian explorer **Thor Heyerdahl** proposed that the first Polynesians came from South America rather than Asia. To substantiate his theory, he constructed a boat from balsa logs and other materials found in Peru. In the *Kon-Tiki*

Thor Heyerdahl's balsa raft

expedition in 1947, Heyerdahl proved that it was possible to travel in a balsa boat from Peru to the island of Tuamoto in the Pacific. While many scientists rejected Heyerdahl's claims, he demonstrated that his theory was a possible answer to the question of where the original inhabitants of the Pacific islands came from.

European Discovery and Impact

Of the many islands claimed by European countries, only a few were heavily colonized. As in other endeavors, colonization brought positive and negative consequences.

The negative consequence that was most obvious was the introduction of diseases that ravaged many of the islands. Not having been exposed to common European diseases, the island peoples had not developed immunity against them. As in the Americas, diseases such as smallpox wiped out large portions of the island populations on some islands.

One change that had both negative and positive consequences was the introduction of European culture. The Europeans brought new clothes, new trade goods, and new customs. Some islanders embraced the new ways, while others longed for the culture that existed before Europeans arrived.

The most important positive impact on the people of the Pacific islands was the arrival of missionaries. We will briefly look at two missionaries to the Pacific and examine their ministries to the island peoples.

John Paton left Scotland with his new bride, Mary Ann, and sailed for the South Pacific in March 1858. They landed on an island in the New Hebrides in November. Their child, Peter Robert, was born three months later. Nineteen days after the birth, Mary Ann died of a tropical fever. A few days later, the baby died as well. Despite these overwhelming losses, John Paton continued his ministry among the hostile islanders.

His life was constantly in danger, and the native peoples made many attempts to kill him. Despite these threats, he endured, married again, and developed a thriving ministry on Aniwa Island. Maggie, John's second wife, held classes with the women and taught them to sew, make hats, and read. The Patons built two houses for orphans, a church, and a printing house to produce a printed New Testament in the language of the people. More than thirty years of ministry by the Patons on Aniwa led to the professed conversion of everyone on that island. By 1899 the Aniwa New Testament was printed and missionaries were established on twenty-five of the thirty islands of the New Hebrides.

James Chalmers, also from Scotland, arrived in Papua New Guinea in 1877 with his wife Jane and worked tirelessly to establish a ministry among the Papuan peoples. Those who accepted Christ were carefully nurtured in the faith. Chalmers was careful to baptize only those who demonstrated a genuine transformation and a growing desire to know the Word of God.

In 1901 Chalmers attempted to contact an isolated tribe that had been especially hostile toward outsiders. He and his assistant, Oliver Tomkins, accompanied some of the Papuans. Later, the Papuans returned without Chalmers and Tomkins. British investigators found that the Papuans had killed and eaten Chalmers and his assistant. Chalmers died as he had lived, striving to meet the spiritual needs of the indigenous peoples of New Guinea.

John Paton

James Chalmers

Section Review

1. What is the largest island of Oceania?

2. What type of island provides fertile volcanic soil?

3. Which group of Pacific islands is composed of small islands?

4. Where did James Chalmers serve as a missionary for twenty-four years?

✶ What theory did Thor Heyerdal propose? How did he demonstrate that his theory was plausible?

✶ What impact did Europeans have on the Pacific islands?

▪ II. Early European Exploration

The Europeans did not stop exploring when they discovered the New World. Within one hundred years of Columbus's discovery, Europeans began directing their attention to the lands across the Pacific Ocean and the wealth they believed these lands possessed.

Europeans also believed a great land existed at the southern pole of the earth. Mapmakers called this land the unknown southern land. They found support for this idea in the writings of the early Greek astronomer Ptolemy, who proposed that there must be a land in the Southern Hemisphere equal in size or mass to Europe and Asia in order to keep the world from toppling over. The Europeans pictured a huge continent, probably as large as Asia, overflowing with riches and treasures. Each European country sought to be the first to find the mythical southern land.

Spanish Exploration

The Incas told their Spanish conquerors of a great Incan king who had traveled west over the ocean and discovered a land filled with riches. Whether it was true or the Incas just wanted to draw attention away from themselves, Spanish interest was aroused.

In 1567 the viceroy of Peru commissioned an expedition into the Pacific to find this great land. The first expedition, led by **Alvaro de Mendaña**, included two ships. This expedition sailed west for two and one-half months before discovering land. The island at which they arrived appeared fruitful at first, and hopes ran high that they had found the mythical Incan land. They named the island chain the **Solomon Islands** after King Solomon of the Bible since he was

Solomon Islands

Guiding Questions

1. What were the motivations and patterns of Spanish exploration?

2. What discoveries resulted from Dutch exploration?

Alvaro de Mendaña

Justice on the Islands

Too often in encounters between Europeans and islanders, the principle of "might makes right" ruled. But because all humans are image-bearers of God, all humans have rights that other humans ought to respect. Respecting these rights is just. Disregarding them is unjust. Genesis 9:6 teaches that because humans bear God's image they have a right to life. Thus, humans have a duty not only to refrain from murder but also not to steal another's life by enslaving him (Ex. 21:16). People also have a right to keep their property (Ex. 21:1, 4, 7-13), which means other people have a duty not to steal from them. These basic principles of justice were often ignored by European explorers.

Santa Cruz

famous for his great riches. After an initially friendly welcome and a brief time of peace, the Spanish offended their hosts. The Spanish, rather than trying to trade with the islanders, used force to get food. They fired shots and wounded or killed several islanders. The Spanish were no longer welcome on the island.

When a ten-man landing party tried to go ashore after that incident, they were attacked. Only one man escaped to swim back to the ship. The next day reinforcements rowed toward shore to save the missing men. However, they were prevented from landing by angry islanders.

Mendaña wanted to continue exploring for other islands but was forced to return to Peru because the water and food supplies were running low. The Solomon Islands that the Spanish discovered were not visited by other Europeans for another hundred years.

However, Mendaña was not discouraged by this failure, and he led another expedition in 1595 with a young navigator named **Pedro Fernández de Quirós**. This time the expedition had four ships and carried settlers, including women and children. Among the passengers were Mendaña's own wife, Doña Isabel, and her three brothers. They were pampered aristocrats and brought their own supplies of animals, water, oil, and wine for their personal use.

The expedition charted a course for the Solomon Islands but miscalculated. Instead, they came to a new set of islands that they named the **Marquesas** after the viceroy of Peru. The islanders were friendly, and Mendaña invited them aboard. But when the islanders began to steal supplies, the Spanish crewmen shot and wounded several people. Sadly, the Spaniards continued to deal brutally with the islanders; they had killed two hundred people by the time the Spaniards resupplied the ship.

Mendaña and Quirós continued to search for the Solomon Islands. However, the next island they found was not the intended goal. Mendaña tried to communicate with the island peoples without success. He decided to settle this island that he named **Santa Cruz** (holy cross). Fever soon spread among the settlers and many died, including Mendaña. Quirós took over the command of the ships and rationed supplies in order to survive the voyage. However, Doña Isabel and her brothers still had a large supply of animals, water, oil, and wine.

With his ships wearing out due to shipworms, Quirós headed northwest for the Philippines, where the Spanish already had an established colony. Three months later, the one remaining ship of the expedition arrived at Manila Bay. The Spanish authorities were shocked to find almost one hundred men, women, and children starving to death while two of Doña Isabel's pigs rested on the deck. The authorities ordered the pigs to be slaughtered to feed the starving travelers.

Quirós requested and finally received support for another expedition. During the voyage Quirós became ill, and his navigator took control of the ship. This voyage ended with no significant discoveries and marked the end of Spanish exploration. Spain could not afford to continue sponsoring expeditions that failed to bring home riches.

Dutch Exploration

The Dutch authorities in Batavia, the chief Dutch base of the East Indies, called on one of their best captains, **Abel Tasman**, to search for the mythical unknown southern land. In 1642 Tasman took two ships and began his voyage. He started in southern India and sailed east. This way, Tasman thought, he could not miss the huge landmass that he believed to be the southern land.

Tasman sailed on, vainly looking for the unknown land. He sailed south of Australia and landed on the island now named for him: **Tasmania**. The Dutch sailors found signs of life on the island but could not find the shy islanders.

Tasman soon realized that this island was not the continent that he sought, so he sailed even farther east. He crossed a large body of water (now called the Tasman Sea) and discovered another set of islands that we now call **New Zealand**. Tasman and his men made contact with the indigenous peoples there and discovered that they were not friendly. The tall, fierce **Maoris** (MOU reez) resisted Dutch attempts to land. As the Dutch sailors explored one of the bays, the Maoris killed four sailors and drove the others back to the main ships. Tasman named this place Murderer's Bay.

On a second expedition in 1644, Tasman mapped out parts of the western coastline of Australia. Even though the west coastline looked uninviting, the Dutch knew that in such a sizeable land there might be better places for settlement. However, the Dutch lacked the manpower and the money to explore and colonize. To avoid drawing attention to the area, the Dutch East India Company suppressed many of Tasman's findings. They claimed the land they found and named it **New Holland**. Tasman retired in 1652, having failed to locate the mythical unknown southern land. However, he had discovered three new and important islands: Australia, Tasmania, and New Zealand.

Abel Tasman National Park, New Zealand

Section Review

1. How did Mendaña treat the island peoples during his visit to the Solomon Islands?

2–4. What three islands did the Dutch discover?

★ How did Doña Isabel and her brothers avoid suffering from starvation like the others on the Spanish ship?

★ Why was Quirós forced to sail to the Philippines?

■ III. European Exploration in the 1700s

During the sixteenth and seventeenth centuries, the English and French stayed busy developing territory in the American colonies. However, when circumstances changed in their colonies in the 1700s, the French and British renewed efforts to explore. Several French and British explorers sailed the Pacific during the 1700s, but only one man from each country will be examined.

Guiding Questions

1. What discoveries resulted from French exploration in the Pacific?

2. What impact did the English exploration have on the search for a southern continent?

Louis Antoine de Bougainville

French Exploration

In the midst of his training to become a lawyer, **Louis Antoine de Bougainville** (BOO gun vil) became bored with his studies and decided to pursue the challenge of a military career. He served with the French in Canada and witnessed the loss of Quebec to the British.

Hoping to regain power and respect for France, Bougainville organized an expedition to settle the Falkland Islands off the coast of Argentina. With thirteen colonists from Nova Scotia, he set sail for the Falklands in the fall of 1763. Due to English and Spanish claims to these islands, Bougainville was ordered to close his settlement. The French then sent him in search of the mythical unknown land to the south.

Two scientists accompanied Bougainville on the voyage. Philibert Commerson, a naturalist, was brought along to describe and classify the animals and plants discovered. Antoine Véron, an astronomer, sought to work out new ways to determine longitude. Their contributions to the voyage were perhaps the most significant. Bougainville's idea of taking a naturalist and an astronomer became the custom for other explorers.

On his journey across the Pacific, Bougainville revisited and claimed for France several islands, including **Tahiti**. These explorers were influenced by the concept of the "noble savage." Contrary to the Bible doctrine of original sin (all humans are born sinners), Enlightenment philosophers claimed that humans are born good and are then corrupted by civilization. They supported their claims with Bougainville's reports that the Tahitians were good and lived simple lives in harmony with nature. They ignored or were unaware of reports that the Tahitians practiced cannibalism, performed human sacrifices, and engaged in frequent tribal warfare.

English Exploration

English captain **James Cook** became the most famous explorer of the Pacific. His fame is especially amazing since he came from a working-class background and had little formal education. He rose in rank during a time when the wealthy and well-educated were usually the only men put in high-ranking positions such as captain.

Cook was one of the best sailors and explorers of his time. His mission for the British was to discover the truth about the unknown southern land and claim land for England. In three voyages he crisscrossed the Pacific. First, Cook sailed around New Zealand. Later he sailed north and nearly reached Antarctica before sailing south of the Pacific islands in search of a mythical continent. On his third voyage, he sailed north between Alaska and Russia before returning to Hawaii. Cook and his crew became the first men to sail completely around Antarctica, although they never actually saw that continent. Information gathered during his voyages proved that there was no great southern land.

During Cook's voyages, danger was often present. Once while sailing along the Great Barrier Reef off the coast of Australia, Cook's ship grounded on a reef. Cook ordered his men to lighten the ship, hoping that the tides would lift it off the reef. When the ship broke free, a large piece of coral broke off as well, plugging the hole until the ship could be repaired.

In his travels, Captain Cook discovered many islands in the Pacific, notably the Hawaiian Islands. He differed from other explor-

James Cook

ers by treating the island peoples fairly and generously. Cook often noted in his diaries good characteristics and abilities that he observed in the islanders. He treated people with respect, tried to make friends, and avoided violence whenever possible. Cook became one of the first white men to make peaceful contact with the Maoris of New Zealand.

One way that Captain Cook dealt with problems with the island peoples, however, led to his death. When islanders stole an item from the English ships or camps, Cook would capture a chief or other important person. Then he would announce that the captive would not be freed until the thief returned the stolen items. This method worked well until he tried it in Hawaii in 1779. After some Hawaiians stole tools and a canoe, Cook tried to take an old chief hostage. However, a mob of angry Hawaiians attacked Cook and his men. Cook's men escaped, but he did not. The furious Hawaiians beat Cook to death with their war clubs.

Death of James Cook

Section Review

1. Why did Bougainville establish a colony on the Falkland Islands?

2. What idea did Bougainville develop that became a custom for other explorers?

3. Who was the most famous explorer of the Pacific?

4. What was Captain Cook's mission?

5. On what chain of islands did Captain Cook die?

★ Why were tropical islands like Tahiti described as proof that man was born unspoiled? Why were these claims inaccurate and unbiblical?

■ IV. European Settlement in Australia

We may never know which European explorer was the first to see the coast of Australia. The Portuguese may have seen Cape York Peninsula when they passed through the Torres Straits in 1606. The Dutch followed Australia's coastline many times as they explored the region in search of the mythical southern land. Captain Cook

Captain Cook and Sauerkraut

Captain James Cook was one of the greatest explorers in history, and he owes a small part of his success to sauerkraut.

On long voyages, sailors often suffered from **scurvy,** a deadly disease caused by a lack of vitamin C in their diet. Captain Cook convinced his officers to eat large amounts of sauerkraut (fermented cabbage) and set an example for the crew. His men learned to eat the sauerkraut to meet their vitamin C needs, and few ever came down with scurvy.

Maori chief

Guiding Questions

1. How did the original Australians live, and what was their culture like?

2. How did English colonization in Australia affect the original Australian people?

3. How did Australia develop into a nation?

*Olympic gold medalist Cathy
Freeman from Australia*

and his men landed in Botany Bay on August 23, 1770, and then surveyed the entire eastern coastline. All these countries viewed Australia as a land ready to be claimed and developed by Europeans. However, Australia already had a population.

When Captain Cook landed in Botany Bay, he met a group of people who had no name for themselves. The Europeans called these people **Aborigines**. The word *aborigine* comes from a Latin word that means "origin" or "original."

The Original Australians
Life and Culture

The indigenous (in DIJ eh nus; original) Australians were among the most isolated groups of people in the world. They were separated not only from other countries but also from each other within Australia. The rugged coastline of the west and north created one barrier. This hostile front helped to prevent earlier European and Asian contact. Australia's rugged and dry terrain also separated groups of indigenous Australians from each other. In a continent the size of the United States, the small population of the indigenous Australians was spread far and wide.

The people of Australia followed a lifestyle similar to many hunter-gatherer tribes. The men spent time hunting and worshiping the tribal gods using a variety of rituals. The women gathered food early in the day and spent the rest of the day preparing dinner and caring for the children.

The indigenous Australians developed forms of music as part of their worship. They used pieces of eucalyptus wood that had been hollowed out by termites to make an unusual musical instrument, the **didgeridoo** (DIJ eh ree doo). While this instrument produces a single note, the person blowing through this tube can add his own vocal sounds to vary the final sound. The length of the didgeridoo determines the pitch of the sound, with longer instruments making a deeper drone.

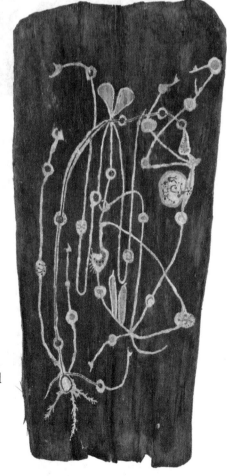

Another reflection of their religious expression is found in Aboriginal art. Indigenous Australians painted their bodies, rocks, and pieces of bark. The paintings often depicted religious stories, including the Aboriginal accounts of Creation.

Some of the indigenous Australians in western Victoria developed a game called **Marn Grook**. This game has elements of football and soccer and is played with a ball shaped like a football and made out of possum hide. Australian Rules football may have developed from this Aboriginal sport.

*Aboriginal didgeridoo player, Kings Park in
Perth, Australia* (above); *bark painting* (right)

Impact of European Immigration

Although the indigenous Australians were often involved in tribal conflict, they were very rarely hostile to the early settlers. The English settlements became well established and began to push into Aboriginal territory and hunting grounds. When the native population tried to resist, they were no match for the weaponry of the English. Gradually the Aborigines lost more and more of their land and rights.

Perhaps the most lethal things the Europeans brought with them were diseases such as smallpox. In Chapter 7 you learned that many Indians in the Americas died from European diseases. In a similar manner, the indigenous Australians had not been exposed to or developed immunity to these diseases. The outcome in Australia was tragically similar to that of the Americas. Many indigenous Australians died from diseases to which the Europeans exposed them.

England Claims New South Wales

The Dutch had claimed an area called New Holland in northern Australia, but that did not mean the Dutch could claim all of Australia. Various European countries claimed land in Australia as they had in North America. Claims were based on a first-come-first-served basis. For example, when the *Endeavour* sailed into the harbor of Botany Bay, Captain Cook claimed the land he saw for England. He called this land **New South Wales**.

When the American colonies declared their independence from England, the prison colony of Georgia was no longer available to Britain. The English decided to rid themselves of many of the occupants of the overflowing British prisons and poorhouses by relocating those people to the land Cook had claimed in Australia. The **First Fleet** left England in May of 1787 and sailed to New South Wales. Of the more than one thousand people on these ships, over eight hundred were convicts.

Replica of Captain Cook's ship

After traveling for about eight months, the fleet's captain, **Arthur Phillip** (later the colony's first governor), sighted Australia. He had sailed ahead with the intention of preparing a small settlement before the other ships arrived. However, the remaining ships arrived two days after he had sailed into Botany Bay. Phillip soon realized that this bay was too shallow and exposed to the open ocean to provide protection for the fleet. He found a more suitable port a few miles to the north (Port Jackson). This bay had a deep harbor and included many protected coves. Phillip chose to settle in a cove that became known as **Sydney Cove**. This bay had a deep, sand-fringed harbor with a freshwater stream. The Fleet arrived on January 26, 1788. This date is now celebrated as **Australia Day**.

The future of the colony depended on building homes and cultivating the land. However, there were no skilled laborers among the crew or convicts. In addition, the eucalyptus and other gum trees that were in abundant supply were very hard and quickly ruined the axes. When the settlers were finally able to cut down one of these trees, it took up to twelve men a full day to dig out the stump. In order to

Arthur Phillip

177

Eucalyptus trees

survive, the settlers resorted to building houses from cabbage trees covered with wattle and daub (sticks and mud plaster).

Another problem soon surfaced. On the long voyage Phillip had kept his crew and the convicts healthy, but much of the transported grain and flour was ruined. Without flour or grain the settlers would have no bread. In addition, many settlers began to show signs of scurvy. In desperation, they resorted to eating plants that they found around them to survive.

Phillip carefully rationed the remaining flour while the settlers waited for the supply ship that was scheduled to arrive within the first year. Unknown to the colonists in Australia and authorities in England, the supply ship struck an iceberg during the voyage and sank. The colonists had to survive for two years before they received any news from England. By that time the colony faced famine.

Governor Phillip had stationed an outpost at Botany Bay to look for ships that would arrive from England since the colonists had first planned to settle there. Finally the news came that an English ship had been sighted, and the settlers were excited when they received this report. However, their excitement soon turned to disappointment when the ship was found to be another transport ship with over two hundred convicts and few supplies. Providentially, a well-stocked supply ship soon arrived. The famine ended, and the colony became firmly established.

Expansion and Establishment

For several years the colonists remained near the coast. The **Great Dividing Range**, with its steep rock faces and giant gorges, effectively confined the colonists to living along the ocean. However, settlements continued to be established. Many convicts finished serving their prison terms and became profitable members of the colony.

Settlers soon learned how to live entirely off the land. Using crop rotation and fertilizer, more and more farmers established suc-

Great Dividing Range

cessful farms on land grants from the colonial authorities. In order for the colonists to receive this land, they had to accept convict laborers to work the farms. The greatest problem with this arrangement proved to be thievery by the convict laborers.

The crossing of the Great Dividing Range provided a great opportunity for expansion into the interior of Australia. In May 1813 **Gregory Blaxland** and two companions started out from Blaxland's farm at the foothills of the mountains. After three weeks of exploring, these men looked down from a cliff edge and saw a stream running through the center of a valley. Further exploration revealed a passage to the western plains that enabled the exploration and colonization of the outback (remote, dry region located in the center of the island).

In 1836, explorers traveled southwest from Sydney around the coast and founded a new colony called **South Australia**. In 1852, sheep farmers in search of more pasture traveled south overland and discovered a river that they named the Murray. South of this river they founded the town of Melbourne and called the colony **Victoria** after Queen Victoria of England.

Find It!

Ayers Rock
25.353°S, 131.034°E

The Outback Geography

This region contains a mixture of desert regions, plains, and mountains. Agriculture is usually limited to grazing animals in areas where rainfall supports adequate vegetation. Tourists enjoy the beautiful vistas afforded them in many parts of this area. In addition, explorers have discovered vast mineral deposits such as iron, aluminum, diamonds, and gold. As a result, mining has become a major industry in the outback.

Mount Connor (above); Ayers Rock in the Uluru-Kata Tjuta National Park (left); Karlu Karlu, Devils Marbles in outback Australia (below)

The Outback: Wildlife

day and become active during the cool of the night. Vast flocks of cockatoos and many other birds also add color and noise to the outback.

Kangaroo (left); *koalas* (below); *dingo* (right)

Despite the harsh conditions found in much of the outback, this region has an abundance of wildlife. Animals ranging from camels, kangaroos, and koalas to dingos and wild pigs rest during the

A New Nation

All the Australian colonies were under the rule of England when gold was discovered in New South Wales, and a gold rush resulted in 1851. Around that time the convict transports to the east coast stopped, and with the rush of gold-hungry immigrants, the percentage of free citizens increased dramatically. About 400,000 people lived in the Australian colonies in 1850. Within ten years the population had increased to over one million.

These new colonists wanted more freedom to govern themselves. In 1856, England responded by granting self-government to

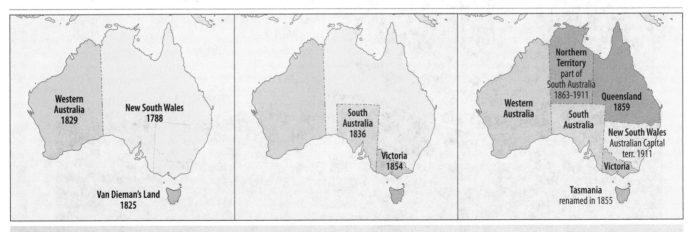

Australian History

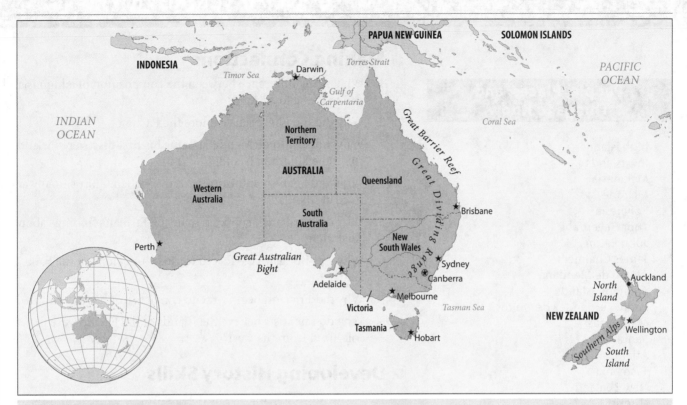

Australia and New Zealand

most of the colonies. However, England still protected the colonies and intervened in foreign affairs.

In 1901, after intense discussions, Australia became the **Commonwealth of Australia**, made up of six states—Queensland, New South Wales, Victoria, Tasmania, South Australia, and Western Australia—and two federal territories. Instead of each colony governing independently, the Commonwealth formed a single federal capital. By 1927 the government buildings in the new capital of **Canberra** were ready for use. Canberra is similar to Washington, D.C., in the United States. It is the seat of government but is not part of any state.

Section Review

1. What did Captain Cook call the indigenous peoples that he found in Australia?

2. What musical instrument is made from hollow eucalyptus trees?

3. What did the Europeans bring to Australia that proved lethal to the native population?

4. Who was the first colonial governor of New South Wales?

5. What did the colonies of Australia become in 1901?

★ Why did Australian colonists remain along the coast for several years?

CHAPTER REVIEW

■ Making Connections

1. What is the difference between the composition of a high island and that of a low island?

2. Why did the Europeans explore the Pacific?

3. Why did Alvaro de Mendaña name his first discovered island chain the Solomon Islands?

4. What did Spanish authorities discover when Quirós finally arrived at Manila Bay?

5. Why did the Dutch suppress many of Tasman's findings about Australia?

6. Why was Bougainville forced to close his colony in the Falklands?

7. Why did England begin to send convicts to Australia in 1787?

8. Why do scientists believe the islands of the Pacific were first colonized from the west?

■ Developing History Skills

1. Locate the following on the map below:

   a. Australia

   b. Easter Island

   c. Hawaiian Islands

   d. Melanesia

   e. Micronesia

   f. New Zealand

   g. Polynesia

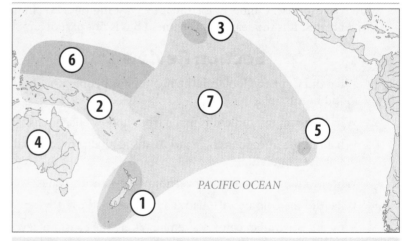

The Islands of Oceania

2. Based on the information in this chapter, write a list of the barriers the explorers found when surveying and exploring Australia. Briefly describe how they overcame these barriers.

■ Thinking Critically

1. How did the myth of the "noble savage" appear to support the claims of the Enlightenment philosophers? Is the concept of the noble savage biblical in light of Romans 1 and 3:23?

2. Why do you think the Australians wanted more freedom to govern themselves? Was this desire right or wrong?

■ Living in God's World

1. Divide into groups. Each group should plan a missionary venture to Australia or a Pacific island in the late 19th century. Research the area where you plan to work and detail how you plan to establish and maintain a ministry there.

2. Imagine that you are an islander in the Pacific or an indigenous Australian. Write an account of your encounter with explorers.

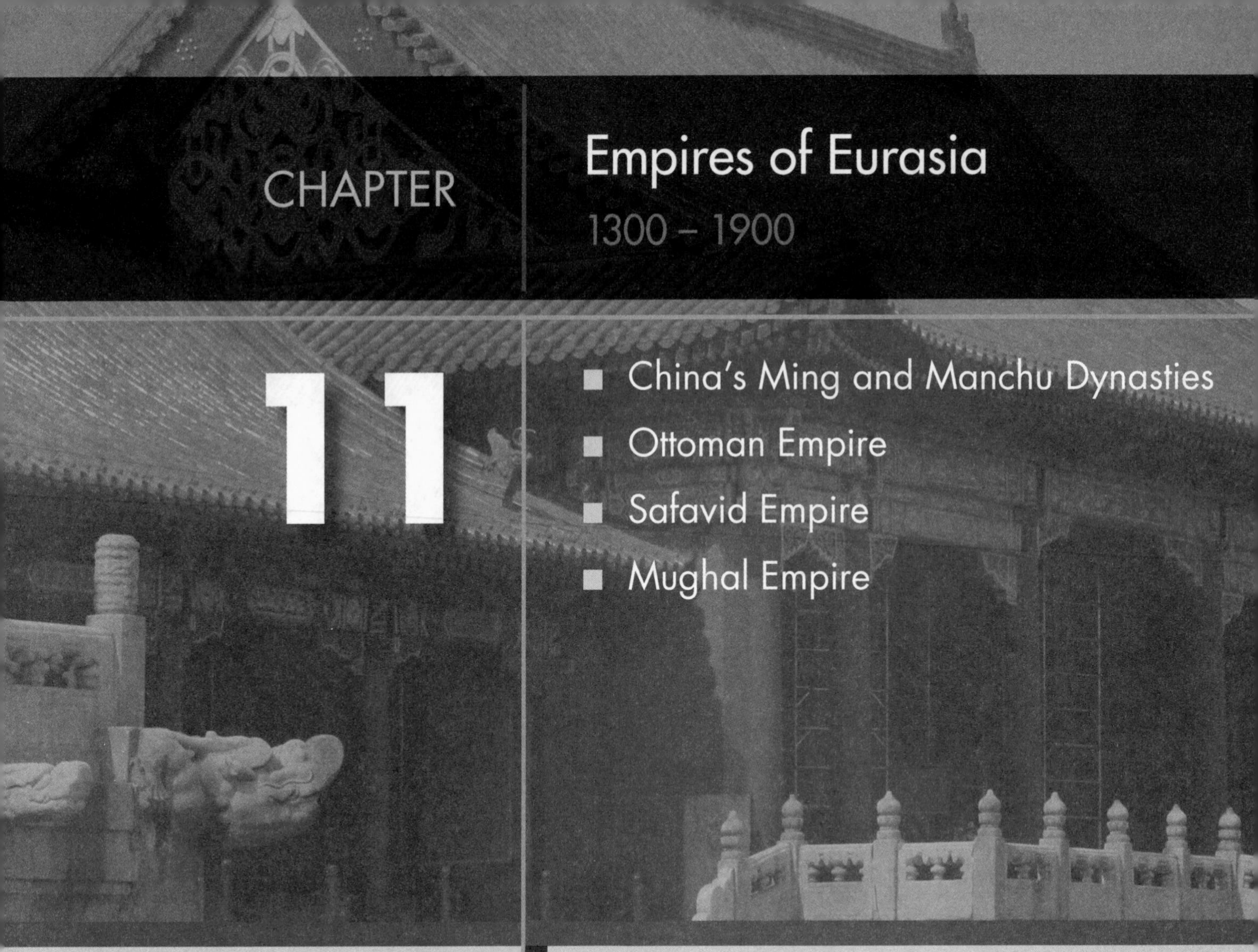

CHAPTER

Empires of Eurasia
1300 – 1900

11

- China's Ming and Manchu Dynasties
- Ottoman Empire
- Safavid Empire
- Mughal Empire

1300 – 1900

Zheng He naval fleet
of China travels to
Asian and African
countries 1406–36

Mehmed II rules the
Ottoman Empire
1451–81

■ Shah Ismail I founds the
Safavid dynasty 1501

■ Babur invades India and founds
the Mughal Empire 1526

■ China's
Grand Canal
is restored
1417

■ Akbar becomes
the ruler of the
Mughal Empire
1556

■ Emergence of the Ottomans
c.1300

1300　　　**1400**　　　**1500**

Ming dynasty rules China 1386–1644

Ottoman forces capture Constantinople 1453 ■

Abbas begins rebuilding the Safavid empire 1587 ■

Big Ideas

1. How did China develop into a regional power under the Ming and Manchu dynasties?
2. How did the Ottomans unify Southeast Europe and Southwest Asia?
3. How did the Safavid Empire form?
4. What led to the rise and expansion of the Mughal Empire?

Across eastern Europe and Asia, empires were forming and expanding while others were declining and collapsing. During the period spanning the fourteenth through the eighteenth centuries, kingdoms such as China and Persia struggled to break free from foreign oppression. The Ottomans built an empire and destroyed an ancient kingdom. India finally succumbed to Turkish-Mongol domination. Obstacles of age and circumstance were overcome to accomplish great things. For example, two of these empires were built or revived by young people about your age.

■ Europe stops Ottoman threat at Vienna 1683

■ Safavid dynasty overthrown by Afghan forces 1722

The British East India Company controls Indian trade with Britain 1803–74

| 1700 | | 1800 | 1900 |

Manchu, or Qing, dynasty rules China 1644–1911

Chapter 11

Guiding Questions

1. Was imperial absolutism exercised wisely in China's Ming and Manchu dynasties?

2. Why did China consider itself the "middle kingdom," and what was its relationship with other Asian countries?

3. Why did China exclude the outside world after the Zheng He voyages?

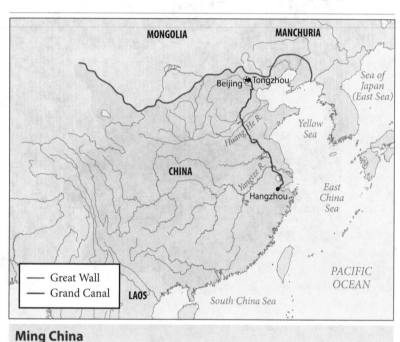

Ming China

■ I. China's Ming and Manchu Dynasties

The Chinese called their land *Chung Kuo*, the **Middle Kingdom**. For two thousand years China existed as the central nation and great power in Asia. Its borders have changed over the years, and one dynasty has overthrown another, but China has remained. Other empires that traded with the Chinese have come and gone. The Babylonians, the Persians, the Greeks, the Romans, all great at one time, have fallen, but China has carried on as a central power among the other Asian nations.

The Ming Dynasty

You learned in Chapter 4 that China was briefly ruled by a foreign power—the Mongols. Their rule was called the Yuan dynasty. After a little more than a hundred years, Chinese forces overthrew the Mongols and established a new dynasty called the **Ming dynasty** (1386–1644).

The Ming dynasty restored native Chinese rule. A renewed national pride caused the Chinese to look down on all foreigners, including European traders. The Ming rulers turned their attention to rebuilding the grandeur of China, and the people enjoyed an era of peace and prosperity under this dynasty. The Ming attempted to maintain a government based on absolutism. In addition, they concentrated on the arts, reconstruction, and exploration.

Imperial Absolutism

Taizu founded the Ming dynasty and established a pattern of absolute rule that his successors followed for the next three centuries. He was a harsh ruler and demanded that his ministers kneel before him. During previous dynasties the ministers had been allowed to sit or stand in the emperor's presence.

Taizu also labored to manage every aspect of Chinese society, including households. He used a secret police force to discover any who opposed his controls. Officials who dared to ignore or resist imperial control were subjected to public beatings that sometimes resulted in death.

Chengzu became the third emperor after defeating the second emperor, Huizong, in a civil war. He continued Taizu's harsh policies when dealing with his enemies, but he also sponsored many scholarly events. Chengzu collected a vast literary treasury that employed over two thousand scholars. He also reversed Taizu's policy of preventing naval expansion and sent out the Zheng He voyages that will be discussed in more detail later in the chapter.

Succeeding emperors began to entrust more and more authority to government officials known as grand secretaries. In the long term, delegating power led to political corruption and a weakened central government. In the short term, it freed the ruler to explore interests in arts, including porcelain, painting, poetry, and bronze work.

The Arts

Ming craftsmen perfected **porcelain** production, which helped to continue the demand for exports. During different periods of the Ming and succeeding dynasties, various colors of porcelain were developed. Blue and white porcelain was produced for the royal family alone, but imitations were soon available to sell at home and abroad. Enamel colors were added, and five-colored enamels became highly prized during the fifteenth century.

As in Europe during the Renaissance, increased wealth provided the opportunity for increased literacy and expanded literature. Bookshops sold samples of the examinations that all students had to pass in order to gain government employment. Novels and short stories also became popular. Men who did not pass the rigorous exams for government employment often developed literary careers to support themselves. Many oral stories were written down and sold in collections.

Drama developed into long and complex plays in the Ming dynasty. Language, form, and music combined to produce plays that often lasted for hours and contained more than forty scenes. Over time, plays were reduced by the combining of selected scenes from various plays to shorten the performance.

Porcelain

Porcelain is formed when objects made from materials such as kaolin clay are heated in a kiln to between 1200°C and 1400°C. The finished ceramic product is strong, hard, and translucent (light will pass through it). Artisans make a variety of porcelain products, including vases, plates, cups, tiles, and false teeth.

Artisans during the Ming dynasty perfected the art of making porcelain and exported porcelain products on a massive scale. Ming porcelain was sold literally around the world.

Most people simply refer to porcelain as china.

Ming ewer with fruit, foliage, and a dragon

Manchu vase with a court scene and three star gods

Ming Dynasty, Fishing beside a brook, *16th century*

Great Wall of China

This great line of stone and earth began as a series of isolated fortresses in the fifth century BC. Over the centuries, Chinese leaders linked and rebuilt these structures. The Ming dynasty built most of the portions of the Great Wall that survive today.

Ming Dynasty, painting on silk, 14th century

During the Ming dynasty, painting **landscapes** (nature scenes) became a popular form of expression. Some painters drew the trees and other natural scenes in a way that invited the imagination of the viewer. Poems were written about the paintings that described imaginary creatures such as dragons and giant birds in conflict.

Reconstruction

The Ming rebuilt broken portions of the Great Wall and extended it even farther. They repaired roads and bridges and built the **Imperial City** in their capital city, Peking (later called Beijing). Chengzu rebuilt Peking into a magnificent city and completed the

Forbidden City in Beijing

Grand Canal

Temple of Heaven in Beijing

restoration of the **Grand Canal**. The construction of a canal had begun about 700 BC. Over the centuries, various canals were dug and finally connected as one continuous canal. It had fallen into disrepair before Chengzu restored it to a functional canal extending more than eleven hundred miles.

Exploration—The Zheng He Voyages

During a thirty-year period in the early fifteenth century, Ming emperors sent out seven naval expeditions. Around sixty large ships and over two hundred smaller ships were sent out to represent a renewed China. The emperor desired to gain control over trade and demonstrate Chinese superiority over countries along the Indian Ocean. This fleet also reduced the ever-present threat of piracy.

Zheng He was made the admiral of this great convoy, with an army and crew that may have numbered almost thirty thousand.

Ming Tomb in Beijing

Artist's conception of one of Zheng He's huge ships alongside a ship used by Columbus

These ships sailed to many countries, including Arabia, East Africa, India, Indonesia, and Siam (Thailand). Zheng presented gifts of gold, silver, porcelain, and silk to foreign rulers.

The treasures he brought back to China included unusual animals such as ostriches, camels, and giraffes. On these voyages Zheng used diplomacy when possible and his large army when necessary in order to enhance China's reputation and bring countries into submission. On his fourth voyage, Zheng brought envoys from several nations to China. These officials came to honor the Ming court.

Over the course of these journeys, Zheng and his fleet traveled more than 30,000 miles. He extended Chinese influence beyond the Indian Ocean and may have traveled as far as Iran. Zheng died on the seventh voyage and was buried at sea.

The naval voyages ended with the death of Ming emperor Xuanzong in 1436. The restoration of the Grand Canal around 1417 had reduced the need for an ocean navy to transport and protect food supplies to the capital. In addition, a system of locks enabled the Chinese to maintain the water level needed to transport grain by way of the canal to the capital throughout the year.

One of the negative consequences of the reduced navy was the return of piracy and smuggling. Despite attempts to control these problems through regulation, the practices continued. Profits proved to be more powerful than government decrees.

Decline

While the Ming directed their attention to the south and east, foreign invaders from the north slowly gained control. The last four emperors became distracted with matters not related to governing China. One emperor even spent his life building furniture rather than attending to government. As a result, the power of the emperors diminished, and local officials ruled without fear of royal hindrance. Infighting and corruption further weakened the Ming dynasty. Seizing upon this opportunity, Manchurians from a region north of China steadily gained access to and then control of the Imperial City.

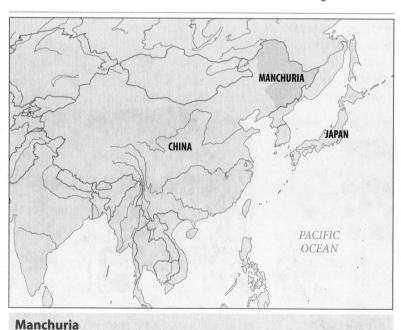

Manchuria

The Manchu Dynasty

In 1644 the **Manchu dynasty** seized power from the failing Ming dynasty. They had previously been invited into China to help the Ming government defeat a group of rebels. Once invited into the country, however, the Manchus steadily took power from the weak Ming rulers. The Manchus established the second foreign dynasty to rule in Chinese history. The Manchu (Qing) dynasty ruled from 1644 to 1911, when dynasty rule ended in China.

Inclusive Rule

The Manchu rulers worked hard to build a good relationship with the people of their newly conquered empire. They knew that to retain power and succeed in governing, they needed the support of the people. The Manchus tried to become Chinese rather than make the Chinese become Manchurian. The Manchus allowed the Chinese to have a part in the government. At the higher levels of government, a Chinese and a Manchu often shared the same office. At the local level, almost all government officials were Chinese.

Imperial Absolutism

The Manchu government differed little from the early Ming government. The emperor still held supreme power and could order any policy to be enforced throughout the empire. Scholars continued to receive positions in government by receiving a high score on civil service exams. Many Chinese scholars held important positions at the imperial court in Peking. In addition, each level of government was responsible to the next higher level so that local governors had little control over their own affairs. This process enabled the Manchus to successfully govern their Chinese subjects for nearly two centuries without major discontent.

The Middle Kingdom

Throughout much of their history, the Chinese have had an attitude of superiority toward all other countries. They called themselves the Central Nation or the Middle Kingdom because they considered themselves to be the center of the world. In many ways China truly was much more advanced than other countries. For example, during the Middle Ages in Europe, China had a period of great achievement. You learned in Chapter 4 that the Chinese invented many technologies, including printing, papermaking, gunpowder, and chemical processing. Before Europe entered the modern age, China was the most technologically advanced region in the world.

The Manchus continued to promote this attitude of superiority. They especially tried to keep China from having any contact with the West through trade. China closed all but one or two ports to Western trade during the eighteenth century.

However, this policy created problems for China. It not only kept the West from receiving quantities of desirable Chinese goods but also prevented the Chinese from receiving the new inventions and learning of the West. While the Western world moved rapidly into the modern age, the Chinese refused to change their traditional culture. Their pride in their culture blinded them to the valuable achievements of other cultures. Isolation caused the Chinese to fall behind in many areas, including technology and the military.

Power

The task of subduing the earth is too great for one person to achieve. This is why God commanded Adam and Eve to be fruitful and to multiply. While individuals and cultures have been blessed by God with greater abilities in certain areas than others, God intended for humans to work together to wisely rule over the earth. But when a person or a culture becomes proud of accomplishments and does not choose to help others or learn from others, people suffer.

Section Quiz

1. What did the Ming dynasty restore to China?

2. Who founded the Ming dynasty?

3. What clay product did Chinese craftsmen perfect?

4. Who commanded the Chinese fleet during the fifteenth century?

✯ Why was the Ming dynasty vulnerable to conquest?

✯ Why was the Chinese concept of the Middle Kingdom contrary to a biblical worldview? Reference Bible verses such as Genesis 1:26–27; Acts 17:26; Daniel 4:17, 30–35; and 1 Cor. 4:7 and explain your answer.

Guiding Questions

1. How did the destruction of the Byzantine Empire contribute to the expansion of the Ottoman Empire?

2. What were the poltical, institutional, and economic developments of the Ottoman Empire?

3. How did Muslim, Orthodox, and Jewish populations coexist under Ottoman rule?

■ II. The Ottoman Empire

The **Ottoman Empire** emerged during the beginning of the fourteenth century in the land east of the Byzantine Empire called **Anatolia**. Its beginnings were small, and most of its population was Turkish and practiced Islam. The Ottomans gained and lost territory over the next century as they wrestled with Byzantine forces for control of the Anatolian Peninsula and endured civil wars. When the Ottoman Empire emerged from internal strife under **Mehmet II** (r. 1451–81), the goal became the conquest of Constantinople.

Destruction of the Byzantine Empire

The Byzantine Empire had survived many wars and assaults over its thousand-year history. However, by the fifteenth century, its age was showing. The days of this empire were numbered.

Decline

As is often the case with empires throughout history, weak leadership and internal strife had undermined the strength of the once-mighty Byzantine empire. European crusaders had attacked Constantinople in 1204 and had severely weakened it with a wound from which it would not recover. Byzantine emperors regained power but concentrated on building defenses west of the city rather than rebuilding aging defenses in the eastern provinces. The Ottomans steadily moved west and captured one Byzantine city after another. Final defeat of the remaining Byzantine forces was imminent.

Defeat

The Ottomans, led by Mehmet II, prepared for the attack by occupying a fort on one side of the Bosporus Strait and building a second fort on the other side of the strait. Using these forts, the

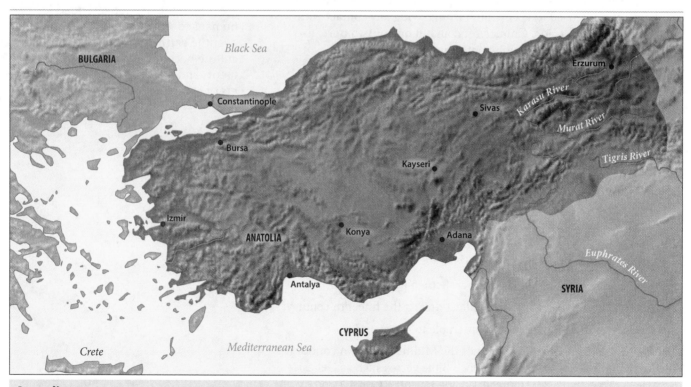

Anatolia

Ottomans sought to prevent ships from coming to defend Constantinople. The greatly-outnumbered Byzantine forces repelled many assaults on the ground and prevented siege towers from sending Ottoman forces over the walls. Byzantine defenses also prevented the Ottoman ships from getting close to the city. However, the massive Byzantine walls could not withstand the continual assault of Ottoman cannons. On May 29, **1453**, Ottoman forces breached a section of the wall and poured into the city. They killed the defenders and pillaged (looted) the city for three days.

Constantinople was rebuilt, and the name was changed to **Istanbul**. This city became the permanent capital of the Ottoman Empire.

Fortress built by Mehmet II between 1451 and 1452, before he conquered Constantinople

Ottoman Military Successes

After the defeat of Constantinople, the Ottomans consolidated territory in eastern Europe and swept south into northern Africa and east across Asia Minor. The Ottoman navy turned the Mediterranean Sea and the Black Sea into Muslim-controlled waters.

The Ottoman army became one of the most advanced fighting forces in the world. They were among the first to use small cannons, called falconets, and muskets on the battlefield. The Ottoman cavalry also developed techniques similar to those used by the Mongols. They used bows and short swords and advanced on fast Arabian horses to attack their enemies. When necessary, the Ottomans also pretended to retreat. Then they surrounded their opponents in a crescent shaped formation and killed the enemy forces when they left the safety of the city walls.

The European nations struggled against repeated Ottoman attacks for the next two centuries. The Ottoman threat finally ended when the European forces were providentially enabled to repel the Ottoman attack on Vienna in 1683. Once again, Europe was delivered from a Muslim invasion. After this defeat, Europe continued to improve militarily while the Ottoman Empire slipped further and further behind.

Ottoman Development

The Ottomans built a strong, powerful, and wealthy empire that endured for six centuries. Rather than a complicated system of government and heavy taxing of wealth, the Ottoman Empire developed a simple system of rule. They also controlled income flow by limiting taxation of the wealth generated by the working class.

Political Organization

The Ottomans developed a two-dimensional form of government: military and civil. The sultan held the highest position and served as both civil and religious leader of this Islamic empire. However, he delegated his authority to advisors and ministers who governed the various areas of the empire. During the period when the

Mehmet II entering Constantinople in 1453

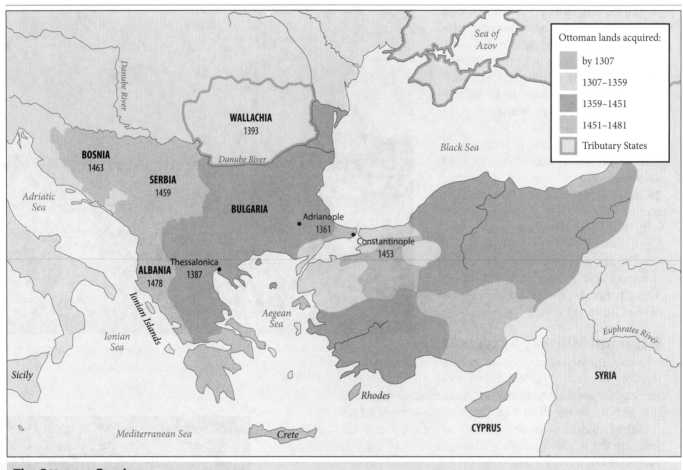

The Ottoman Empire

Map legend:

Ottoman lands acquired:
- by 1307
- 1307–1359
- 1359–1451
- 1451–1481
- Tributary States

Map labels: WALLACHIA 1393, BOSNIA 1463, SERBIA 1459, BULGARIA, ALBANIA 1478, Thessalonica 1387, Adrianople 1361, Constantinople 1453, SYRIA, CYPRUS, Rhodes, Crete, Sicily, Danube River, Adriatic Sea, Ionian Islands, Ionian Sea, Aegean Sea, Mediterranean Sea, Black Sea, Sea of Azov, Euphrates River

Providence

Some Christians might wonder why God would allow Muslims to conquer a leading Christian city and allow a Christian empire to be destroyed.

When God's purposes are not specifically revealed in Scripture, they can be difficult to discern. The Bible says that God disciplines the disobedient (Ps. 39:11; 94:12). Given the departure of the Byzantine church from biblical teaching, the fall of the empire could have been discipline for disobedience. The Bible also teaches that Christians should expect to encounter opposition and even persecution (Mk. 10:30; 2 Cor. 12:10; 2 Tim 3:12). So the temporary triumph of false religions should not surprise Christians.

Ottoman Empire was quickly expanding, loyal and skilled subjects from many nationalities were appointed to administer the affairs of the empire. Albanians, Hungarians, Greeks, Jews, and others were recruited to help manage this vast empire. This preference for qualified and talented officials strengthened the government and resulted in a stable empire during the early years of its development.

Economic Strategies

The leaders of the Ottoman Empire concentrated economic development in key cities like Adrianople and Istanbul. These cities were transformed into important commercial and industrial centers. The Ottomans viewed the merchants and artisans (skilled craftsmen) as essential to the economic success of the empire. These productive classes of society were enabled and encouraged to prosper. As a result, state revenues increased through a controlled taxation that did not hinder the prosperity of those who created the wealth.

In addition, the Ottomans welcomed Jews who fled other parts of Europe due to persecution. The Jews brought skill and diligent labor in fields such as medicine, trade, and banking to the Ottoman Empire. Their economic success contributed to Ottoman economic success.

Key military conquests had placed the Ottoman Empire between the West and the East. Thus spices, silk, porcelain, and other Eastern treasures had to pass through Ottoman lands. Ottoman merchants made an immense profit by buying these goods and then selling them to the West at a much higher cost. However, this strategy of wealth had negative consequences for the Ottoman Empire. You learned in Chapter 7 that European nations responded by seeking water routes to India and China in order to bypass the Ottomans. The success of European nations at finding alternate routes to the East resulted in a significant economic decline in the Ottoman Empire.

Diversity

The Ottoman Empire grew into a vast and varied state which ruled over many conquered states. Within this empire a variety of religions, cultures, languages, and nationalities existed. The Ottomans used this diversity to their advantage.

Religious Mixture

Muslims, Christians, and Jews were all allowed to worship in the Ottoman Empire. Only those who practiced polytheism were not tolerated. Since the Ottoman Empire was Islamic (Sunni), Christians and Jews were required to pay the government an annual tax. In exchange for paying this tax, Orthodox and Armenian Christians and the Jews were allowed limited and monitored opportunities to worship. For example, Christians were forbidden to share the gospel with Muslims. Consistent with the teaching of Islam, conversion by a Muslim to Christianity was not allowed. In addition, no Orthodox or Armenian church building could be larger than the local mosque. As a result, many large cathedrals were destroyed or converted into mosques. The Muslim authorities even regulated the size and ringing of the bells in Orthodox churches. Christianity was permitted, but Christians were not allowed to practice Christianity in the way God commanded. Religious persecution of Christians and Jews did occur from time to time. As the Ottoman Empire began to disintegrate in the 1800s, persecution increased and intensified.

Cultural Variety

The Ottoman Empire began as a Turkish-dominated state. However, as the empire expanded through conquest, it gained control of territory on three continents. As a result, the Ottoman Empire became a collection of many cultures and languages. The Ottomans made provision for this variety and turned it into a means of strengthening the empire. Careful treatment of the various cultures and minorities enabled the Ottoman Empire to remain strong for several centuries.

Hagia Sophia and the Bosporus strait in Istanbul

Christian Activities in a Muslim Land	
List the activities that are restricted or forbidden and those that are mandated in Scripture.	
Restricted or Forbidden	**Mandated in Scripture**

Section Quiz

1. Who led the Ottoman forces in the assault on Constantinople?

2. What weapon did the Ottomans use to break through the Byzantine defenses?

3. What did the Ottomans rename Constantinople?

4. What type of religion was not tolerated in the Ottoman Empire?

✶ Why is it not accurate to call the Ottoman Empire "Turkish"?

✶ What economic strategy did the Ottomans use to strengthen their empire?

Guiding Questions

1. How did Persia unify under the Safa-vids and Ismail I?

2. What Safavid political and cultural achievements occurred under Shah Abbas?

■ III. The Safavid Empire

In the region that lay between the Ottoman Empire and India, the Persians reemerged in a new state. Remarkably, this empire grew out of a boy's desire to avenge the murder of some of his family.

Ismail and his family belonged to the Safavid clan. A rival clan killed his father and older brother, making Ismail the head of his family at the age of seven. To survive, he went into hiding until he was twelve. Then he began his military career by leading forces to take revenge on those who murdered his father. Ismail's embrace of Shia Islam contributed to his rise in political prominence.

Once he had exacted his vengeance, Ismail's fame quickly spread, and he gathered supporters, including Shiites from various regions. Ismail continued to seize territory and began to build a state. With the conquest of the city of Tabriz in 1501, his empire was established. He became **Shah Ismail I** and founded the **Safavid dynasty** (1501–1722). He built this fledgling state into a growing economic and political power. Ismail formed a strong centralized government and brought stability to this region. He also attempted to develop diplomatic relationships with neighboring states. Working with nearby countries was essential because of this region's location along the trade route between the East and the West.

Whereas the Ottoman Empire was primarily Sunni Muslim, the Safavid Empire became Shia Muslim under Ismail's influence. The Safavids often struggled with the Ottomans, Uzbeks (to the north), and even Portuguese forces for control of disputed territories and to determine which group would dominate this region. Ismail had developed a reputation for being invincible. However, this reputation was shattered in 1514 when the Safavid forces were defeated by

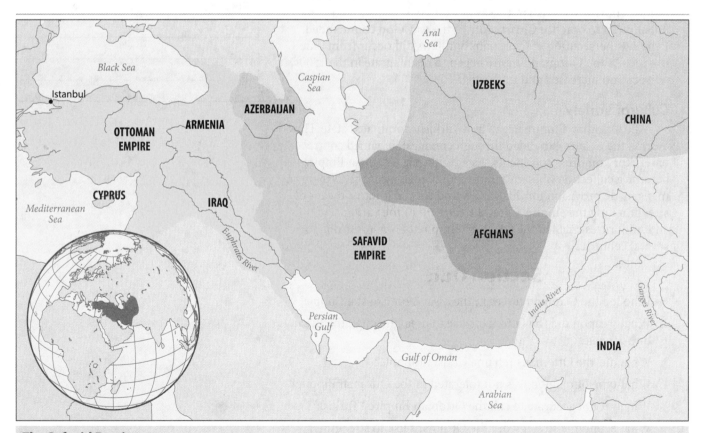

The Safavid Empire

Jame Abbasi mosque, an example of Safavid architecture in Iran

a much larger Ottoman force. Ismail withdrew from an active role in governing the empire, and it became vulnerable to internal struggles and attack from neighboring states.

During a time of weakness in 1587, a rival family leader replaced the Safavid ruler with his sixteen-year-old son **Abbas**. Abbas proved to be a strong leader and rebuilt centralized authority for the Safavid Empire. Abbas is regarded as the second founder of this empire. He reorganized the army and conquered land that had been taken from the Safavids by the Ottomans and others. Abbas regained control of Baghdad and allied with the British to capture the Strait of Hormuz to enhance trade. Abbas also became a great builder of religious architecture, royal palaces, and public buildings. Under his leadership, a new style of architecture developed.

As with most empires, the Safavid Empire declined due to a lack of qualified successors. Neighboring states, including the Ottomans, invaded and took away territory. Internal strife led to revolts. In 1722 this empire was overthrown by Afghan forces. However, the foundation of the modern state of Iran had been laid.

Section Quiz

1. Where was the Safavid Empire located?

2. Who founded this empire?

3. Who became ruler as a youth in 1587 and proved to be a strong leader?

4. What modern country was founded on the Safavid Empire?

✶ Why did the Safavid Empire adopt Shia Islam as its official version of Islam?

Guiding Questions

1. How did the Mughal dynasty develop in central and southern India?

2. What type of relationship existed between Muslims and Hindus during Akbar's rule?

3. What led to the decline of the Mughal Empire?

The Taj Mahal, an example of Mughal architecture

British East India Company

The East India Company was an early English joint-stock company that was formed to develop trade with the East Indies. The company soon turned its attention to India and China. At first, the company engaged in trading cotton, silk, tea, and other products. Later, with the assistance of British forces, it gained enough power to rule large areas of India and abandoned commercial activity. Company officials proved to be poor governors, and the Indians resisted British efforts to force Western ideas on the Indian people. Following Indian rebellions, the British government took over direct control of India in 1857, and the East India Company was later dissolved in 1874.

■ IV. The Mughal Empire

The Mongols had attempted to conquer India for centuries. Despite many attempts and the terrible slaughter of Indians by Tamerlane (Chapter 4), the Mongols had only been able to retain control of northern India. During the sixteenth century, a descendant of the Mongols and Turks finally gained control of most of India.

Conquest

The Muslim leader **Babur**, "the Tiger," became the leader of the Turkish-Mongol tribes of modern Afghanistan. In 1526 he invaded northern India with an army of twelve thousand men and overthrew the Muslim government. Babur was a descendant of two great Asian conquerors, Chinggis Khan (Mongol) and Tamerlane (Turk). He established the **Mughal** dynasty (from *Mongol*) and conquered a large region in northern India.

Following the brutal example of his predecessors, Babur directed his forces to practice Muslim jihad by slaughtering their way into control of northern India. When they had destroyed all opposition, the Mughal rulers rebuilt India according to Islamic law and acquired great wealth. Over time, the Mughal culture experienced a renewal of the arts, including a distinct type of architecture.

The most effective Mughal ruler came to power at the age of thirteen following the death of his father. **Akbar** (r. 1556–1605), the grandson of Babur, continued the brutal conquest of India begun by his grandfather. Under Akbar's military leadership, the Mughal Empire expanded to the west, east, and south to central India.

Reform

Having conquered central India through military conquest by means of the Muslim practice of jihad against non-Muslims, Akbar gradually began to institute reforms in Indian society. He is said to have abolished the tax on non-Muslims and to have begun including Hindus in government, although he continued to endorse periodic slaughter of non-Muslims as commanded in the Qur'an.

Decline

The last effective Mughal ruler, Aurangzeb, consumed most of the Mughal Empire's resources in conquering lower India. His death in 1707 ended the expansion of the empire and was followed by rapid decline. Successive rulers had little power and were dominated by rising warlords. Persian and Afghan forces frequently invaded and carried off treasures from Indian cities, including Delhi.

In 1803 the nominal Mughal ruler Shah Alam II agreed to the offer of protection from the **British East India Company**. The British maintained the appearance of working under the Mughal rulers until 1857, when they exiled the last Mughal emperor and imposed direct rule.

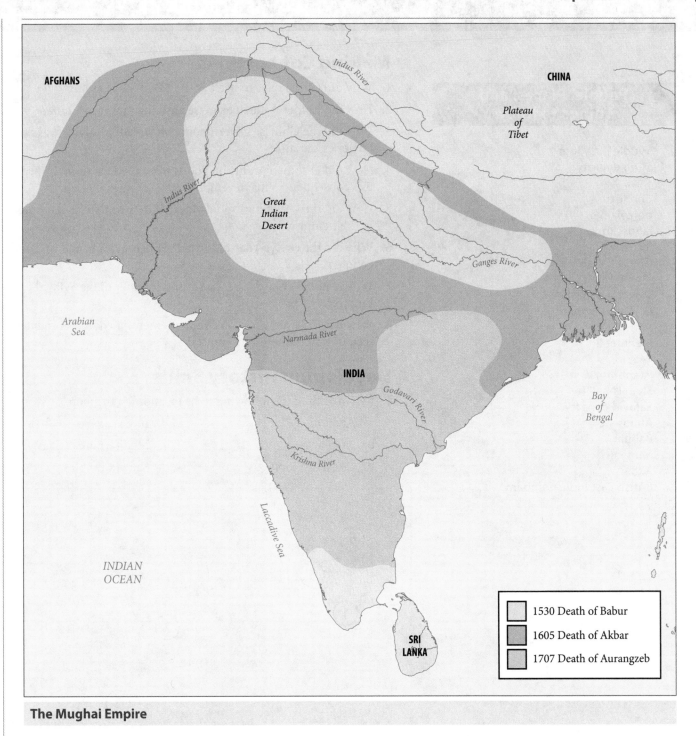

AFGHANS

CHINA

Indus River

Plateau of Tibet

Indus River

Great Indian Desert

Ganges River

Arabian Sea

Narmada River

INDIA

Godavari River

Bay of Bengal

Krishna River

Laccadive Sea

INDIAN OCEAN

SRI LANKA

	1530 Death of Babur
	1605 Death of Akbar
	1707 Death of Aurangzeb

The Mughai Empire

Section Quiz

1. When were the Mongols finally able to gain control of most of India?

2. Who founded the Mughal Empire?

3. How did Akbar treat Hindus?

4. What nation gained control of India in 1803?

★ Who was the most effective Mughal ruler? Why?

CHAPTER REVIEW

■ Making Connections

1. Why did China refer to itself as the Middle Kingdom?

2. How did Emperor Taizu exercise absolute power in China?

3. Why did the Chinese government conclude that a navy was no longer essential?

4. How did Ottoman profits on goods from the East result in negative consequences for the empire?

5. How did the Ottomans initially deal with the mixture of religions in their empire?

6. Why did the twelve-year-old Ismail gather an army and begin to conquer?

7. Why is Abbas regarded as the second founder of the Safavid Empire?

8. Why did the two European countries mentioned in this chapter seek to gain influence in Eurasia?

■ Developing History Skills

1. Match each of the following to its location on the map.

   a. Anatolia
   b. Arabian Sea
   c. Constantinople
   d. India
   e. Mediterranean Sea
   f. Safavid Empire

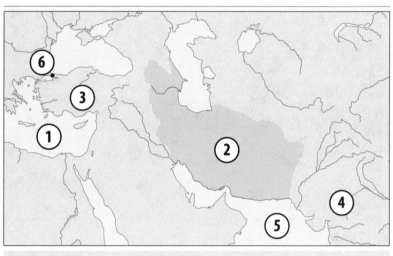

Asia

2. Why were the Manchurians able to seize control of China? What history lessons can you draw from this?

■ Thinking Critically

1. In what way did God construct the church so that local assemblies could weather the kind of religious restrictions placed on it by the Ottoman Empire? Consider Matthew 28:18-20 and Acts 2:42 as giving the mission of the church.

2. What were the long-term consequences of China's exclusion of foreigners during this period?

■ Living in God's World

1. Imagine that you are a Christian historian analyzing the Ming and Manchurian periods of Chinese history. Write a paragraph analyzing China's dislike of foreigners in light of the Christian command to love one's neighbor. Be sure to draw on your answer to the previous question.

2. Imagine that you are a Christian leader in the Ottoman Empire. Write a brief speech to be delivered before the emperor in defense of the Christian duty to evangelize. Address the issue of tolerance. Refer to Acts 4:19.

UNIT

The Revolutionary Age
1750 – 1900

4

Following the lead of Britain, European states began to turn the many raw materials from the colonies into finished goods and transformed much of the world during the Industrial Revolution.

Soon the demand for raw materials and the greed of men led to the conquest of regions, including Africa and Asia, in order for Europeans to take full advantage of resources. Rivalries developed as nations competed for control of these resource-rich regions.

CHAPTER 12

Political Turmoil in Europe

1776 – 1850

- French Revolution
- Rise and Fall of Napoleon
- Revolts Across Europe
- German and Italian Unification

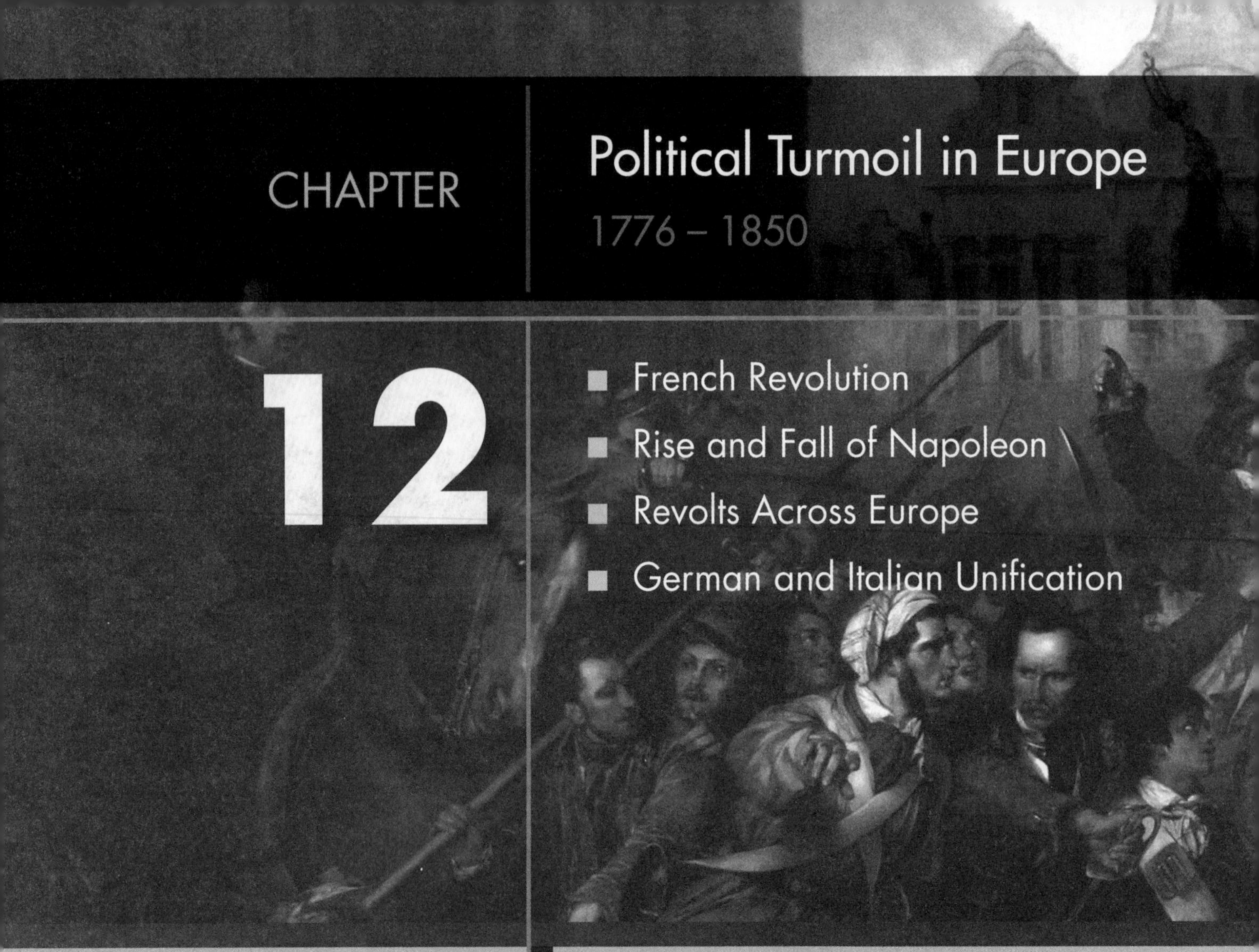

1650 – 1900

Louis XIV ends religious toleration of Huguenots 1685

Seven Years' War 1754–63

1650 | 1700 | 1750

Big Ideas

1. **What events led to the French Revolution?**
2. **How did Napoleon come to power, and what led to his fall?**
3. **What circumstances led to revolts across Europe in the nineteenth century?**
4. **How did German unification differ from Italian unification?**

Nineteenth-century Europe struggled with the consequences of decisions made by previous generations regarding the Reformation. In addition, the desire for nationalism intensified. Core ideals such as liberty, equality, justice, and citizenship transformed from Enlightenment writings into political movements. Some territories combined to form nations, while others won independence from outside control. Still others tried and failed to gain their independence. This period was a time of great turmoil in Europe.

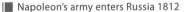

Napoleon's army enters Russia 1812

Napoleon defeated at Waterloo June 18, 1815

Poland ceases to be a country 1831

Greece wins independence from Ottoman rule 1832

Louis XVI convenes the Estates General May 5, 1789

Mazzini forms an Italian unification group called Young Italy 1832

Parisian mob storms the Bastille July 14, 1789

Bismarck becomes chancellor of Prussia 1862

Belgium becomes independent from the Netherlands 1835

The Declaration of the Rights of Man is signed August 26, 1789

Germany is united 1871

1800

1850

1900

Napoleon ends the Directory and starts the Three Councils 1799

Hungary unsuccessfully rebels against Austrian rule 1848

Guiding Questions

1. How did political incompetence, social problems, and economic troubles prepare France for revolution?
2. How did the French Revolution lead to the rise of Napoleon?
3. How did the Revolution affect French society?
4. How was the French Revolution different from the American Revolution?

Voltaire

Population of France

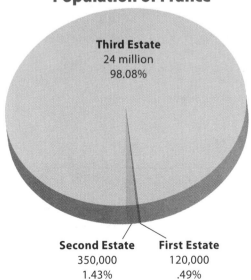

Third Estate
24 million
98.08%

Second Estate
350,000
1.43%

First Estate
120,000
.49%

I. French Revolution

French writers such as François-Marie Arouet (better known as **Voltaire**) wrote volumes of literature to describe and endorse Enlightenment ideals. Voltaire produced over twenty thousand letters, up to two thousand books, and many pamphlets. This flood of literature from Voltaire and other Enlightenment philosophers inspired the French to demand equality, civil liberties, and religious freedom. But these freedoms were only a dream for most of the French people in the eighteenth century.

You learned in Chapter 6 that France had rejected the Reformation in favor of Roman Catholicism. The Church of Rome taught its followers to submit to papal authority. This submission supported the concept of an absolute monarchy. Yet many people in France embraced the Reformation. These French Protestants became known as Huguenots (HYOO guh NAHTS). The limited toleration of Huguenots ended under Louis XIV in 1685. By royal decree they were required to convert to Catholicism. Many chose instead to flee the country. Their departure removed pressure to retain checks and balances on the king's power.

In addition, the French had retained a corrupt social structure that gave the king absolute power and the elite members of French society immunity from most taxes. As a result, the nation placed a terrible financial burden on the middle and lower classes. Continued mismanagement of the government, refusal to modify the existing system, and the spread of Enlightenment ideals provided an opportunity for violent social turmoil.

Reasons for Revolution

Social Discrimination

On the French social ladder, the leaders of the French church occupied the highest position. The upper tier of the **First Estate** (1.2 percent), the archbishops and bishops, numbered about ten thousand. They managed land for the Roman Church that amounted to about 10 percent of the country, and they also owned valuable properties in the cities. Under French law, these wealthy churchmen and their properties were exempt from most taxes. Their luxurious lifestyle differed drastically from that of the poor priest or monk (98.8 percent of the First Estate) who interacted with the French population. These common clergymen struggled to exist and supported the revolution when it finally swept across France.

The **Second Estate** was composed of about three hundred fifty thousand nobles and other aristocrats who owned or controlled about 20 percent of the land. They too were exempt from many taxes. Members of this class gained their wealth by charging rent to the peasants who farmed their land and charging fees for the use of their mills, wine presses, and bakeries. Given their enviable financial and social standing, they opposed any changes to the status quo.

The great majority of French men and women were confined to the **Third Estate**. This group of at least twenty-four million people contained a wide variety of citizens, including the middle class, artisans, townsmen, and peasants. The middle class accounted for about 10 percent of the Third Estate and owned between 15 and 20 percent of the land. The remaining 90 percent were peasants, and they owned or rented up to 50 percent of the land.

In the French society, those who were wealthy produced little or no wealth and were protected from most of the tax burden. Ironically, many of those who produced the nation's wealth were not allowed to benefit from their earned prosperity. Under this imbalanced system, the government oppressively taxed and the nobility charged rents and other fees to groups such as merchants, farmers, and artisans. This system reduced many to poverty, and it limited opportunities for economic growth. At the same time, those who paid the most in taxes, rents, and fees were denied basic freedoms and political representation in the governing of France. Such injustice would not be sustained indefinitely.

Economic Collapse

French kings had spent the nation's wealth lavishly since the reign of Louis XIV. The cost of frequent wars and the building and maintenance of the Palace of Versailles had drained France of much wealth. Louis XV continued to drain French resources during the Seven Years' War (1754–63) with England. French support of the American War for Independence also placed French finances under a great strain. During the reign of Louis XVI, the French government borrowed its way into near bankruptcy. Payments on the national debt consumed nearly half of the annual income from taxes and other fees. By 1787 the French government faced a major economic crisis. After much delay and hesitancy, Louis XVI convened the **Estates-General** in 1789. This was the only political body with the authority to reform the tax system. The Estates-General had not been convened since 1614 due to the rise of absolute monarchs and the ability of French kings to bypass the assembly. But France faced a financial crisis, and nothing less than a meeting of representatives of the three estates would suffice. Once this meeting occurred, events quickly spiraled out of control.

Political Incompetence

The political and financial collapse in France occurred during the reign of **Louis XVI** and **Marie Antoinette**. It is only fair to say that they inherited many of the problems from previous monarchs. But they proved to be totally unqualified to lead the nation and diffuse the mounting crisis.

In 1770 sixteen-year-old Louis married fifteen-year-old Marie Antoinette, and France celebrated this union as the hope for the future of France. Upon the death of Louis XV in 1774, Louis became king. Initially the royal couple enjoyed great popularity among the French people. But Louis quickly demonstrated that he was weak and incapable of making difficult choices. Marie-Antoinette convinced Louis to dismiss his father's ministers. The tax reforms

The Estates-General

As the French royal power extended across the territories of France, the king recognized the need for an assembly to represent the people and provide counsel. In 1302 the first assembly was held, and for the next three hundred years it met whenever called by the king. Until the sixteenth century, representatives of the First and Second Estates were selected by the king. The Third Estate was distinct in that its representatives were elected by the people.

At some point prior to and during the Hundred Years' War, this assembly held the power of the purse and retained a measure of control over the French king. After the war, however, the assembly surrendered that right and allowed the king greater freedom to tax without restriction.

Following the meeting of the Estates-General in 1614, Louis XIV and his successor avoided calling the assembly into session. The dire economic condition of France in 1789 forced Louis XVI to call this body into session. The rest is history.

Louis XVI

Marie Antoinette

Tennis Court Oath

The members of the Third Estate promised not to disband until a constitution had been approved that guaranteed basic rights to everyone in France. The assertion of human rights, due process, and representation was good and necessary. But this declaration was unhinged from a solid moral viewpoint. For instance, article four states, "Liberty consists of doing anything which does not harm others." But people with different moral viewpoints will disagree about which actions actually harm others.

The great expectations reflected in the Tennis Court Oath and the Declaration of the Rights of Man were dashed by the revolutionary manner in which they were undertaken. France rapidly declined into anarchy, and the French constitution became a meaningless document within one year.

that Louis XV had started near the end of his reign to restore financial stability ended with this unfortunate decision. Louis and Marie-Antoinette quickly moved from popular to unpopular. Before long, unpopularity gave way to hatred as the French people saw their hopes vanish under their monarch's lavish but ineffective rule.

Course of the Revolution

On May 5, 1789, Louis XVI convened the Estates-General. From the outset, Louis humiliated the representatives of the Third Estate and gave preference to the members of the First and Second Estates. Traditionally each estate had one vote. However, the representatives of the Third Estate demanded one vote for each representative. This voting method would provide a clear advantage for those representing the large majority of French citizens.

When the First and Second Estates refused to change the rules for voting, the representatives of the Third Estate left the meeting in anger. Members of the Third Estate formed the **National Assembly** of France and signed the famous Tennis Court Oath three days later.

At this point, the members of the National Assembly had no intention of transforming France into a democracy or ending the monarchy. They simply wanted a constitution that would guarantee basic rights to all French citizens and limit the government to a constitutional monarchy. Conditions changed rapidly as the French king continued to aggravate the situation.

Louis made the situation much worse when he ordered troops to assemble outside of Paris. When the citizens learned of this action, they began to panic. They responded by searching for weapons to defend themselves. On July 14 a crowd gathered at the Bastille, a fortress-prison formerly used to house political prisoners. When they encountered resistance, possibly even gunfire into the crowd, the mob stormed the building and killed those assigned to guard it. July 14 has since been celebrated as France's day of independence.

Riots and demonstrations continued and grew increasingly violent. Rioters attacked government buildings and destroyed documents that recorded debts and rents due to members of the First and Second Estates. The king remained passive and failed to

Royal tennis court where the famous oath was signed

use troops to end the violence. Louis remained king in name only from this point on.

Destruction of the Old Regime

On August 26, 1789, the National Assembly signed the **Declaration of the Rights of Man**. This document demanded the end of many of the abuses suffered by the French people and advocated ideals that included innocence until guilt is proven and liberty to do anything that does not injure another. The sovereign will of the people became the basis for law, and the false precepts of humanism became the standard for France.

The National Assembly confiscated lands owned by the Roman Church in an effort to pay off the massive national debt. This move resulted in a verbal attack from the pope and great concern among many loyal Catholics in France. Many conservatives and nobles fled France and settled in neighboring countries. They labored to overthrow the revolutionary government and regain their privileged positions. Even Louis XVI attempted to flee the country on June 20, 1791, but he and his family were captured and imprisoned.

Many of the wealthy French citizens had fled to Austria. The National Assembly demanded that Austria and other countries send these citizens back to France. Austria refused to comply with this demand. In response, the French government declared war on Austria, Marie Antoinette's homeland, in April 1792. Prussia entered the war as Austria's ally. When the Prussians warned the French not to harm the king, the revolution took a radical turn. Louis was tried and executed.

Reign of Terror

With the mounting problems of dealing with internal and international strife, the French leaders appointed committees to manage the government. The most important of these, the **Committee of Public Safety**, soon gained absolute authority in France.

To maintain control, this group of radicals called for the removal of all opponents and instituted a period of mass execution known as the **Reign of Terror**. At least twenty-five thousand men and women from all levels of society were sent to the guillotine, including Marie Antoinette. Many members of the Third Estate who had supported the revolution became victims of this violent purge.

Following the rejection of this form of government, a new government was formed that was headed by a five-man committee known as the **Directory**. This government quickly made peace with Prussia and Spain but remained at war with Austria and Britain. The

Revolutionary Ideals

While the French Revolution failed to accomplish its many lofty goals, the ideals survived for future generations. The concepts of social equality, human rights, and constitutionalism continue to have an influence on modern society. These concepts have great value. But they can be interpreted differently from various worldviews. For example, a democracy of citizens who believe in the importance of Christian virtues will be very different from a democracy of citizens that believe in the freedom to do whatever one wishes as long as it does not bring physical or financial harm to others.

Citizenship

In Genesis 1:26-28 God gave all humans the right to rule over His creation. This universal right to rule does not abolish all order of authority (even in the garden Adam had the task of leading his family). But it does mean that a political system that does not give a voice to the majority of people is out of step with the world as God created.

Effect on French Society

The French Revolution had a profound effect on French society. The Roman Church never regained its former power and wealth. Social relations were drastically altered by the secularization of marriage, and divorce became much easier. The legal and political position of women changed because women often took a leading role in the uprisings and demonstrations. While women did not achieve equality with men during the French Revolution, they did achieve a greater voice in government and society.

With the introduction of state-controlled education, children became the property of the state, and the role of parents was diminished. Although many more students received an education, they were taught to support and serve the state. This child control, along with easier divorces, had a negative impact on the family in France.

The enormous loss of life during the French Revolution had dreadful consequences for France that defy calculation. From 1798 to the end of the Battle of Waterloo in 1815, an estimated 1.4 million French soldiers died in battle. It would take France generations to recover from these losses. When one adds in the twenty-five to forty thousand people who were executed during the French Revolution, the human cost is staggering.

Minutemen facing British soldiers on the North Bridge in Concord, Massachusetts, April 19, 1775

Enlightenment

Enlightenment thought encouraged freedom, but it was not a freedom tempered by responsibility and accountability to a higher power. Enlightenment philosophers had taken God and His Word out of the equation. Therefore, the freedom that the Enlightenment proclaimed led to certain failure and, finally, to anarchy in France.

Reformation Heritage

In the early days of the Reformation, German nobles protested against attempts to use the government to halt the Reformation. Reformers developed a heritage of holding rulers accountable for the manner in which they ruled. They realized that human depravity affects the actions of leaders. To limit the tendency to abuse power, they developed checks and balances.

leaders came to rely more and more on the army for support since they lacked the support of most of the French. These circumstances created a rare opportunity for one man to seize power and rule France.

Contrast with the American Revolution

While many attempt to compare the American Revolution with the French Revolution, there are few similarities. France had rejected the Protestant Reformation and persecuted the Huguenots. In stark contrast, the American colonies had been founded and populated to a large degree by Protestants who fled persecution in Europe. Enlightenment ideas influenced both France and the American colonies. However, the French accepted these ideas without the biblical restraints recognized by many American colonists.

The French Revolution also opposed religion and established a secular state. In America, colonial religious leaders typically supported the war effort. The form of rational religion that was common among some colonial elites retained a belief in a god and taught that religion was necessary to impart virtue to the populace. In addition, the American colonies experienced a great spiritual awakening prior to the war and an extended period of revival following the war. In striking contrast, French revolutionaries exalted the goddess of Reason and elevated Enlightenment philosophy to a religion.

Causes

These differing views of religion and reason led to different goals for the French and American revolutions. The American colonists insisted on the same liberty that had been won by the British in the Glorious Revolution. They were seeking to preserve the economic, political, and religious liberties that American colonists had enjoyed for more than a century. The Americans had greater concerns about human sinfulness, and this limited their aims. French revolutionaries, by contrast, were attempting to overthrow a tradition of tyranny and social, political, and economic inequality. The French, believing that humans are perfectible, undertook a revolution that went to the roots of their society.

These different goals led to different approaches to revolution. American colonists were led by local, elected leaders. Though they were seeking to free themselves from the oppression of the British crown, the Americans were seeking to preserve their own local forms of government. By contrast the French citizens rushed to sweep away the existing government and replace it with an entirely new one of their creation.

Character and Consequences

In America, elected leaders were guided in many ways by a biblical viewpoint. They balanced liberty with responsibility. Rather than massive rejection of local authority and unrestricted violence, the American colonists limited their resistance to repelling the invaders and defending their freedom. The American Revolution did not lead to mass executions and anarchy. Rather, it led to the birthing of a nation that would be governed by laws and a constitution with a bill of rights to protect its citizens. The American Revolution tempered Enlightenment ideals with scriptural principles.

The French were led by students of the Enlightenment who sought liberty without responsibility. The French leaders were humanists who had rejected the scriptural view of man as fallen. Believing that man was perfectible, the leaders were confident that they could reshape the entire society. The cost of this unrestrained idealism was terrible in terms of loss of life. The result was anarchy and an opportunity for a dictator to seize control.

Section Quiz

1. Briefly describe the members of the three estates in France.
2. What political body had the authority to reform the tax system in France?
3. Who ruled France at the beginning of the revolution?
4. How long did the first French constitution remain in force?
5. What was the impact on France when the Committee of Public Safety came to power?
★ How did France respond to the ideas of liberty and equality?
★ Why is a biblical view of man more compatible with reforming an existing government rather than sweeping away the old to bring in an entirely new government?

■ II. Rise and Fall of Napoleon

Napoleon Bonaparte took advantage of the chaos in France and used his power to take control of the government. He had risen through the military ranks, becoming a general in 1793. Napoleon had led French forces to many victories by using unusual battle tactics that included marching his troops all night and launching surprise attacks on unprepared enemy troops. However, his ambitions extended far beyond defeating France's enemies.

Rise

In 1799 Napoleon supported the overthrow of the unpopular Directory. Three consuls led the new government. Napoleon served as one of the three, but he quickly pushed the others aside to become the **First Consul**. He then turned this position into that of dictator of France when he became emperor in 1804.

Contribution

Napoleon set about to win the support of the French people. He began by signing peace treaties between Britain and France. In addition, he initiated several public works projects, including the building of roads, bridges, and canals. To stabilize currency and enhance trade, Napoleon founded the Bank of France. He developed

Guiding Questions
1. How did Napoleon seize power and become the dictator of France?
2. What contributions did Napoleon make to France?
3. How was Napoleon initially successful in battle, and why was he defeated at Waterloo?

Napoleon Bonaparte

211

Power

In 1789 the French revolted against the abuses of an absolute monarchy. Within ten years, however, France found itself under the control of another absolute dictator. In the years in between, the French learned that handing absolute power to the people is no less dangerous than handing absolute power to a king or dictator. A government that has a democratic element while ensuring that actual rule is carried out by wise and virtuous men is the biblical ideal for government. To emphasize one element to the exclusion of the other leads to tragedy.

Duke of Wellington at Waterloo

an improved tax system and stabilized the national debt—problems that had long plagued France. Napoleon also established a system of public education and placed it under the guidance of the University of France. Finally, he set up a commission to organize the many laws that were passed during the revolution. The result was a codification of French law that became known as **Code Napoleon.**

Fall

Over the next decade, Napoleon conquered several nations in Europe and, initially, played the role of liberator. However, his seizure of each nation's wealth and placement of a relative on each throne revealed his true intentions. French abuses stirred national pride in the conquered nations, and Napoleon faced mounting resistance.

In addition, Napoleon tried to block European trade with Britain in an effort to destroy the British economy. Russia and a few other nations ignored Napoleon's economic blockade. This defiance led to war between France and Russia. Napoleon entered Russia in 1812 with about six hundred thousand troops. The outnumbered Russians withdrew and lured the French deep into Russian territory. When the French finally retreated, the Russian forces and the Russian winter destroyed the French army. Fewer than one hundred thousand French soldiers made it safely out of Russia.

Napoleon suffered another defeat in 1813 at Leipzig, Germany. An alliance of European leaders forced Napoleon to step down as ruler of France and go into exile on an island just off the western coast of Italy. However, while the European leaders met to restore order in Europe, Napoleon escaped early in 1815 and returned to France to raise another army.

On June 18, 1815, the armies of Prussia and Britain confronted Napoleon and his forces in modern Belgium at **Waterloo**. Napoleon launched a surprise attack on the Prussian forces and separated them from the British army. Following thunderstorms and a delay while the ground dried, Napoleon sent his forces directly into the British line. However, the British forces held their position, and the Prussians regrouped and trapped the French forces. Napoleon's army collapsed, and he was sent into a final exile on the island of St. Helena in the South Atlantic.

Section Quiz

1. What contribution did Napoleon make to French law?

2. What role did Napoleon play in conquering several European states?

3. What nation's trade did Napoleon attempt to block in order to destroy that nation's economy?

4. In what country was Napoleon defeated by a harsh winter?

★ Why was Napoleon able to rise to the level of First Consul?

■ III. Revolts Across Europe

Following the defeat of Napoleon, European leaders met and tried in vain to restore Europe to the state it had been in before the French Revolution. However, a growing sense of **nationalism** (intense devotion and loyalty to one's own people) could not be contained. Revolts soon broke out all over Europe.

The revolts came in three waves. The first wave hit in the 1820s. The second wave arrived in the 1830s. The third wave came in 1848. Many of these revolts failed, but some states succeeded in gaining their independence. Greece and Belgium gained their liberty, while Poland and Hungary suffered crushing defeat. Despite many setbacks, the movement toward nationalism could not be stopped.

Greece

Greece came under Ottoman control following the conquest of Constantinople in 1453. The Greeks repeatedly sought to break free from the Ottomans over the next three centuries. In 1819 the Greeks renewed their struggle. Finally, in 1829 the Greek forces received support from Russia, Britain, and France. The combined naval support of these nations destroyed the Ottoman fleet. French troops then assisted Greek forces in their struggle to drive the Ottoman forces out of Greece. In 1832 Greece gained recognition as an independent state.

Belgium

This small nation was formed out of the southern provinces of the United Kingdom of the Netherlands. Due to differences in religion and language, this region had little in common with the rest of the Dutch kingdom. The people from this region were Roman Catholic and spoke French, while most in the Netherlands were Protestant and spoke Dutch. This region also suffered from high levels of unemployment and unrest among many in the working class. These differences and the resulting discontent led to uprisings in 1830. Some Belgian leaders took advantage of this strife and supported the idea of secession (becoming independent). Despite intense fighting, efforts to settle the question of Belgian independence on the battlefield were unsuccessful. The king of the Netherlands appealed to the **Great Powers** (major European nations) for a peaceful resolution. A

Guiding Questions

1. Why did the desire for nationalism sweep across Europe?

2. Why were some European countries able to achieve independence while others were not?

Nationalism

The longing of a group of people to form a nation may be a positive desire, depending on the motivation. Some groups pursued nationalism to escape the control of an oppressive power and seek equality for citizens. For example, the Greeks desired independence from the oppressive Ottoman Empire and fought for national independence. Others sought nationhood in order to combine regions with a common language or culture. Nation states can lead to patriotism. If the values shared by people are good, then nation states often reinforce these ideals.

However, nationalism can also be an effective way to justify oppressing others. For example, the Russian government oppressed the citizens of Poland. Other examples would include Ottoman slaughter of the Armenians and German slaughter of the Jews. In addition, nationalism can provide another way for a corrupt ruler to oppress his own people. Hitler, Mussolini, Stalin, and Mao provide ready examples.

Romanticized scene of Polish forces at the Battle of Stoczek, 1831

conference of European powers met in London and recognized Belgian independence in 1831. However, the Dutch continued to resist Belgian independence until 1835.

Poland

This country endured many foreign invasions and partition attempts by neighboring countries. The Poles often rallied against the invaders and tried to expel them in a desperate attempt to regain their independence. This cycle was repeated in the nineteenth century. In 1807 Napoleon invaded a partitioned Poland and established a Polish state. While Napoleon liberated the Poles from other European powers, he also placed Poland under his rule. In 1815, following the defeat of Napoleon, Poland was again invaded. The Allied powers at the Congress of Vienna again partitioned Poland among its neighboring countries. Russia controlled the eastern portion of Poland and soon annexed this region to Russia. The Russians steadily reduced the freedoms of the Poles and installed a brutal regime. In November 1830 some Polish cadets revolted and led an armed rebellion against Russian oppression. As the resistance spread, many Polish citizens joined the uprising. Initially, the Poles succeeded on the battlefield. But Russia sent a large army and crushed the Polish forces in 1831. Poland did not regain its independence until after World War I.

Hungary

Hungary had been under the control of Austria for centuries. In 1848 the Hungarians carried out mass demonstrations and demanded rights such as freedom of the press, trial by jury, and religious liberty. Initially, the Austrian ruler had to accept these demands due to internal problems. However, a new Austrian ruler rejected Hungary's demands and sent an army to subjugate the Hungarians. Hungarian forces won the first few battles. The Austrian ruler then enlisted the support of Russia, and the combined forces overwhelmed the Hungarians. Many of the Hungarian leaders were executed, and the rest escaped into exile. Like Poland, Hungary gained its independence after World War I.

Section Quiz

1. What movement led to revolts in Europe?

2. What nations came to the aid of Greece in order to help Greece gain its independence?

3. What powerful nation controlled the eastern portion of Poland?

4. What European nation assisted Austria in subduing the Hungarian revolt?

★ How did religious differences contribute to Belgium's revolt against the Netherlands?

★ Why were Greece and Belgium able to achieve independence while Poland and Hungary were not?

■ IV. German and Italian Unification

Unification in Germany and Italy grew out of the surge of nationalism. German intellectuals attempted to revolt against the dominant powers in 1848, but other factors would eventually lead to

Guiding Questions

1. How did Germany attain unification, and what role did Bismarck play in this?

2. How did Italy attain unification, and what contributions were made by key leaders?

the formation of the German state. Italy's efforts at unification began with the growth of patriotic societies. In both of these nations, strong leaders used diplomacy and military strategy to work toward unity.

German

Initial progress toward German unification resulted from an economic union called the **Zollverein**, which was formed to enhance trade between the German states. Prior to this agreement, trade was limited between the German territories. This union reduced the cost of selling goods and greatly increased the volume of trade among the member states. Enhanced economic cooperation helped build support for political union.

In 1862, King **Wilhelm I** appointed Count **Otto von Bismarck** as the chancellor of Prussia. Bismarck became the driving force behind political unification of the German states. He used diplomacy, propaganda, and military might to unite the Germans.

War with Denmark and Austria

Bismarck's first opportunity to promote German unification came in 1864. He provoked a war with Denmark over a dispute regarding the two small territories of Schleswig and Holstein. These regions lay between Denmark and Prussia. Bismarck convinced Austria to side with Prussia against Denmark, and the Danes were easily defeated. Austria took control of Holstein, and Prussia gained control of Schleswig.

Then Bismarck convinced Russia and France to remain neutral while he tricked the Austrians into declaring war on Prussia. This war lasted only seven weeks, with Prussia emerging as the clear victor. As a result, Austria surrendered control of Holstein to Prussia. In addition, Prussia gained a dominant influence over the newly formed North German Confederation.

Otto von Bismarck

Unification of Germany 1866–71

215

Giuseppe Mazzini

Count Camillo di Cavour

With Austria and Denmark neutralized, one nation lay between Prussia and a unified German state. Bismarck planned carefully to use France as a tool to complete German unification.

Franco-Prussian War

Though Prussia had gained dominance in northern Germany, the southern German territories remained fragmented and independent of Prussian control. Bismarck believed that a war between the German states and France would convince the southern territories to align with Prussia.

The Franco-Prussian War resulted from a controversy over the next king of Spain. At first, Leopold, a man related to the Prussian ruling family (Hohenzollern), was invited to become the next Spanish king. France felt threatened by this action and protested loudly. Even though Leopold declined the offer, the French were not satisfied. The French sent an ambassador to meet with the Prussian king and demand a promise that no member of the Hohenzollern family would ever rule Spain.

The Prussian king refused to make such a promise and sent a dispatch (report) of this meeting to Bismarck. Bismarck carefully changed the wording to imply that the Prussian king and the French ambassador had insulted each other. Then he published the revised dispatch. Both nations were furious, and the French declared war on Prussia.

Bismarck's plan worked, and the southern German states sided with Prussia in the war against France. The German forces invaded France and trapped the French forces within two months. Ten days before the French surrendered, Kaiser Wilhelm I was declared ruler of the German Reich (empire) in the Palace of Versailles, near Paris. German unification had been accomplished.

Italian

For centuries the Italian peninsula had been divided into many small kingdoms and controlled by foreign powers. But the drive toward nationalism surged in Italy as it had in other countries. A movement called the **Risorgimento** ("resurgence") contributed to the movement for nationalism.

Mazzini

In 1832 an Italian named **Giuseppe Mazzini** formed a group called **Young Italy** for the purpose of accomplishing Italian unification. The struggle proved to be slow and frustrating, but men like Mazzini persisted in their efforts.

Cavour

Count **Camillo di Cavour** proved to be the most successful at uniting Italy. He was the prime minister of the Kingdom of Sardinia (see map on p. 221). Much like Bismarck in Germany, Cavour used whatever means necessary to promote Italian unification. He sent troops to support Britain and France in wars against Russia. While his support was largely symbolic, Cavour used these alliances to build support for unification. On another occasion Cavour supported Napoleon III against Austria in order to remove Austrian control of regions in Italy. Cavour's efforts were frustrated when Napoleon III abruptly made peace with Austria to prevent Cavour from gaining too much power.

Garibaldi

While Cavour unified the regions of northern Italy, a disciple of Mazzini, **Giuseppe Garibaldi**, formed an army known as the "Red Shirts" and conquered the island of Sicily in 1860. Garibaldi and his forces then moved to the Italian Peninsula and captured the city of Naples. Garibaldi planned to capture Rome and gain control of the Papal States, but Cavour traveled south and intervened. Since the French supplied forces to protect Rome, Cavour feared that Garibaldi's assault would draw the French into this conflict. Instead, Cavour convinced Garibaldi to turn his conquered territory over to **Victor Emmanuel II**, the king of Sardinia. In the spring of 1861, an Italian parliament declared the formation of the Kingdom of Italy. They named Victor Emmanuel II as the first king. By 1870 the Papal States and Rome were added to the Italian kingdom despite furious papal opposition. In 1871, Rome became the national capital.

Unification of Italy 1859–71

Giuseppi Garibaldi

Victor Emmanuel II

Section Quiz

1. Who was appointed to be the chancellor of Prussia in 1862?

2. What methods did Bismarck use to unite the German states?

3. Who formed a group of patriots that worked to bring about Italian unification?

4. Who formed an army known as the "Red Shirts" and conquered the island of Sicily?

✶ What role did the Zollverein play in German unification?

✶ What role did Count Cavour play in accomplishing Italian unification?

CHAPTER REVIEW

■ Making Connections

1. Why was the French Revolution unable to build a stable society based on Enlightenment ideals?

2. How did Louis XVI turn his initial popularity into hatred by the French people?

3. How did the National Assembly offend the Roman Catholic Church and cause great concern among loyal Catholics?

4. Why is the name "Committee of Public Safety" ironic?

5. Why was Napoleon successful at defeating one army after another for more than a decade?

6. Why did the Belgians desire independence from the United Kingdom of the Netherlands?

7. Why did Bismarck publish an altered dispatch of a discussion between the king of Prussia and the French ambassador?

■ Developing History Skills

1. Locate the following on the map:

   a. Austrian Empire   d. Rome

   b. France   e. Sardinia

   c. Papal States   f. Sicily

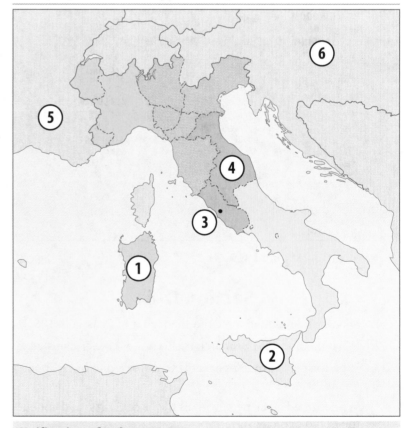

Unification of Italy 1859–71

2. Construct a timeline of events leading to Napoleon's rise to power and ultimate fall.

■ Thinking Critically

1. Beginning with information in this chapter and adding what you know about American and French history, contrast the impact of the American Revolution and the French Revolution on our world today.

2. What lessons can be learned from the social, political, and economic problems in France prior to the revolution?

■ Living in God's World

1. Pretend that you are part of the National Assembly and you have the responsibility of reading and voting on the Declaration of the Rights of Man. If you had the ability to change these rights according to a Christian worldview, how would you do so?

2. You are an editor of a German newspaper watching the events of the Franco-Prussian war unfold. Write an editorial to the German people explaining the pros and cons of nationalism.

13

- Laying the Foundation for Industry

- Expansion of Industry and the Rise of Social Reform

- End of the Slave Trade in the West

1700 – 1900

Eli Whitney invents the cotton gin 1793

Andrew Meikle develops a threshing machine 1786

Introduction of an improved cast iron plow 1763

Jethro Tull develops the seed drill 1701

Great Awakening in the American colonies 1720–60

James Hargreaves invents the spinning jenny 1764

1700

1750

John Kay invents the flying shuttle 1733

James Watt improves the steam engine 1760s

William Wilberforce wins a seat in Parliament 1780

Big Ideas

1. How did industrialization develop in England?
2. How were European societies transformed by industrialization?
3. What were the causes and consequences of the transatlantic slave trade?

A revolution can be defined as an abrupt or monumental change. The transformations described in this chapter did not occur quickly, but they were immense and often costly. Changes in agriculture and industry produced a remarkable increase in wealth. These changes, however, produced problems as well, and solving the problems proved to be a very difficult task. Often, solutions would create new problems while solving old ones.

Cyrus McCormick invents a horse-drawn reaping machine 1831

Parliament passes a bill to end slavery in the British Empire 1833

The Factory Act places limits on child labor 1833

Parliament ends the importation of slaves in the British Empire 1807

The Mines Act bars women and boys below ten from working in mines 1842

Congress ends the importation of slaves in America 1808

Ten Hour Bill restricts women and children to working a ten-hour day 1847

1850

1900

John Fowler develops a self-propelled steam tractor 1850s

Crop Rotation

Farmers learned that planting different crops in the same fields each year enriched the soil. For example, wheat would be planted one year and cotton the next. Corn would be followed by soybeans. Each crop added some nutrients to the soil and took some from it. The next crop replaced the missing nutrient and consumed another left by the previous plant. Using this method, all farmland could be used each season, and none would need to be left untilled as in the past. This greatly increased food production.

■ I. Laying the Foundation for Industry

In the beginning, Adam and Eve cared for the garden that God had entrusted to them under the Creation Mandate (Genesis 1:28). Succeeding generations continued to farm and carry on basic industry. However, methods remained largely unchanged for centuries. Most farming was done with wooden tools and human or animal power. It involved loosening the soil by pulling a crude device through the ground in order to plant seed. Crops were harvested by hand or with a sharp tool. The labor was intense, and the harvest varied from season to season.

Most industry remained primitive and required a strong back and long hours to produce items required for daily life. Shoes, clothing, tools, and other items were made by hand, and each was slightly different from the rest.

However, with the coming of modern industry and improved farming methods in the eighteenth century, life in Europe entered a period of monumental change. Life would never be quite the same, and the consequences would affect people around the world.

Agricultural Revolution

Over time, farmers developed methods that resulted in an increased food supply. The earliest examples of these improvements appeared in Great Britain. British landowners increased crop production by using four-field **crop rotation**, fertilization, and recently invented machines. A better understanding of animal breeding and care also increased quantities of milk and meat. These changes marked the beginning of modern scientific farming.

Transition to the City

Because of the increased food supply, families were able to provide for more children, who were needed to work on the farm. These changes contributed to a large growth in the British population—from six and one-half million to nine million between 1750 and 1800.

Greater demand for food also led landowners to enclose the land in order to increase productivity. Many poor farmers were unable to support their families on the small plots of land left to them. They

Early spinning wheel

Early weaving loom

were forced to seek work in the cities, leaving their lands available for wealthier landowners to claim.

As more land became available, landowners raised more sheep. The sheep's wool provided a cash crop. The landowners sold the wool to weavers who labored in the emerging textile industry in Britain. The downside was that sheep farmers needed fewer workers than other types of farms. Lack of work opportunities in agriculture led families to develop **cottage industries**, where wool was spun and merged to make cloth. Early spinning wheels and looms could fit in a home or a shop and provided income for the family.

Inventors and Their Machines

Many inventions improved the planting, cultivating, and harvesting of crops. A few of the key inventors and their inventions will be briefly examined.

Jethro Tull developed a **seed drill** in 1701 that efficiently placed seeds in rows across a plot of land. However, farmers were slow to use this tool. For nearly a century, they continued to scatter their seed by hand. When the seed drill gained popularity, it enabled a farmer to grow more crops using much less seed. This invention also paved the way for the use of other farming inventions since it produced evenly spaced rows.

Several men worked to develop an iron plow. The first plow to enjoy wide use was developed around 1730. An improved cast iron plow was produced in 1763. This plow turned the soil more easily and enabled the field to be plowed more quickly. Continued improvements to the plow's design made it possible to plow land that formerly could not be farmed due to the composition of the soil.

For centuries wheat and other grains had been harvested and separated from the husk by hand. The process was exhausting and required many laborers. **Andrew Meikle** developed a **threshing machine** in 1786. His machine enabled a few men to separate the wheat from the husks and stalks quickly.

Land Enclosure

Most English farmland was open, and many could use it for grazing their livestock. Land enclosure, however, prevented common use. The enclosed land could be tilled or otherwise used for the private benefit of the landowner.

Creation Mandate and Population Growth

In 1700 the earth could not have sustained the 7 billion people that now live on the planet. But the growth of the human population has not led to worldwide starvation. The technological developments of the Industrial Revolution—and developments that followed—enabled more people to live on earth. As people fill the earth, they subdue it, and as people subdue the earth, they make it possible for more people to fill the earth.

Seed drill

Early threshing machine

American inventors also contributed to the agricultural revolution. For example, in 1793 **Eli Whitney** invented the **cotton gin**. This device enabled one worker to process fifty pounds of cotton per day. Prior to Whitney's invention, one worker could process only one pound per day by hand. From inventions such as this, raw materials could be processed at a much faster rate. Inventors of textile machines soon had to increase the speed of processing products such as wool and cotton. They did this to keep pace with the speed at which the landowners could provide the raw materials.

Another American, **Cyrus McCormick**, invented a horse-drawn **reaping machine** in 1831 that enabled farmers to cut wheat much more quickly. Prior to his invention, many laborers were needed to cut the harvest by hand, and the process was very slow. With McCormick's reaping machine, more acres could be harvested in less time. This device, along with Meikle's threshing machine, led to increased wheat production while reducing the number of farm laborers needed.

Eli Whitney (above)
Whitney's original cotton gin (right)

Cyrus McCormick

Early reaping machine

Steam power (discussed on pp. 225–26) also assisted the agricultural revolution. During the 1850s and 1860s, an engineer named **John Fowler** developed one of the first known self-propelled steam engines. Fowler designed this **steam tractor** to plow fields and dig drainage channels. His machines lowered the cost of plowing fields.

John Fowler's Steam Tractor

Fowler's engines were far too heavy to pull a plow across fields. Instead, he would place one engine at the edge of the field and place a second engine on the opposite edge. Then, using cables, one engine would pull a two-directional plow across the field, and then the other engine would pull it back. The plow made a furrow back and forth with each pass.

John Fowler

Reducing the number of laborers needed and replacing teams of horses or oxen with steam engines lowered costs. The channels also drained water from previously unusable land, thus making more land available for planting.

Industrial Revolution

Industry also benefited from new inventions during this time period. The changes in manufacturing were so great that the eighteenth and nineteenth centuries are called the **Industrial Revolution**. As with farming, the industrial changes began in Great Britain.

Transition to the Factory

The development of larger weaving machines led industry to migrate from cottages and shops to large buildings or **factories** that were centrally located. Animals initially provided power for some of the larger machines. Where running water was available, mills and factories used water to turn large wooden wheels and power various machines. However, animals could not produce enough power, and water did not provide a constant source of power. A drought or flood could shut down a mill or factory that depended on flowing water to power its machines. Factories needed a more reliable source of power.

Inventors and Their Machines

One of the most important inventions during this period was the **steam engine**. While **James Watt** did not invent this device, he

Why Britain?

By 1815, after Napoleon's defeat, Britain was the most thriving nation in Europe. The British had cottage industries that made many goods. Their large merchant fleet transported those goods abroad.

Britain also had a stable banking system and government. A growing population combined with many natural resources, especially iron ore and coal, made Britain an ideal location for the advance of industry.

Some may conclude that this combination of factors was merely an accident of history. However, Christians can see the hand of God in arranging all of these details and making possible the Industrial Revolution in Britain. We refer to this as divine providence.

James Watt (above); *a working model of an early engine* (right)

made important improvements in the design during the 1760s that greatly increased its efficiency. Soon steam engines powered machines that had been driven by water or animals. The steam engine also provided the necessary power to pull heavy loads in the form of tractors and locomotives. In addition, steam was used to power ships and even some early automobiles. Steam engines provided consistent and reliable power for the Industrial Revolution.

Inventors developed several machines early in the eighteenth century to support the growing textile industry. Weaving cotton thread into cloth was a slow and tiring process until **John Kay** invented a small device known as the **flying shuttle** in 1733. When added to a weaving machine, this invention enabled workers to weave the strands of cotton into cloth much more rapidly. This speed created a growing demand for spools of thread to supply the

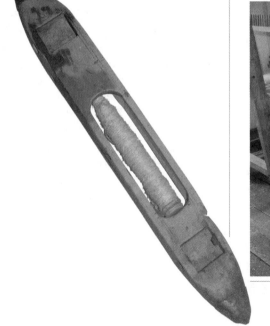

Loom with flying shuttle

weavers. To meet this demand, **James Hargreaves** invented the **spinning jenny** around 1764. This machine could quickly spin many strands of cotton into thread.

As demand increased, inventors responded by developing new machines to make cloth more quickly. Another new invention enabled a person to spin the yarn at a faster pace. In addition, production of iron and steel improved and increased to supply the metal needed for many of these inventions. Improvements in one industry often led to growth and job opportunities in many other industries.

Connections Between Industrial and Commercial Relations

Men who developed businesses and sold their inventions were known as **entrepreneurs**. *Entrepreneur* is a French word referring to one who undertakes between two different parties. These businessmen undertook to connect industry to the market. They often risked their personal wealth to develop a market for these laborsaving devices. **Richard Arkwright** became one of the most famous entrepreneurs. While Arkwright is credited with inventing many machines, he also got the government to protect several inventions with a **patent** that prevented others from making a similar device for several years. Then he raised funds to build and sell those inventions.

Men like Arkwright developed contacts with banks and wealthy persons. The bankers and wealthy investors provided the needed **capital**, or money. The entrepreneurs then bought supplies, built factories, and paid wages in order to sell the products. In return, the investors received a share of the profits made by a thriving business. However, they also shared in the losses if the business failed.

Factors that Encouraged the Rise of Industry

Several of the factors already mentioned made the rise of industry possible. A growing population provided the labor force. Abundant raw materials, including wool, iron ore, and coal, fed the growth of industry. Also essential to the rise of industry was a stable government. Patents, among other safeguards, provided inventors with legal protection that ensured an exclusive right to make a product.

As we have already noted, the Industrial Revolution began in Britain. At first, the British tried to prevent knowledge of manufacturing equipment from spreading beyond their borders. However, the British soon realized that they could not prevent this knowledge from going abroad. So they decided to make money by exporting this equipment.

Soon the British exported their inventions to other European countries and North America. British laborers traveled to these countries and helped them set up and operate the machines. British investors also helped to finance industrial growth in European countries such as France. Many nations profited from the spread of industry, and Britain played a leading role in this growth.

Reconstruction of Hargreaves's original spinning jenny

The Patent

Imagine making a new product at great cost. Then you discover that someone has copied your product and is selling it at a lower cost. This action would prevent you from making a profit on your invention.

The modern patent is a set of special rights that a government gives to an inventor for a certain period. During this time no one else can legally copy and sell the invention.

This protection gives the inventor time to recover the cost of developing the invention and to make a profit. In exchange, the inventor must give the government a complete description of the invention.

Once the patent expires, anyone can then make and sell the product without breaking the law.

Section Quiz

1. What contributed to the large growth in the British population between 1750 and 1800?

2. Why did landowners enclose their land?

3. How did Andrew Meikle's invention lead to increased wheat production?

4. What role did the steam engine play in the Industrial Revolution?

☆ Why did industry transition from cottages to factories?

☆ What does the precise combination of events and resources that made possible the Industrial Revolution in Britain suggest?

Guiding Questions

1. What is the connection between population growth, industrialization, and urbanization?

2. How did industrialization and urbanization affect class distinctions, family life, and the daily lives of people?

3. How did industrialization impact movements for political and social reform in Europe?

■ II. Expansion of Industry and the Rise of Social Reform

Although society profited from the Industrial Revolution, problems also developed. Cities were unprepared for the tremendous growth in population and the pollution that came with industry. Workers often labored under terrible conditions, and many lived in filthy and crowded housing. In time, conditions improved and government enacted reforms to protect the workers and their families.

Growth of Cities

Villages became towns and towns became cities as the British population increased and industry expanded. Fewer and fewer workers were needed on the farm, and families moved in order to find work. This migration supplied much-needed labor for the factories and other industries that abounded in the urban areas.

Towns and cities tended to grow quickly. However, adequate housing, roads, and sanitation did not keep pace with the rapid growth. As a result, multiple-story tenement buildings that housed many families were quickly built and crowded together. Traffic often congested roads. Water supplies were often impure, and smoke from coal-fired furnaces polluted the air.

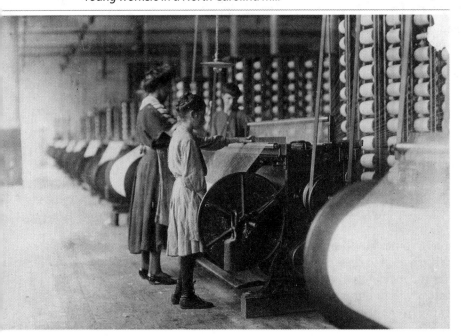
Young workers in a North Carolina mill

Effect on Society

In the short term, society struggled to meet the problems and challenges that accompanied the Industrial Revolution. Skilled craftsmen often found themselves out of work as mass-produced and cheaper goods poured out of the factories. Conditions in the factories were dangerous. Wages were low, and everyone (including women and children) had to work long hours to meet financial needs. Family members often had to work different shifts and seldom had time together. Life in crowded cities was difficult, and diseases spread quickly by human contact or impure water.

In the long term, however, the Industrial Revolution benefited many people. The size of the middle class dramatically increased, and the wages of the average worker gradually improved. In time, children no longer had to work to help support their families. Wages slowly increased to the point that the parents could provide for the financial needs of the family. The mass-produced goods from mills and factories improved the lives of rich and poor alike. Clothing, shoes, and various household items were available at prices most people could afford.

Nonetheless, these advances came at a great cost to many people. Many children were unable to receive an education, workers were severely injured or killed, and the quality of life for many was initially degradingly low. The injustices produced by the Industrial Revolution led to cries for reform.

Boys began to work in factories at an early age.

Class Distinctions

Class distinctions had existed for centuries in Britain and other European countries. The Industrial Revolution tended to break down these barriers. Families that had endured poverty for generations worked, saved, and improved their lives. Men like Cyrus McCormick and James Watt rose from humble beginnings and became very wealthy through their inventions and hard work.

Those who had recently become wealthy also tended to reject the widely accepted view that poverty and ignorance were acceptable. They built libraries and schools to make learning available to everyone. Some wealthy industrialists donated up to half of their annual earnings to improve the standard of living for others. This access to learning continued to break down the distinctions between the classes and provided opportunity for all people.

The Industrial Revolution produced new distinctions as the middle class expanded into the upper and lower middle class. Industrialists and wealthy investors composed the upper middle class. Merchants and small business owners composed the lower middle class. Remaining at the bottom of the social ladder, poor workers composed the lower class.

However, people could move up or down in these classes in one or two generations. For example, in one generation a poor man could work his way up from poverty to the upper middle class by diligence and hard labor. His children or grandchildren could waste the inherited wealth and slide back into poverty. Therefore, carefulness or carelessness in managing family resources tended to determine someone's position in society during the Industrial Revolution.

Family Life

Family life in the industrial cities changed in many ways. At first, several members of the family worked in factories. Industrial labor also required many hours of work without the opportunity to

The Industrial Revolution	
List some examples for each topic below.	

Topic	Examples
Problems during the Industrial Revolution	
Legal reforms	
Religious transformation	

Markets and Morals

Some people define justice as equality, and thus they see economic inequality as an injustice that the government ought to correct, usually by taxing the rich and giving to the poor. However, the Bible does not define justice in terms of equality. In the parable of the minas, the faithful servant who earned ten minas was placed over ten cities. The servant who earned five minas was placed over five cities (Lk. 19:11-27).

Others resist government interference in economic matters since this limits people's freedom. However, when God set up a government, He regulated the treatment of workers and provision for the poor (Ex. 21:26-34; 22:25-27; 23:10-12; Deut. 24:14; cf. Mal. 3:5).

These passages indicate that justice in Scripture involves treating image-bearers of God as befits image-bearers of God. Justice involves ensuring that workers are paid fairly for their labor, that they are given rest from their labors, that the working environment is safe, and that provision is made for the poor.

take a break between jobs. Parents were unable to spend time with their children.

There were differences between working in the city and working on the farm. Laborers performed the same task repeatedly in the factory instead of working a variety of jobs on the farm. However, the long hours of work in a factory at a low wage were similar to the long hours of work required to survive on the farm. While working conditions were terrible, the family, in time, developed greater financial security.

Workers endured dangerous working conditions and health problems due to pollution. Women and children labored in dreadful conditions and endured abuses. However, they labored under these circumstances to survive in an economy that was undergoing large-scale transitions.

With the coming of each generation, families found greater opportunities for economic and social advancement. Children had greater access to a free education than their parents had. Higher education became possible for more and more people. The society of an industrialized nation reaped the benefits of an educated people.

Movements for Social Reform

Most modern historians focus on the negative aspects of the Industrial Revolution and minimize the positive contributions. A few may reverse this emphasis. The truth lies somewhere in between.

Problems that Called for Reform

The working class found itself in a desperate situation. Many individuals and families could not survive in the cities unless they labored in a factory. With an abundant work force, some industrialists took advantage of the workers. Inventors tended to make machines that maximized production rather than worker safety. Many employers allowed conditions in the early factories to be dirty and dangerous. Workers often became injured or sick. Many employers would replace their employees when they became ill or injured due to poor working conditions.

Greed may have motivated many who provided housing for the growing numbers of people moving to the cities. They built large buildings with many small apartments that lacked proper sanitation. Safety and comfort were not priorities among many of the owners. The buildings were often built close together to maximize the use of the property. Conditions in these tenement buildings were often terrible.

In addition, some mills and factories dumped their waste into rivers and polluted the water supply. Factories burned coal to fuel the steam engines

Each worker, even those as young as the girl pictured here, had to keep several lines of thread winding on the spindles.

and created terrible air pollution. People complained to their elected officials about the injuries and diseases that resulted from these conditions.

Historical Perspectives: The Industrial Revolution

Historians J. L. and Barbara Hammond argue that life for industrial laborers became worse with the Industrial Revolution. The worker lost the freedom of working his own ground with some of his time. He also lost control over his time, including most leisure time. Machines were time-saving devices, but they were expensive. Owners wanted workers to keep them running as long as possible to make them as productive as possible. This meant longer work hours. Some owners saw leisure time as work time wasted. Education was thought to make workers less obedient, so employers were not inclined to provide it. Children were also no longer working alongside parents at a home industry but were working long hours at work that destroyed their health.

Source: J. L. Hammond and Barbara Hammond, *The Skilled Labourer, 1760-1832* (1919; repr., New York: Harper, 1970), 3-7.

Ludwig von Mises argues that the old economic system was not able to handle the increasing population of Great Britain. Thus increasing numbers of people ended up in the poorhouse, workhouse, or military. This is why people came to work in factories despite the conditions being "shockingly bad." In addition, mass production was producing affordable goods for the growing population, which means factories benefited the poor. Mises attributes the rising standard of living to market forces. Therefore, government intervention to ensure just treatment reduced industurial productivity and therefore actually delayed the rising standard of living. The higher standard of living that resulted from the Industrial Revolution was a great benefit for many, but it was necessary for workers at the beginning of Industrial Revolution to live and work in "deplorable" conditions in order for those benefits to be reached.

Source: Ludwig von Mises, *Human Action: A Treatise on Economics* (New Haven: Yale University Press, 1949), 613-619.

1. What assumption of the Hammonds' did Mises challenge in his writing?

2. With these two perspectives in view, write a brief summary of the Industrial Revolution from a Christian perspective.

Growth of Unions

Some workers also sought to improve their wages and working conditions by forming unions. The results were mixed, and opinions differ on the outcome.

Some historians point out that gains made by unions resulted in less money for the factory owner to invest in new machinery. They also argue that unions punished the consumers, who had to pay higher prices for the manufactured goods.

Others believe that it was right for unions to force owners to take a cut in profits and to make consumers pay higher prices in order to provide workers a better wage. This situation provides a good example of the tug-of-war that occurs between men in a fallen world.

England's Struggle

Government Reform

During the 1830s and 1840s, Parliament began to enact laws to protect workers. For example, the **1833 Factory Act** placed limits on child labor. Children under nine years of age could not work in a textile mill. Children from nine to thirteen years old could not work more than eight hours a day. In addition, the children were required to attend school three hours a day. Parliament appointed inspectors to check the mills and enforce mill owner cooperation.

Instead of submitting to this law, some mill owners responded by dismissing child workers rather than enduring the government inspections. Other government attempts to improve working conditions included the **Mines Act** (1842), which barred women and boys under the age of ten from working in the mines. In addition,

John Wesley

George Whitefield

Whitefield and the Great Awakening

Whitefield also played a key role in the **Great Awakening** in the American colonies (1720–1760). This spiritual movement brought many to salvation, started many churches, and prepared the American colonies for independence.

the **Ten Hour Bill** in 1847 prevented women and children from working more than ten hours per day in any British industry. While these laws were important means for curbing the unjust treatment of workers, women and children were working out of necessity, and wages were often inadequate to support an entire family. Additional societal changes were needed to address the problems that arose during the Industrial Revolution.

Religious Transformation

During this period God sent an evangelical revival to Britain. British pastors and evangelists spent countless hours preaching all over England. Plant owners, managers, and government officials responded to the preaching of God's Word. Every level of society changed as people were converted. Owners and managers determined to better care for their workers. Government officials passed laws that improved working conditions and addressed many of society's problems.

Nor were the workers forgotten in this revival. Evangelists preached to coal miners and factory workers. As laborers turned to Christ, they not only worked with a new sense of purpose but also abandoned vices that would have prevented them from improving their lives.

John Wesley became one of the greatest preachers in Britain during this period. He traveled throughout the country on horseback and preached around 42,000 sermons. He organized his converts into Methodist societies, with laymen serving as leaders.

Thousands from all walks of life were converted under the preaching of Wesley and the witness of many of his followers. Wesley and his followers also supported many reforms, including improved prison conditions and better working conditions. When Wesley died, there were 630 lay preachers and 175,000 members in the Methodist societies.

George Whitefield, another influential preacher, had an international ministry. He preached throughout England, Wales, and the American colonies. Whitefield introduced the Wesleys to the practice of preaching outdoors to masses who did not attend church. It is estimated that Whitefield preached to as many as twenty thousand people at a time. He often preached thirteen times a week to both large and small groups. Many thousands of people trusted Christ during his ministry.

The gospel transformed Britain as large numbers of men, women, and children trusted Christ. Crime rates dropped, and movements for industrial reform remained largely peaceful. The British nation was spared much of the violence that plagued other European nations. The drunkenness that plagued Britain declined as men trusted Christ.

The Struggle in Other European Countries

You learned in Chapter 12 that France endured a terrible revolution as the people sought reform. In the middle of the nineteenth century, Paris again became the scene of several riots over issues including poor working conditions and low wages.

Labor unrest and a desire for freedom characterized several western European countries in 1848. Workers in France, Hungary, the German territories, and Russia resorted to armed resistance during these disputes. Few if any improvements resulted. Government oppression or indifference continued, and conditions for the laborers did not improve.

Section Quiz

1. What problems were created by the lack of adequate housing in the city?

2. What were two positive results for society brought about by the Industrial Revolution?

3. Who could afford most of the goods produced in the factories?

4. Which English preacher played a key role in the Great Awakening in the American colonies?

★ Why were government reform and religious transformation both needed to correct injustices that occurred during the Industrial Revolution?

★ If God made possible the Industrial Revolution, why did many bad things happen in the course of its development?

■ III. End of the Slave Trade in the West

Although slavery has a long history, the enslaving of Africans became a large and profitable industry during the Age of Exploration. African tribes found a ready market for those captured in war. Muslim, Portuguese, and Dutch traders purchased the African

Guiding Questions

1. What brought about the abolition of the slave trade and the abolition of slavery?

2. What role did Europe play in suppressing the transatlantic slave trade?

3. To what degree did emancipated slaves and their descendants achieve social and economic equality?

Diagram of a typical slave ship

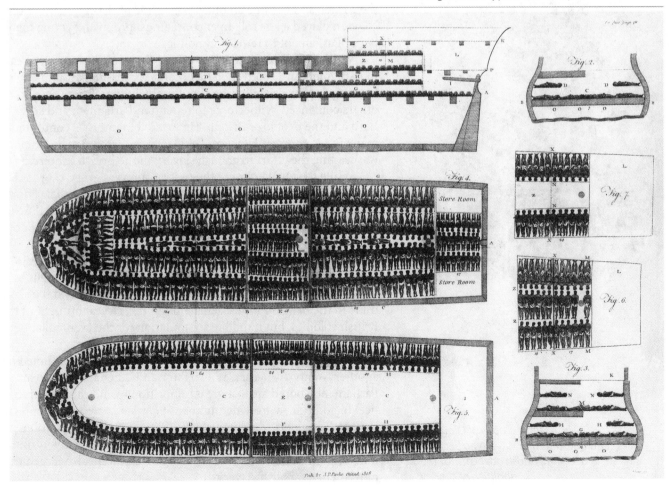

William Wilberforce

The autobiography of Olaudah Equiano, a former slave, who became a leading British advocate for the abolition of slavery

slaves. The Portuguese and Dutch carried the slaves to Europe and the New World to be sold at a profit. Over time, more and more Europeans were confronted with the terrible realities of the slave trade. In response, a growing number found slavery to be a wicked abuse of fellow human beings.

The British were among the first to seek an end to slavery. After decades of debate, the practice of slavery ended peacefully in Britain. Many in America opposed slavery as well. However, Americans were divided over this issue, and the abolition of slavery did not occur through a peaceful process. During the eighteenth century, slavery thrived in French colonies. The French abolished and then restored slavery for a time in the nineteenth century.

Britain

Quakers were the first known religious group to challenge slavery. Initially, Quakers owned slaves and did not oppose this practice. However, some Quakers began to question the right of one person to own another person. By the 1750s, many Quakers rejected slavery and supported abolition.

Around the same time, John and Charles Wesley also promoted the abolition of slavery. Under their influence, many Methodist laymen became involved in a growing abolitionist movement in Britain.

Best known for writing the words to the hymn "Amazing Grace," **John Newton** (1725–1807), a former slave-ship captain, became a Christian in 1748. He had witnessed the horrible conditions of the slave trade and became an outspoken critic of slavery. In addition, Newton played a key role in encouraging a promising young member of Parliament to remain in politics.

William Wilberforce (1759–1833) first won election to a seat in Parliament in 1780. When he became a Christian around 1785, he struggled over whether he should remain in politics. Newton and others convinced Wilberforce to remain in Parliament and serve the Lord and the people of Britain. He worked to improve conditions for many in his country. However, Wilberforce's greatest achievement was leading the effort to abolish slavery in the British Empire.

While the Quakers were the first to oppose slavery, they had no voice in Parliament. Quakers and Anglicans united their efforts with the formation of the **Committee for the Abolition of the Slave Trade** in 1787. Wilberforce supported this committee but did not officially join until 1791.

From 1791 until 1807, Wilberforce overcame setback after setback in Parliament as he sought to end British involvement in the slave trade. In 1807 Parliament finally passed a bill to end the slave trade in the British Empire. This did not free slaves throughout the British colonies, but it did lay a foundation for the eventual abolition of slavery.

The struggle to end slavery in the British Empire continued for another twenty-five years. Wilberforce and other abolitionists in Parliament labored against great opposition to end this evil practice. In addition, a growing number of Christian reformers opposed slavery. Pamphlets were published to expose its evils. Abolitionists also refuted the claims that the Africans were inferior. Over time, industrial workers, including women and children, also joined the movement to abolish slavery.

While the struggle in Parliament continued, abolitionists purchased land in West Africa to settle freed British and American slaves. They pressured African chiefs to end the trading of slaves. The British navy played a key role by intercepting ships to search for slaves. The navy's diligence resulted in the rescue of thousands of African slaves.

Wilberforce had spent most of his adult life pressuring a reluctant Parliament to end one of the most shameful practices in modern history. He died in July of 1833 with that goal in sight. One month after his death, Parliament passed a bill that effectively ended slavery in the British Empire.

America

In America, as in Britain, Quakers were among the first to speak out against slavery. Organized as the Society of Friends, the Quakers became a consistent voice in early America in opposition to slavery.

Thomas Paine published the first known article in the American colonies that supported the freeing of slaves. He titled the article "African Slavery in America," and he advocated the abolition of slavery by the emerging nation. Two students of Jonathan Edwards, another important figure in the Great Awakening, also published their support for abolition. Some slave owners shared this desire, choosing to make provision in their wills for their slaves' freedom.

The Students of Jonathan Edwards

One of Edwards's most prominent students, Samuel Hopkins, published a work in 1776 denouncing slavery. His stated goal was to emancipate, or free, all African slaves.

Jonathan Edwards's son, known as Jonathan Edwards the Younger, also published a work that confronted and condemned slavery in 1791.

Even though Edwards owned at least one slave, several students who sat under his training concluded that slavery was a great evil that had to be abolished.

Leading American Abolitionists

William Lloyd Garrison (1805–79)

William Lloyd Garrison became one of the most important and outspoken opponents of slavery in the North. As the editor of the abolitionist newspaper *The Liberator*, he exposed the evils of slavery using fiery language. His writing enraged many in the North and the South. Many in the North took offense at his description of discrimination toward free blacks in the North.

While some in the North preferred the gradual emancipation of slaves, Garrison would have none of it and demanded immediate emancipation. To build support for his position, he helped found the American Anti-Slavery Society.

William Lloyd Garrison (above);
Frederick Douglass (below)

Frederick Douglass (c. 1818–95)

First known as Frederick Augustus Washington Bailey, Frederick Douglass was born a slave in Maryland. Despite laws that prohibited teaching slaves to read, Douglass received basic reading lessons at the age of twelve. His determination to master the skill of reading changed his world. He read newspapers and every book he could find. Douglass also taught other slaves to read the New Testament on Sundays.

After several failed attempts to escape and brutal beatings by at least one slave owner, Douglass boarded a train dressed as a sailor in the fall of 1838 and escaped to Philadelphia.

Douglass quickly became an active and eloquent spokesman for abolition. Garrison wrote of Douglass's life in *The Liberator* and helped to spread his message of the evils of antebellum slavery.

Even political opponents often agreed to cooperate to abolish slavery. For example, the New York Manumission (to free from bondage) Society was composed of Federalists John Jay and Alexander Hamilton and Democratic-Republican Aaron Burr.

Congress banned the importation of slaves beginning on January 1, 1808. Authorities did not consistently enforce this ban, but slavery seemed to be declining. However, one laborsaving invention changed the course of American history and ended the trend to abolish slavery.

As we noted previously, Eli Whitney invented the cotton gin. Although he did not personally profit from his invention, this machine turned cotton into a highly profitable crop. Slave labor in the cotton fields became the key to southern prosperity. The majority of slaves were owned by about one percent of southern landowners. However, the one percent controlled large plantations and exerted a great influence over government officials. America did not abolish slavery until the end of the Civil War in 1865.

William Lloyd Garrison and **Frederick Douglass** became two of the most famous American abolitionists. Garrison was the editor of the newspaper *The Liberator*. Through his writing, he influenced many to support abolition. Douglass, a former slave, was a persuasive spokesman for abolition.

France

During the French Revolution, the government abolished slavery. However, Napoleon revived this practice when he became the First Consul. He sent troops to put down slave rebellions in various colonies, including Haiti.

For the Haitians, the cost in human lives was immense. However, they would not submit, and thousands of French soldiers died in a failed effort to subdue the Haitians. In 1804 Haiti became one of the first French colonies to gain independence and to end French-imposed slavery.

In the Muslim World

Slavery thrived in the Middle East and Africa before, during, and after the period when Europeans practiced slavery. Some Muslim nations, including the Sudan in East Africa, continue to practice slavery. Estimates vary, but several million people live in slavery in Muslim nations today.

Section Quiz

1. When did slavery become a profitable industry in Europe?

2. What religious group was the first to oppose slavery?

3. What former slave-ship captain became an outspoken opponent of slavery?

4. What invention led to an increased demand for slave labor in America?

5. What island population successfully revolted against French control?

★ What role did William Wilberforce play in the abolition of slavery in the British Empire?

Making Connections

1. How did crop rotation increase food production?
2. Why did an increased number of sheep on farms lead people to move to towns?
3. How did Jethro Tull's seed drill lead to a greater food supply?
4. How did Eli Whitney's cotton gin increase the value of cotton as a crop?
5. Why was James Watt's steam engine so important to the Industrial Revolution?
6. What effect did the Industrial Revolution have on class distinctions in Europe?
7. What political and moral victory did Wilberforce win in 1807?
8. Prior to the invention and widespread use of the cotton gin, what seemed to be the direction of slavery in America?

Developing History Skills

1. Based on the information in this chapter, draw a timeline that includes inventions that were developed during the Industrial Revolution.
2. Based on the information in Chapter 9 and this chapter, answer the following question: Why did the Industrial Revolution originate in Britain?

Thinking Critically

1. Identify the positive and negative effects of the Industrial Revolution. Make a list of each on a separate sheet of paper.
2. Evaluate the role of government in regulating industry based on the information in this chapter.

Living in God's World

1. Pretend that you are William Wilberforce. A vicar has recently argued in a newspaper that Christianity is spiritual and thus should not be used to oppose the slave trade. Write a newspaper response defending the role of Christianity and the Bible in the shaping of public policy.
2. You are a Christian historian writing about the period after the Industrial Revolution. As a Christian, you know that missions is very significant and should be included in the writing of history. Explain how the Industrial Revolution, in God's providence, opened the way for British and American missionaries to spread the gospel around the world in the nineteenth and twentieth centuries.

People, Places, and Things to Know

crop rotation
cottage industries
Jethro Tull
seed drill
Andrew Meikle
threshing machine
Eli Whitney
cotton gin
Cyrus McCormick
reaping machine
John Fowler
steam tractor
Industrial Revolution
factories
steam engine
James Watt
John Kay
flying shuttle
James Hargreaves
spinning jenny
entrepreneurs
Richard Arkwright
patent
capital
1833 Factory Act
Mines Act
Ten Hour Bill
John Wesley
George Whitefield
Great Awakening
John Newton
William Wilberforce
Committee for the Abolition of the Slave Trade
William Lloyd Garrison
Frederick Douglass

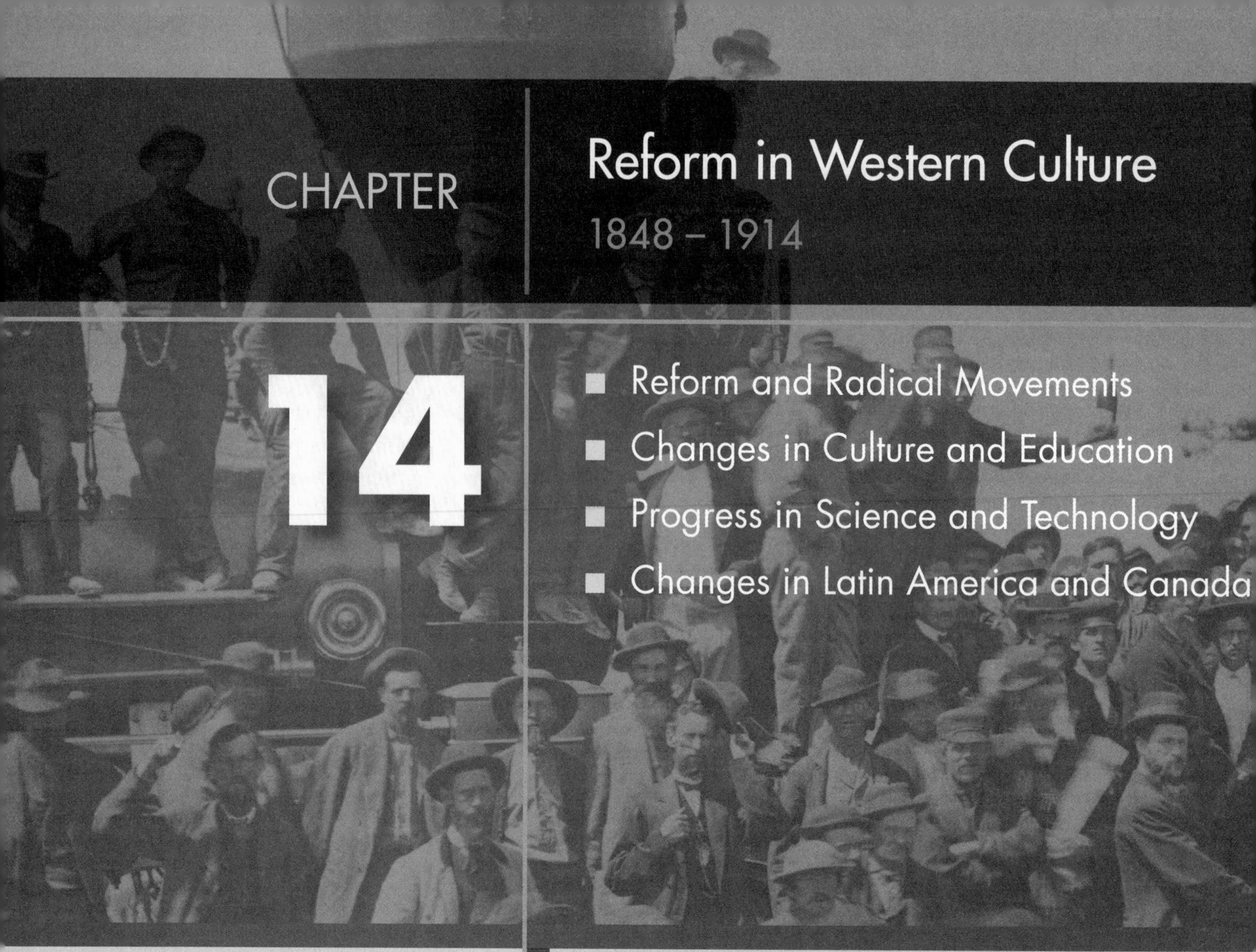

Reform in Western Culture

1848 – 1914

14

- Reform and Radical Movements
- Changes in Culture and Education
- Progress in Science and Technology
- Changes in Latin America and Canada

1830 – 1920

Porfirio Diaz elected president of Mexico 1876

Louis Napoleon Bonaparte establishes
France's Second Empire 1852

Unification of Germany completed 1871

Karl Marx and Friedrich Engels publish
the *Communist Manifesto* 1848

France's Third Republic begins 1870

Parliament repeals the Corn Laws 1846

Reform Act grants voting privileges
to all British male homeowners
1867

Reform Bill entitles the middle
class to vote 1832

British North America Act creates
the dominion of Canada 1867

Samuel Morse patents
the first known telegraph
1837

Laying of the first successful
trans-Atlantic cable 1866

1830	1840	1850	1860	1870

Mexican-American War
1846–48

Charles Darwin's *Origin of
Species* is published 1859

Big Ideas

1. What was the impact of new social movements and ideologies on nineteenth-century Europe?
2. What cultural, intellectual, and educational trends developed in nineteenth-century Europe?
3. How did developments in science and technology during the nineteenth and early twentieth centuries lead to progress?
4. What political, economic, and social changes occurred in Latin America and Canada in the nineteenth century?

Many changes occurred during this brief period in Western history. These developments came in many forms and affected a number of issues. Changes in political representation, education, technology, and many other areas that influence us today can be traced back to this period.

Change also occurred in the Americas as Latin American states struggled to become stable nations. In the north, Canada progressed from being a British colony to a self-governing nation.

British women over thirty receive the right to vote 1918

The Dreyfus Affair occurs in France 1894

The Wright brothers make their first successful flight in North Carolina 1903

Parliament Bill gives the House of Commons power over the House of Lords 1911

| 1880 | 1890 | 1900 | 1910 | 1920 |

Guiding Questions

1. What are the main ideas of Marxism, and how do they compare with a Christian worldview?

2. How did women's suffrage and other popular movements develop in Europe and North America?

3. How did Britain and France become more liberal and democratic in the nineteenth century?

4. What led to the return of anti-Semitism in Europe?

Karl Marx

Friedrich Engels

■ I. Reform and Radical Movements

The second half of the nineteenth century witnessed many reforms and the development of several radical movements. Socialism initially developed from the ideal of equality for all people. Thus, any kind of inequality was considered to be evil. Popular movements, including those supporting the universal privilege to vote and the regulation of alcohol, emerged during this period. In response to popular pressure, governments in countries such as Britain and France enabled more citizens to vote and recognized other liberties that tended to provide a more stable society.

Socialism

Socialism has many applications. As an economic term, it refers to government ownership of business. As a philosophy, socialism emphasizes the welfare of the group.

Socialism was a reaction against the capitalistic system. It saw the capitalism that emerged from the Industrial Revolution as unjust because a small number of men controlled the wealth of society. The solution, as socialists saw it, was to press for social equality by restructuring society so that workers controlled the wealth they produced. The socialists also emphasized harmony and cooperation throughout society. Instead of a society developed through competition, they sought a classless society in which everyone cooperated for the common good.

Socialism has developed into several forms, including Utopian socialism, Christian socialism, and Marxist socialism. We will briefly examine the first two before discussing Marxism.

Utopian socialists generally believed that people were the products of their environment. Therefore, education, labor reform, and other improvements to man's cultural environment would improve man's character.

Christian socialists tried to combine Christianity with socialism. They rightly criticized abuses against workers. But, like all socialists, they tended to abandon the biblical teaching that all people are born sinners. They assumed the human problem resulted from a corrupt and unequal society. Christian socialists believed these problems could be reformed if Christians would challenge people to rise to their full potential. They did not challenge the key points at which socialism departed from a biblical worldview.

Marxism

Karl Marx (1818–83) was a student of philosophy and history. During his years of study, Marx developed radical political views. His support of violent revolution led government officials to expel him from several countries. In Paris, Marx met Friedrich Engels (1820–95), and they became close friends. Together they wrote and published the *Communist Manifesto* in 1848.

In this work, Marx and Engels insisted that history is a series of class struggles. They declared that these struggles would end when the **proletariat** (laborers) united against the **bourgeoisie** (BOOR zhwah ZEE; capitalists). Then the workers would violently overthrow the middle class and establish a classless society.

Marx believed that private ownership of property and private control of wealth were evil. Like other socialists, he believed that a small number of men controlling most of the wealth was wrong.

Marx thought that an item's value came from the cost of materials plus the cost of the work that went into making it. He thought that a business owner who took the profits from sales were unjust because the owner did not work for those profits. Marx did not consider the costs of building and running factories. Therefore, Marx sought to end what he considered unfair practices. He insisted that only violent revolution would end these problems. Marx believed that **communism** (common ownership of property) would result when the proletariat established a dictatorship where the worker would be in power.

Marx and Religion

Marx was a materialist; that is, he believed that only matter was real. Rejecting belief in spiritual things, Marx took a negative view of religion—especially Christianity. He claimed that belief in God, sin, and salvation through Jesus Christ kept the proletariat in bondage, blinding them to their real needs and their power to change society. Marx famously claimed that religion was the "opium of the people." It drugged people and kept them from seeing reality as they needed to see it. As a result, Marx rejected the idea that a sovereign God superintended the course of history. Instead, history moved forward according to a set course determined by social conflicts.

Popular Movements

During the nineteenth century, various groups pressed for reform in society. Two popular movements centered on women's suffrage and the problem of drunkenness.

Women's Suffrage

The privilege to vote, or **suffrage**, became a popular movement in English-speaking countries during the nineteenth and twentieth centuries. Men who had not previously gained the right to vote demanded this privilege. At the same time, women worked to share this freedom. Middle class men in England soon found supporters in Parliament to represent their demands. However, women struggled to overcome decades of resistance and reluctance on the part of British officials. Even when women found a measure of support in Parliament, the majority refused to grant them suffrage. Women in America encountered the same resistance from their elected officials.

Under the leadership of women such as Lydia Becker, British women established suffrage committees beginning in the 1860s. By 1879 these committees united to form the National Union of Women's Suffrage Societies. They presented a united front and relentlessly pressured Parliament. Despite their persistence, British women did not gain the right to vote until after World War I.

While most women sought only to gain suffrage, others developed ambitions that were more radical. They moved beyond petition to heckling political figures and practicing civil disobedience. A minority of radical leaders sought to erase some of the distinctions between men and women.

Justice

Socialism emerged in part out of concern for justice. Socialists were concerned about the plight of the poor and oppressed. Nonetheless, God did not intend His world to work without hierarchies (Matt. 19:28; 1 Tim. 2:12) or private property (Ex. 20:15). Several socialist nations have imposed their system on unwilling people—leading to some of the most horrific human rights abuses and deadly injustices known to history.

Suffragettes parade down Bedford Avenue in Brooklyn.

American Women's Suffrage

The struggle to win the privilege of women's suffrage also continued in America. With the passage of the Nineteenth Amendment to the Constitution, the law of the land guaranteed women the privilege to vote. Congress ratified this amendment in 1920.

Citizenship

Christians can support the efforts of women to vote. God gave mankind, both male and female, the right to rule over His creation (Gen. 1:26-28). In addition, both men and women are made in God's image and are deserving of just treatment. This meant that some of the laws of this time needed to be reformed.

Members of the Women's Christian Temperance Union (WCTU) who marched on Washington D.C. to present a petition supporting prohibition

Temperance Movement

Britain

Christians and other members of British society became deeply troubled by the increased abuse of alcohol. Various societies were formed to battle drunkenness by supporting **temperance** (drinking in moderation). Other groups viewed **abstinence** (no drinking of alcohol) as the most effective way to prevent drunkenness. Two examples of these groups are the British Association for the Promotion of Temperance, which formed in 1835, and the Band of Hope, which formed in 1847 to protect working-class children from becoming victims of alcohol.

A division within the British temperance movement occurred over proposed laws to ban drinking. Some preferred to use moral persuasion rather than making drunkenness a legal matter. Legal efforts lost ground when restrictions on beer sales led to rioting. Laws that limited or prohibited the sale of alcohol were overturned, and additional efforts met with stiff resistance.

While legal options proved elusive, efforts to reduce drunkenness continued. In 1873 a Catholic abstinence group formed the League of the Cross. Concerned women also formed the British Women's Temperance Association in 1876 to convince men to stop drinking alcohol.

America

America struggled with drunkenness as early as the late eighteenth century. Temperance societies began to form at this time and continued to multiply through the nineteenth century.

Concerned women in America formed the Women's Christian Temperance Union in 1880 to educate the public regarding the evils of alcohol. They worked with students to warn them before they were tempted to begin drinking.

The goal of many of the American temperance groups was the passage of an amendment to the Constitution (the Eighteenth Amendment) that would make the manufacture, sale, and transportation of alcohol illegal. They sought legal means to protect families from the destructive effects of alcohol.

Reform in Western Europe

Britain and France provide two examples of economic and political reform in Europe during this period. Some of the decisions that preserved Britain from unrest and revolution continued to bless that nation. Likewise, some of the decisions that led the French into revolution and political instability continued to plague them. In the midst of change in Europe, the ugly reality of anti-Semitism reemerged and continued to become more prominent as the nations rushed toward the twentieth century.

Britain

Economic

Prior to the middle of the nineteenth century, the British government had maintained high tariffs (taxes on imports and exports) on commodities such as imported grain. These taxes protected those who produced these items in Britain. However, the high prices also burdened the British people.

In 1846 Parliament removed one of these tariffs by repealing the **Corn Laws**. This decision allowed merchants to import cheaper grain and lowered the cost of food for everyone. By repealing laws that had protected a segment of the market, Britain began to shift toward a free trade economy. This transition resulted in a dramatic increase of trade and brought great prosperity to Britain.

Political

While most of the British population had moved from the country to the cities, representation in Parliament did not reflect this change. The growing middle class began to demand a voice in government. They persisted, and the **Reform Bill of 1832** entitled the middle class to vote. However, members of the working class remained excluded.

Chartism developed among the working class as an effort to accomplish several goals. Members of this movement demanded universal manhood suffrage. In other words, they sought the right for every Englishman to vote. They also supported the use of the secret ballot in elections. The secret ballot protected the voter from pressure or bribery. Though Chartism failed, many of the issues it raised became law over time.

Following the Reform Bill of 1832, additional reform met with stiff resistance. Finally, in 1867, **Benjamin Disraeli** supported a bill that doubled the number of men who could vote. In the **Reform Act of 1867**, Parliament granted voting privileges to all male homeowners. This act increased the number of voters to two million out of a population of around five million men. Later reforms provided more representation for those who lived in rural communities.

Despite their many years of demanding the privilege to vote, women were the last to achieve this goal. In 1918 Parliament voted to allow British women who were over thirty to vote. Due to the persistence of reformers, all British women over the age of twenty-one received this privilege in 1928.

Disraeli's political opponent, **William Gladstone**, stressed domestic reform during his terms as prime minister. Among his many accomplishments, Gladstone helped to establish a national court system and voting by secret ballot. In addition, he labored to improve public education. Gladstone believed an educated public would produce informed voters.

Throughout this period in Britain, the House of Lords struggled to retain power over the House of Commons. However, the **Parliament Bill of 1911** changed the balance of power. The House of Lords could no longer veto laws passed by the House of Commons. This bill established the supremacy of the House of Commons over the House of Lords.

France

France suffered great political instability because of Napoleon's failed attempts to control Europe. European leaders restored the monarchy, but it did not last. The French overthrew the next government during the Revolution of 1848.

Benjamin Disraeli

William Gladstone

243

Napoleon III

Captain Dreyfus being stripped of his rank

The French then elected **Louis Napoleon Bonaparte** as president of the newly formed Second Republic in 1848. He followed his uncle Napoleon Bonaparte's example and declared himself president for life. In 1852 he gave himself the title of emperor of France, as Napoleon III, and established the **Second Empire**. He remained in power until the people revolted in 1870.

During Louis Napoleon's reign, France experienced growth in several areas. Industry developed, and many French families moved from the country to the cities. The French economy expanded as the Industrial Revolution reaped the benefits of English machinery and British financing.

Louis Napoleon also allowed freedom of the press and the development of labor unions. In addition, suffrage increased to include many more citizens.

However, a disastrous war with Germany led to a humiliating defeat of the French forces. Louis Napoleon lost favor with the people. The forces of the newly formed **Third Republic** (1870–1940) captured and deposed Louis Napoleon. He spent the rest of his life in exile in England.

Jews in Europe

Hostility toward Jews, or **anti-Semitism**, has a long history. You learned in Chapter 5 about violent attacks on the Jews during the Middle Ages. Animosity toward Jews ebbed and flowed in intensity during succeeding centuries. However, it remained like a smoldering ember ready to burst into flame.

Germany

German composer Richard Wagner provided a glimpse into German anti-Semitism in 1850 when he wrote an essay attacking Jewish composers, including Felix Mendelssohn. He opposed the Jewish influence on German culture. Another glimpse surfaced in 1878 when the Lutheran court chaplain to Kaiser Wilhelm I formed the Christian Social Party to resist Jewish influence in Germany.

France

The **Dreyfus Affair** exposed a strong undercurrent of anti-Semitism in France. Alfred Dreyfus, who was Jewish, served as an artillery captain in the French army. In 1894 the French government accused him of passing military secrets to the Germans. Despite his innocence, the government convicted and sentenced him to life in prison on Devil's Island.

The French government later secretly tried and acquitted (found not guilty) the real spy. The French people became divided over the treatment of Dreyfus and his guilt or innocence. However, a large majority of the French press condemned Dreyfus. Under pressure, the government eventually released Dreyfus from prison and restored his rank in the French army. However, the Dreyfus Affair left an ugly stain on French history.

Russia

Many Jews had migrated to Russia over the centuries. Some fled persecution in western Europe (see chapter 5). The czars welcomed them because of their skills and strong work ethic.

However, by the nineteenth century, more and more Russians began to view the Jews with jealousy and suspicion. As the level of

Cartoon showing Russian oppression of the Jewish population. Teddy Roosevelt is seen rebuking the czar.

violence in Russia increased, Russians often blamed the Jews for assassinations and other crimes. Russian authorities and citizens murdered Jews without regard for age or gender. The term **pogrom** (puh GROM) was first used to refer to a sweeping, targeted, and repeated attack on Jews in Russia.

Section Quiz

1. According to Marx, what would end the cycle of class struggle?
2. What privilege did the woman's suffrage movement seek?
3. What did the American temperance groups seek in order to make alcohol illegal in the United States?
4. What were two goals of the Chartist movement?
★ How did the Dreyfus Affair expose anti-Semitism in France?
★ Marx claimed that only matter is real and that religion is just a drug. Marx also claimed that oppression of the proletariat is wrong and ought to be opposed. How do these ideas contradict each other?

▪ II. Changes in Culture and Education

Culture in Europe shifted from an idealist view of man to one that emphasized reality. Writers and artists created works that reflected what they saw rather than what they imagined. Leaders also realized that citizens required a basic education in order to become a productive and informed society. Public education became more widely available as a result.

Culture

Romanticism

The nineteenth century was an age of change and philosophy, and the arts were no exception. **Romanticism** dominated the first half of the century. Several themes characterize romanticism.

Guiding Questions

1. What led to expanded educational opportunities and increased literacy in nineteenth-century Europe?
2. How did major movements in literature, music, and the visual arts shape social and cultural values in nineteenth-century Europe?

The Bible and Romanticism

Romanticism and realism both picked up on parts of the truth as it is found in God's world. Romantics rightly recognized that humans are not just minds. The emotions play an important part in the human life. Indeed, the greatest commandments are to love God and to love others. But God did not design a world in which emotions should function apart from the mind. Creativity and freedom are good, but God also built laws into His world. Creativity and freedom are beneficial when exercised within those laws, and they are harmful when they push beyond God's laws. Similarly, in a fallen world, one cannot say that nature is good and culture is bad. Both nature and culture are part of God's good plan for the world (Gen. 1:28, 31), and both have been twisted by the Fall.

Romanticism is still a powerful force in American culture. It is present when people oppose religion but concoct their own personal spirituality, when people claim to be able to shape their own identity into whatever form they choose, or when they break cultural norms for the sake of expressing their individuality.

Romanticism and Realism

List characteristics of romanticism and realism.

Romanticism	Realism

Emotion triumphs over reason. Freedom is exalted over the rules of any system. As a result nature is preferred to culture. Romantics preferred creativity to prudence. Truth was not a single thing to be found through science but was instead found in multiple perspectives.

Romantic novels and poetry of this period celebrated nature in contrast to industry and mysticism in contrast to the organized religion of the church. Novels exalted heroic lovers who followed their hearts or mystics who sought forbidden knowledge even if it led to their destruction. Romanticism taught that it was right for a person to do what his heart told him. In other words, it would be better to rise up against impossible odds and do the heroic thing than to rationally weigh the possible outcomes.

Romantic paintings are often peaceful scenes of rural life or landscapes. Some artists also painted scenes from the revolutions. In music, composers reacted to the orderly, classical style by changing to the full, emotion-filled romantic style. Ludwig van Beethoven (BAY toh vun) is perhaps the best-known composer of this age. He mixed classical and romantic elements in his works.

Realism

By the middle of the nineteenth century, **realism** had replaced romanticism as a new art form. Realism reacted against romanticism's dreamlike quality by emphasizing, as its name suggests, what life is really like. In writing and painting, realists pictured everyday life in realistic detail.

However, realism, like romanticism, failed to portray correctly the sum total of life. Realism tended to show life as pessimistic and hopeless. Realists seemed to be suspicious of redemption, and their literature implied it would be dishonest to have a happy conclusion.

Charles Dickens

Literature

Realist authors did not abandon emotion in their writings. Instead, they sought to describe events that occurred in everyday life. At times, the events they described were sad or unpleasant. For example, **Charles Dickens** wrote about the negative aspects of the Industrial Revolution, including the slums where many workers lived. He vividly described the terrible conditions in the industrial cities and provided the reader a glimpse into the British debtors' prisons. Another realist author, **Leo Tolstoy**, described the difficulties of life in Russia. In his novel *War and Peace*, he emphasized the struggles of all kinds of people rather than focusing on leaders such as Napoleon or the czar.

Leo Tolstoy (left); Young Women from the Village *by French realist Gustave Courbet (right)*

Visual Arts

Realist painters produced works of art that portrayed everyday life. Scenes included common events such as friends meeting and engaging in conversation. Photography developed during this period, and the reality captured by a photograph may have contributed to the appeal of realism in paintings.

Education

Opportunities for education were very limited in Europe prior to the nineteenth century. The Roman Catholic and Anglican Churches still operated most schools and emphasized religious education. However, in Britain and France public education became a priority during the nineteenth century. The government established and financially supported schools. Literacy and a basic education finally became available to most children in these countries.

Britain

Early private education in Britain began with the Sunday school movement. Though we tend to think of Sunday school as a time for Bible training in church, it began as an effort to teach poor children how to read. The teaching occurred on Sunday, so it became known as Sunday school. By 1831 over one million British children had attended these sessions and learned to read. The goal for these students was to be able to read the Bible and learn God's Word.

The public school system began in 1833 when Parliament voted to spend money to build schools for poor children. The government became increasingly involved in education by determining the courses for grammar school in the 1840s. Through successive legislation, the government required children to attend school from ages five through ten. In 1893 the government provided educational opportunities for blind and deaf children. By 1918 the British government required education for five- to fourteen-year-old children and part-time education until eighteen years of age.

Germany

During the 18th century Prussia became one of the first European states to provide a free primary education that was required for all children. Improvements included certification for teachers and special schools to train people how to teach.

Shortly after achieving unification in 1871, Germany continued to make great advances in education. For example, the new nation established one of the first separate secondary schools for girls in Europe. Continued improvements led to secondary schools that trained German students in ancient and modern languages. Students also received training in science and math. Those students who did not qualify for a college education could receive technical training in preparation for an industrial job.

By the end of the nineteenth century, Germany had developed one of the finest systems of education in Europe. The state regulated these schools and demanded the right to set educational standards.

France

Modern French education began near the end of the nineteenth century. Jules Ferry, the Minister of Public Instruction, formed the republican school system. He required all children to attend school until the age of fifteen. Ferry made public education required, free, and secular. Prior to these changes, Roman Catholic clergy had played a central role in education. The system established by Ferry has continued with little change.

Section Quiz

1. How did realism differ from romanticism?
2. What did Charles Dickens write about?
3. What new invention possibly influenced realist painters?
4. What was the earliest form of private education in Britain? What was its goal?
★ How did Germany develop one of the finest education systems in Europe?
★ Evaluate romanticism in light of Jeremiah 17:9.

■ III. Progress in Science and Technology

Science and technology continued to make important discoveries and provide significant contributions to society. However, advances did not always lead to a positive impact on culture. Progress in these fields produced mixed outcomes.

Science

Major scientific advances occurred during this period, especially in the fields of physics, chemistry, and microbiology. However, the results from one man's study of nature led to an epic shift in science that caused an ongoing assault on Christianity and the Scripture.

James Clerk Maxwell

James Maxwell (1831–79), a Scottish scientist, made major contributions to the fields of physics and astronomy. Regarded by many as a scientific genius, he predicted the existence of radio waves before their discovery. Perhaps his greatest contribution was com-

---

Guiding Questions

1. What was the social significance of the work of such scientists as Maxwell, Pasteur, and Darwin?
2. How did inventions such as the railroad, steamship, telegraph, and telephone transform global communication and trade?

Maxwell, Man of God

While others recognized Maxwell for his great intellect, he acknowledged himself to be but a humble sinner. His mother trained him at home until her death in 1839. Maxwell experienced a spiritual conversion and matured into a devout man of God.

bining the sciences of electricity, magnetism, and optics into one model. Other great scientists, including Albert Einstein, built on the foundations laid by Maxwell.

Louis Pasteur

Louis Pasteur (1822–95), a chemist in France, made many important discoveries that prevented several diseases. For example, he developed a method of heating milk and other liquids in order to slow the development of disease-causing microbes. Today we call this process **pasteurization**.

Pasteur also made an immense contribution to science by proving that spontaneous generation (the idea that life is generated from non-living materials) is a myth. He placed a mixture of sugar and yeast in a special flask and heated it to sterilize the mixture. The design of the flask allowed air to enter, but prevented dust and microbes from coming into contact with the mixture. If the theory of spontaneous generation was correct, some basic life form should have developed from the sugar-yeast mixture. However, no life forms developed. This discovery struck at the very foundation of the emerging theory of evolution.

Charles Darwin

Charles Darwin (1809–82) was born into a Unitarian family that had a history of freethinkers. As a child, he became very interested in nature. At the University of Edinburgh he studied medicine, and in his free time he learned about the study of nature. His classes, however, bored him, and his father then sent him to Cambridge to study to be a pastor. Darwin eventually gave up becoming a pastor as well. In 1831 Darwin sailed on a five-year voyage as a naturalist on the HMS *Beagle*. His discoveries led him to question whether creatures changed over time or not.

Darwin also struggled with the question of how a good God could design and sustain a world filled with pain and suffering. He concluded that God had little or nothing to do with the creation or

Louis Pasteur

Charles Darwin

249

Do Christianity and Evolution Mix?

Many Christians have felt pressured to fit the biblical Creation narratives into the evolutionary story told by the Darwinists. They think that in doing so they remove a great scientific objection to belief in Christianity. But in making this concession to Darwinism, Christians remove the answer to the great philosophical objection that Darwin himself raised against Christianity: how a good God could design and sustain a world filled with pain and suffering? The Bible's answer to this question is that death and suffering are a result of the Fall (Rom. 5:12; 8:20-21). Any attempt to fit the Bible and the theory of evolution together places death and suffering before human sin. It deprives the Christian of the answer to the question that Darwin struggled with. Instead of attempting to fit the Bible to evolutionary theory, Christian scientists should work to show the errors in the theory of evolution and develop alternative scientific explanations that are consistent with Scripture.

maintaining of this world. The death of his beloved ten-year-old daughter, Annie, seemed to him to prove his point.

Darwin's observations, combined with this conclusion, provided the foundation for an evolutionary theory to explain the origin and changes of life. His theory assumed a natural explanation for man's origins. His premise also assumed that spontaneous generation was possible. Darwin's observations led him to believe that all living things had developed from a single life form. His works, *Origin of Species* in 1859 and *The Descent of Man* in 1871, led to fundamental changes in the direction of science and its influence on society. As scientists began to apply this theory, they excluded God and the Bible from consideration as a source of reliable information.

Technology

Inventive minds continued to develop improved methods of transportation and communication. Scientists and inventors produced great discoveries. At the same time, society gradually came to replace faith in the God of the Bible with faith in science and human achievement. As a result, improvements in technology tended to increase man's self-confidence and reduce his dependence on God.

Transportation

Railroad

Britain has the distinction of developing the first known railway system in the world. Initially, several local railroads operated over short routes. During the 1840s these routes were combined into a national network. The railroad became an important method of transporting goods and people across Britain and, later, across Europe. While canals were frozen and unavailable in the winter, railroads could operate year-round. With continuing improvements, the railroads operated at great speeds and provided transportation

Promontory Summit in Utah, where the Union Pacific and Central Pacific connected to form a transcontinental railroad in 1869

at reduced cost. This provided a variety of benefits to the British economy.

America imported its first steam locomotives and steel rails from Britain and gradually developed rail lines along the east coast. Railroads proved to be strategic during the Civil War as they delivered supplies and troops. The nation quickly recognized the tremendous importance of the railroad, and workers completed the first transcontinental railroad in 1869. The railroad became a vital asset in colonizing the West.

Steamship

With the development of steam-powered engines, several inventors sought to power ships using this new device. For a time, wind-powered ships could travel faster than the early steamships. However, use of Watt's steam engine, combined with improvements by other inventors, led to faster and faster steamships.

American Entrepreneur

Robert Fulton, an American, quickly saw the potential of the steamship in Britain and built a steamboat using a Watt steam engine. He delivered passengers between New York City and Albany, New York. His idea became a commercial success.

Steamship

With continued improvements, steamships replaced sail-driven ships and traveled across the ocean. Soon ships carrying hundreds of passengers, mail, and other items traveled between Britain and America.

Internal Combustion Engine

While the steam engine received its power from outside the engine, the **internal combustion engine** produced power inside the engine. Powered by gasoline or diesel, this engine revolutionized transportation. Automobiles developed as a combination of many inventions after years of trial and error. While Europeans probably developed the first working automobiles, American entrepreneurs like Henry Ford took the automobile and made it an essential part of mobility in America and around the world.

Early gasoline engine

251

Flight

Man has dreamed of flying for centuries. Sketches by Leonardo da Vinci reveal his interest in human flight. However, the first successful flight did not occur in Europe. Wilbur and Orville Wright, two brothers who owned a bicycle shop in Ohio, built the first successful airplane. On the sandy beach of Kitty Hawk in North Carolina, the **Wright brothers** made their first successful flight on December 17, 1903.

First flight by the Wright Brothers

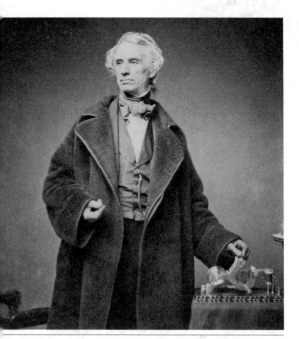

Samuel Morse

Communication

Inventions such as the telegraph and the telephone laid the foundation for global communication. Messages that previously took days or weeks to be delivered could now be transmitted and received in a matter of minutes or seconds. While instant communication was convenient, it also enabled a rapid response. Demands could be made and responses could be sent in the heat of the moment. Not all the consequences were positive.

Telegraph

The word telegraph combines two Greek words *tele* ("far") and *graphein* ("to write"). The **telegraph** enabled people to write messages to others who lived far away. Operators sent the first messages over wire lines using a code developed by **Samuel Morse** and his assistant. In 1837 Morse patented the first known machine to send these coded messages. By 1861 telegraph lines stretched across the country to the west coast. Continued developments enabled operators to transmit many messages at the same time through existing wire.

In 1866 the first successful telegraph cable was laid across the Atlantic Ocean. This cable enabled operators to send messages directly to Europe. By 1870 Britain had laid a submarine cable to India. Within a few years, operators could literally send messages around the world.

Telephone

Similar to the word *telegraph*, the word **telephone** combines the Greek word *tele* with the Greek word *phone* ("voice"). While many men worked to develop the technology that resulted in the telephone, **Alexander Graham Bell** was the first to patent it. The great inventor Thomas Edison also worked to improve Bell's invention. Edison had lost most of his hearing as a child. When he first tried to use a telephone, he could not understand what he heard. As a result, Edison made improvements to Bell's phone that enabled Edison (and many others) to hear the caller clearly.

Section Quiz

1. What did James Clerk Maxwell combine into one model?
2. What theory did Louis Pasteur prove to be a myth?
3. Over what issue did Darwin struggle?
4. What two modes of transportation developed because of the invention of the steam engine?
5. Why couldn't Edison use Bell's early version of the telephone?
* Evaluate some of the improvements in technology. How might they have increased man's self-confidence and decreased his dependence on God?

Alexander Graham Bell

■ IV. Changes in Latin America and Canada

While most of Europe and the United States benefited from stable governments and growing economies, Latin and Central America searched for stability. Far to the north, Canada slowly advanced toward its goal of becoming a self-governing nation.

Latin America

Latin and Central America struggled for stability following independence from Spanish and Portuguese control. Although this region is rich in natural resources, many of the people lacked opportunity to develop those resources. The vast percentage of the wealth and power resided in a tiny portion of the population. A large majority of the people remained in poverty and had no voice in the governing of their nation.

In the Region as a Whole

Successes

The Latin American states of Uruguay, Chile, Costa Rica, and Colombia developed some form of democracy. These countries avoided some of the political instability that much of Latin and Central America suffered.

Some of the leaders ruled in a responsible manner and gained the support of a majority of citizens in the country. They tended to share more of the wealth generated by the natural resources sold to Europe and America.

Failures

Most of the countries in Latin America tried for many years without success to develop a sense of nationality. Often the states warred with one another over territorial disputes and access to natural resources.

Guiding Questions

1. What were the successes and failures of democracy in Latin American countries that gained their independence in the nineteenth and early twentieth centuries?
2. What led to nation-building and self-government in Canada?

LATIN AMERICA

For example, in one war (1864–70) Argentina, Brazil, and Uruguay defeated Paraguay. Due to the war and other factors, Paraguay's population dropped from over five hundred thousand to two hundred thousand. In a later war, Chile defeated the combined armies of Bolivia and Peru (1879–84) to gain control of mineral-rich areas.

The gap between the rich and poor also remained great in Latin America. By 1910 about 1 percent of the population controlled 85 percent of the land. Wealthy landowners controlled gold mining and food production. Wages for the average worker remained very low, and opportunities for improvement were rare.

In Mexico

Mexico's struggle resembled that of other countries in Latin America. This young country tried in vain to overcome economic and political instability. In addition, the Mexican-American War (1846–48) resulted in Mexico losing a large section of its territory to the victorious United States.

Under the leadership of Louis Napoleon Bonaparte, France forced Mexico to submit to a foreign ruler during the 1860s. Archduke Ferdinand Maximilian of Austria served as the puppet ruler for Bonaparte. However, this foreign rule ended in 1867 when the Mexican government regained power and then tried and executed Maximilian.

Mexicans elected **Porfirio Díaz** in 1876 based on his promises of a constitutional democracy and prosperity. Once elected, Díaz maintained order and welcomed investments from foreign businesses. Under his leadership, Mexico became one of the most prosperous nations in the region.

However, Díaz transformed his government into a dictatorship and ruled for another thirty-one years. Over time, the people saw

Mexico

Located in the southwest region of North America, Mexico has been inhabited for thousands of years. Ancient Indian civilizations built empires in this area, although many had disappeared or suffered great decline prior to the arrival of the Spanish in 1519.

For the next three centuries, the Indian population of Mexico endured Spanish control and adopted the Spanish language. Even after gaining independence from Spain in 1821, Mexico endured foreign rule under Maximilian and dictatorships under leaders such as Porfirio Díaz.

Ferdinand Maximilian

Porfirio Díaz

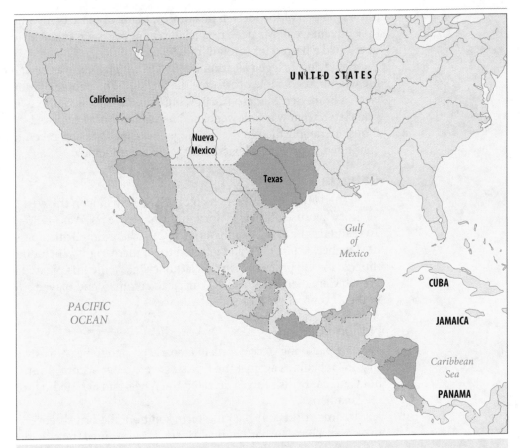

Mexico in 1821

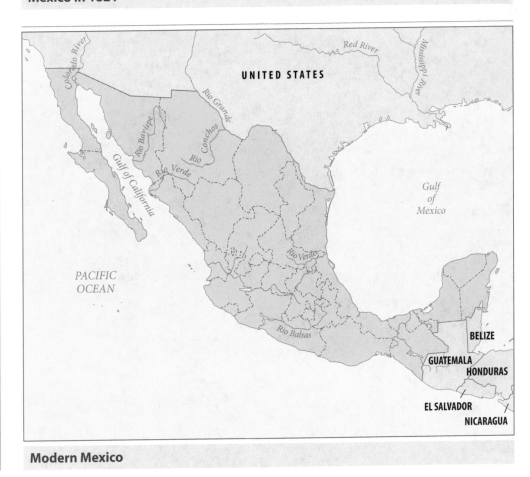

Modern Mexico

him as a pawn of the foreign businesses. Many of these companies took advantage of Mexico's financial weakness. As a result, Mexicans developed a hatred for foreign influences.

Following a rigged election in 1910 in which Díaz was declared the winner, the people overthrew the dictator. The people of Mexico elected Francisco Madero in 1911, but an assassin killed him two years later. Civil war followed, and an estimated nine hundred thousand people died in the fighting. Assassinations and revolutions continued to prolong Mexico's struggle for democracy.

Canada

Canada began as a French colony. The British won this vast territory because of their victory in the Seven Years' War (1756–63). To maintain the loyalty of the French Canadians, the British passed the Quebec Act in 1774 and granted them many rights, including the freedom to practice Roman Catholicism. While this pleased the French Canadians, it alarmed American colonials and played a role in their eventual War for Independence.

Nation Building

The pacifying of colonists in Canada proved to be short-lived. In 1837 rebellions against the British government occurred throughout Canada. British forces defeated the rebels and arrested hundreds of Canadians.

In order to establish a long-term solution, the British government sent Lord Durham to investigate. He examined the situation

Canada

in Canada and returned to Britain with a report. Durham recommended that Parliament grant the Canadians the right to govern themselves in domestic matters while Britain would control foreign dealings. He also recommended that Parliament unite the Canadian provinces. Parliament accepted the second recommendation and made this formal with the Act of Union in 1840.

The **British North America Act** in 1867 created the dominion of Canada with four provinces: Ontario, Quebec, New Brunswick, and Nova Scotia. The government established the province of Manitoba in 1870. British Columbia and Prince Edward Island became provinces in the 1870s. In 1905, Alberta and Saskatchewan also became provinces. Newfoundland and Labrador became the tenth province to join the Canadian Confederation in 1949.

Self-Government

In theory, a constitutional monarchy governs Canada. In fact, the British Crown serves as a merely symbolic head of government. The federal and provincial governments wield the actual power to govern. An elected House of Commons and an appointed Senate provide the Canadians with representation.

The party with a majority of seats in the House of Commons retains the legislative power to govern. To strengthen its influence, the party in power nominates its supporters as senators. The influence of the Senate becomes more noticeable when a new party wins a majority of seats. Then the ruling party nominates new senators to replace those appointed by the previous administration.

Section Quiz

1. List Latin American countries that developed some form of democracy.

2. What country invaded Mexico in the 1860s and set up a puppet ruler?

3. What act initially secured French Canadian loyalty to Britain?

4. What role does the British monarch play in Canadian government?

★ Why did many Latin American countries fail to develop stable governments?

★ Contrast the treatment of Canada and the American colonies by the British government.

CHAPTER REVIEW

■ Making Connections

1. Why did several European countries expel Karl Marx?

2. Why did the British temperance movement divide over supporting regulations to ban drinking alcohol?

3. What was the result of Britain's shifting toward a free trade economy?

4. Why did the British seek the right to use a secret ballot for elections?

5. How did German composer Richard Wagner demonstrate an anti-Semitic attitude?

6. Which type of painting would probably be more bright and colorful, romantic or realist? Why?

7. Describe Louis Pasteur's immense contribution to science.

8. What impact did Darwin's work have on the direction of science?

■ Developing History Skills

1. Based on the information in this chapter, draw a timeline that shows the development of Canada from British colony to self-governing nation. Provide the significance of each date.

2. Based on the information in previous chapters and this chapter, explain why Britain consistently enjoyed greater prosperity and political stability than France did.

■ Thinking Critically

1. Darwin struggled with the question of how a good God could design and sustain a world filled with pain and suffering. He resolved the question by proposing that God had little or nothing to do with the creation and maintaining of this world. How would you resolve this question according to the Bible?

2. The following is a famous quotation from Karl Marx. Evaluate this statement from a Christian worldview: "Religion is the sigh of the oppressed creature, the heart of a heartless world, and the soul of soulless conditions. It is the opium of the people. The abolition of religion . . . is the demand for [the people's] real happiness. To call on them to give up their illusions about their condition is to call on them to give up a condition that requires illusions."

■ Living in God's World

1. Divide into two groups. One group should create a story or piece of artwork according to the description of romanticism in this chapter. The second group should do the same according to the description of realism. Evaluate the creations as a class and review the elements of romanticism and realism. Note ways in which romanticism and realism may be used contrary to the Christian worldview and ways in which they may be compatible.

2. Sometimes Christians are attracted to socialism because of its emphasis on righting injustices. Imagine that you are an author for a Christian magazine tasked with explaining why socialism is not compatible with Scripture. Use the following Scripture passages as the basis for your article: Exodus 20:15; 21:33-35; Numbers 36; Proverbs 10:4; 12:24; 13:11, 18, 22; Acts 5:4; Galatians 6:10; James 1:27; 2:14-16.

Colonial Africa
1750 – 1950

15

- Transition from Trading Partner to Possession

- Partitioning of Africa for Imperialism

- Consequences of Imperialism

1810 – 1910

The Second French Colonial Empire begins with France's invasion of Algeria 1830

Robert Moffat begins missionary work in South Africa 1817

Samual Ajayi Crowther helps establish a mission in Nigeria 1843

1810	1820	1830	1840	1850

David Livingstone explores Africa 1840–73

Big Ideas

1. How did Africa transition to modern states?
2. Were European motives for the partitioning of Africa justified?
3. What were the consequences of European imperialism in Africa?

Africa, newly freed from the influence of the slave trade, made great strides in the second half of the nineteenth century. As long as outside forces did not interfere, many Africans were able to modernize their states and improve their way of life. However, by the end of the nineteenth century, European powers began to interfere in the development of the African states to take greater advantage of their resources. The conquest of one or more nations by another nation, known as **colonialism**, became Europe's goal in its quest to control Africa. In addition, the dominance and power asserted by one nation over less powerful nations, known as **imperialism**, became the accepted practice of Europe into the twentieth century.

John Africanus Horton's *West African Countries and Peoples* is published 1868

The Fante Confederation is formed in Ghana 1868

Belgian government takes control of the Belgian Congo from King Leopold 1884

European leaders divide Africa among themselves at the Berlin Conference 1885

Samuel Ajayi Crowther finishes work on African Bible translations 1891

Ethiopians reject colonization at the Battle of Adowa 1896

| 1870 | 1880 | 1890 | 1900 | 1910 |

Scramble for Africa 1880–1910

Guiding Questions

1. Why was there a rapid growth of African slavery between 1600 and 1800?

2. What led to the opening of the African interior?

3. How did Christians evangelize Africa?

■ I. Transition from Trading Partner to Possession

Growth of the Slave Trade

Before 1600, about two thousand slaves were captured each year by African raiders and taken from the coasts of Africa by Europeans. One hundred eighty years later, this wicked trade had expanded to over seventy thousand slaves per year. The settlement of the Americas was the major reason for this growth. (These numbers do not take into account the slaves taken by Middle Eastern slave traders for transit to Muslim countries.) European landowners developed large plantations throughout South America, the Caribbean, and North America, and they needed laborers to work the land.

Rather than farm the land themselves, many landowners enslaved Indians and forced them to work the land. When most of the Indians died or fled, Europeans turned to Africa for slave labor. They reasoned that the Africans were used to the hot climate and

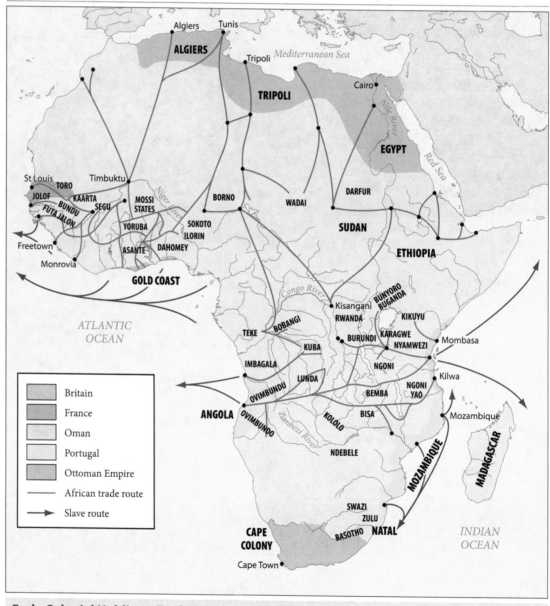

Early Colonial Holdings, Trade Routes, and Tribes

hard work. Many Europeans convinced themselves that the slave trade served as a respectable way to farm the land.

European slave traders (mostly from Britain, France, and Portugal) anchored their ships off the western coast of Africa to pick up their human cargoes. African raiders brought slaves from the interior to the coast. Held captive in chains, ropes, or yokes, the slaves were forced by the raiders to walk many miles to the coast.

After the harsh treatment received during the land journey, the slaves' sea voyage proved to be even worse. The traders crammed the slaves into their ships, which had decks too low to stand between and were often too crowded to move in. Sailors chained each slave to the ship to prevent his escape. For two months they lived—or died—in these hot, filthy quarters. At times they were allowed fresh air and exercise above deck, but in poor weather they were kept below with no fresh air. As many as 25 percent of these men, women, and children died before reaching the New World.

Africa had entered the nineteenth century with a few powerful leaders engaged in supplying slaves to European and Muslim nations. When Europeans stopped participating in this evil practice, African states found positive and productive ways to produce wealth.

Progress in Africa After the Slave Trade

As they had for centuries, several states in Africa maintained their independence during most of the nineteenth century. Kings and chiefs continued to rule over expanding states, and a modern Africa began to emerge.

Trade in slaves had ended along the coasts of Africa, thanks in large part to efforts of the British and their navy. Much of the African economy changed from selling slaves to providing raw materials needed by industrial countries. These materials included ivory, beeswax, honey, cotton, and rubber. Palm oil remained the leading export because industrial nations used it to lubricate their machines.

Justice

All people are required to obey God's law because of who He is. He has a right to command obedience from all people. In a similar way, all humans have rights and duties toward each other based on who they are as image bearers of God. God clearly states in Genesis 9 that humans have a right to life based on their position as bearers of the divine image. This entails the duty of not murdering humans. Humans also have right not to be enslaved, because stealing a man is stealing a life. Thus a duty exists not to steal humans or to buy stolen people. It is for this reason that God prescribed the same penalty for murdering a man as for stealing and selling him–death (Gen. 9:6; Ex. 21:16).

Tapping a rubber tree (left); *oil palm tree* (above); *oil palm tree fruit* (below)

Cocoa pod

Transition in Africa

The transition of the African economy brought many benefits. We will briefly examine a few of them.

Warfare and raiding of enemy tribes did not begin with the advent of slavery. However, the growing demand for slaves in the New World led to a great increase of both. When the British navy effectively ended the slave trade from western Africa around 1850, the warfare and raids declined significantly.

Powerful leaders of African tribes had controlled the slave trade and the wealth it generated. Once slavery ended, most Africans enjoyed an improved distribution of wealth. Since anyone could harvest the natural resources, many Africans took advantage of this opportunity. Known as a **gathering-based economy**, this change allowed more Africans access to the wealth that poured into Africa. Crops that could quickly be sold for cash included cocoa and peanuts (in addition to those mentioned above).

With the decline in warfare and the end of the slave trade, Africa experienced a steady increase in population. Tribes also gained a measure of stability. Peaceful conditions allowed the African tribes to settle rather than continue to migrate. One exception to this reduction in warfare occurred in areas of West Africa dominated by Islam, which spread primarily through jihad. Muslim rulers conquered their weaker neighbors and enforced the practice of Sharia (Muslim law).

In addition to the long history of trade and economic prosperity along the coasts of Africa, the internal or rural economy of Africa began to develop. As a result, more and more Africans experienced the benefits of trade.

Most important of all, according to noted African historian A. Adu Boahen, was the changed status of the African himself. After centuries of being treated as an object for sale, he claimed his place as a fellow human being and became a producer of merchandise to sell to others.

Unification of Africa

African commerce had been regional for centuries. For example, the coast bordering the Atlantic Ocean served as one market. The Mediterranean Sea formed another commercial region. Yet another centered on the coast bordering the Indian Ocean. However, during the nineteenth century these commercial routes merged and unified. This unification resulted in a large expansion of trade and brought great wealth to Africa and its people.

The old African empires were crumbling, but new ones were growing. As previously mentioned, some African states grew because of Islamic conquest. The Sokoto (in modern Nigeria) and Tukulor (in modern Mali) empires are two examples of Islamic expansion. In addition, nations such as Ethiopia and Egypt expanded by conquering neighboring states. However, even through conquest, Africa moved toward unification as these conquering states imposed a common language and culture on subject states.

Modernization of Africa
Industry

African states began to modernize by setting up factories. For example, Egypt developed textile and cotton mills. This nation also developed mills to process wood, make glass, and produce paper. Some African states also began to experiment with constitutional forms of government.

Military

Some African states in North and West Africa, including Morocco, Tunisia, and Ethiopia, began to modernize their armies in anticipation of possible threats from European nations. For example, **Menelik** of Ethiopia replaced his poorly trained volunteer army with well-equipped and well-trained soldiers. He also built factories to build modern military equipment. West African general **Samori Ture** also developed a modern army with current weapons to defend the **Wassoulou** Empire.

Education and Representation in Africa

Many Africans gained access to education and insisted on a voice in their governments. Some struggles led to violence, while other areas transitioned without bloodshed. For example, states on the West Coast of Africa won representation without violence.

The **Fante Confederation** formed along the coast in Ghana in 1868. This African organization, led by African pastors and teachers, provides an excellent example of Africans working to maintain self-rule and improve the lives of their people. The confederation produced a constitution that reflected a spirit of cooperation, promoted male and female education, and advocated the development of African resources to benefit Africans.

The goals of this organization were progressive. For example, its educational objectives included technical training in addition to a basic education for all African children. Members of this confederation also promoted the development of self-reliant citizens. Finally, this organization supported cooperation between educated Africans, who tended to abandon traditions, and those who retained African traditions. Sadly, conflict with the British and the Asante Empire (located in central Ghana) destroyed the possible attainment of these lofty goals.

Opening the Interior

The interior of Africa, or the regions inland from the coasts, became more accessible to the world during the second half of the nineteenth century because of at least two factors. First, tribes from the interior increased trade with other African states. Second, European exploration dramatically increased knowledge of and interest in the African interior.

Increased Trade

As previously stated, cash crops provided a growing income for many Africans. As a result, African states that had not previously engaged in trade began to do so. Natural resources increased in value as demand increased. Increased trade and economic opportunity spread into the heart of the African continent.

European Exploration

Many Europeans explored Africa in search of answers to a number of questions. For example, Sir Richard Burton searched for the answer to a mystery that began in ancient Egypt: the elusive source

Samori Ture

Citizenship

Education is an essential element for informed citizen participation in government. When African Christians and Christian missionaries educated Africans, they were laying the groundwork for more stable and democratic governments in the future for those regions.

British Intrusion

Even as the Fante Confederation was forming, the British were determined to gain control over portions of the Gold Coast in West Africa. To solidify these gains, they purchased a Dutch fort along the coast. However, the Asante Empire had worked in cooperation with the Dutch and used this region to gain access to the coast. The British intrusion threatened Asante trade. The Asante responded by invading this region. The British dispatched well-trained soldiers and eventually forced the Africans to retreat. British forces seized control of this region in Ghana in 1873. This seizure by Britain forced the Asante Empire to submit to British control. It also effectively ended the Fante Confederation.

David Livingstone

Robert Moffat

Victoria Falls

of the Nile. He and another explorer concluded that the Nile originated in a lake called *Ukerewe* or *Nalubaale* by the Africans. Burton's former associate later named the lake Victoria in honor of Queen Victoria.

The most famous European explorer in Africa during the nineteenth century was **David Livingstone** (1813–1873). Born in Scotland, he arrived in South Africa in 1840 and traveled throughout Africa until his death in 1873. His few trips to Great Britain allowed him to set before Europe the need for missionaries in Africa.

Livingstone ventured inland to places no known European had ever visited. He followed the Zambezi River and discovered the falls that the Africans called *Mosi-oa-Tunya* (the Smoke that Thunders). Other Europeans named these falls **Victoria Falls**.

Livingstone also traveled to Lake Tanganyika, and it was there in 1871 that **Henry Stanley**, a Welsh reporter, found him. The *New York Herald* newspaper had sent Stanley to find Livingstone after he had been out of contact for several months. Livingstone later died near this lake. Livingstone's African companions buried his heart in Africa. Then they took Livingstone's preserved body to the coast. The British returned it to England for burial in Westminster Abbey.

Early Christian Outreach

Europe's initial missionary outreaches did not include Africa. Instead, early mission societies focused on recruiting missionaries for India and China. However, despite a slow beginning, British Christians played a great role in evangelizing Africa.

British Missionaries

Scottish-born **Robert Moffat** became one of the earliest missionaries from the British Empire to serve in Africa. At the age of eighteen, Moffat came into contact with Methodist laymen. After weeks of searching the Bible for answers, he trusted Christ for salvation in 1816. Shortly after his conversion, Moffat decided to serve abroad as a missionary. In 1817 Moffat landed in South Africa and began a ministry that spanned fifty-three years. His fiancée joined

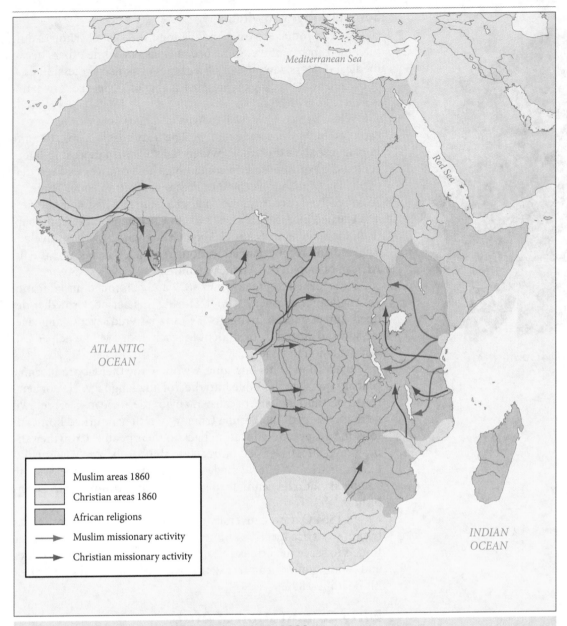

The Spread of Islam and Christianity 1860–1900

him in South Africa two years later. They were married in December 1819.

Moffat took the gospel to many tribes and established a mission that became a way station for later missionaries. He established friendships with several tribal leaders and worked to bring peace to the area. Moffat also translated the Bible and other works into one of the African languages. His work continued to the next generation when his daughter, Mary, married David Livingstone.

In response to the plea for workers from men like Moffat and Livingstone, many more missionaries took up the work in Africa. In addition, new missionary societies formed with the specific goal of recruiting missionaries for Africa. These men and women trusted God to deliver them from the many dangers in Africa while they worked among the various African tribes. In addition to sharing the gospel, missionaries established schools, provided medical care, and trained Africans in a variety of occupations.

Samuel Ajayi Crowther

Samuel Ajayi Crowther

Africa produced a long and distinguished list of scholars during the nineteenth century. Some became pastors, while others became medical doctors, lawyers, or other types of skilled professionals. One of the most fascinating biographies is that of a Nigerian boy named Ajayi (c. 1809–1891).

When he was only twelve, Ajayi and his whole village were captured by Muslim slave raiders. The Muslims then sold them to Portuguese slave traders. Providentially, a British navy ship intercepted the Portuguese ship containing these captives and rescued them. The British took them to Freetown, Sierra Leone. There Ajayi received care from the Anglican Church Missionary Society and learned English. He converted to Christianity and, upon baptism, took the name **Samuel Ajayi Crowther**. Crowther traveled to England and received an education. Years later, he became the first African bishop in the Anglican Church.

He returned to Freetown in 1827 and continued his education at an Anglican missionary school. During this period, Crowther developed a great interest in linguistics and mastered several languages. He soon advanced from student to teacher. In 1843 he helped establish a mission in Nigeria.

In addition to his missionary work, Crowther labored for many years to translate the Bible into the **Yoruba** language. He concentrated on this language because many of the Africans at Freetown were members of the Yoruba tribe. When they returned home, they took the gospel and education back to their people. Crowther also promoted an African-led outreach to the Yoruba and, eventually, to all of Africa. While he made great progress in his endeavors, the Anglican Church eventually decided to replace him with a European bishop.

In 1864 Oxford University recognized Crowther's great contribution to Africa by giving him a Doctor of Divinity degree. He continued to serve in various roles, including overseeing the production and refining of African translations of the Bible, until shortly before his death in 1891.

Early Colonization of Africa

Initial European colonization of Africa involved setting up colonies on uninhabited islands to establish trade with mainland Africa. Over time, European nations began to lay claim to more coastal territory in Africa. Portugal, Britain, and France established some of the earliest coastal settlements in Africa.

Portugal

In Chapter 7 you learned that Portugal was one of the first European states to sail around Africa and visit port cities in East Africa. While Portugal lacked the ability to develop into a major power, the Portuguese retained control of these coastal settlements and profited from the ongoing trade. Portugal claimed territory in the southern regions of West Africa and East Africa.

Britain

In Chapter 10 you learned that Britain expanded its exploration following the loss of the American colonies in the eighteenth century. In addition to major discoveries in the South Pacific, British explorers established trade colonies in West Africa. Early British trade with Africa primarily involved slaves. British ships transported about three and one-half million African slaves to the Americas and the British Caribbean. When the British ended this terrible practice, African raw materials grew into a large and profitable industry for British merchants. The expanding Industrial Revolution provided a growing demand for several of these raw materials.

France

In the eighteenth century, the British frustrated and ultimately ended early attempts by the French to establish their first colonial empire. However, the French viewed themselves as a world power, and a world power must have colonies. As a result, the **Second French Colonial Empire** began in 1830 with the invasion of Algeria in North Africa. However, the Algerians resisted for several years before French forces triumphed. Another fifty years passed before France acquired additional territory in Africa. France's renewed efforts to colonize had a catastrophic effect on Africa.

Section Quiz

1. What did Africans transition to for income following the abolition of the slave trade?

2. Why were African tribes able to settle in one place rather than be forced to migrate?

3. What unified Africa prior to European colonization?

4. What language did many of the Africans in Freetown speak?

★ How did David Livingstone contribute to the growth of missions in Africa?

★ Who do you think was more effective in evangelizing Africans: Samuel Ajayi Crowther or David Livingstone? Explain your answer.

■ II. Partitioning of Africa for Imperialism

Between 1880 and 1910, Africa went from a continent filled with many independent, sovereign states to forty artificially created colonies subject to European control. In a brief span of time, the Africans lost their freedom to govern and make independent decisions.

In 1879 several events occurred in rapid succession, triggering a rapid conquest and partitioning of Africa. The French made the first move by sending three French groups to determine routes for a trans-Saharan railway. Then the French appointed a commander in North Africa to expand French interests farther inland. King Leopold of Belgium and the French made the next move by sending diplomats to secure treaties with the African tribes in the Congo basin.

Since Britain and Portugal had previously laid claim to this region, these moves created great alarm. Continued expansion by France and Belgium resulted in claims by Britain and other European states. Soon, almost all of Africa came under European domination.

European Motives

Today it is difficult to understand why the Europeans would treat Africans in such a harsh way. However, the Europeans did not

Guiding Questions

1. Were the European motives for imperialism justified?

2. What were the three phases of the Scramble for Africa?

3. How did Africans react to the forced colonization of Africa?

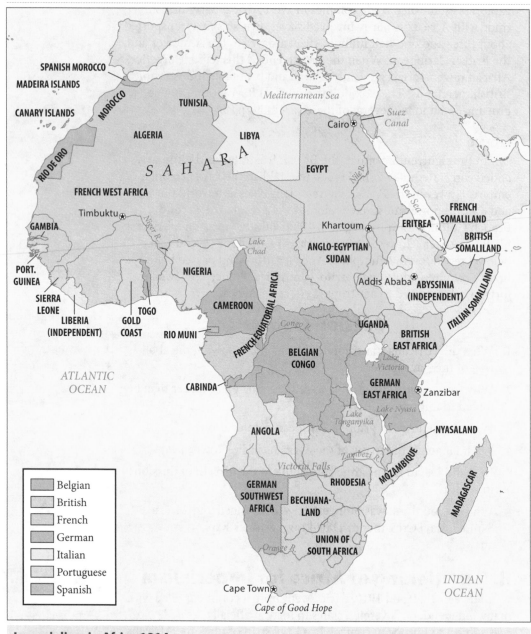

Imperialism in Africa 1914

Motives for Colonialism

Describe the various motives for colonialism and evaluate them from Scripture.

Motive	Description	Biblical Evaluation
Economic		
Nationalistic		
Religious		
Racist		

see themselves as behaving cruelly or unjustly. Their motives conditioned them to see the colonization of Africa as good. Understanding these motives enables the Christian to evaluate the reasoning that led to this behavior.

Economic

Because of the Industrial Revolution and free trade policies, international trade grew rapidly. As more European nations fostered a growth in industry, competition for foreign markets increased.

Nations reacted to the increased competition by abandoning free trade. To protect their markets from lower priced foreign goods, they raised tariffs. This increased the price of foreign goods, but it also hindered trade between nations. These shortsighted responses to competition created a demand for colonies that European states could force to buy European products and support the European economies.

The increasing need for raw materials also made control of resources in Africa appealing to the European states. Africa already supplied a growing quantity of raw materials to industrialized Europe. However, European powers decided that Europeans could better manage Africa's resources and increase their profits by taking direct control.

In addition, industrialists and investors in Europe enjoyed a quickly rising amount of profit (capital). As the Industrial Revolution produced greater wealth, investors sought new places to invest these funds in order to continue to increase their profits. Africa appeared to present a vast potential for great economic profit. Whether the Africans had a say in this seemed to be unimportant to government officials and entrepreneurs.

Nationalistic

Nineteenth-century Europe displayed an exaggerated spirit of nationalism. This extreme sentiment was especially dominant in the recently unified states of Germany and Italy. These nations were barely a decade old when they set out to prove themselves worthy of being world powers. Colonization of regions in Africa provided them an excellent opportunity to compete with the established European powers.

You may remember from previous chapters that France had suffered from internal and international defeats. The latest humiliating defeat by Germany in 1870 left France desperate for a victory. French pride was at stake, and the conquest of African states provided France with a way to regain its standing in the world.

Religious

Some people, especially in Britain, viewed colonialism as a way to open Africa for expanded evangelistic outreach. For some people, evangelization simply provided religious cover for sinful treatment of the Africans. Others genuinely saw colonialism as a way to spread the gospel but were blinded to the negative aspects of colonialism.

Some missionaries–especially those who were not sent by a state church–opposed colonialism. They were often in conflict with the colonial rulers. Because the missionaries lived among the Africans, they often developed close relationships with them and tried to understand life from the Africans' point of view. As a result, these missionaries protested the ill treatment of Africans by colonial rulers.

Whether colonialism was helping or hindering evangelism, the colonial era was a time of great missionary advance. By the end of the nineteenth century, almost six thousand British missionaries had traveled to foreign lands under British control. Many of these missionaries were in Africa.

Racist

Tragically, many Europeans used the lie that Europeans were superior to the African race to justify colonialism and imperialism. As Darwin's theory of evolution became more popular, it offered support for the idea that some people groups were more advanced than others. Using Darwin's theory of the survival of the fittest, Europeans assumed they were part of a superior race. This attitude of superiority was reflected in some of the literature of the day, such as Rudyard Kipling's poem "The White Man's Burden," which asserted the white man's obligation to civilize the "heathen."

King Leopold of Belgium

Leopold had tried using his family fortune to purchase existing, undeveloped colonies in Africa from other European countries. However, his efforts failed.

Leopold then took advantage of pleas by men like Livingstone "to heal the open sore of Africa" from its slave trade and spiritual darkness. He played the role of a humanitarian (one concerned for human welfare). His motives, however, were anything but noble.

Leopold hosted a convention of explorers in 1876 and offered to help pay for the cost of exploration. He also encouraged investments by other countries in an organization called the **International African Association (IAA)**, but he retained control of the organization as president.

Europeans initially saw Leopold as the leader of the crusade against slavery. The fact that he used his own money led others to call him a great humanitarian. Leopold had finally gotten access to Africa. By 1882 Leopold owned the company that resulted from the IAA. His questionable actions began to make the other European nations nervous.

Investors in the IAA later found that Leopold encouraged the harsh treatment and torture of African workers (slaves) on his plantations. Leopold's detestable actions caused an outcry that persuaded the Belgian government to take control of the territory itself in 1908. The territory in the interior of Africa along the Congo River was called the **Belgian Congo**.

John Africanus Horton

Many African scholars sought to challenge this prejudice against Africans. For example, **John Africanus Horton** disproved the claims that the black man was racially inferior. His work *West African Countries and Peoples: A Vindication of the African Race*, published in 1868, argued that different stages of civilization had nothing to do with race.

The Scramble

As previously stated, the French and Belgians began to lay claim to African territory. They also pressured African states to sign treaties giving the Europeans exclusive rights to trade and mining. In response, the rush for European conquest of Africa was set in motion. In what is known as the **Scramble for Africa**, or the Race for Africa, European nations advanced in three phases to control the continent. By the end of the third phase, all but two African states (Liberia and Ethiopia) had lost their independence and had become the possessions of European powers.

Phase One

This phase began when Europeans convinced African rulers to sign treaties with a particular European state. On the surface, these treaties reserved trade and natural resources solely for that European power. In exchange, the Europeans often promised to protect the African peoples from enemy attack. Those promises, however, were empty and were merely a means of deception in order to gain exclusive access to an African state. Lord Lugard, an enthusiastic British agent of the British East Africa Company, made an incriminating note in his diary about these treaties.

> No man if he understood would sign it, and to say that a savage chief has been told that he cedes all rights to the company in exchange for nothing is an obvious untruth. If he had been told that the [British East African] Company will protect him against his enemies, and share in his wars as an ally, he has been told a lie, for the Company have no idea of doing any such things and no force to do it with if they wished.

Often the African rulers signed documents they could not read and surrendered control of their states without realizing it. Some were willing to sign because they faced great threats on their borders and believed the European state would provide them with a valuable ally.

However, some African rulers refused to sign treaties. For example, African king **Macemba** of the Yao tribe wrote to the German authorities who pressured him to submit to a treaty. Macemba eloquently explained that he saw no need to submit to their pressure. He expressed a desire for friendship with Germany but rejected any thought of subjection. Macemba even cautioned that he was prepared to fight to protect the freedom of his people rather than meekly bow to German demands.

Phase Two

To make sure the jostling for territory in Africa did not lead to war, representatives of European nations met with each other to work out agreements. They signed treaties that defined their regions of interest and agreed on boundaries to avoid conflict. They signed

Berlin Conference

these treaties in Europe with no Africans present. Therefore, Africans remained unaware of the existence of these treaties and their dreadful consequences.

Several European powers established key agreements by 1885 at the **Berlin Conference**. They agreed to allow unrestricted access to the Niger and Congo Rivers for the free flow of trade. But they also carved up the continent of Africa with no regard to the wishes of Africans.

African Reaction

Phase three began with the arrival of ships and troops off the coast of African states. Though the Europeans had carefully planned this phase, the Africans received little or no advance warning of this invasion and conquest by European powers. We will examine three broad responses by the Africans, understanding that they varied over time, depending on a number of circumstances.

Submission

Some African leaders immediately recognized they could not protect their people through armed resistance. They chose to protect their people by submitting. Given the modern weapons of the Europeans, most Africans would have been slaughtered had they chosen to fight. Some submitted with no thought of eventual resistance, while others did so either to buy time and seek a peaceful resolution or to prepare for an armed resistance.

Alliance

Other African leaders accepted European forces and saw them as a means of protection from hostile neighbors or internal forces that threatened their rule. Often the Europeans would allow a ruler

Samori Ture's Resistance

Samori Ture had established a Muslim empire in West Africa. When the French attempted to take control of his land, he resisted and defeated them in many battles. However, he realized that he could not overcome the French completely, so he signed a treaty with them in 1886. Despite signing the treaty, the French continued to undermine Ture's rule. Ture spent two years preparing for one major battle to defeat the French. Despite heroic efforts, Ture's men could not defeat the well-equipped French forces. Following a move by the British to establish a new empire on the Ivory Coast and Ghana, Ture set out to form an alliance with other African states. British and French forces responded by moving against Ture, capturing him in 1898. He died in captivity two years later.

Power

European nations were able to subdue African nations because technology and organization gave the Europeans greater power. Possession of this power was not wrong. It was gained through living out the Creation Mandate. But in a fallen world, the God-given abilities can be put to evil purpose. Sadly, many European nations claimed Christianity as their religion. In their colonial dealings, however, they failed to observe Christianity's foremost ethical teachings: "Love thy neighbor as thyself" (Matt. 22:39) and "whatsoever ye would that men should do to you, do ye even so to them" (Matt. 7:12).

to maintain a semblance of power in order to gain the cooperation of the people. Some African leaders embraced an alliance with Europeans with the hope that their place on the throne would remain secure.

Unfortunately, the Africans often discovered that these alliances offered them no protection at all. Some European powers made promises to the ruler of an African state while supporting his enemies at the same time. This treachery left some African leaders no option but to submit or confront the European forces. Some committed suicide rather than embrace either of these choices.

Confrontation

Many African states chose to confront the European forces who demanded control of their land and resources. This confrontation took two forms, and African leaders used one form or the other depending on the situation at hand.

Diplomacy was the more restrained form of confrontation. African leaders negotiated with the Europeans to try to maintain as much control over their land as possible. Some sent diplomats to Britain or one of the other European nations to seek a solution that would preserve African independence. The European powers often refused to meet with these diplomats or proceeded to invade the African nation even as they met with the African diplomats. Diplomacy only worked to the extent that Africans were able to slow down the process of colonization.

Other African tribes resorted to armed resistance as soon as they realized the Europeans' true intentions. Muslim rulers were determined not to submit to rule by the infidel Europeans. They offered stiff resistance and died in large numbers because of the advanced weapons used by the Europeans. With few exceptions, even the most advanced African forces still used flintlock weapons, while the Europeans returned fire with rapid-firing guns like the **Maxim gun.** Often, a small European force could defeat a much larger African force because of their technological advantage in weapons.

Technological Advances

Transportation, including railroads and roads, could be used to enhance trade or to move troops and supplies where they were needed to suppress rebellion. Communication methods included telegraph and telephone lines to rapidly issue instructions for a purchase or sale. They could also quickly transmit battle plans and alarms when resistance was discovered. Superior European technology effectively suppressed the Africans.

Flintlock musket

Early Maxim gun

Section Quiz

1. What two recently unified nations quickly joined the race to colonize Africa?

2. Which European leader used the pretense of humanitarianism to gain access to territory in Africa?

3. In phase one, what did the European states use to establish claims in Africa?

4. Why didn't the Africans object to the treaties signed between the European states in phase two?

★   Complete the graphic organizer on page 270. Evaluate each motive for colonialism based on the following Scripture passages: Economic: Matt 7:12; 22:39; Nationalistic: Ps. 56:1-2; Prov. 15:25; Religious: Rom. 1:5, 16; Acts 9:15-16; Racist: Gen. 1:26-28; Acts 17:26.

★   How did Europeans use technology to subjugate Africa?

■ III. Consequences of Imperialism

While it is easy to condemn European imperialism, evaluating the actual results is a bit more complicated. Europeans can take little or no credit for any positive results of imperialism. It would not be an exaggeration to state that most of the positive results of European imperialism were accidental rather than intentional. However, there were positive results mixed in with many negative results. The Christian should not be surprised to find that God can bring good things out of the worst actions of fallen man.

Political

Evaluating the political consequences is like unwinding the many strands that compose a cable. Some strands were positive, while others brought terrible long-term consequences. Together, they form the political consequences that resulted from colonialism and imperialism.

Peace and Stability—At a Price

Over time, European forces captured or killed the leaders of rebellions. Weapons were confiscated, and armed resistance declined. New African leaders emerged who had no choice but to work within the system to benefit their people. As long as the African leaders submitted to European control, African states experienced a temporary peace and stability. However, Africans paid a great price for this artificial tranquility: the loss of their freedom.

Formation of New African States

Gradually, over fifty new African states emerged from colonial rule. While this appeared to be an improvement over the hundreds of tribes that existed before, these divisions were artificial states. Europeans often drew boundaries on maps with little regard for the actual location of tribes. As a result, they divided tribes or combined segments of various tribes at the stroke of a pen and without African input. Europeans often thrust together groups that had little in common and even spoke different languages. These differences led to unrest in several of the states, especially as they gained independence in the twentieth century.

Development of Political Organization

European powers did succeed in establishing bureaucracies of civil servants needed to manage and govern the African states. The British system produced well-trained and effective civil servants. The French proved to be much less successful in developing civil servants. However, the Portuguese had the dubious distinction of producing the worst-trained civil servants of any European colonial power. A bureaucratic structure proved beneficial to African states as they later gained their independence.

Another positive development for African states was the formation of modern judicial systems. These have undergone very little change since their formation and have been very successful.

Development of Professional Armies

Prior to the colonial period, few African states had armies; those they had were often poorly trained volunteers. However, that situation changed dramatically when Europeans took control of African states. They trained professional armies to control the population and put down armed resistance. Tragically, these armies became a chronic source of instability, confusion, and anarchy that continues in some African states today.

Delayed Development

At the time of European colonization and imperialism, many African states were in the process of developing into modern countries. Some had made much progress, and others were just beginning to develop. However, European conquest effectively ended the natural development of modern states in Africa.

In addition, the loss of sovereignty and independence had a long-term negative effect on the African states. At least two generations of Africans grew up under the control of Europeans and had

Two Major States that Withstood European Conquest

Joseph Jenkins Roberts served as president of Liberia from 1848 to 1856 and again from 1872 to 1876. He combined protection afforded by the United States with wise diplomacy to preserve Liberian independence.

Menelik, king of Ethiopia, refused to submit to Italian demands. When he had exhausted efforts to negotiate with the Italians, he prepared for battle by importing thousands of rifles and several cannon. At the battle of Adowa, 100,000 well-trained and well-armed Ethiopians easily defeated the 17,000- man Italian force. The Ethiopians killed or wounded nearly 40 percent of the Italian army in this decisive battle in January 1896.

Joseph Jenkins Roberts

Menelik

no experience in self-government. Much of the progress made by their parents and grandparents was lost and forgotten.

Under European control, the Africans became isolated from the rest of the world. European nations limited all economic and political activity with other countries. These restrictions prevented the normal development of African states for many years.

Economic

The economic consequences of European control of African states produced mixed results. Clearly, there were positive results, but even these often had negative aspects. Other results had no redeeming qualities.

Positive

The Europeans built a modern **infrastructure** in Africa. They laid thousands of miles of track for railroads and built many miles of roads. In addition, the Europeans strung miles of wire for telegraph and, later, telephone communication.

While the Africans were already harvesting natural resources, the Europeans introduced improved farming methods and greatly increased production of many natural products. The railroads and roads enabled much larger harvests to be delivered to markets.

The Europeans also brought with them an understanding of the value of land. The Africans learned that the vast lands of Africa served as a great asset. As a result, the value of land in Africa increased dramatically.

Africans were already developing cash crops. European management techniques simply improved and elevated this agriculture to a new level. European control also hastened the decline of the traditional barter-based economy. It was quickly replaced with a money-based economy.

Finally, along with a money-based economy, the Europeans introduced Africans to modern concepts of banking. This system, along with other contributions, became a great asset to the African states as they regained their freedom from European control.

Negative

Even though the Europeans brought a modern infrastructure to Africa, they established it to benefit themselves rather than the Africans. As a result, the Europeans distributed transportation and communication improvements unevenly. Some areas experienced great improvements in their infrastructure while areas that were of no interest to the Europeans received no improvements.

In addition, when the Europeans carved Africa into manageable regions, the result was an uneven development of regional economies. Some regions had access to the coast, rich mineral deposits, and other natural resources. Others were landlocked and had access to few natural resources. These arbitrary decisions left some African states with little opportunity to prosper.

Even though the Europeans brought industry and technology to Africa, they denied Africans the opportunity to develop industry and technology on their own. This had a long-term effect of hindering natural African development in these areas.

Another problem developed as the Europeans forced the people to concentrate on growing cash crops rather than food to feed their

Giraffe

Elephants

277

Historical Perspectives: Missions and the Colonies

The role of Christian missions during colonization and imperialism is often viewed negatively by historians. Some authors link missions work with racism. One high-school textbook, next to the label "racism" reads, "The sense of moral duty and cultural superiority there was not limited to missionaries." Another notes that some Europeans felt a "duty to civilize the inferior races," which "included bringing Christianity to the heathen." While these books acknowledge the benefits of education and even efforts to soften colonial rule, they frown upon the attempt to impose foreign Christian values like monogamous marriage on peoples with their own morality and customs.

Richard W. Bulliet, et al., *The Earth and Its Peoples: A Global History*, 5th ed. (Boston: Wadsworth, 2011), 772-73.

Robert W. Strayer, *Ways of the World: A Global History with Sources*, 2nd ed. (Boston: Bedford/St. Martin's, 2013), 884, 905-7.

Noted sociologist Robert Woodberry set out to determine if there was a link between democracy and Protestantism and spent years sifting through historical records. He concluded that the "impact of missions on global democracy was huge," and he had the research and statistics to prove his claim. According to Woodberry, "Areas where Protestant missionaries had a significant presence in the past are on average more economically developed today, with comparatively better health, lower infant mortality, lower corruption, greater literacy, higher educational attainment (especially for

women), and more robust membership in non-governmental associations." In addition, he found that missionaries of independent churches tended to oppose injustice practiced by colonial powers. For instance, missionaries smuggled pictures out of the Congo to raise public awareness of horrible abuses taking place there. Missionaries in South Africa spearheaded an agreement that protected the peoples in what is now Botswana from further European land grabs.

Andrea Palpant Dilley, "The Surprising Discovery about Those Colonialist, Proselytizing Missionaries," *Christianity Today*, January 8, 2014.

Robert D. Woodberry and Timothy S. Shah, "The Pioneering Protestants," *Journal of Democracy* 15, no. 2 (April 2004): 47-61.

Robert D. Woodberry, "The Shadow of Empire: Christian Missions, Colonial Policy and Democracy in Postcolonial Societies," PhD diss. (Chapel Hill, NC: University of North Carolina, 2004).

Which view looked at the actions and results of the missionaries themselves? Which view looked primarily at European thought at the time? Which approach is likely to give a better understanding of the missionaries' own views?

1. Why is racism and a sense of cultural superiority wrong?

2. Why is it wrong to assume that all cultural customs and moral views are equally valid?

3. Why would certain Christian mission endeavors result in benefits that reach far beyond the original goals of the missionaries?

people. The Europeans imported food from other areas to supply the Africans' dietary needs. Unfortunately, Africans have found it difficult to change their agricultural practices and instead continue to depend on other nations to provide food for their people.

Furthermore, as we learned earlier in the chapter, the African states had developed a maturing inter-African trade before the colonization of Africa. European colonization effectively ended this trade, and African states have yet to restore it.

Finally, European colonization resulted in great wealth for European investors. These investors, however often took their wealth back to Europe rather than reinvesting it in Africa. As a result, Europeans left Africa with an underdeveloped and underfunded economic system.

Social

European colonization and imperialism also brought social consequences. As with other aspects of European control, some results were positive. Others created long-term problems for Africans.

Positive

After an initial decline, Africa began to experience a significant population growth. The initial decline was due to contact with

European diseases and armed conflict with European forces. But as violent resistance subsided, African population growth rebounded.

In addition, villages grew into towns, and towns expanded into cities. Under European control, Africa experienced significant urbanization. This development proved to be an important long-term contribution to Africa.

In some African states, especially those controlled by the British, Europeans encouraged the spread of religion and education. In addition to proclaiming the gospel, missionaries also provided most of the education for the Africans.

Finally, African historian Adu Boahen notes that European colonization created a new social order based on merit and achievement. Prior to European control, many Africans based their social order on birth. Under European management, Africans who worked hard and cooperated with the system could advance and gain promotion.

Negative

Although the Europeans urbanized Africa, they also created a large gap between the urban and the rural areas. The urban areas had access to most of the modern infrastructure, while the rural areas remained undeveloped. African cities also had most of the medical facilities and schools. The Europeans constructed few of these facilities outside the urban areas.

In addition, Europeans tended to downgrade the status of African women. Europeans built more educational facilities for boys than for girls. Lacking equal educational opportunities, women could not gain access to many professions, including medicine, law, and civil service. The colonial world favored men, while the women were restricted to menial tasks.

Finally, Europeans, including many missionaries, condemned everything African. They opposed African names, music, art, and anything else that originated in Africa. They even forced the Africans to wear European-style clothing. These measures disrupted the cultural development of Africa.

Section Quiz

1. What was the price of African peace and stability during the colonial period?
2. Which European nation produced the most well-trained civil servants?
3. Why did the development of African professional armies produce long-term problems for African states?
4. What new social order did the Europeans establish in Africa?
* Why did European formation of new African states create many problems?
* Evaluate the modern infrastructure established in Africa by European states.

CHAPTER REVIEW

People, Places, and Things to Know

colonialism
imperialism
gathering-based economy
Menelik
Samori Ture
Wassoulou
Fante Confederation
David Livingstone
Victoria Falls
Henry Stanley
Robert Moffat
Samuel Ajayi Crowther
Yoruba
Second French Colonial Empire
International African Association (IAA)
Belgian Congo
John Africanus Horton
Scramble for Africa
Macemba
Berlin Conference
Maxim gun
infrastructure

■ Making Connections

1. Distinguish colonialism from imperialism.
2. Why did Menelik of Ethiopia establish a modern army?
3. Why did the efforts of the Fante Confederation abruptly end?
4. Why did Samuel Ajayi Crowther labor for years to translate the Bible into the Yoruba language?
5. How did the abandoning of free trade contribute to the pressure to colonize Africa?
6. How did France's struggle to regain national glory play a role in the colonization of Africa?
7. What impact did Darwin's work have on the justification of colonialism and imperialism?
8. How did King Leopold of Belgium take advantage of calls "to heal the open sore of Africa"?

■ Developing History Skills

1. Based on the information in this chapter, draw a timeline that shows important events outlined in this chapter. Provide the significance of each date.
2. Evaluate this excerpt from a letter to the British by a king of an African state in northern Ghana. What did he desire to gain by signing this treaty?

> Tell my friend, the Governor of Accra, I like his friendship, I like a man who is not a foolish man. I like a man who is truthful. Tell my friend I like my country to be quiet and secure; I want to keep off all my enemies and none be able to stand before me. . . . Let plenty guns, flint, powder and cloth, and every kind of cost goods be sent here for sale. I want a rare magnificent cloth myself to put on. Tell him also to send for sale here those short small guns firing many times [revolvers].

■ Thinking Critically

1. Evaluate European colonialism in light of the Ten Commandments in Exodus 20. Link each of your points to the relevant commandment and give the Bible reference.
2. Given the European rejection of everything African, evaluate how the biography of Samuel Ajayi Crowther may reflect this bias.

■ Living in God's World

1. Imagine that you are a modern missionary to an African country. Do a research report that investigates the culture of that country. Discuss aspects of that culture that need to be challenged by the Bible. What aspects of the culture are perhaps more in line with Scripture than Western culture is?

2. Imagine that you were a Christian journalist from Europe who was covering the Congo during the Scramble. Write a report of what you observed.

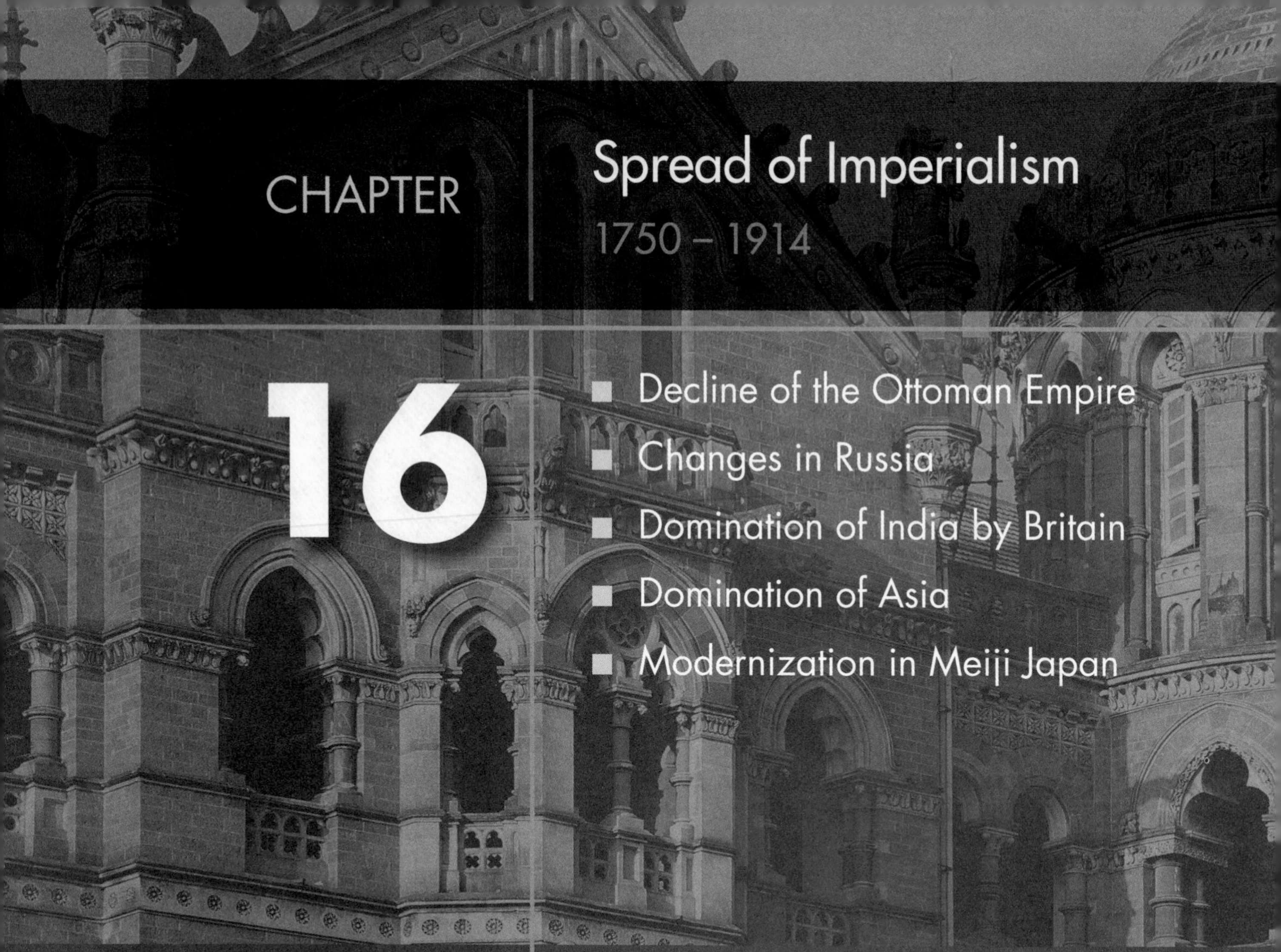

CHAPTER

Spread of Imperialism
1750 – 1914

16

- Decline of the Ottoman Empire
- Changes in Russia
- Domination of India by Britain
- Domination of Asia
- Modernization in Meiji Japan

1750 – 1900

Decembrist Revolt in Russia 1825 ▪

Nicholas I becomes the czar of Russia 1825

Charter Act gives the British crown control of all ▪
British East India Company possessions 1814

Napoleon invades Russia 1812 ▪

Alexander I becomes the czar of Russia 1801 ▪

Seven Years' War between England
and France 1756–63

Napoleon invades Egypt 1798 ▪

1750	1775	1800

Battle of Plassey breaks France's
▪ strength in India 1757

Mahmud II rules the Ottoman
Empire and lays the foundation
for modern Turkey 1808–39

Big Ideas

1. How did the Ottoman Empire respond to the challenges of territorial loss and imperialism?
2. Why did Russian reform fail to address the nation's problems?
3. What were the consequences of European imperialism in India?
4. How did China's Qing dynasty respond to economic and political crises?
5. How did Japan transform into a modern nation-state?

In the last chapter you learned about western European imperialism in Africa. This chapter reveals that regions of eastern Europe and Asia were also victims of empire building. Russia and Japan sought to expand their territory at the expense of other established nations. Old empires crumbled and new ones emerged during the nineteenth century.

Treaty of Kanagawa between America and Japan 1854

Alexander III becomes the czar of Russia 1881

Hundred Days' Reform in China 1898

Crimean War 1854–55

Boxer Rebellion begins 1899

Alexander II becomes the czar of Russia 1855

Opium Wars between China and Britain begin 1842

Sepoy Mutiny in India 1857–58

Russo-Japanese War 1904–5

1850   **1875**   **1900**

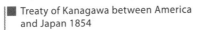

Taiping Rebellion in China 1851–64

Guiding Questions

1. Why was the Ottoman Empire forced to retreat from the Balkans and the Black Sea region?
2. What did the French invasion of Egypt in 1798 reveal?
3. What modern nation emerged from a declining Ottoman Empire?

Crimean War (1854–55)

Russian expansion threatened the balance of power in Europe. European nations, including Britain, sided with the Ottoman Empire in the Crimean War in 1854 to stop the increase of Russian influence in this region.

■ I. Decline of the Ottoman Empire

At its height, the Ottoman Empire had ruled a vast kingdom that spanned three continents. The Ottomans controlled large regions of southeastern Europe and western Asia as well as areas in North Africa. However, by the beginning of the nineteenth century, the empire began to show definite signs of decline. Political corruption, failure to modernize the military, and other common ailments of aging empires plagued the Ottomans. Neighboring states began to seize Ottoman land. A weak response resulted in an increasing loss of the empire's territory. During this decline, the central Ottoman government proved to be unable to respond to external as well as internal threats.

Loss of Territory

In Chapter 12 you learned that Greece gained its independence from the Ottoman Empire. Later in the nineteenth century, other subject states declared their independence.

The Balkans

The **Balkans**, a large region in southeastern Europe, received its name from the Balkan Mountains. The Ottoman Empire had ruled this territory for centuries. However, during the nineteenth century, several of the Balkan states declared their independence. Russia extended its influence by supporting these struggling states and helping them to break away from Ottoman control. For example, Serbia, Montenegro, and Romania led the way in gaining their freedom.

Other states, including Bulgaria, gained their independence from the Ottoman Empire following the Russo-Turkish War in 1877. The Ottoman Empire continued to lose large portions of its empire.

The Black Sea Region

The Ottoman Empire had maintained control of territory around the **Black Sea** for centuries. However, during the nineteenth century the Ottomans lost control of most of this land. As previously stated, some states gained their independence, but others, such as Moldova, came under the control of an expanding Russian Empire. In addition, Russia seized control of Ottoman lands along the eastern shore of the Black Sea. This region transformed from one of Ottoman control to one of Russian dominance.

External and Internal Pressures

In addition to revolts by subject states, the Ottoman Empire suffered assaults from foreign powers including France and Russia.

The Black Sea Region (present day)

Internal instability further weakened the aging empire. Weak rulers invited uprisings and plots to seize power.

French Invasion of Egypt

Napoleon I attempted to conquer Egypt, an Ottoman territory, in 1798. The French forces easily defeated the Ottoman forces in Egypt. However, Lord Nelson and the British fleet destroyed the French ships anchored off the Egyptian coast. This attack greatly hampered the French forces.

Napoleon in Egypt

The Ottomans tried to defeat Napoleon by sending two armies to Egypt. He responded by attacking one of the Ottoman armies in Syria before it could travel to Egypt. This tactic failed, and Napoleon was forced to retreat to Egypt. He initially held off the second Ottoman force in Egypt but soon decided to abandon his army and return to France rather than risk loss of popular support at home.

Napoleon's forces in Egypt continued to suffer from attacks and disease. They finally surrendered to the British in 1801. While the Ottoman Empire regained control of Egypt, this invasion had demonstrated how vulnerable the empire had become.

Mahmud II

Mahmud II (r. 1808–1839) came to power in the Ottoman Empire during a period of decline and political instability. His half-brother staged a coup, murdered the sultan, and then ordered Mahmud's execution. Mahmud barely escaped this attempt on his life. A palace rebellion ended the coup and placed Mahmud on the throne.

Decline of the Ottoman Empire
List reasons for the Ottoman Empire's decline.
Reasons for Ottoman Decline

Mahmud II

Three apprentices hauling water

Mahmud ruled the Ottoman Empire during the period when Greece, the Balkans, and other regions gained their independence. In addition, Mahmud found himself powerless to stop the French from seizing Algeria, an Ottoman province, in 1830.

However, in the midst of decline, Mahmud laid the foundation for a modern Turkey. For example, he abolished the military organization developed in the fourteenth century and replaced it with a modern Ottoman army. In addition, Mahmud enacted reforms that resulted in social and legal changes. As a result, the Turks began to embrace European clothing, European laws, and land reform.

Section Quiz

1. Where are the Balkan states located?

2. What empire had maintained control of the Black Sea region for centuries?

3. What Ottoman territory did Napoleon attempt to conquer in 1798?

4. Who came to power in the Ottoman Empire during its period of decline?

☆ How did the Ottomans respond to the emperor's reforms?

■ II. Changes in Russia

In Chapter 4 you learned that the Russians gained their independence from Mongol control around 1480. By the eighteenth century, Russia had grown to become the largest state in the world. Under leaders such as Peter the Great, Russia controlled an immense territory from the Baltic Sea to the Pacific Ocean.

However, much of Russia suffered from a harsh climate, and limited growing conditions restricted the food supply. As a result, this vast state had a population of only about fourteen million people. Successive rulers moved west and south to seize new lands, gain access to warm-water ports, and increase Russian influence.

While Russia expanded its control over neighboring states, much of the Russian population remained in virtual slavery as **serfs**. Uprisings increased as Russian citizens grew increasingly impatient with the status quo. In order to survive, Russia would have to make major reforms to benefit its people. Failure to do so would provide fertile ground for the growth of violent revolution.

Territorial Expansion

Russian imperialism continued during the reign of **Catherine the Great**. Catherine was a German princess who married a German heir to the Russian throne. Her husband proved to be a weak leader. He soon died under mysterious circumstances, and Catherine became the ruler of Russia.

Under her aggressive leadership, Russia continued to move west. During her reign, Russia seized Ottoman land that lay between Russia and the Black Sea. Catherine also joined with other nations in partitioning Poland in order to continue the expansion of Russian political control westward.

Alexander I became the czar of Russia following Catherine's death in 1796. He continued Russia's expansion by seizing control of Finland from Sweden in 1809. Alexander also took control of additional Ottoman territory in 1812.

Reform

While Russian rulers succeeded in gaining territory, they continued to tolerate the oppression of nearly one-third of the Russian population. Millions of Russians lived on land owned by nobles and spent most of their time working to support the nobility. As a result, they were little more than slaves and lived in terrible, impoverished conditions.

Internal Influences

In 1773 Catherine made life for the serfs even worse by making it legal to sell serfs separate from selling the land. In response, the peasants revolted and nearly entered Moscow before royal forces brutally defeated them. Succeeding Russian rulers tended either to work for reform or to react to violence and suppress the people in order to prevent reform.

Popular Opposition Movements

Nicholas I (r. 1825–1855) came to power in the midst of a revolt. Several well-educated Russian officers had traveled to Europe on various military assignments. They learned of representative government in western Europe and brought this idea back to Russia. As a result, a small group of nobles and army officers sought to replace Nicholas with his brother in order to establish a constitutional monarchy. This rebellion occurred in December 1825 and became known as the **Decembrist Revolt**.

Nicholas and his forces defeated this revolt. However, such a threat led Nicholas to reject the westernization begun by Peter the Great and embrace "Orthodoxy, Autocracy, and Nationality." As a

Orthodoxy, Autocracy, and Nationality

The czars assumed the right to rule without question and tolerated no criticism. They used several kinds of power to keep Russia firmly under their control. They wielded military power and suppressed rebellion through force. They exercised power through the church, which encouraged the people to submit to the state. The czars also retained power by promoting nationalism; they emphasized individual sacrifice for the good of the nation.

In the right hands, these types of power could be used for good. The government should have power to protect the innocent and to ensure justice (Rom. 13:1-7; 1 Tim. 2:1-2). The church should have the power to disciple Christians in the ways of Christ (Matt. 28:19-20). Finally, God established nations, and there is something good about loyalty to one's nation.

However, some of the czars abused these powers without ensuring justice. They used the power of the church to protect themselves rather than to teach the people how to live righteously. And many abused the loyalty of the people by failing to repay patriotism with justice.

Decembrist Revolt

Anarchy

In simple terms, *anarchy* means "without law" or "the absence of law." We often use this term to describe a state of lawlessness and political disorder. The French Revolution provides a clear example of the anarchy that follows the overthrow of government.

However, Tolstoy imagined a theoretical state where there is simply no law or government and where man has the liberty of governing himself. Tolstoy dreamed of achieving this state without resorting to violence and disorder.

Even though Tolstoy envisioned a peaceful anarchy, his vision of the world conflicted with the way God designed it to work. It is unrealistic to think that a fallen world could exist without government to ensure justice (Rom. 13:1-7). Even in eternity, government continues with Jesus ruling as king and others ruling under Him (Rev. 20:4).

Justice

Freeing the serfs without giving them land or other resources to support themselves did not ensure justice. In Deuteronomy 15:12–18, God established a principle for freeing a servant. God commanded His people to generously provide for the needs of a freed servant. This practice provided the servant with the resources he needed to survive and become a productive citizen.

result, opposition groups became more popular, and more people began to accept radical proposals to solve Russia's problems.

Michael Bakunin became one of the Russian radicals to emerge during this period. Known as the Father of Anarchism, Bakunin supported **anarchy**, or the concept of society without government. To escape imprisonment, Bakunin fled to western Europe. However, his participation in an uprising in Dresden, Germany, led to his imprisonment and deportation to Siberia. Bakunin managed to escape and return to Europe, where he worked with Karl Marx.

In addition, Russian authors, including Fyodor **Dostoyevsky** and Leo Tolstoy (refer to Chapter 14), provided their readers with a glimpse into Russian society during this period. Their conclusions, however, were polar opposites. For example, Dostoyevsky embraced Eastern Orthodoxy and opposed the anarchists and atheists who were becoming popular in Russia during this period.

Fyodor Dostoyevsky

Tolstoy, on the other hand, rejected Eastern Orthodoxy and emphasized the Sermon on the Mount. However, his interpretations of the Sermon conflicted with the rest of Scripture. He interpreted the command to "turn the other cheek" to teach pacifism (refusal to fight), denial of sexual desires, and the abolition of private property. In fact, Tolstoy played a key role in developing anarchist reasoning. In works such as *The Kingdom of God Is Within You*, he attacked the church, the state, and the principle of law in Russian society.

Imperial Reforms

Following Napoleon's failed invasion of Russia, Alexander I discussed possible constitutional reforms and introduced a few minor changes. However, the fundamental problems remained, and pressure continued to mount for reform.

Alexander II (r. 1855–81) sensed the growing demand for reform in Russia. Rather than wait for reform to occur through violent revolution, he made a bold move in 1861. Alexander II abolished serfdom and freed twenty-three million people out of a total Russian population of sixty-seven million. This emancipation created a great supply of free laborers to move to the cities and fill jobs created by developing industries.

However, freed peasants did not receive free land along with their new status. Instead, the government required them to pay a huge tax in order to continue to farm the land. The government then used this money to pay the nobles large sums for the land the government had taken. The peasants often ended up with the least productive land, and this land belonged to the village community rather than to individual farmers.

In the end, simply abolishing serfdom did little to improve the lives of millions of Russians. Russia needed fundamental reforms to correct centuries of repression. Because the Russian government did not implement these reforms, conditions did not improve. The support for revolution continued to grow.

Imperial Reactions

Despite Alexander II's attempts to bring reform to Russia, his efforts proved to be in vain. In 1881, he died at the hands of assassins. His successor, Alexander III (r. 1881–94), suppressed all real and imagined threats to the monarchy. He censored the press and persecuted many groups, including the Poles and Finns. Pogroms (mentioned in Chapter 14) became a brutal tool of the government to terrorize those considered a threat. These vicious policies continued under Alexander's son Nicholas II (r. 1894–1917).

External Influences

Napoleonic Invasion

Napoleon had allied France with Russia in order to prevent the British from trading with countries in Europe. However, by 1811 this alliance began to collapse. When Napoleon learned that Russia was preparing for war, he ignored all warnings and invaded Russia in June 1812.

The Russians refused to engage Napoleon's forces and drew them deep into the heart of Russia. When the Russians did stand and fight, they suffered defeat. Russian retreats pulled the French into Russia but denied the French any significant victories.

Despite Napoleon's capture of Moscow, the Russians would not surrender. Concern over unstable conditions back in France and the approaching Russian winter led Napoleon to retreat, and the Russian people rallied to destroy the French forces as they tried to flee. Ninety percent of Napoleon's army died in battle, from the harsh Russian winter, or from Russian attacks.

Napoleon's forces retreating from Russia

Napoleon's invasion had disrupted much of Russian society and led those who suffered most to expect reform. The serfs had played a major role in defeating Napoleon. In return, they demanded major reforms that would free them from their virtual slavery. However, as we have seen, Alexander I offered only minor changes. No significant reform followed Napoleon's invasion.

European Economic Growth

In Chapter 13 you learned about the tremendous changes that occurred in western Europe because of the Industrial Revolution. Economic growth from this revolution propelled western Europe far ahead of Russia economically. While Russia had the necessary natural resources, it lacked the free and mobile laborers, stable government, and other ingredients needed to develop industry on a large scale.

Russia continued to expand its empire by seizing land from weaker states, but it lagged further and further behind economically. Western Europe became wealthy through industry, expanding sea trade, and the exploitation of African colonies. Russia could not compete or catch up. Western success exposed the great weaknesses of the Russian Empire. Radical groups used these weaknesses to attract increasing support for their efforts to overthrow the existing system in Russia.

Section Quiz

1. By the eighteenth century, which country had grown into the largest state in the world?

2. What kind of group led the Decembrist Revolt?

3. Who became known as the Father of Anarchism? Briefly define *anarchy*.

4. What did Czar Alexander II decree in 1861? Did it accomplish his intended goal?

★ How did Catherine become ruler of Russia?

★ Briefly contrast Dostoyevsky's and Tolstoy's interpretations of Scripture and their views on anarchy.

Guiding Questions

1. How did Britain increase its power over India in the nineteenth century?

2. What were the consequences of British control of India?

■ III. Domination of India by Britain

As you learned in Chapter 11, the English initially came to India for trade. However, as the Mughal Empire declined, England gradually took control of most of the country. Britain was not the only European country to seek influence in India. France also labored to establish and maintain trade with this vast country.

Advance of British Power to 1850

The East India Company developed extensive trade relations with states in India. Over time, the British government became more involved and eventually took control of British affairs in India. However, Britain had to deal with its main competitor before extensive trade could continue.

Conflict with France

Britain soon ended the threat of French competition by winning the Seven Years' War (1756–63). At the **Battle of Plassey** in 1757,

Consequences of British Rule

The British faced many problems in ruling India. The country had over one hundred million inhabitants who spoke over a hundred different languages. In addition, they followed several religions.

British officials in India often misunderstood the Indians and had little desire to learn about Indian culture. The British rulers also tended to isolate themselves from the Indian population and assumed the role of master over their Indian subjects. Indians found employment as servants and performed other menial tasks the British would not lower themselves to do.

Many British officials also hindered missionary efforts to evangelize the Indians. They feared that this evangelism would lead to unrest and instability as the missionaries revealed the error of Indian religions and idolatry. For example, British officials compelled William Carey to carry out his translating and printing work from the Danish settlement of Serampore.

To reduce the strife in India, Queen Victoria proclaimed a policy of noninterference. This policy, though proclaimed with good intentions, hindered missionary efforts to spread the gospel and to bring about reforms to protect women, children, and the outcastes of Indian society.

Despite these negative aspects of British rule, there were positive results for India as well. These results included improvements in agriculture, industry, transportation, and education. In addition, British and American missionaries were able to evangelize much of India. When the British government restricted direct evangelization, missionaries often used the meeting of medical and educational needs to provide opportunities to witness.

To improve agriculture, the British brought in better equipment, introduced fertilizers, and taught the Indians improved methods of farming. To increase production, they also built many miles of irrigation canals.

The British also developed raw materials such as tea, cotton, and jute into products for export. India soon exported more tea than China.

British officials planted the first rubber trees on the island of Ceylon (Sri Lanka). These plants thrived, and Ceylon became a major exporter of rubber.

In addition, Britain laid thousands of miles of track to construct a massive railroad system. They also set up a telegraph system and reorganized the postal system.

Cotton boll farmer in India

Irrigation ditch in India

British commander **Robert Clive** defeated a much larger Indian force whose leader supported the French. With only three thousand men, Clive routed a disorganized Indian force of eighty thousand. This battle broke France's strength in India. Within three years the French were defeated in India.

Conquest of India

Following the end of French influence, British trade with India grew over the next hundred years. The British government began to exercise greater control over the East India Company in 1773 due to the company's financial mismanagement. As the British government became more involved, officials quickly realized the importance of stabilizing India to enhance British trade. British commanders such as Lord Cornwallis put down rebellions and enforced stability.

During the late 1700s and early 1800s, the British government continued to exert more control over the activities of the East India Company. In 1814 the **Charter Act** gave the British crown control over all that the company possessed. The final incident that led to the British government taking complete control occurred when Indian soldiers called **sepoys** (SEE poyz) revolted.

The **Sepoy Mutiny** (1857–58) began because of a rumor that the cartridges for a newly issued rifle had been greased with either pork or beef fat. In order to use the cartridges, the soldiers had to open them, usually by biting them. The Hindu soldiers were offended because the cow was sacred to them. The Muslim soldiers were offended because they considered pork unclean.

When the British commanded the sepoys to load the new rifles, they refused and the British stripped them of their uniforms and pensions. British forces arrested and imprisoned other sepoys when they also refused to obey this command. As news spread of the British actions, a mutiny arose. Before the British could restore order, both sides had massacred many innocent people.

The British suppressed this mutiny within a year. Queen Victoria responded by proclaiming India under control of the British crown and by declaring that the Indian people had the right to a voice in their own government. Yet at the same time, with no input from the Indian people, Britain absorbed India into its empire.

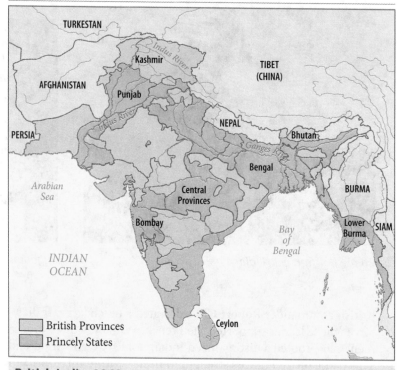

British India, 1860

Patterns of British Trade with India and China

British merchants, with the support of the British government, developed extensive trade between India and China. The British became very wealthy in the process. The massive flow of wealth tended to blur the lines between legitimate trade and the growing trade in a destructive drug.

Ganges Canal

The British developed cotton production and weaving in India. British ships transported goods, including cotton cloth and raw cotton, to Chinese ports. In exchange, the Chinese traded rhubarb, tea, and silk. However, the goods brought from India were worth less than those offered by the Chinese merchants. As a result, British merchants had to pay the difference in silver. This situation created a negative balance of trade for British merchants.

However, the British also produced **opium** from poppy plants in India and exported it to China. Soon, the Chinese demand for the addicting and destructive opium reversed the balance of trade. Now silver flowed from China to Britain. In addition to the terrible damage inflicted on the Chinese due to opium addiction, this reversal became a great financial drain on China.

Section Quiz

1. Why did the English originally travel to India?
2. What other European state sought to compete with Britain for control of India?
3. What act in 1814 gave the British crown control over all the East India Company's holdings?
4. What rumor led to the Sepoy Mutiny?
5. What drug did British merchants sell to the Chinese in order to gain a favorable balance of trade?
* In light of Exodus 20:13 and 17, evaluate the British motives for selling addictive opium to the Chinese.

Justice and Trade

Trade has the potential to bring about great good. Ideally, trade can result from love for one's neighbor. The goods exchanged bring mutual benefit, and the profits made can be used for good.

Of course, in a fallen world, this is often not the case. When the sole standard of whether an economic transaction is good or bad is profit, much evil results. Every Christian businessman ought to consider whether or not he can sell his product out of true love toward his neighbor. Some products, like opium, are so destructive that it is appropriate for the government to ensure justice by banning the sale of those products. During the mid-1800s, however, the British government went to war to ensure an open market for a life-destroying drug.

Immature growing poppy

Mature poppy flower

Guiding Questions

1. What caused the governmental breakdown and social collapse in China?

2. Why did China resist political contact and trade with Europeans?

3. What were the causes and consequences of the Taiping Rebellion?

4. What type of missionary efforts occurred in India and the rest of Asia?

Hong Xiuquan and Christianity

Hong was a gifted student who tried repeatedly to pass the government exam for civil service. Whether it was true or not, he believed his failures to pass resulted from corrupt officials. His frustration led to a serious illness. During his illness, he believed that he had visited heaven and received a calling to rid China of demon forces.

After his illness, Hong met Chinese Christians who gave him a Bible. He read the Old Testament and concluded that he had indeed met with God and that God had chosen him as a son. When Chinese Christians pointed out his errors, he rejected their counsel and formed his own cult, known as the God Worshippers Society. In this cult, God was the Father, Christ was the Son and Elder Brother, and Hong was the Younger Brother.

■ IV. Domination of Asia

You learned in Chapter 15 that Europe dominated Africa during the second half of the nineteenth century. During this same period, European nations and one Asian state also dominated Asia. China came under domination as the Manchu or **Qing** dynasty weakened. In addition, most of Southeast Asia became subject to European imperialism.

Weakening of the Middle Kingdom

The Manchus seized control of China in 1644. Although their formal rule did not end until 1911, the Qing dynasty experienced serious decline in the nineteenth century. Growth of trade with the West and the imperialism of European nations played a role in this decline. However, China had remained isolated from the rest of the world for centuries. China's continued resistance to change ultimately led to the collapse of its central government.

Opium Wars

For many years British merchants bribed Chinese officials in order to bring chests of opium into China. When the Chinese government finally tried to end this destructive trade, the British strongly objected. The British government intervened on behalf of the merchants and became directly involved in the opium trade. Mounting tensions resulted in the **Opium Wars**. Following the first Opium War in 1842, Britain forced China to open more ports to British merchants. During the second Opium War (1856–60), France joined Britain to gain even more trade concessions from the Chinese. These wars and the increased influence of European countries continued to weaken the Qing dynasty.

Rebellions

Throughout China, more and more people rebelled to express their rejection of the Qing government. The heavy taxation and government corruption especially angered the people. Famine became another serious problem for China. The Chinese population had rapidly increased, but the people had no additional farmland on which to grow more food. During some years, the farmers could not produce enough food to pay taxes and feed their families. Hungry and angry peasants often joined revolts against the government.

A frustrated Chinese student named Hong Renkun became the leader of one of the worst rebellions in Chinese history. Hong channeled his frustration into the development of a cultic political movement that attracted a huge number of the roaming peasants. As his movement grew, he changed his name to **Hong Xiuquan** ("Heavenly King") to reflect his claims that he was the younger brother of Jesus.

The weakness demonstrated by the Qing government during the Opium Wars caused more people to join Hong's movement. By 1851 he had a ten-thousand-man army with which he could attack the Manchurian forces.

The resulting **Taiping Rebellion** lasted from 1851 to 1864. Hong's movement quickly grew to over one million peasants who joined him in rebellion. At first, the rebels were difficult to suppress because they remained mobile. However, once they established a capital in Nanking, the British and Chinese forces were able to mount an attack and end this serious threat. During the many

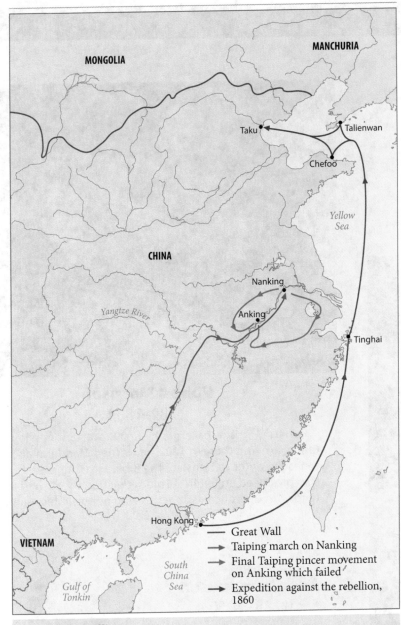

Taiping Rebellion

Member of the Boxer Rebellion

battles required to suppress this rebellion, between twenty and thirty million people died.

Unrest again erupted when the **Boxer Rebellion** broke out in 1899. The Boxers were members of a secret society officially named the *Society of Righteous and Harmonious Fists*. The Europeans nicknamed the group Boxers because the martial arts they practiced looked like shadowboxing. Initially, this society opposed the Chinese government. However, they concluded that an alliance with the Imperial government against European imperialists would better represent Chinese interests. The Empress Dowager Tz'u-Hsi (or Cixi; see p. 298) discouraged the Imperial government from restraining this movement.

In the early months of 1900, the Boxers began by killing missionaries and other foreigners in northern China. About two hundred and fifty foreigners died in the attacks. The Boxers also slaughtered thousands of Chinese Christians.

Missions in the Far East

Robert Morrison
1782–1834

Robert Morrison became the first Protestant missionary to China, arriving there in 1807. He learned Mandarin and Cantonese in order to translate the Bible into Chinese. Morrison also produced an English-Chinese dictionary. He had to contend with Catholic missionaries who opposed his ministry.

William Carey
1761–1834

William Carey was an English Baptist preacher and linguist who translated the Bible into many languages, including Bengali and Sanskrit. His motto ("Expect great things from God; attempt great things for God") and book, *An Enquiry into the Obligations of Christians to Use Means for the Conversion of the Heathens*, published in 1792, show his passion for missions. Carey is considered the Father of Modern Missions.

Adoniram Judson
1788–1850

Adoniram Judson became America's first foreign missionary, arriving in Burma in 1813. In spite of various afflictions, including imprisonment and the deaths of his first and second wives, he completed a Burmese Bible translation so precise that it is still used today.

Samuel R. Brown
1810–1880

Samuel R. Brown, a New Englander who attended Yale in 1832, founded China's first Protestant school at Canton. After a visit to America in 1847, he left for Yokahama, Japan, in 1859. Brown became one of the first Christian teachers in this city. During his years of ministry in Japan, he translated the Bible into Japanese and wrote a grammar entitled *Colloquial Japanese*.

James Hudson Taylor
1832–1905

James Hudson Taylor established the China Inland Mission (CIM) in 1865. Over time, this mission agency guided hundreds of missionaries to China. Taylor adopted Chinese customs and dress, a practice uncommon among most Western missionaries.

J. C. Hepburn
1815–1911

J. C. Hepburn served as a missionary-doctor in Japan. He spent many years producing an English-Japanese dictionary. Hepburn started a school that later became Meiji Gakuin University. The Japanese government recognized his contribution by awarding him the Order of the Rising Sun.

Jonathan and Rosalind Goforth

Canadian missionary **Jonathan Goforth** and his family, along with other missionaries, began their escape on June 28, 1900. They faced a journey of about twenty-four days through territory overrun with Boxers.

The Chinese Christians at their mission urged them to go. They knew that the Boxers had a special hatred for Chinese converts to Christianity. (They believed these Christians had denied traditional Chinese culture and heritage.) However, the Chinese Christians could blend into their villages or hide in the countryside, while the foreigners could not.

On July 8 Boxers attacked Goforth and his group but failed to kill Jonathan, despite several blows with swords and a club. The Boxers soon became more interested in the goods in the missionary's carts, and the missionaries slipped into the crowd to safety. Two years later the Goforths returned to China and their mission.

Empress Dowager Cixi

Foreign navies from eight countries began to expand their presence on the northern China coast by the end of April 1900. Initially, European commanders dispatched 435 troops to help put down the rebellion. However, the crisis deepened, and marine and army forces numbering over 49,000 were required to crush this violent and deadly rebellion.

In addition to Britain, France, and the United States, Japan and Russia sent large numbers of warships and troops. Germany, Italy, and Austria-Hungary also provided a token force to complete the Eight-Nation Alliance.

Continued Opposition to Contact with the Outside World

A child born with the name Zaitian became the tenth emperor of the Qing dynasty in 1875. He became token ruler at the age of four and received the name of **Guangxu**. The **Empress Dowager Cixi** adopted Guangxu as her son and served as the actual ruler of China for the first fourteen years of his reign. She used her considerable power to oppose reform and change in China.

Once Emperor Guangxu began to rule on his own, he worked to modernize China and develop a constitutional monarchy similar to the one developed by Japan. In June 1898 the young emperor began the **Hundred Days' Reform** with the goal of implementing sweeping political, legal, and social changes in China. By September the Empress Dowager had staged a coup and imprisoned Guangxu. She issued an edict stating that Guangxu was not fit to be emperor and quickly reversed his efforts to reform China.

Guangxu remained under house arrest until his mysterious death at the age of thirty-seven. The next day Empress Dowager Cixi died. Theories about the possible murder of Guangxu abound.

Foreign Intervention

As foreign nations saw the Qing dynasty continue to weaken, they began to take advantage of China. The emerging state of Japan made the first move. Europeans nations quickly moved to limit Japan's access to Chinese territory.

Korea

For many years Korea had been under token Chinese control. In 1876 Japan forced the Koreans to sign a treaty declaring their independence from China. China immediately began to maneuver to recover control of Korea. When a Korean secret society rebelled, the pro-Chinese king of Korea requested military assistance from China. The Japanese also sent troops. In 1894 the **Sino-Japanese War** began. The Japanese easily defeated China and humiliated the Manchu government. The Japanese took possession of Korea and received Taiwan along with other Chinese territories.

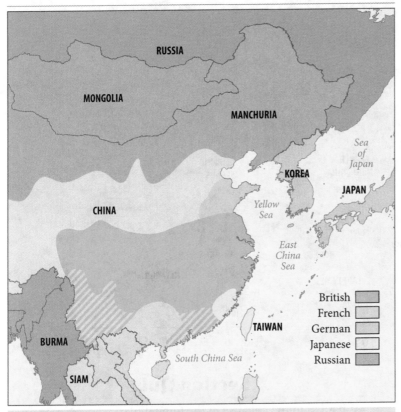

Foreign Influences in China, 19th Century

Fearing that Japan would gain control of more Chinese territory, several European nations sought ways to claim territory for themselves and establish **spheres of influence** in China. Like children eyeing a huge pie, each nation demanded a "slice" of China. Britain, France, Germany, and other European countries all chose areas they wished to control. The weak Chinese government had little say in these decisions except to give away land.

Southeast Asia

The area east of India and south of China is called Southeast Asia. Several regions of this area had come under European control prior to 1800. However, the nineteenth century witnessed European assimilation of the entire region, with the exception of Siam (Thailand). Siam escaped European control by serving as a buffer between French and British territories. Europeans seized control of many states and islands in the area for strategic and economic reasons. For example, the Europeans exported many natural resources from this area, including rubber, tea, and food not grown in Europe.

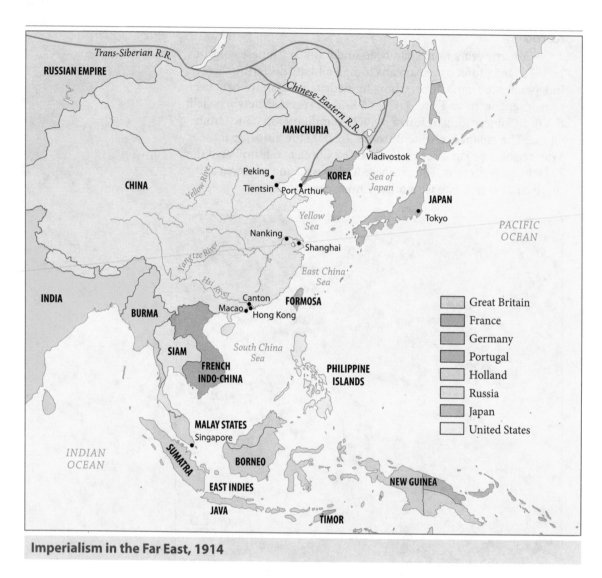

Imperialism in the Far East, 1914

Section Quiz

1. What led to the collapse of the Qing dynasty?

2. What motivated more and more Chinese peasants to rebel?

3. Whom did Hong Xiuquan claim to be? What rebellion did he lead?

4. What rebellion resulted in the deaths of many missionaries?

✶ Why was Emperor Guangxu imprisoned while in office?

✶ Evaluate Japan's actions toward a weakened China.

■ V. Modernization in Meiji Japan

Over two hundred years of Japanese isolation ended in 1853. In that year **Commodore Matthew Perry** of the United States visited Japan with his fleet and pressured the Japanese to open to trade. In 1854 Japan and the United States signed the **Treaty of Kanagawa**. This treaty opened Japan to trade with other nations.

In a later visit, Perry brought with him several inventions that amazed the Japanese people. One was a telegraph system, which could send messages from one town to another. Another was a miniature train and railroad track. The Japanese realized that they had much to learn if they were to catch up with the rest of the world.

Guiding Questions

1. What led to the Meiji Restoration, and how did it impact Japan's modernization?

2. How did Western ideas and reformed Shintoism influence Japan in the Meiji period?

3. How did Japan's relations with China and Western powers change from the 1850s to the early 1900s?

Impact of Western Ideas

The Japanese began to trade with the United States and many other countries. Soon the Japanese adopted the Western way of life. They built factories to make new products. The Japanese also sent some of their young men to the United States and Europe to learn more about Western ideas and new developments in industry. In addition, Japanese commissions studied Western governments, schools, and militaries.

The Meiji Restoration

In 1868 the emperor used the title **Meiji** (MAY jee; "enlightened rule") to describe his reign. He led the transformation of Japan from a feudal society (refer to Chapter 4) to a modern state. Japan became

Emperor Meiji

the first nation in Asia to become industrialized. In addition, the Japanese developed a constitutional form of government. They also developed modern educational and judicial systems modeled after the West.

Japan transformed its feudal military forces into a modern, well-trained army and navy. Despite a lack of raw materials including coal and iron ore, the manufacture of modern weapons and a modern naval fleet quickly made Japan a powerful nation in Asia. We noted earlier that Japan supplied warships and thousands of well-armed troops to help suppress the Boxer Rebellion in China. Japan soon demonstrated imperialist desires toward its weaker neighbors.

Expansion of Japan

As we mentioned in the section on China, Japan began to expand its territory at the expense of China in 1894. A few years later, Japan astonished the European states by quickly and decisively defeating the Russian army and navy during the **Russo-Japanese War** (1904–5). This war forced the world to notice that Japan had developed into a world power.

Decision to Modernize Japan

Once Perry and his fleet had ended Japanese isolation, the Japanese had to decide how to respond to the West. Would they follow China's example of resisting change? The Japanese fought a civil war to decide this issue. In the process, the victorious forces overthrew the shogun and recognized the Japanese emperor as the leader of Japan. The emperor embraced contact with the West and led Japan to become a great power in Asia.

Japan and Shintoism

In Chapter 4 you learned about this ancient Japanese religion. During the Meiji Restoration, political leaders transformed Shintoism into a tool of the Japanese government. They sought to unify Japan under the rule of the emperor.

Shinto priests taught the young people Shinto theology that supported the divinity of Japan's national origins and the emperor. Shintoism also became a tool to motivate improvements, such as industrial growth, in a way that would enhance extreme nationalism and promote militarism.

Section Quiz

1. What treaty opened Japan to foreign trade?

2. What European developments did Japan study?

3. What does the term *Meiji* mean?

4. What did Japan manufacture to become a powerful nation?

5. What major power did Japan defeat in 1905?

✶ How did Japan's transformation into an industrial nation differ from Britain's (refer to Chapter 13)?

CHAPTER REVIEW

■ Making Connections

1. Why did Europe side with the Ottoman Empire in the Crimean War?

2. Why did Napoleon abandon his army in Egypt?

3. Why was Russia able to support only a meager population?

4. Why were serfs unable to escape terrible poverty?

5. Why did a small group of nobles and army officers seek to replace Czar Nicholas I?

6. Why did the Chinese effort to end the sale of opium lead to war with Britain?

7. Why did several European nations seek ways to claim Chinese territory for themselves?

8. What did the Meiji Restoration in Japan quickly lead to?

■ Developing History Skills

1. Locate the following on the map. Then match each area with the corresponding number on the map.

   a. Burma   d. Japan

   b. China   e. Russia

   c. Indian Ocean   f. South China Sea

2. Contrast the imperialism of Europe in China with that in Africa (refer to Chapter 15).

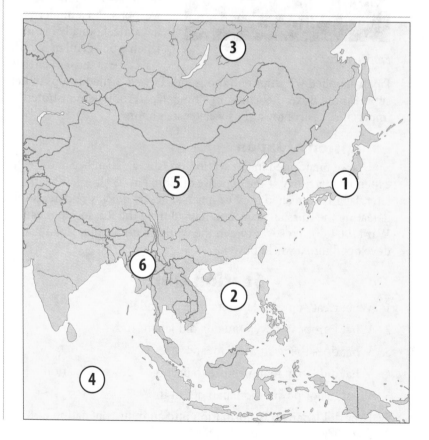

■ Thinking Critically

1. Evaluate British rule of India.

2. Contrast the British rule of India with the European and Japanese imperialism in China.

■ Living in God's World

1. Dostoyevsky wrote short stories and novels that confronted people with human sinfulness and the importance of the Christian religion. His works were very influential and are still read today. Write a short story dealing with problems in modern culture. Throughout your story, suggest that the Bible and a right relationship with God can solve these problems.

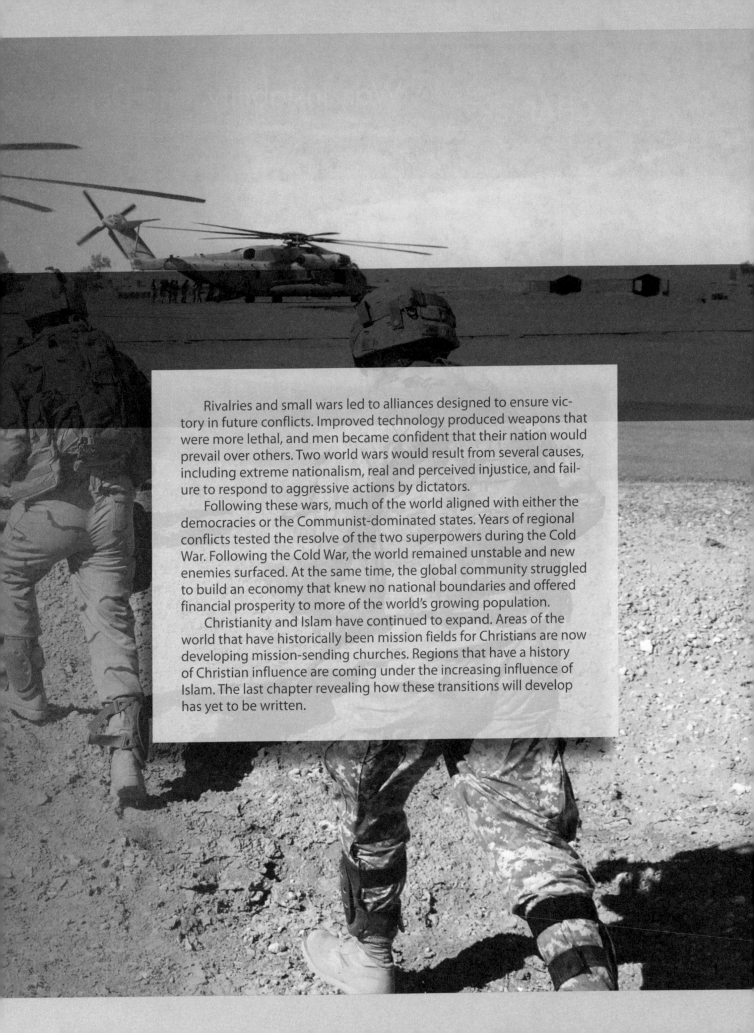

Rivalries and small wars led to alliances designed to ensure victory in future conflicts. Improved technology produced weapons that were more lethal, and men became confident that their nation would prevail over others. Two world wars would result from several causes, including extreme nationalism, real and perceived injustice, and failure to respond to aggressive actions by dictators.

Following these wars, much of the world aligned with either the democracies or the Communist-dominated states. Years of regional conflicts tested the resolve of the two superpowers during the Cold War. Following the Cold War, the world remained unstable and new enemies surfaced. At the same time, the global community struggled to build an economy that knew no national boundaries and offered financial prosperity to more of the world's growing population.

Christianity and Islam have continued to expand. Areas of the world that have historically been mission fields for Christians are now developing mission-sending churches. Regions that have a history of Christian influence are coming under the increasing influence of Islam. The last chapter revealing how these transitions will develop has yet to be written.

CHAPTER

War, Instability, and Depressio
1914 – 39

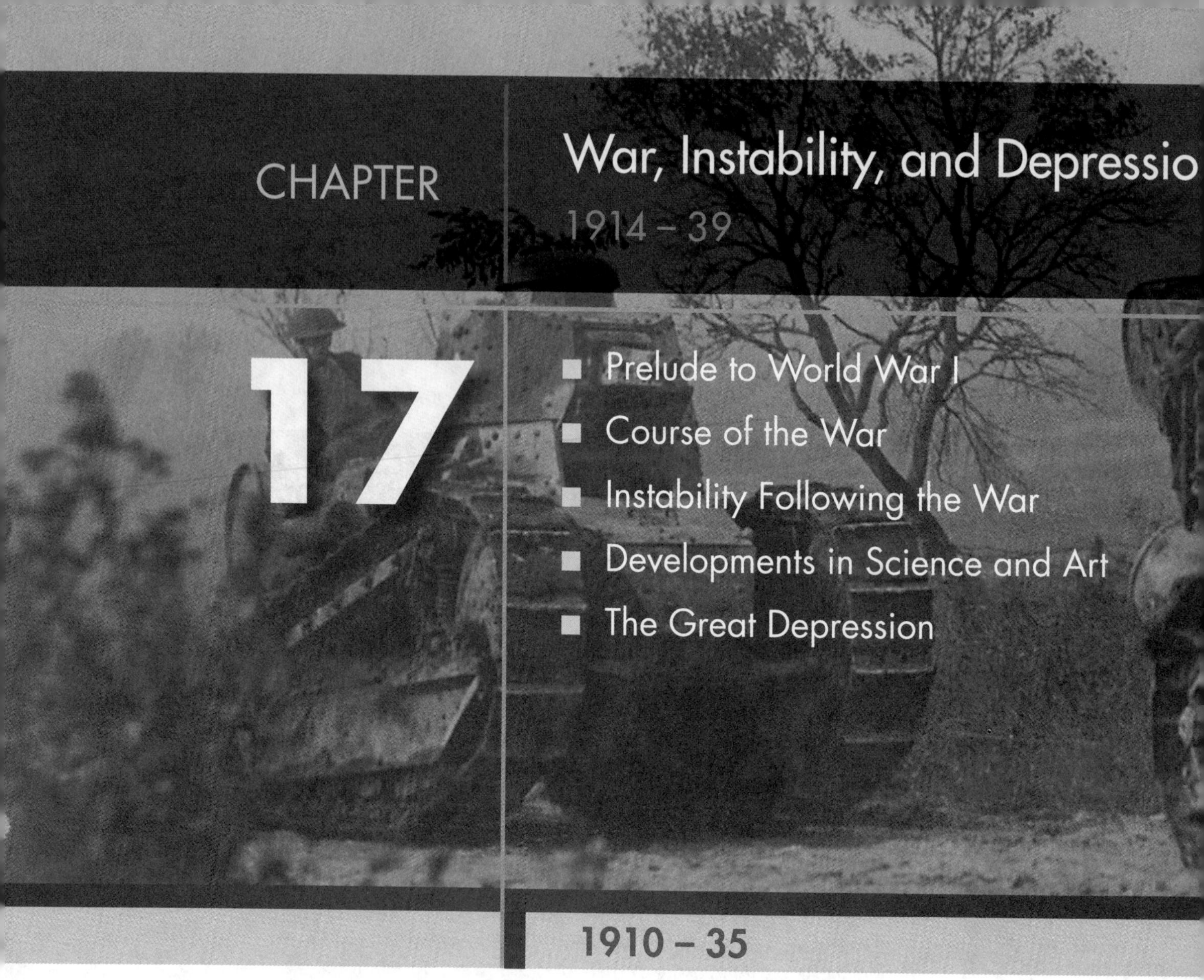

17

- Prelude to World War I
- Course of the War
- Instability Following the War
- Developments in Science and Art
- The Great Depression

1910 – 35

■ Vladimir Lenin becomes the first Communist
dictator of Russia 1917

■ America's Congress declares war on Germany April 6, 1917

■ Lenin signs a treaty with Germany and
takes Russia out of the war 1918

■ Paris Peace Conference 1919

Washington
Naval Conference
1921–22

■ Chinese revolution ends
the Qing dynasty 1911

■ Archduke Francis Ferdinand is
assassinated, leading to World
War I June 28, 1914

1910   **1915**   **1920**

Mussolini seizes power in Italy 1922 ■

Big Ideas

1. What events led to World War I?
2. What were the key aspects of World War I?
3. Why did instability follow the war and result in the rise of dictatorships?
4. What were important developments in science and art during this period?
5. What caused the Great Depression?

The period between 1900 and 1939 was filled with turbulence and radical change. Nations sacrificed tremendous human and natural resources in vain attempts to conquer one another. Sadly, the period following World War I provided little relief and resulted in a terrible economic depression. The 1920s began with great optimism but ended with many living in despair. Too many failed to learn from the First World War and blindly stumbled along toward another season of destruction.

Joseph Stalin becomes Russia's second dictator 1924

Chiang Kai-shek becomes leader of the Kuomintang Party 1925

Locarno Pact 1925

Kellogg-Briand Pact 1928

Stalin launches first Five-Year Plan 1928

Lateran Treaties between Italy and Rome 1929

America's stock market crashes 1929

The Great Depression begins 1929

Hitler becomes chancellor of Germany 1933

1925

1930

1935

F. D. Roosevelt is elected U.S. president 1932

1. What role did European alliances play leading up to war?
2. How did science and technology contribute to a more lethal war?
3. What role did the Balkans play in triggering the war?

THE DOGS OF WAR.

British cartoon showing Russia and the Balkan countries trailing the aging Ottoman Empire while Britain looks on with concern

■ I. Prelude to World War I

Competition between nations continued during this period. However, the struggle for additional territory or disputed territory often became heated. Nations continued to have an exaggerated sense of nationalism, and in Europe war remained a popular way to demonstrate a nation's importance. In addition, states that had been conquered in the last century struggled to regain their freedom. Alliances formed and dissolved as nations played a dangerous game of checking and blocking their opponents. In addition, old opponents became new allies as European powers sought to gain an advantage against a neighboring state or potential foe in battle.

Rivalries

England, France, and Spain had traditionally regarded each other as rivals. However, during this period newly formed nations, such as Germany, surged forward and turned former rivals into allies. In addition, former allies changed priorities and often became rivals.

Economic

Recently unified Germany quickly industrialized. By the beginning of the twentieth century, Germany came close to its goal of replacing Great Britain as Europe's primary industrial nation. Other European countries lagged behind and struggled to modernize their industries.

Political

In 1870 Germany humiliated France. France remained hostile, and Bismarck, Germany's chancellor, made alliances with other European powers to isolate the French diplomatically. Later in the chapter we will briefly examine some of these alliances.

The English worked to maintain their isolation from the political strife that plagued western Europe. However, Britain could not remain neutral forever. Soon the British would have to give their support to one of these feuding countries.

Russia, always looking for more Ottoman territory, encouraged the Balkan states to drive the Ottoman Turks out of the Balkans. Russia sought to influence and later dominate the Balkan region.

Faith in Science and Technology

Faith in science, technology, and progress became prominent at the beginning of the twentieth century. Men began to believe that they could solve any problem and cure all of society's ills. Ultimately, this confidence led nations to stumble into a war that could not be resolved quickly. This war would exhaust the greatest military and scientific minds as they desperately attempted to overcome their enemies.

Science

Scientists made a number of discoveries about the atom and its structure. For the first time in history, scientists leaped from using the term *atom* as a philosophical term to using it as a scientific term.

Additional experiments led to the discovery that the atom had negatively charged particles called electrons. Continued research greatly expanded understanding of the nature of the atom and its enormous potential.

In addition, physicians developed a process to reveal and confirm the causes of certain diseases. For example, in the 1870s German physician Robert Koch discovered the cause of a disease called anthrax. This disease spreads from animals such as cattle to humans and can be deadly. Koch's discovery helped others learn how to understand the spread of other diseases.

Ongoing research led to a number of other scientific discoveries by the end of the nineteenth century. These findings opened new fields of experimentation and study. Such revelations encouraged men to believe they could ultimately unlock the secrets of the universe.

Technology

Improvements in processing steel and the production of electricity and chemicals led to a tremendous growth of technology during this period. European countries used these advances to build infrastructures, modernize their militaries, and multiply wealth as new products became available.

In addition, developments in chemicals resulted in mass production of paper, soaps, and fertilizer. Germany became the largest producer of chemicals. Among other achievements, German scientists developed synthetic dyes and improved ways to refine oil.

Causes of the War

There are many theories about the causes of World War I. We will look at some of the basic causes that led to this destructive period of warfare between nations.

Militarism

Several European nations built militaries with capacity far beyond the need for defense. A large army and navy became an expression of national glory and a symbol of power. In addition, the military dominated the government of some nations. Sadly, during the early twentieth century, citizens often glorified war without regard for its justification.

Imperialism

You learned about imperialism in Chapters 15 and 16. The competition for colonies continued into the twentieth century. Nations such as Germany and Italy still sought to gain access to foreign lands in order to compete with Britain and France. This increasing rivalry led to tension and suspicion among the European states.

Rival Alliances

Bismarck made an alliance with Russia and Austria-Hungary that protected Germany against an attack by France. When this agreement fell apart, he allied Germany with Austria-Hungary and Italy. In addition, Bismarck arranged a secret treaty with Russia known as the **Reinsurance Treaty**. He considered this treaty crucial to protecting German interests.

However, when **Wilhelm II** became the ruler of Germany in 1888, he dismissed Bismarck and allowed the Reinsurance Treaty to

Robert Koch

Power and Technology

The development of science and technology gave humans access to greater power. This period of history raises the question of whether humans used that power wisely. In Genesis 6:11 God warns of the danger of great power in the hands of fallen humans.

Justified War

God gave government the power of the sword (Rom. 13:4), and John the Baptist gave instruction to those who were seeking to behave uprightly within the military profession (Luke 3:14). When Christian theologians debate what kinds of wars are right and what kinds of wars are wrong, many conclude that the second great commandment governs all of our relationships with others. Wars fought out of love for others are permissible. Wars fought for selfish reasons are not.

expire. France took advantage of this blunder and convinced Russia to sign an alliance with the French. Wilhelm then proceeded to provoke Britain by ordering the construction of a massive naval fleet. Continued German miscalculations convinced England to end its isolation. To defend against German aggression, Britain and France developed an *Entente Cordiale* (friendly understanding).

In 1907 Russia joined this loose confederation, and these three nations formed the **Triple Entente**. Germany and other European states would soon test this system of alliances, which would ultimately lead to a world war.

The Balkans

The Balkan region, located in southeastern Europe, has a long history of conflict, whether it was between ethnic groups or from invading forces. In addition, several states, including Russia, the Ottoman Empire, and Austria-Hungary, had overlapping claims to land in this region. These overlapping claims, combined with a growing sense of nationalism in the Balkans, made this area the "powder keg" of Europe. In other words, any spark of war in this region could ignite a major war throughout Europe.

In 1912 several Balkan states united to drive out the Ottoman forces. Following a brief war, the Balkan states decisively defeated the Ottomans. However, they fought among themselves over the remaining Balkan territory.

The spark that ignited the crisis that became World War I began on **June 28, 1914**. On that date, a Bosnian radical (based in Serbia) assassinated Archduke **Francis Ferdinand**, heir to the throne of Austria-Hungary. The Austrian government then made demands that the Serbian government could not meet. Germany responded by pledging its support to the Austrians, while Russia mobilized in order to defend Serbia.

Germany demanded that Russia stop mobilizing its forces within twelve hours. When Russia failed to comply, Germany declared war on Russia. This decision led to a rapid series of declarations of war. Germany, Austria-Hungary, and the Ottoman Empire formed the **Central Powers**. On the other side, Russia, Serbia, and France formed the **Allies**.

Archduke Franz Ferdinand with his wife, Sophie, and their three children

Guiding Questions

1. What were the major turning points of the war?

2. What was the significance of nationalism and propaganda in the promotion of a total war?

3. How did industrial production and innovation affect the tactics, scale, and duration of the war?

Section Quiz

1. What nation did Germany strive to replace as the industrial power of Europe?

2. How did advances in science and technology change the way people thought about the world?

3. What country became the largest producer of chemicals during this period?

4. What country took advantage of Germany's failure to renew the Reinsurance Treaty with Russia?

★ Why did European nations develop large militaries?

★ Why were the Balkans known as the "powder keg" of Europe?

■ II. Course of the War

As Europe rushed to war, both sides were confident that they would win and that the war would be over quickly. German forces made the first move, and the French quickly responded. However, the war dragged on, and casualties swiftly climbed into the millions with little to show for the massive loss of life. After four brutal years, the war finally ended, but its conclusion laid the groundwork for another war in less than twenty-five years.

Initial Movements

Germany had the initial advantage and sought to make short work of the French by quickly attacking Paris. The French did not initiate the conflict, but they responded with surprising speed. The Russians surprised everyone and disrupted Germany's carefully planned strategy.

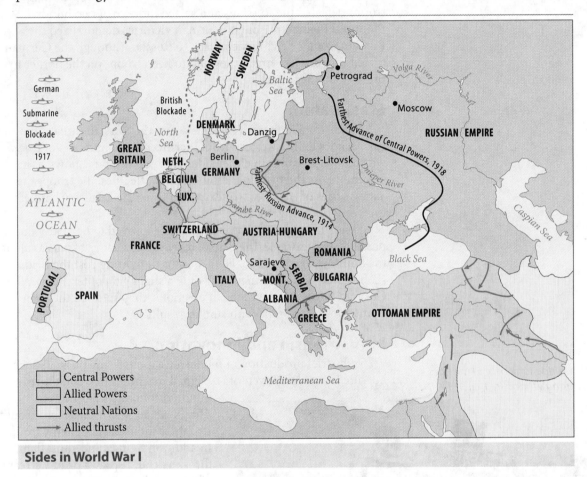

Sides in World War I

Germany

With France on the western front and Russia on the eastern front, Germany found itself fighting a two-front war. However, this did not take the Germans by surprise. Several years earlier a German general named Alfred von Schlieffen prepared a strategy that would enable Germany to win a two-front war. The **Schlieffen Plan** called for the Germans to send most of their forces west through neutral Belgium and quickly surround Paris. Once France surrendered, the German forces would rush to meet the advancing Russian forces on the eastern front.

When the Germans demanded the right to travel through Belgium, the Belgians refused. However, the Germans broke their treaty with Belgium and forced their way through. This violation brought Britain into the war on the side of the Allies.

France

The French stopped the German advance outside of Paris and reinforced their troops at the Marne River. Taxicabs from Paris helped to deliver troops to the front. Despite the German push into France, the French held their position. British forces soon joined the French and helped to prevent German forces from advancing.

Russia

The Russian army surprised the Germans by mobilizing more quickly than anticipated in the Schlieffen Plan. Russian forces enjoyed initial success against German and Austrian forces. However, under the command of General Paul von Hindenburg, German troops defeated the Russians and seized more than two hundred thousand Russian prisoners. German victories demoralized the Russian troops, driving them back to Russia. Although the Germans ended the Russian threat, they had to keep troops on the border to prevent another attack.

Stalemate

While the Germans were able to end the Russian threat from the east, armies on the western front sacrificed large numbers of troops without major gains on either side. This condition is known as a **stalemate**. As the two sides established battle lines, the troops dug a long series of trenches that extended from the English Channel to the border of Switzerland.

Overrunning these entrenched forces proved to be nearly impossible. For example, the British carried out a series of battles along the Somme River in 1916. Four months of fighting cost the British six hundred thousand men with only a slight gain of territory. When German forces attacked French positions, they suffered the same tremendous loss of life with similar results.

Industrialism and Innovation

Industrial production of modern weapons made possible such horrific loss of life. Inventors designed machines that could fire hundreds of bullets per minute. Thus, a small, well-armed force could slaughter thousands of enemy troops. In addition to machine guns, flame-throwers could spray a deadly stream of burning liquid into trenches and foxholes.

Designers of artillery invented shells filled with poisonous gas. Many on both sides suffered terrible burns and agonizing deaths from the deadly contents of these shells. Once fired, the deadly gas was blown by the wind. No one was safe, not even civilians.

The British gained a temporary advantage by secretly developing the tank. Tanks finally enabled the Allies to overrun the German trenches. However, the Central Powers quickly

British-made tank behind the lines during World War I, circa 1918

Plane used during WWI

German zeppelin

Captured German submarine

developed measures to stop the tanks. Adapting rapidly, the Germans also developed tanks. By the end of the war, both sides had produced more than eight thousand of these offensive weapons.

In addition, aircraft changed the dynamic of war. Both sides initially used airplanes to monitor the troop activities of their enemies. However, planes were soon equipped with bombs and machine guns to enable them to kill enemy troops and pilots. The Germans also used zeppelins (aircraft similar to blimps) to bomb civilian areas of England.

While the British enjoyed naval supremacy, the Germans introduced a lethal weapon to neutralize Britain's advantage. German submarines sank over six thousand Allied ships. The British started using blimps to spot German submarines and developed depth charges to destroy them.

Propaganda posters

Justice and Total War

Christian leaders have pointed out that wars need to to be fought properly in addition to being righteous. Distinctions must be made between guilty parties (enemy soldiers) and innocents (civilians, especially women and children). In addition, the force used should only be that which is needed to achieve the goal. Revenge has no place in a righteous war.

Propaganda and Total War

Governments on both sides used every available form of media to maintain support for their side while demonizing the enemy. They also tied war to religion. Sacrifice for the nation was often portrayed as sacrifice for Christianity. Both sides often presented the war as a moral crusade against a wicked enemy. This use of religion to promote the goals of the state is called **civil religion**. Propaganda emphasized national pride and the atrocities (real and exaggerated) committed by the enemy to mobilize civilian support for **total war**. A total war is a war in which there are no limits on targets or the kinds of weapons used.

In addition, total war brought the war to civilians, who became targets during the war. As previously mentioned, Germans bombed civilian areas with zeppelins. They also fired artillery from great distances, and exploding shells often struck civilian targets. As the war took its terrible toll, food became scarce and strikes became common among those who were suffering. Civilian deaths from attack, disease, and famine climbed into the millions.

Major Turning Points

Russia's disastrous defeats at the hands of the Germans resulted in the collapse of central government in Russia. Czar Nicholas II stepped down on March 15, 1917. In 1918 the new Communist Russian leader, **Vladimir Lenin**, signed a treaty with the Germans and took Russia out of the war. This freed the German forces to concentrate on the western front and possibly defeat the Allied forces.

The Germans had angered the United States on several occasions, including their sinking of two American vessels. Also, the United States sought to maintain a balance of power in Europe. Therefore, at the request of President Woodrow Wilson, Congress declared war on Germany on April 6, 1917. At first the American forces had little influence on the war. However, during the war's final months, America sent over two hundred and fifty thousand troops to France every month. The American forces provided the Allies with a much-needed advantage and helped defeat the German forces.

Armenian Genocide

Armenian orphans deported

Most of the Armenians came under control of the Ottoman Empire in the 1400s. When the empire began to decay in the 1800s, the Ottomans began to view the Armenians as a threat. The Armenians were Orthodox Christian, whereas the Ottoman Turks were Muslim.

In addition, many Armenians lived in nearby Russia. The Russians hoped to use the Armenians in the Ottoman Empire in their ongoing attempt to seize more Ottoman territory. When the Armenian people began asking for more self-rule, the Ottomans responded violently.

Over one hundred thousand Armenians died in the first round of killing in the 1890s. Another round of repression in 1909 saw the deaths of over thirty thousand more. The Ottomans resorted to genocide (the planned killing of a race of people) during World War I.

When the war broke out, some Ottoman leaders feared the Armenians might side with the enemy.

Others saw an opportunity to settle "the Armenian question" permanently. At first there was the harassment, torture (such as nailing horseshoes to the feet of victims and making them dance), and killing of individuals.

In 1915 the violence dramatically escalated. Ottoman officials decided to eliminate all the Armenians living in the Ottoman Empire without regard for women, children, and the disabled. The Ottomans had determined that Armenian existence must come to an end.

Soldiers killed Armenians without restraint. They shot them, bayoneted them, or burned them to death in their houses. Then the Ottomans decided to march the survivors over two hundred miles to detention camps in Syria and Palestine. Guards killed some on the march, and a vast majority of the others died of hunger, abuse, or disease. For example, one group began the journey with eighteen thousand Armenians. When they arrived at the detention camp, only one hundred and fifty had survived.

Estimates vary, but approximately 1.5 million Armenians died between 1915 and 1923. This attempted genocide forced another half-million Armenians to live in exile.

Only a small population of Armenians remains in Turkey today. Despite a large body of evidence supporting the attempted genocide, the nation of Turkey denies that the slaughter ever took place and refuses to use the term *genocide*.

Aftermath of the War

The war had led to the deaths of millions and resulted in immense destruction of property. Representatives from major nations met and worked out treaties. However, World War I did not end with a decisive defeat. The Germans agreed to sign an armistice (truce or ceasefire) because they believed that the Allies would treat them fairly. The outcome proved to be very different.

The Paris Peace Conference

Delegates from thirty-two nations attended the **Paris Peace Conference** in January 1919. The Allies excluded countries that had supported the Central Powers. They also excluded Russia because of its early withdrawal from the war.

Representatives formulated five treaties, with the **Treaty of Versailles** being the most important. This treaty between the Allies and Germany contained harsh demands and blamed Germany for the war. Germany lost territory and its colonies and was ordered to pay massive reparations (payment for war damages). In addition, Germany would have to reduce its military capability dramatically.

The Cost

It is almost impossible to comprehend the losses that both sides sustained in this terrible war. Ten million men died in battle, and twenty-six million more were wounded or missing in action. Civilian deaths may have equaled the number of those killed in battle. About fifteen thousand people died for each day of the war.

In addition to the tremendous cost in human lives, the direct and indirect costs of the war exceeded three hundred and fifty billion dollars. Some believed that the cost had been so great that no nation would ever go to war again. They would tragically be proven wrong within a few years.

Section Quiz

1. Who made the first military move in World War I?

2. How did the Russians upset the Schlieffen Plan?

3. What weapon did the Germans use to reduce the impact of British naval superiority?

4. Briefly define "total war."

5. What were two major turning points in World War I?

★ How did industrialism and innovation increase the death toll in World War I?

★ After tens of millions of dead and wounded, many thought that World War I was the war to end all wars. But roughly two decades later a second world war broke out. Why would such devastation not actually cause war to cease, as many thought? Reference James 4:1–3 in your answer.

■ III. Instability Following the War

The world following the war proved to be much different than it had been before the war. Democracies struggled to survive, and nations turned to dictators who promised them security and stability. The United States and several European powers labored to secure a

Guiding Questions

1. Why did dictatorships develop following the war?

2. How did nations struggle for a lasting peace through organizations and agreements?

3. What changes occurred in Asia, Africa, and the Middle East following World War I?

long-term peace, but their reasoning excluded the reality of man's fallen nature.

In addition, major changes occurred in Asia and other areas as European imperialism began to lose its influence. The world proved to be very unstable, and no amount of precaution could overcome the human drive to seek power and dominate weaker nations.

Rise of Dictators

Russia—The Rise of the Soviet Union

In Chapter 16 you learned about the conflict in Russia. Despite brutal suppression by the czar and the central government, unrest continued to grow. During the reign of Czar Nicholas II, many radical parties formed in Russia. One of the most radical, the Social Democratic Party, soon split. The more radical faction took the name **Bolsheviks**, and the more moderate faction became known as the **Mensheviks**. The Bolsheviks supported violence, while the Mensheviks sought change through peaceful methods.

While many events contributed to the overthrow of the Russian monarchy, violent strikes and riots beginning on March 8, 1917, quickly led to Nicholas's abdication on March 15. Initially, a temporary government led by Menshevik Alexander Kerensky tried to stabilize the chaotic conditions in Russia. However, the Bolsheviks sabotaged these efforts and stirred up Russian workers to prevent the possibility of Menshevik success.

While exiled in Switzerland, Vladimir Lenin led the Bolshevik party. In a strategic move, the German government enabled Lenin to return to Russia from exile. As we learned earlier, Lenin signed the peace treaty that removed Russia from the war and aided the German cause in World War I. On November 7, 1917, Lenin's forces took over the government offices in St. Petersburg. With little effort, Lenin became the virtual dictator of Russia.

While Lenin embraced Marxist teaching, he disagreed with Marx on several issues. First, Lenin rejected the possibility of peaceful change in favor of violent revolution. Lenin also believed that revolution would only occur under the direction of strong leadership, instead of the spontaneous revolts by the working class taught by Marx. Third, Lenin limited power to a small elite group who would exercise great authority, rather than Marx's dream of a dictatorship by the masses.

Lenin also became a strong opponent of religion. He declared that atheism was a vital and inseparable part of Marxist teaching. Agreeing with Marx, Lenin declared religion to be "the opium of the people." He viewed religion and churches as tools used to take advantage of the working class.

Lenin's hatred of religion quickly transformed from rhetoric to bloodshed. For example, in 1918 when pastors and

What's in a Name?

The violent wing of Russia's Social Democratic Party represented a minority of the party. Yet, for propaganda purposes, they took the name *Bolshevik*, which means "majority." The moderate wing of this party comprised a solid majority of the Social Democrats, yet their opponents called them the Mensheviks, or minority wing. The fact is that the Communists never had anything like a majority in the Soviet Union. It is remarkable that less than 10 percent of the population could control the Soviet Union for nearly seventy years.

Nicholas II (above);
Vladimir Lenin (left)

Joseph Stalin

Adolf Hitler

priests opposed Lenin's violent tactics and his orders to empty the churches of valuables, he ordered the military to put down their resistance with great brutality. In addition, Lenin instructed his forces to execute large numbers of religious leaders.

When Lenin died in 1924, two of his followers, Leon Trotsky and **Joseph Stalin** (1879–1953), struggled for control of the Communist Party in Russia. However, Stalin quickly outmaneuvered Trotsky and became the second dictator of the Soviet Union.

In 1928 Stalin instituted the first of several Five-Year Plans. With these plans, Stalin tried to build up industrial production and brought agriculture under central government control. However, many peasants opposed Stalin's plan to control agriculture. Stalin used the secret police and army to burn the homes of offending peasants. Authorities also deported or executed those who resisted. Stalin's forces crushed the resistance and, in the process, destroyed over half of the homes in Russia.

Stalin also continued and intensified oppression of religion. The Soviet government systematically closed thousands of churches and religious schools. Stalin also ordered the execution of an unknown number of pastors and priests. Many Christians suffered terrible persecution during the vicious assault on Christianity under Communist rulers like Stalin.

Germany—The Rise of the Nazi Party

At the end of World War I, German delegates formed the **Weimar** (VY mar) **Republic** (named after the town in Germany where the republic was organized). Despite early optimism, this German government had little opportunity to succeed. Most Germans did not support it. In addition, the large number of political parties in Germany made it very difficult for one party to win a majority in elections.

With the growing unpopularity of the Weimar Republic and continued political instability, radical groups became more popular. One group, the National Socialist German Workers' Party (commonly known as the **Nazi** Party), became a contender for power. Led by **Adolf Hitler**, the Nazis used the political process to gain control of the German government in 1933.

However, once in power, Hitler suspended the republic and declared himself the dictator of Germany. Using the principles of fascism, the Nazis controlled industry and used it to rebuild Germany for future military conquest. One example is the modern highway system throughout Germany. This road system would enable German troops to move rapidly from one front to another in the event of another two-front war. Hitler also worked to make Germany self-sufficient (able to produce everything needed by the country). Self-sufficiency would limit the ability of enemy forces to cut off supplies in a time of war.

Italy—The Rise of Fascism

Italy had supported the Allies during the war and had suffered the loss of five hundred thousand men. However, Italy received no territory or colonies. Instead, the Italian economy suffered from a large war debt and strikes by discontented workers. The wealthy looked for protection from a possible Communist revolution, and the masses wanted a strong leader to restore Italy's national pride.

Benito Mussolini had been a member of the Socialist Party in Italy, but he proved to be too violent for the Socialists. As a result, he formed the Fascist Party and quickly gained popularity. In his writings and speeches, Mussolini promised order and stability. Sensing that the government was vulnerable, Mussolini led thousands of followers in a march on Rome in October 1922. King Victor Emmanuel III agreed to the Fascists' demand that he appoint Mussolini the leader of Italy.

Mussolini gradually transformed Italy into a dictatorship. While he maintained the image of a representative government, Mussolini and the Fascists sought to gain total control over the government. Within three years, the transition was complete, and Mussolini became the absolute ruler of Italy.

Like Hitler, Mussolini set about to make Italy economically self-sufficient. To accomplish this goal, he organized Italy's work force into thirteen groups. The Fascists carefully monitored and controlled all economic activity. They also determined wages, prices, and other policies that affected the economy.

In order to add the appearance of legitimacy to his rule, Mussolini ended the long-standing dispute with the Roman Catholic Church. In 1929 Mussolini and Catholic representatives signed the **Lateran Treaties**. These agreements ended Rome's opposition to the unification of Italy that had continued since 1870. Until 1929 the papacy had refused to cooperate with succeeding Italian governments. However, in exchange for money and a small independent region known as Vatican City, the pope recognized Mussolini's government and ended the papacy's prior claims to additional territory.

Struggle for a Long-Term Peace

Led by men like President Wilson, many nations sought a way to guarantee that the world would never again experience a major conflict like World War I. Leaders formed organizations to promote peace and enable the nonviolent resolution of conflicts. Others embraced disarmament (doing away with weapons) as a way to prevent future conflicts.

League of Nations

Following World War I, U.S. president Woodrow Wilson led in the formation of the **League of Nations**. Wilson and other founders believed such an organization could bring about international cooperation. They hoped to achieve peace by preventing future wars.

However, the United States Senate refused to ratify the treaty that formed this League. The League only had power to recommend action. It had no power to enforce its recommendations. The League soon proved to be weak and ineffective, especially when dealing with powerful nations.

Disarmament and Nonaggression Pacts

In a continuing effort to prevent future wars, nations signed three pacts or agreements. These agreements were doomed to fail because they did not take into account man's fallen nature.

Several nations met in 1921–22 for the **Washington Naval Conference** and agreed to limit the number of war ships each could build. The participants assumed that nations could avoid war by simply reducing or eliminating the weapons. However, Japan's

Benito Mussolini

Basic Principles of Fascism

1. Businesses are privately owned but tightly controlled by the government.

2. Fascists place an extreme emphasis on nationalism and glorify the state.

3. Dictators supported by the military often govern in a fascist state.

Citizenship and Nationalism

Citizens should be grateful when they live in a country they can love, celebrate, and support. There are values, traditions, and freedoms that nations protect which citizens should be willing to die to preserve. But nationalism becomes a great evil when a nation is made into an idol. When nationalism demands loyalty to the state that takes precedence over family, friends, church, or God, such a demand is idolatrous.

Sun Yat-Sen

Chiang Kai-shek

Mao Zedong

participation in the conference did not prevent it from continuing to build a large naval fleet.

In 1925 European nations met in Locarno, Switzerland. At this meeting, Germany signed an agreement with France and Belgium recognizing its present borders with those two nations as permanent. In theory, this would have prevented World War II. The **Locarno Pact** briefly offered the promise of peace in Europe.

In 1928 the American secretary of state, Frank Kellogg, decided that the best way to prevent war was to get nations to agree to renounce offensive war. Those who signed the **Kellogg-Briand Pact** agreed to settle their disputes by negotiation rather than force. Kellogg naively believed that this agreement could prevent wars from being started. However, three years after signing this pact, Japan invaded Manchuria.

Shifts in the Post-War World

European imperialism, described in Chapters 15 and 16, changed after World War I. Sadly, colonies did not gain their freedom, although many demanded it. However, China entered into a struggle for reform and independence that continued after the end of World War II. Japan made a radical shift from being a European ally in the First World War to being a major threat heading into the Second World War. African nations that had been governed by Germany now came under French and British rule. Finally, the Middle East transferred from Ottoman rule to French and British rule.

China—The Struggle for Power

In Chapter 16 you learned about the decline of the Qing dynasty and its continued resistance to change. By 1911 young Chinese officials, along with military officers and students, staged a revolution to replace the Qing dynasty with a republic. Led by **Sun Yat-Sen**, the Chinese worked to bring reform to China. However, others pressured Sun Yat-Sen to postpone reform and allow the last Qing monarch to abdicate. He soon regretted agreeing to this compromise. Chinese prime minister Yuan Shikai took advantage of Sun Yat-Sen's restraint and used his influence to dismantle the new republic before he was forced to step down in 1916. As a result, a power vacuum developed, and Sun Yat-Sen struggled to bring unity to China through the **Kuomintang** (KWO min TAHNG) or Nationalist Party.

Following the death of Sun Yat-Sen in 1925, **Chiang Kai-shek** (CHANG KYE-SHEK; 1887–1975) assumed the leadership of the Kuomintang. In 1927, a radical element of this party split off into what became the **Chinese Communist Party**. Led by **Mao Zedong** (1893–1976), the Communists stirred up peasant revolts in order to undermine the conservative government of Chiang Kai-shek. These two forces fought a civil war to gain control of China. The Japanese invasion in 1931 postponed this struggle until the conclusion of World War II.

Japan—The Rise of Militarism

The military developed a strong influence in Japan during the Meiji Restoration. As Japan became more aggressive toward China and other countries, this influence grew into control. Japanese leaders viewed a strong military as essential for expanding and controlling Japan's overseas empire.

Japan developed a form of fascism to manage the growing economy. Fascism combined with the growth of monopolies (when a person or company has control over a product or service) enabled Japan to quickly grow into a major financial power. A strong economy and a strong military combined to form a military state with a growing appetite for foreign territories.

Mandate System and Colonial Rule

The League of Nations established a procedure that enabled France and Britain, primarily, to take possession of colonies previously ruled by the Central Powers. Some American observers complained that Britain and France merely divided the colonies to suit their interests. The map indicates which regions in Africa and the Middle East the British and French governed under the mandate system.

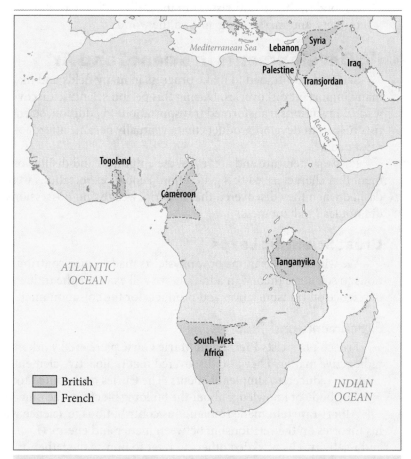

Mandates in Africa and the Middle East

Middle East

During World War I, Arabs began to seek a united state of Arabia and an Arab League that would spread from the west coast of northern Africa to Saudi Arabia. This secular movement, known as **Pan-Arabism**, suffered several setbacks, including the Balfour Declaration in 1917, which authorized the British to administer Palestine. Later, the creation of the nation of Israel provided a major obstacle that resulted in many failed attempts to destroy this tiny country. The destruction of Israel continues to be the goal of Arab nations, in part because of the dream of Pan-Arabism. More recently, this has transformed into a religious movement with the growing influence of what many refer to as militant Islam.

Section Quiz

1. Into what two groups did the Social Democratic Party (Russia) split? What do their names mean?
2. Who were the first two dictators of Russia?
3. What German republic fell to the Nazis?
4. What nation supported the Allies during the First World War but became a dictatorship after the war?
5. What was the goal of the Kellogg-Briand Pact?
6. Name the first two leaders of the Kuomintang Party.
* Respond to the new atheist claim that religion is the root of wars, conflicts, and mass killing around the world.

■ IV. Developments in Science and Art

Scientists continued to make progress in many fields and made many important discoveries. During this period scientific discoveries and inventions transformed transportation. In addition, scientists helped to develop products that eventually became affordable to most people.

Postwar literature and art reveal the emptiness and disillusionment that characterized this generation. People's expectations were dashed when they discovered that material wealth and possessions did not lead to happiness.

Great Scientific Leaps

We will briefly examine how physicists made major contributions to scientific theory. In addition, we will examine the influence of science on transportation and products for the common man.

Experiments and Theories

French physicists **Pierre and Marie Curie** pioneered work in radioactive matter. They also discovered that radioactive elements could be reduced to simpler elements. The Curies contributed to the growing body of knowledge about the building blocks of the universe.

Albert Einstein made tremendous contributions to science with his theories on the relationship between matter and energy ($E=mc^2$) and relativity. His work led others to refer to him as the father of modern physics. In addition, he theorized about the existence of black holes in space and other celestial concepts that helped man realize the vastness of the universe.

Transportation Advances

Scientists used discoveries in fields such as math, physics, and chemistry to develop many improved modes of transportation, including the airplane. Between the first flight and the end of World War I, the airplane changed dramatically. World War II would elevate the airplane to an essential tool for war.

In addition, many scientific discoveries combined to produce a vehicle that was self-propelled. We refer to this scientific marvel

Guiding Questions

1. What great scientific advances occurred between the wars?
2. How did the art of this period reflect the pessimism of the age?
3. How did the media communicate Western ideas and culture around the world?

Albert Einstein

as the automobile. Scientists continued to play a role as larger and more powerful engines powered cars, trucks, and weapons such as tanks.

Another invention that underwent tremendous change because of science was the railway. From slower wood-powered steam locomotives to faster coal- and then diesel-powered engines, the railway continued to progress. Important during times of peace, it became essential during the next war.

These various modes of travel affected commerce positively. Industry relied on these forms of transportation to get goods to the market quickly. In addition, these vehicles enhanced migration within and between nations. For example, laborers could more easily travel to locations where they could find work. The middle and upper classes could also travel in comfort for work or vacation.

Mass Consumption

Additional products became mass produced and available to an eager public. Products such as bicycles, refrigerators, and radios became very popular in many nations. Continued scientific discoveries and improvements made these products less expensive to produce and thus affordable to more people. Credit enabled the eager customer to buy the latest product immediately and make payments later on the balance.

Chemists continued to experiment with natural materials and chemical combinations. Artificial fibers made from wood included rayon and acetate. Scientists developed the first synthetic fiber, nylon, in 1939 as a substitute for silk. Gradually artificial and synthetic fibers became the raw materials for products used around the world.

Postwar Art

The Allies had triumphed over the Central Powers, and many people in the victorious countries experienced financial wealth after the war. However, much of American and European society found life to be empty and ultimately futile. To them, feelings became more important than facts. These feelings found expression in literature and art. Even architecture changed during this period.

Literature

Literature following World War I often reflected the despair and emptiness of modern life. For example, T. S. Eliot (1888-1965) wrote an intricate poem entitled "The Waste Land" that attempted to describe this emptiness. German writer Thomas Mann (1875–1955) wrote works whose main characters were passive victims of forces beyond their control. Much of the literature from this period expressed misery and gloom.

Painting

Two schools of art emerged during this period, **Expressionism** and **Cubism**. Expressionist painters created art that reflected how the artist felt about his subject, rather than what he saw as he painted his subject. Cubist painters reduced their subjects to geometric shapes (often cubes). This school of painting attempted to depict the subject from several perspectives at once. Cubist painters often designed their works to astonish the observer and confront his view of the world.

The Scream *by Edvard Munch, an example of Expressionism*

The portrait of Pablo Picasso by Juan Gris is an example of cubism.

Fallingwater designed by Frank Lloyd Wright within the Bear Run Nature Reserve in Pennsylvania

The Bauhaus designed by Walter Gropius in Dessau, Germany

Architecture

Using concrete, glass, and steel, architects designed buildings with a sense of openness and functionality. American architect Louis Sullivan (1856–1924) developed the concept of skyscrapers. Walter Gropius (1883–1969) developed the concept of functional architecture in Europe. Frank Lloyd Wright (1868–1959), an American architect, added his own personal touch by designing buildings that blended in with their surroundings.

Media

Improved printing machines and mass production of paper from wood pulp lowered the cost of producing various forms of print, including newspapers and magazines. Commercial advertising also multiplied as companies paid to get the public to notice and buy their products.

During this period, moving pictures developed, and scientists soon found a way to add sound. Movies became a popular and inexpensive form of entertainment. Continued improvements to the radio led to mass production, and soon no home was complete without one. Through print, picture, and sound, ideas and aspects of culture were effectively communicated around the world.

Section Quiz

1. With what type of matter did the Curies make discoveries?

2. What sciences contributed to improved modes of transportation?

3. What did Expressionist painting reflect?

4. What characterized architecture during this period?

5. How were ideas and culture spread around the world during this period?

★ Why did materialism fail to result in happiness?

The Prudential Building designed by Louis Sullivan in Buffalo, New York

V. The Great Depression

Following World War I, some nations seemed to recover and prosper financially. Others struggled and found themselves awash in national debt. The United States appeared to be able to absorb massive war debt and yet prosper. However, that apparent prosperity faded, and economic fractures began to appear. Many blame the stock market crash in 1929, but that was only a symptom of underlying problems. The costs of the Depression created a great burden for the world to bear, and the consequences endure to this day.

Causes of the Depression

The causes for the **Great Depression** are many, and historians continue to debate this subject. However, we will briefly look at three basic problems that the United States experienced leading up to the Depression. By this period, America had grown into one of the most prosperous nations in the world. Therefore, when America experienced an economic downturn, many other nations also suffered.

Financial Devastation of World War I

The United States had loaned the Allies over ten billion dollars during the war. This increased the national debt from about one billion dollars to twenty-four billion dollars in three years. While most of the Allies promised to pay back their debt, only Finland actually followed through. When European nations experienced financial problems, they simply refused to pay their war debt to America. This placed immense stress on the American economy.

Failure of the Federal Reserve

In 1913, the U.S. Congress created the **Federal Reserve** to control the money supply and help protect the American banking system. To accomplish these goals, the Federal Reserve had the power to set interest rates and loan money to banks.

However, the Federal Reserve raised interest rates four times during 1928 and 1929, from three and one-half to six percent. This doubling of the interest rate had a negative impact on the U.S. economy. Increased rates made it very hard for businesses to borrow money and invest. This hindered economic growth and contributed to the stock market crash in October 1929.

Protectionism

As the U.S. economy weakened in the late 1920s, American companies began to pressure presidential candidate Hoover and members of Congress to pass tariff legislation that would raise the prices on foreign goods and protect American-made products. In response, Congress debated and passed the highest tariff (duty or tax on foreign products) in U.S. history. In 1930 President Hoover signed the **Smoot-Hawley Tariff Act**, and many European states quickly responded with restrictive tariffs of their own.

This tariff resulted in American exports dropping from seven billion dollars in 1929 to two and one-half billion dollars in 1932. The loss of trade devastated the American economy, and the damage spread throughout many nations as one government after another imposed tariffs on imported goods.

Guiding Questions

1. What caused the Great Depression?
2. What were the costs of the Great Depression?

The Danger of Tariffs

The Smoot-Hawley Tariff made many foreign products much more expensive. For example, this tariff increased the price of Swiss watches. The Swiss responded by placing a high tariff on automobiles and other products made in America. However, the Swiss had been buying more American cars than Americans bought Swiss watches. Therefore, the American automobile industry and other industries suffered more than did the Swiss watch industry. This shortsighted tariff cost many American jobs.

Causes and Costs of the Depression

List the causes and costs of the Depression.

Causes	Costs

Costs of the Depression

The United States and other nations had experienced financial panics and brief depressions many times prior to 1929. However, this time, the federal government in America and national governments throughout Europe took a much more active role in trying to revive their economies. Consequently, natural economic corrections did not occur. The Great Depression endured for many years with little improvement, despite massive spending of the taxpayers' money.

Unemployment

Massive unemployment was one of the immediate effects of the Depression. Up to one-third of the work force lost their jobs, and many people looked to government to meet their needs. Since the Depression began during the administration of Herbert Hoover, many blamed him for this economic downturn and pressured him to do something to help those in need.

Contrary to popular opinion, President Hoover did not sit idly by and refuse to act. He spent large amounts of taxpayer dollars to assist various areas of the American economy. However, despite his spending over two billion dollars, the unemployment rate remained high and recovery proved elusive.

Growth of Government

President Hoover began to increase the size of the federal government by supporting the Federal Farm Board to shore up the price of farm products. In addition, he endorsed the Reconstruction Finance Corporation and its efforts to help failing businesses.

Franklin D. Roosevelt, the Democratic candidate for president, repeatedly attacked Hoover's efforts as an unwarranted growth of federal government and wasteful spending of the nation's wealth. Ironically, following his election in 1932, Roosevelt set about to substantially grow and transform the federal government.

For example, Roosevelt established a growing number of federal agencies that were supposed to create jobs and bring America out of the Depression. His administration spent billions of dollars and created thousands of temporary make-work jobs. Yet the unemployment rate never dropped below 14 percent, and the Depression continued.

Section Quiz

1. Why did the U.S. national debt grow from one to twenty-four billion dollars in just three years?

2. What did American companies demand from Congress to protect the competitiveness of American products?

3. How did the Federal Reserve make it difficult for businesses to borrow and invest?

4. Why did President Roosevelt establish a growing number of federal agencies? Did they help to end the Depression?

★ Why did the Great Depression last longer than previous depressions?

★ What may have been the divine purpose for the Great Depression?

Making Connections

1. Why did England side with the Allies in World War I?

2. Why did Russia mobilize its troops at the beginning of the war?

3. Why did the Germans send most of their forces against France at the beginning of the war?

4. Why were the Central Powers and the Allies unable to attain a quick victory?

5. Why did both sides resort to propaganda?

6. Why did Hitler rebuild the German infrastructure, including a modern highway system?

7. Why did the Kuomintang and the Chinese Communist Party temporarily stop fighting each other?

8. Why did the Smoot-Hawley Tariff lead to a drastic decline in American exports?

Developing History Skills

1. Compare and contrast German methods for acquiring land and using war to bring about German unity in Chapter 12 and this chapter.

2. Respond to the following statement: "The isolation of the United States following World War I contributed to the conditions that led to World War II."

Thinking Critically

1. Evaluate President Roosevelt's expansion of the federal government during the Great Depression.

2. Evaluate conditions leading to World War I in light of Bible passages such as Exodus 20; 2 Chronicles 16, 18; Psalm 20:7; and James 4:1.

Living in God's World

1. Write an essay for a technology magazine presenting a Christian view of a recent advance in communications technology. The essay should discuss how Christians can wisely use the technology.

2. Read Amos 1:3–2:8. Imagine that you are a pastor who lived during World War I. Write a brief essay addressing Europe in light of Amos 1–2.

People, Places, and Things to Know

Reinsurance Treaty
Wilhelm II
Triple Entente
June 28, 1914
Francis Ferdinand
Central Powers
Allies
Schlieffen Plan
stalemate
civil religion
total war
Vladimir Lenin
Paris Peace Conference
Treaty of Versailles
Bolsheviks
Mensheviks
Joseph Stalin
Weimar Republic
Nazi
Adolf Hitler
Benito Mussolini
Lateran Treaties
League of Nations
Washington Naval Conference
Locarno Pact
Kellogg-Briand Pact
Sun Yat-Sen
Kuomintang
Chiang Kai-shek
Chinese Communist Party
Mao Zedong
Pan-Arabism
Pierre and Marie Curie
Albert Einstein
Expressionism
Cubism
Great Depression
Federal Reserve
Smoot-Hawley Tariff Act

World War II

1939 – 45

18

- Causes of the War
- Course of the War
- Consequences of the War

1935 – 46

Munich Conference is held September 1938

Pact of Steel is formed
May 1939

Rome-Berlin Axis is formed
October 1936

Nonaggression Pact
between Germany
and the Soviet Union
August 1939

Anti-Comintern Pact is
signed November 1936

Italy's army conquers
Ethiopia October 1935–
May 1936

Japan invades China
July 1937

Germany invades
Poland September
1939

| 1935 | 1936 | 1937 | 1938 | 1939 | 1940 |

Francisco Franco becomes fascist dictator in Spain July 1936–April 1939

Big Ideas

1. What were the causes of World War II?
2. What were the course, outcome, and human costs of the war?
3. What were the philosophical and religious consequences of the two decades following the war?

The two decades that followed the First World War were filled with unrest. Some nations responded by expanding their militaries and planning for conquest. At the same time, other states, disillusioned by the war, determined to avoid future conflict at almost any cost. Tragically, the perceived weakness of one group led to the unrestrained aggression of the other.

Germany invades Russia
June 1941

Japan attacks Pearl Harbor
December 1941

Allies invade France
June 1944

Allies defeat Axis powers in Europe
May 1945

Allies defeat Axis powers in the Pacific
September 1945

| 1941 | 1942 | 1943 | 1944 | 1945 | 1946 |

■ I. Causes of the War

Fascism multiplied and spread in Europe and Asia. In addition, old wounds created by the harsh treaties signed following World War I refused to heal. Land-hungry states began to seize territory from weaker neighbors. The democratic states hesitated to respond with the threat of force. This situation became a recipe for another world war.

Spread of Dictatorships

In addition to Italy and Germany, Spain came under the leadership of a dictator. Furthermore, Japan's military continued to gain power even as the civilian government steadily lost influence. This military growth enabled the figurehead emperor to gain real power because he supported the Japanese military.

Europe

In the last chapter you learned about the rise of fascism in Italy and Germany. In 1936 **Francisco Franco**, a Spanish general, overthrew the republican government and imposed a fascist dictatorship in Spain. Mussolini and Hitler supported Franco and used the Spanish Civil War to test their new weapons and tactics in preparation for future conquest. This war served as a practice run for World War II.

Japan

In addition to adopting fascism, Japan transformed into a society where the representative civilian government declined in influence as the military steadily gained more power. As a result, the power of the emperor also increased since Emperor **Hirohito** played an active role in military decisions. General Hideki **Tojo** also played a central role in expanding the power of the military in Japan and supporting Japanese conquest. However, rather than dominating the emperor, General Tojo maintained a strong loyalty to Emperor Hirohito. He faithfully carried out the emperor's wishes, including the decision to attack the U.S. naval fleet.

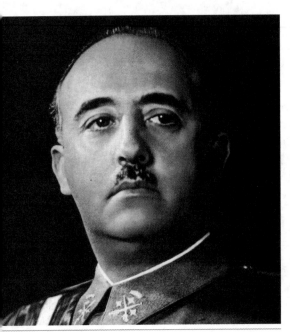

Francisco Franco

Hirohito, 1945 (left);
Hideki Tojo, 1940s (right)

Legacy of World War I

In the last chapter you learned that the Allies treated the Central Powers harshly following their agreement to stop fighting. For example, the war guilt clause in the Treaty of Versailles placed all of the blame for World War I on the Germans and the other Central Powers.

In addition, the Central Powers lost territory at home and abroad. Germany especially suffered great hardship in this loss of land and colonies. A revived and well-armed Germany under Hitler would quickly address this German grievance.

Furthermore, the demand that Germany pay the Allied nations huge sums in the form of war reparations destroyed the German economy and led to the chaos that enabled the rise of the Nazi party. Germany would not be satisfied until these injustices had been corrected.

Aggression in the 1930s

The fascist countries took advantage of their growing military power and expanded their borders at the expense of their neighbors. When the democracies failed to challenge this aggression, the facist states continued their expansion.

Japanese

The Japanese had taken a progressively more dominant role in Manchuria. In 1931 someone destroyed a section of railroad in Manchuria controlled by the Japanese. The Japanese used this event as justification to invade Manchuria and seize additional land. China protested, but no European powers intervened to stop the Japanese aggression.

Japan became increasingly bold and staged a major assault on China beginning in 1937. This attack forced the Nationalist Party and the Chinese Communists to suspend their struggle for control of China in order to resist the Japanese invasion.

When the League of Nations protested this invasion in 1937, the Japanese simply ended participation in the league. Japan brutalized China and seized its many natural resources to build its military.

When war erupted in 1939 with the German invasion of Poland, Japan expanded into Southeast Asia. Japanese forces seized several islands and heavily fortified them. The United States and Great Britain objected to this expansion and blocked shipments of oil to Japan. This move threatened to cripple Japan's fleet and end Japanese imperialism.

Italian

In Chapter 15 you learned that Italy suffered a humiliating defeat when it tried to conquer Ethiopia in 1896. In 1935 Mussolini sent a well-equipped, modern army into Ethiopia and quickly conquered this poor African country. Despite pleas by the Ethiopian leader to the League of Nations, Europe made no serious attempt to stop or punish Italian aggression.

The League of Nations proved unable or unwilling to respond to aggression. Mussolini took advantage of this weak response and seized Albania in 1939. The Italians had been increasing their influence in this strategic country for several years. When the Albanian king refused to submit to Italian domination, Italian forces seized control of Albania.

German and Italian Expansion 1935–39

Rhineland
Sudetenland
Axis Powers
Axis-controlled lands, Sept. 1, 1939

(left to right) *Neville Chamberlain, Édouard Daladier, prime minister of France, Hitler, Mussolini, and Count Ciano, foreign minister of Italy, at the Munich Conference*

German

As soon as Hitler came to power in 1933, he began to carry out his goals to make Germany a world power and a nation free of "defective" and "undesirable" citizens. Later in the chapter we will examine this second goal in detail.

Hitler centralized his nation's resources to construct a new German empire. To defend this **Third Reich**, Hitler needed to establish a military presence in the neutral territory west of the Rhine River. He made a bold move and sent German troops into the Rhineland on March 7, 1936. The French responded with angry words, but no European nation moved to stop German expansion. Germany fortified this region to protect against future attack from France.

According to the Treaty of Versailles, Germany and Austria could not form a political alliance. Despite this restriction, Hitler secretly planned to gain control of this state. In 1938 he arranged to have an Austrian Nazi selected as the chancellor. The Austrian chancellor then invited Germany to send troops and stabilize Austria. Thus Germany and Austria defied the treaty. Germany became the dominant partner in this alliance.

Hitler's successes emboldened him to demand that an area of Czechoslovakia called **Sudetenland** come under German control. To resolve this issue, British and French leaders met with Hitler at the **Munich Conference** in September 1938. Without even consulting the Czech government, the British and French leaders agreed to meet Hitler's demands.

Despite Hitler's promise not to invade Czechoslovakia, German troops marched into the Czech capital six months later and took control of most of the country. The weak response of Britain and France had led Hitler to conclude that he could continue to seize neighboring countries without fear of European interference.

Failure of Democracies to Oppose Aggression

As we have seen, Japan, Italy, and Germany learned that they could attack and conquer weaker states without fear of serious consequences. Much of Europe had not recovered from the destruction of World War I. As a result, leaders remained reluctant to resort to conflict. The empire-building fascist states took full advantage of this paralyzing fear and rushed toward another world war. For a time, the democratic nations failed to intervene and resist these acts of aggression.

Neville Chamberlain served as the prime minister of England. He led the European nations in a policy to avoid war by means of **appeasement** (avoiding conflict by making concessions). Chamberlain used Britain's influence to pressure weaker nations to submit to Hitler's demand for territory. European leaders, including French Prime Minister Édouard Daladier, followed Britain's lead and sought to appease Hitler and Mussolini.

The United States, under President Roosevelt, maintained a policy of isolation. Most Americans wanted to leave European conflict to the Europeans and supported Roosevelt's neutrality. In addition, many Americans continued to suffer under the Great Depression and had little interest in foreign affairs.

Events that Triggered the War

The aggressive nations gambled on the assumption that they could continue to seize land without war and that European leaders would continue to appease. However, the Europeans finally realized that these aggressive states would not stop until forced to do so by threat of war. To prepare for the coming war, or to try to prevent it, nations formed alliances to strengthen their position. Then lines were drawn, and the crossing of those lines would lead to war.

Alliances

Initially, Germany had no allies in Europe after World War I. Even Mussolini had opposed some of Hitler's early attempts at conquest. However, in 1936 Mussolini and Hitler formed an alliance called the **Rome-Berlin Axis**. Later that same year, Germany and Japan formed an agreement known as the **Anti-Comintern Pact**. This pact allied Germany and Japan against Communist Russia. In 1937 Italy and Japan signed a similar agreement. The three nations that would become the **Axis powers** were now connected.

The alliances against the spread of communism provided Europe with a false sense of security. Many European leaders feared communism more than they feared fascism. However, Hitler and Mussolini shattered the illusion of security when they signed a military alliance in May 1939 called the **Pact of Steel.**

The final shock came in August 1939 when Germany and the Soviet Union signed an agreement to refrain from attacking one another for the next ten years. This accord protected Germany from a two-front war and encouraged German conquest. Japan signed a similar agreement with the Soviets and helped to pave the way for continued aggression.

German Invasion of Poland

Over 1.5 million German troops marched across the border into Poland on **September 1, 1939**. Despite Hitler's confidence that Britain and France would continue to appease, these countries demanded an immediate end to the invasion.

When Germany refused to comply with Allied demands regarding Poland, Britain and France declared war. Although the determination of the **Allies** surprised Hitler, he resolved to fight and take control of Europe. The Allies had declared war, but they were in no position to provide Poland with any military assistance.

Japanese Bombing of Pearl Harbor

The Japanese developed a two-track policy for dealing with the United States. Japanese diplomats continued to negotiate in an effort to get the United States to end economic restraints such as the oil embargo. However, the Japanese military, with the consent of the emperor, also prepared for war against the United States. When the Japanese concluded that war presented their best option for conquest of Pacific islands, they planned a major assault to end the American threat.

Soviet Foreign Minister Molotov signs the German-Soviet nonaggression pact; Joachim von Ribbentrop (third from left) and Joseph Stalin (second from right) stand behind him, Moscow, August 23, 1939.

Polish Resistance

The Polish forces fought bravely against the much larger German force from the west and the invasion of the Soviet Union from the east. Polish soldiers destroyed many German vehicles and nearly three hundred aircraft during the brief conflict. Although Poland ultimately fell, Polish forces continued to oppose German and Soviet occupation through a large resistance movement.

333

A burned B-17C (top left); Japanese Zero (top right); USS West Virginia in flames (above)

On **December 7, 1941**, the Japanese launched a surprise attack on the American naval base at **Pearl Harbor**, Hawaii. During this unprovoked assault, the Japanese forces killed more than two thousand Americans, destroyed most of the aircraft, and sank several battleships. Providentially, the American aircraft carriers were away on maneuvers and escaped destruction in the Japanese assault. This brutal attack quickly turned the previously neutral United States into a key Allied power.

Section Quiz

1. Who rose to power in Japan as the military replaced the weak civilian government?
2. What country did Italy invade to avenge a previous defeat?
3. With what country was Germany forbidden to form a political alliance?
4. With what country did Germany and Japan sign an agreement to refrain from war?
5. At what military base did Japan attack American forces and trigger the United States' entry into World War II?
★ Why were the fascist powers able to seize territory without fearing serious opposition?

■ II. Course of the War

The Axis powers had prepared extensively for war and enjoyed the initial advantage. Using brutal tactics, they threatened to destroy the Allied forces. However, they made serious miscalculations and found the Allies to be a formidable force, especially when the United States entered the fight.

Principal Theaters of Conflict

This conflict was truly a world war. Battles occurred on several continents, and soldiers from many nations engaged in this deadly struggle. To varying degrees, nearly sixty countries participated in the Second World War.

Western Europe

In the spring of 1940, Germany invaded Denmark and Norway. Hitler especially wanted to prevent the Allies from developing military bases in Norway. Then the Germans attacked the Netherlands and Belgium. The British and French responded by rushing troops into Belgium to stop the Germans.

However, German forces anticipated this maneuver and slipped past French defenses south of Belgium. Then the German army swept into France, behind the Allied lines. Within one month, the Allied army found itself trapped near the English Channel on the beaches of Dunkirk. The German military could have easily destroyed this force and eliminated all possibility of future Allied military threats.

Nevertheless, Hitler decided to allow the German air force (*Luftwaffe*; LOOFT vahf uh) to wipe out the Allied force composed of more than three hundred and fifty thousand troops. However, Hitler could not control the weather. While fog and clouds made it impossible for the *Luftwaffe* to launch air attacks, British citizens ferried the trapped Allies across the English Channel to safety in Britain.

With the defeat of the Allies, France quickly fell to the German conquerors. Germany occupied more than half of France and allowed a puppet French government to represent German interests in the unoccupied regions of France. However, many French citizens rejected the puppet regime and maintained an active resistance movement to hinder German occupation.

Hitler then began a bombing campaign against Britain to prepare for a land invasion. After destroying many military targets, the

New Leadership for Great Britain

In early 1940 Chamberlain resigned as prime minister. King George VI asked Winston Churchill to accept this position. Despite the opposition of many political leaders in Britain, Churchill proved to be an excellent choice and rallied the British people during one of their greatest trials in history.

Evacuation at Dunkirk

It is difficult to understand the evacuation of Allied forces from the beach at Dunkirk as anything less than an act of God. Fog, rain, and low cloud cover prevented the *Luftwaffe* from bombing this area for nine days. In addition, the channel was unusually calm, and mild winds blew from the east instead of the north as they often do. These conditions made it possible for more than eight hundred vessels, everything from destroyers to fishing boats, to carry the soldiers to safety.

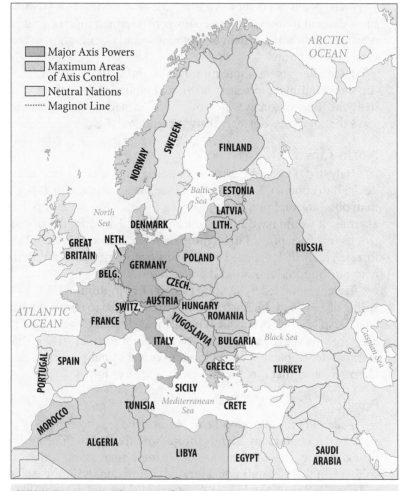

WWII European Theater of Operations

General Erwin Rommel

General Bernard L. Montgomery

Luftwaffe began to bomb London and other British cities in order to kill civilians and destroy British morale. However, the bombing of civilian targets strengthened British resolve. In addition, the Royal Air Force (RAF) destroyed many German bombers and fighter planes. Hitler grew impatient with the resistance of the British and made a change in strategy that doomed the Third Reich to ultimate failure.

Eastern Europe

Russia took advantage of the fighting in Western Europe. As previously mentioned, Russia invaded eastern Poland a few days after the Germans had begun their invasion. In addition, the Russians seized the small countries of Latvia, Lithuania, and Estonia. These conquests provided Russia with control of territory from the Baltic to the Black Sea.

Soviet Union

In 1940 German forces began to prepare for an invasion of Russia. Despite a peace treaty with Russia, Hitler determined to overrun this vast country and take advantage of Russia's many natural resources, including great oil reserves. The attack began on June 22, 1941, with three million Nazi troops rushing into Russia along an eighteen hundred mile front.

German forces quickly captured thousands of Russian prisoners and seized half a million square miles of Russian territory. Despite the fact that the Russians suffered up to five million casualties, the Germans could not achieve victory. The severe winter saw temperatures that fell to forty degrees below zero. German forces could not advance, and most German equipment would not function in these extreme conditions.

Even after several more months of fighting in the spring, the Russians continued to resist and victory eluded the Germans. Gradually the Russian forces wore down the German army. In February 1943 the surviving German army surrendered.

North Africa

Italy had observed Germany's rapid conquest of Europe and decided to conquer North Africa. Since Britain was enduring German bombing and preparing against a possible Nazi invasion, Italy assumed it would have a free hand in Africa. However, the British troops in Africa proved to be more than a match for Mussolini's forces. The British expelled the Italians from Egypt and captured over one hundred thousand Italian troops.

Hitler responded by sending General **Erwin Rommel** in the spring of 1941 with highly trained German troops to rescue the Italians. Despite a lack of supplies and adequate forces, General Rommel advanced into Egypt and nearly defeated the British. In 1942 British commander General **Bernard L. Montgomery** finally defeated the German forces that threatened British control of Egypt.

Pacific

Following the attack on Pearl Harbor, the Japanese military staged attacks on many islands throughout the Pacific. The Philippines became one of the victims of Japanese aggression. American soldiers on these islands concentrated their defenses on the island of Luzon and withstood Japanese attacks for several months. Finally,

President Roosevelt ordered the American commander, General **Douglas MacArthur**, to leave the Philippines in order to escape capture. The Japanese treated captured American forces with great brutality, and hundreds died.

Japan also conquered several Dutch and British colonies with little resistance. However, Japan had conquered more than it could defend. General MacArthur became the supreme Allied commander in the Pacific, and the Allies gradually began to win key victories over Japan.

Two major naval battles in 1942 ended Japanese expansion and preserved Australia from a major Japanese invasion. The first battle occurred in the Coral Sea, northeast of Australia. American planes destroyed many Japanese ships. One month later, American forces discovered that the Japanese planned to attack **Midway Island**. The Americans had an important naval base on this island. Although the Japanese forces far outnumbered American naval forces, the Americans attacked first. American pilots sank several Japanese aircraft carriers and forced the Japanese to retreat.

American forces advanced toward Japan by capturing important islands that the Allies could use for air bases. They bypassed other islands and left the Japanese troops there stranded to await the end of the war.

WWII Pacific Theater of Operations

Major Turning Points

Hundreds of battles occurred during the Second World War. While many important events took place, we will briefly consider several key decisions as turning points in the war. We have already examined Germany's invasion of Russia and Japan's attack on Pearl Harbor. The first event proved disastrous for Germany and resulted in the Nazis facing a two-front war. From this point on, Germany sought to defend against an Allied invasion. Additional conquest was no longer an option. The second event brought the sleeping giant of the United States into the war. As previously mentioned, American forces pushed toward Japan by island hopping, or seizing strategic islands while bypassing others. By the end of 1944, General MacArthur had returned to the Philippines and American forces had destroyed forty Japanese ships as the Allies regained control of these islands. In 1945 American forces captured Iwo Jima and Okinawa with terrible loss of life on both sides. From these islands, American bombers could strike Japan.

To make matters worse for Germany and Italy, when the United States declared war on Japan, Germany and Italy declared war on the United States. This brought America into the European theater of the war. Soon American troops poured into Britain, bringing much-needed supplies and equipment. In 1942, under General **Dwight D. Eisenhower**, U.S. troops landed in North Africa and defeated Axis troops there within a year. Then, in 1943, Eisenhower led a force of

General Dwight D. Eisenhower

337

U.S. troops wade ashore from a LCVP landing craft, off "Omaha" Beach, June 6, 1944.

Landing ships putting cargo ashore at low tide during the first days of the Normandy invasion

Clement Attlee (who replaced Churchill), Harry Truman, and Joseph Stalin at the Potsdam Conference

160,000 during an invasion of Sicily, an island off the coast of Italy. As the Allies advanced to Italy, the Italian government surrendered. However, large numbers of German troops continued to resist the Allied advance north through Italy.

The next important decision for the Allies was where next to invade Europe. After lengthy discussions between Churchill, Roosevelt, and Stalin, they decided to invade France. After much planning, on **June 6, 1944**, the Allies launched a massive invasion of France along a fifty-mile front on five beaches. One hundred and seventy-five thousand men landed and established a beachhead on that first day, which was known as **D-day**. Within three weeks, one million Allied soldiers, five hundred thousand tons of supplies, and nearly two hundred thousand vehicles had landed in France. The fighting in Europe would continue for another year, but this successful landing sealed the fate of Germany.

The dropping of two atomic bombs on cities in Japan became the final turning point in the war. We will examine this event in more detail in the next section.

Conclusion of the War

With the massive infusion of troops and military equipment from the United States, the Allies steadily regained territory from the Axis powers. British, French, and American forces pushed German forces out of one country after another. Soon the Allies had expelled the German army from almost every conquered territory. Continued Allied movements from the west and the east would ultimately compel Germany to surrender.

The Japanese fought with a fierce determination, and few lived to become prisoners of war. Most died in battle or committed suicide rather than allow themselves to be captured. However, their zeal proved to be no match for superior air and naval power. At great cost of life for the Allies and the Japanese, the Americans continued to close in on the Japanese islands. When the Allies demanded the surrender of Japan in 1945, Japanese resistance forced the Allies to use more and more destructive weapons to end the war.

Europe

American and British troops attacked German forces from the west while Soviet troops seized territory in the east that Germany had previously conquered. Allies liberated France and carried out intense bombing of German cities. By December 1944 the Allies in the west had reached the border of Germany. Hitler ordered a final push in order to break through a lightly protected section of the Allied line. This failed attempt became known as the **Battle of the Bulge**.

Germany had consumed much of its remaining military strength, but the Allies held the line and continued to advance into Germany. In the spring of 1945, the Allies waited west of Berlin and allowed the Russians to fight their way into Germany's capital from the east. On May 7 the Germans unconditionally surrendered. The Allies declared **May 8, 1945**, V-E Day for the victory in Europe.

Japan

In April 1945 President Roosevelt died, and his vice president, Harry Truman, became the president of the United States. To him fell the great responsibility of deciding whether to use the secret weapon that American scientists had developed during Roosevelt's administration.

Despite massive bombing of Japanese cities with explosives and incendiary bombs (designed to start fires), the Japanese emperor and his military council refused to surrender. While the death toll continued to rise, the leaders assembled thousands of planes and other war supplies to attack the Americans when they invaded the Japanese islands.

In the summer of 1945, the Allied leaders met in Postdam, Germany, to discuss the end of the war and various post-war issues. They insisted that Japan surrender or suffer terrible consequences. Japanese officials rejected this demand. President Truman responded by ordering that an atomic bomb be dropped on the Japanese city of Hiroshima on August 6. The blast destroyed nearly five square miles of the city and immediately killed an estimated seventy thousand people. Another seventy thousand people suffered terrible injuries from the blast.

Truman again demanded the surrender of Japan and threatened additional destruction if they failed to do so. However, the Japanese leaders refused to surrender. In response, on August 9 an American bomber dropped a second atomic bomb on the Japanese city of Nagasaki. This blast immediately killed about forty thousand people, with another forty thousand injured who died soon after the blast.

Emperor Hirohito walking by a destroyed section of Tokyo in October 1943

Mushroom cloud from the bomb dropped on Nagasaki

Justified War and Killing Civilians

Christian theologians discussing how Christians may and may not conduct war have long maintained that civilians, especially women and children, should not be the targets of warfare. The Bible entrusts the sword to the state, but it forbids using the sword to kill the innocent (Ex. 23:7). Dropping a nuclear bomb on a city, however, specifically targets civilians, including women and children.

Many have made the case that dropping the bombs saved not only American but Japanese lives. As the Americans moved island by island toward Japan, Japanese soldiers fought to the death, even after it was obvious they had lost the battle. Americans knew that when they reached the Japanese home islands they would receive this same kind of deadly resistance from the entire Japanese population. The atomic bomb was seen as the best way to end a war already immensely costly in human lives.

Christians may disagree over the acceptability of targeting civilians even to save many lives overall.

General MacArthur and Emperor Hirohito (above); the "fat man" atomic bomb dropped on Nagasaki (right)

On August 14, the Japanese government finally surrendered. Their only request was that Emperor Hirohito be allowed to retain his position. On **September 2, 1945** (V-J Day), the Japanese and Allied representatives signed the documents that formally ended Japanese involvement in World War II.

Section Quiz

1. In what European country in 1940 did the Allies find themselves surrounded by German forces?

2. What prevented a German victory over the Soviet Union?

3. What general traveled to North Africa to rescue Italian forces and push back the British?

4. What American general had to flee the Philippines in order to avoid capture by the Japanese?

5. What battle became Germany's final attempt to break through the Allied lines?

★ Evaluate the morality of dropping atomic bombs on Hiroshima and Nagasaki.

▪ III. Consequences of the War

World War II resulted in loss of human life and destruction of property on a scale not previously witnessed in human history. The consequences are even difficult to quantify. Statistics alone fail to provide an adequate description of the horrific losses.

It is unlikely that anyone could have imagined a more destructive war than World War I, with about twenty million deaths. However, World War II resulted in more than fifty million deaths. Populations of nations in Europe suffered significant decline as millions of their citizens died in battle or as helpless victims of brutal conquest. For example, the Russians lost over twenty million people during the war. Between eight and ten million Russian soldiers died while fighting the Germans. Over twelve million Russian civilians died as a result of the fighting, disease, or famine.

Communism spread rapidly after the war as the Communists under Joseph Stalin seized most of Eastern Europe. Soviet forces had invaded Poland and virtually every other country east of Germany during the war. Despite promises of free elections, these states quickly became subject to the Soviet Union, and Stalin installed Communist regimes in these countries.

Long-Term Consequences for Society

For centuries European culture was the dominant culture in the world. England, France, and Germany had boasted the strongest armies, the wealthiest economies, and the most advanced centers of learning. However, for generations Europe had been forsaking the Christian worldview that had positively influenced it. Leading Europeans had produced the Enlightenment, had scorned biblical religion, and had emphasized nationalism above allegiance to God and His Word. By the war's end, Europe was crushed. Now the United States and the Soviet Union would dominate the world.

Beginning of the Atomic Age

The United States initially had the advantage regarding the development of atomic weapons. However, the Germans had also been working to develop these weapons. When the Russians invaded Germany, they seized German scientists and information about this new technology. In addition, the Russians used American spies in the atomic industry to obtain valuable American research. As a result, the Russians soon became an atomic power and developed their own crude atomic weapons.

Development of atomic weapons affected the strategy of future wars. The destructive power of these weapons also caused people to realize that scientific and technological developments are not always good. This knowledge played a role in the rejection of Enlightenment ideas that had influenced human reasoning for two hundred years.

Beginning of the Cold War

While Churchill had been one of the first to warn of Soviet intentions toward Eastern Europe, many soon became aware of Russia's intention to dominate world affairs. As a result, a period known as the **Cold War** (political rivalry that stops short of actual war) developed, with America and its allies aligned against continued aggression by the Soviet Union and its allies. We will examine this period in detail in the next chapter.

Disillusionment

The sense of hopelessness and despair that you learned about in the last chapter continued and heightened following the Second World War. Post-war literature and art reflected the view that life has no meaning or purpose. For example, American painter Jackson Pollock developed a form of painting known as **abstract expressionism**. He created many of his paintings by randomly splashing wet paint on the canvas with brushes.

Other artists expressed their hopelessness by writing stories or plays that demonstrated the meaninglessness of life. For example, Albert Camus (kah MOO), a French philosopher, wrote stories dealing with absurdity. He reasoned that people value what is meaningless, since all people value their life even though all die.

Economic Changes

World War II led to dramatic economic changes for countries such as France and Britain. They lost most of their colonies and much of their overseas empires. The few colonies still under their control demanded freedom. Within a few years, the Europeans granted freedom to these remaining colonies. The loss of income

Day of the Lord

Old Testament prophets often warned God's people of coming *days of the Lord* in which God would judge them for turning from the true God to idols. Some of these judgments were locust invasions that destroyed their crops. Others were military invasions, such as those that led to the Babylonian Captivity.

Given Europe's long Christian history and its turn away from God, some Christians may wonder if the world wars were a *day of the Lord* for Europe.

Jackson Pollock

and inexpensive resources from these colonies greatly reduced the prestige and influence of European countries, including France and Britain. They could no longer lay claim to world power status.

Political Changes

World War II ended Europe's domination of the world. Both wars had resulted, in part, from exaggerated nationalism and the illusion that one nationality enjoyed superiority over other nationalities. These errors had been disproved at an incredible cost. Political change emerged as one of the consequences of these wars. Rather than many strong political powers, only two remained. Following the war, power shifted to the United States and the Communist powers. Europe would merely side with one or the other of these political camps.

Return to Materialism

Following the war, many turned back to the emphasis on acquiring material goods that had been prevalent prior to the onset of the Great Depression. With the ever-present danger of atomic warfare and the loss of confidence in government to prevent war, people sought to find temporary comfort by seeking and enjoying the benefits of material wealth.

Philosophical and Religious Consequences

The world wars devastated the illusions upon which most philosophies had been founded. The wars disproved the fantasy that man is born without a sin nature. Philosophies and religions could not explain the outpouring of animosity and hatred that led to the deaths of multiplied millions. They found themselves unable to provide answers for the past or hope for the future.

Philosophical

The horrors of World War I followed by the intensified horrors of World War II altered the thinking of most Europeans. They abandoned the idealism that prevailed in the nineteenth century. This collapse of idealism led to relativism, the idea that truth and moral values are not absolute but rather vary with each person or group.

The philosophy known as **existentialism** became popular during this period. This philosophy stresses a person's uniqueness while encouraging free choice and accepting the consequences of that choice. Existentialists deny that an all-powerful God rules over the affairs of humans. In fact, many leading existentialists were atheists. They also denied the existence of a moral code defining what a human being is or should be. Instead, they believed that humans are free to determine their own values and their own meaning in life. Humans are not obligated to obey the dictates of a government or a church. They are to choose a course of action that seems right to them and then strive to be faithful to that selection.

The most famous existentialist was Jean-Paul Sartre, who wrote the famous book *Being and Nothingness* in which he encouraged people to reject the illusions that deceive them. His philosophy should have led him to oppose every political ideology as mere illusion, but Sartre was inconsistent and supported Marxism.

Besides failing to explain the atrocities of the world wars, human philosophers had not predicted the devastation of the twentieth century. This level of destruction contradicted man's high view of himself and left men without hope or answers.

Consequences of World War II

List the consequences of World War II.

The Holocaust Slaughter of the Weak and the Unfit

Violence against civilians struck a new low under Adolf Hitler. Shortly after coming to power in 1933, Hitler began a program to rid Germany of those he considered weak and unfit. While many have heard of the German attempts to destroy all of the Jews in Europe (commonly called the **Holocaust**), his systematic murder of other groups has received less attention. For example, Hitler ordered the destruction of thousands of Gypsies, the disabled, and the chronically ill. German forces also treated Poles, Russians, Ukrainians, Czechs, and others as inferior and murdered them in large numbers.

Euthanasia

Deceptively calling it "mercy killing," Hitler and others used starvation, lethal injection, and poison gas to purge Germany of the weak. Hitler's definition of the weak included the mentally ill, the disabled, and those with long-term illnesses.

The Nazis assigned the code-name **Operation T-4** to this terrible program. By 1940 they had constructed six centers to kill thousands of these victims. The killing continued until American troops liberated these centers in the spring of 1945. An estimated 200,000 people died in the name of euthanasia, or mercy killing.

The Hunger Plan

Nazi leaders developed a plan to ensure adequate food supplies for the German forces and German civilians. To accomplish this, they limited the amount of food available to Poles and Russians under German control. The Jews in the ghettos of these countries suffered the most, but millions of civilians died of starvation. This horrific plan continued until the Russians drove out the German forces.

Shoah

Many use the word "holocaust" to refer to the mass murder of the Jews. However, many Jews prefer the Hebrew term **Shoah** which means "calamity." Whichever term you use, the Nazi attempt to destroy the Jewish population in Europe has proven to be one of the worst atrocities in history.

Jewish persecution began shortly after Hitler became the ruler of Germany. The Nazis began by pressuring Jews to leave Germany. Of course, they had to leave their wealth behind to fill Nazi coffers. Then German authorities boycotted Jewish businesses and forced them to sell their businesses. Soon the Nazis forced the Jews to relocate to the ghettos (slums). Relocation to concentration camps followed soon after.

A German girl walks past the bodies of 800 slave workers murdered by SS guards near Namering, Germany.

As German armies marched into Russia, the Nazis sent along special mobile killing units to hunt down and kill Jews, Gypsies, and Communists.

Later the Germans developed centralized killing locations in Poland and Germany. The German camp at Auschwitz gained the terrible distinction of killing more people than the other five concentration camps. At least one million two hundred thousand Jews died at this camp. The officials at Auschwitz also murdered one hundred thousand Poles, Gypsies, and Russians.

An Auschwitz crematorium (above); Rows of bodies at the Lager Bordhausen concentration camp (below)

Historical Perspectives

Not all historical perspectives are valid. Emory University hosts the Holocaust Denial on Trial website. Look through the information collected at that site and compare the claims of Holocaust deniers with the conclusions of historians. Identify some of the historical fallacies that are present in the claims of Holocaust deniers.

G. I. Bill

In 1944 President Roosevelt signed the Serviceman's Readjustment Act of 1944. This became known as the G. I. (government issue) Bill of Rights. In this legislation, the federal government helped pay for college or vocational education for returning veterans. Another provision in this bill offered veterans low interest loans to buy homes. This provision enabled millions of veterans to purchase their own homes.

Religious

The world wars discredited religious teaching that assumed humans are basically good. Gone were the dreams of a perfect society. As a result, the churches of Europe began to empty. Atheism grew more popular, and eventually even some prominent theologians concluded that God was dead. Many Jewish people struggled with the idea of God after the Holocaust.

Nevertheless, Christianity also grew during this period. In the United States, many men returned home from war and used the G. I. Bill to attend Christian colleges. These men had seen the world and had seen death. They were prepared to sacrifice to spread the gospel around the world. Many of them returned to minister in places they had been during the war.

Total War and Its Consequences

You learned about the terrible realities of total war in the last chapter. Sadly, improved technology and weapons that were more powerful increased the suffering and death of civilians during the Second World War. In addition, few escaped the consequences of a rigidly controlled national economy. Total war resulted in widespread affliction due to a rationing of food, medicine, and anything else that would contribute to the military effort.

Massive Loss of Human Life

In addition to government control of a nation's economy, total war resulted in the deaths of millions of civilians. Although estimates vary widely, as many as thirty-five million civilians may have died from a variety of causes, including bombing of cities, disease, murder by invading troops, and famine.

Massive Destruction of Property

Entire cities were bombed into rubble or firebombed into ashes. Europe lay in ruins. Her industries and infrastructure suffered almost complete destruction. While the cost of the war had been an incredible one at one-half trillion dollars, the cost of rebuilding would tax the resources of the free world.

Section Quiz

1. What political system spread rapidly over Eastern Europe after World War II?

2. How did the Soviet Union acquire the knowledge to become an atomic power?

3. List five groups that the Nazis systematically murdered prior to and during World War II.

4. Given the failure of philosophy and religion, how did many respond after the end of the Second World War?

★ Why did philosophy fail to predict the devastation of these two world wars?

★ Why did Bible-believing Christians not suffer the same disillusionment common among unbelievers after the war?

■ Making Connections

1. How did Germany and Italy's support of General Franco in Spain prepare their forces for war?

2. Why did Japan become increasingly confident that no nation would come to China's defense?

3. How did seizure of the Rhineland provide a military advantage for Germany?

4. Why did the French and British declaration of war not deter Germany from invading Poland?

5. Why did Hitler invade Russia in 1941?

6. Why was it a mistake for Germany and Italy to declare war on the United States?

7. Why did European nations decline in importance and influence following the Second World War?

8. Why did the Nazis murder Jews, the disabled, and many other groups?

■ Developing History Skills

1. Compare and contrast total war in Chapter 17 and this chapter.

2. Respond to the following statement: "The refusal of the United States to lift the oil embargo against the Japanese forced Japan to attack American naval forces."

■ Thinking Critically

1. Respond to this quotation by a survivor of the Holocaust: "A suffering so great leaves nothing to be redeemed, and precious little to forgive or be forgiven. It is not that God died after Auschwitz; it is that He is no longer needed. The covenant has been broken, not by the people but by their Lord." Use passages such as Hosea 4:6 and Romans 3:10-23 as points of reference.

2. Evaluate conditions leading to World War II in light of Exodus 20; 2 Chronicles 16, 18; Psalm 20:7; and James 4:1.

■ Living in God's World

1. Suppose that you are a Christian historian responding to the denials of an unbeliever regarding God's providence at Dunkirk. Specifically respond to the charge that the events at Dunkirk cannot demonstrate the providence of God because the Germans' conquest of France has its own equally remarkable series of events. Use Genesis 50:20 and Daniel 4:34-35 to prepare your answer.

2. Suppose you are a member of a small church in Germany. It is the summer of 1945, and other members are in despair. In an attempt to explain God's ways, you decide to present a lesson on the topic of the "day of the Lord" from the Old Testament prophets. Develop a Bible lesson on this topic from the following verses: Isaiah 2:12-3:3; 3:8-10; 4:2-6.

People, Places, and Things to Know

Francisco Franco
Hirohito
Tojo
Third Reich
Sudetenland
Munich Conference
Neville Chamberlain
appeasement
Rome-Berlin Axis
Anti-Comintern Pact
Axis powers
Pact of Steel
September 1, 1939
Allies
December 7, 1941
Pearl Harbor
Luftwaffe
Erwin Rommel
Bernard L. Montgomery
Douglas MacArthur
Midway Island
Dwight D. Eisenhower
June 6, 1944
D-day
Battle of the Bulge
May 8, 1945
September 2, 1945
Cold War
abstract expressionism
existentialism
Holocaust
Operation T-4
Shoah

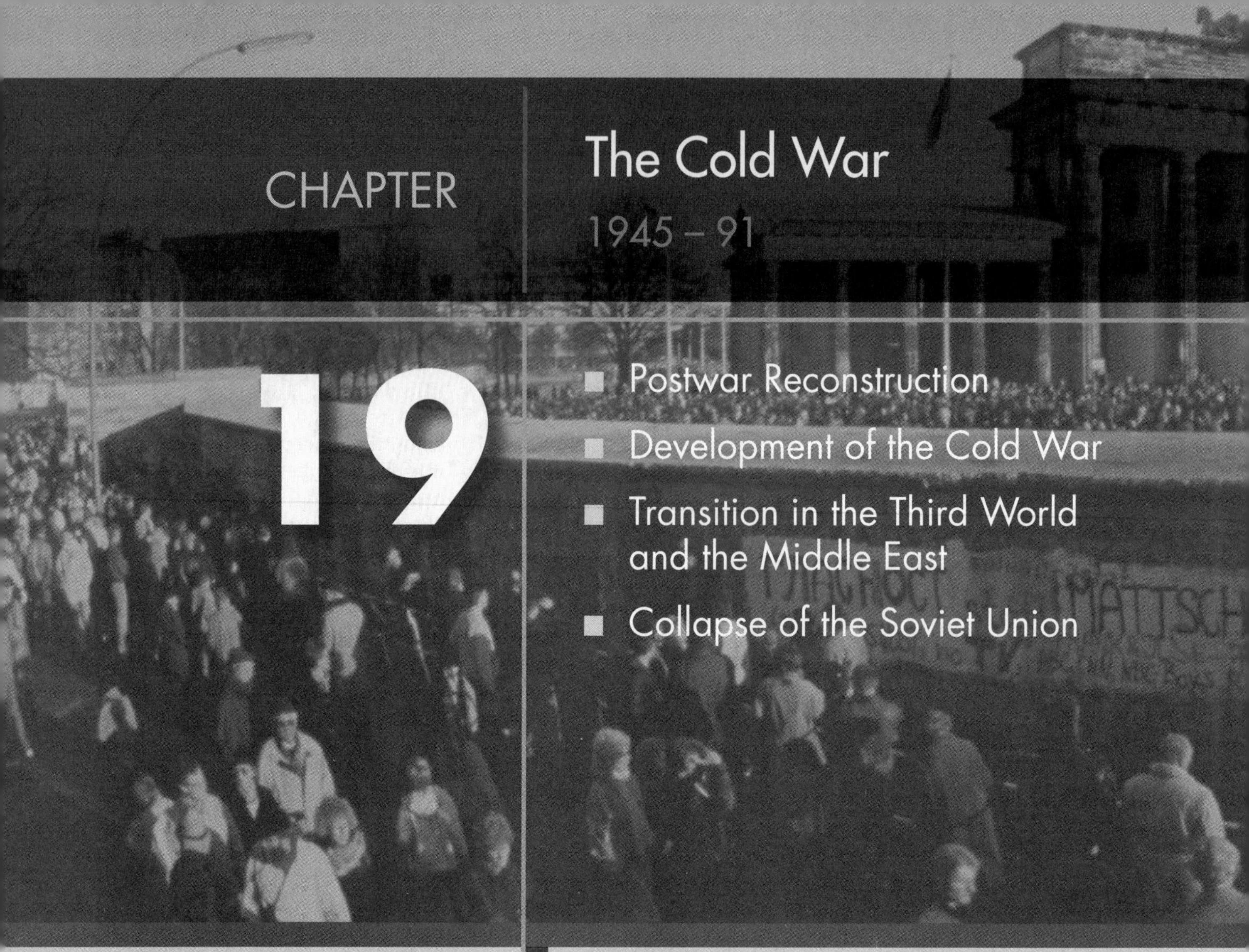

CHAPTER 19

The Cold War

1945 – 91

- Postwar Reconstruction
- Development of the Cold War
- Transition in the Third World and the Middle East
- Collapse of the Soviet Union

1940 – 95

1940 · 1945 · 1950 · 1955 · 1960 · 1965

- Greece endures civil war 1944–49
- Cold War begins 1945
- India gains independence from Britain 1947
- Israel becomes a modern nation 1948
- Arab-Israeli War 1948–49
- Berlin Blockade 1948–49
- Chiang Kai-shek establishes the Republic of China in Taiwan 1949
- Korean War 1950–53
- Battle of Dien Bien Phu 1954
- Ghana becomes the first African colony to gain independence 1957
- *Sputnik* is launched into outer space 1957
- China's Great Leap Forward 1958
- Cuban Missile Crisis 1962
- Six-Day War between Israel and Arabs 1967

Big Ideas

1. What major political and economic changes accompanied the postwar recovery?
2. Why did the Cold War break out after World War II?
3. How did colonies achieve independence following the war?
4. What were the causes and consequences of the collapse of the Soviet Union?

The Cold War was ultimately a war of ideas. Values in the Soviet Union were often the exact opposite of the values Americans held. For example, the Soviet state forced the individual to sacrifice personal goals for the good of the state. Instead of granting freedom, totalitarian rulers dictated every aspect of their subjects' lives. Though communism promised equality, the great class distinction between ruler and ruled soon became apparent.

This clash of values transformed into actual wars when the Soviets attempted to spread their ideology across the globe. The United States, as the opposing superpower, was determined to resist or at least contain the spread of communism.

■ Tiananmen Square massacre 1989

■ Poland gains independence 1989

■ American forces evacuated from South Vietnam 1973

■ Soviet Union collapses 1991

| 1970 | 1975 | 1980 | 1985 | 1990 | 1995 |

Guiding Questions

1. How did Western Europe and Japan achieve rapid economic recovery following the war?
2. What role did the Marshall Plan play in the political and economic stabilization of Western Europe?
3. Why was the United Nations founded, what were its successes, and what were its failures?

Konrad Adenauer

■ I. Postwar Reconstruction

World War II had left most of Europe and Japan in ruins. Extensive bombing and shelling had destroyed whole cities. Europe and Japan would have to be completely rebuilt and infrastructure replaced. The cost would be immense, and the United States would have to provide most of the materials and financing.

Recovery After World War II

Recovery needed to occur quickly. The Soviet Union actively sought to destabilize European countries in order to bring them under Communist domination. A prosperous and stable Europe would be a great deterrent to the spread of communism.

Western Europe

Under the leadership of German chancellor **Konrad Adenauer**, West Germany experienced an incredible recovery known as the *Wirtschaftswunder* (economic miracle). Adenauer tripled national income and led the small nation to produce more goods by 1955 than a larger Germany had produced prior to the war. He also rejected socialism and embraced the principles of the free market. Germany quickly became a major economic force in Europe.

France struggled with instability following the formation of the Fourth Republic in 1946. In addition, France tried to demonstrate that it was still a world power by regaining possession of its colonial empire. However, French forces suffered a catastrophic defeat by the Vietnamese Communist forces in 1954. France gained a measure of stability when **Charles de Gaulle** became the president of France and established the **Fifth Republic** in 1958. This government provided the French with a constitution and strengthened the office of president.

Britain emerged from the war as a nation in decline. The British Empire began to crumble as vast territories, including India and Burma, gained their independence. Rather than continue to have a leading role on the world scene, Britain could only play a supporting role with the United States and European powers.

Japan

Under the initial leadership of General MacArthur, Japan made an astonishing economic and political recovery. MacArthur gave Japan a constitution and helped to establish a stable democratic government.

When the occupation government turned power over to the Japanese, they made a successful transition to a democratic government. In 1955 the Japanese voted the **Liberal Democratic Party** into power. This party ruled Japan until political scandals led the Japanese to replace it with a coalition government in 1993.

Japan took advantage of American financial and technological aid and developed a formidable industrial base. Since the West provided military protection, Japan's financial resources were devoted to creating a competitive heavy industry. Japanese automakers gradually became world leaders in auto manufacturing.

In addition, Japan created new technologies in electronics. By the 1980s, Japan had developed a world market in high-quality electronic equipment such as televisions, radios, and computers.

Stabilization and Growth in Western Europe

To help Europe recover from the devastation of World War II, the United States sent billions of dollars in aid. As a result, Britain, France, West Germany, and others quickly rebuilt their infrastructures. These countries recovered economically at different rates depending on their embracing of capitalism or socialism. This recovery accomplished a key American goal of strengthening Western Europe against Soviet aggression.

Stabilization

Beginning in 1948, under the Economic Recovery Act, the United States poured billions of dollars into Western European countries. Commonly called the **Marshall Plan**, this distribution of funds enabled Europe to rapidly rebuild and retool for a strong economic recovery. As Western Europe recovered economically, communism became less attractive and Communist parties in various countries declined in influence.

Growth

European leaders realized the need for some form of unity to prevent future wars between European countries. While political unity proved to be elusive, economic unity became a reality through at least two organizations.

In 1951 six European states agreed to establish the European Coal and Steel Community (ECSC). France, West Germany, Italy, Belgium, the Netherlands, and Luxembourg coordinated these industries. One of the goals was to prevent future wars, since steel would be essential for any future military buildup. In addition, the ECSC sought to eliminate waste and inefficiency. The resulting industrial products could be produced at a lower cost.

George C. Marshall

Encouraged by the success of the ECSC, these six nations established the European Economic Community in 1957. Known as the **Common Market**, the member states expanded cooperation to include many other products. Removing trade barriers led to lower prices and increased sales. Over the next forty years, the Common Market grew to include nearly thirty countries.

Welfare States and Stagnation

Most developed countries have instituted some form of welfare or government provision of economic and social benefits for their citizens. Some countries are able to pay for limited welfare by taxing a thriving economy. We will briefly examine two European nations that have suffered from the effects of welfare.

After the Second World War, the British government, under the Labour Party, created the National Health Service and took control of key industries, including coal and railroads. By the late 1970s, unemployment and inflation had crippled the British economy. The British responded by voting out the Labour Party and electing the Conservative Party in 1979. In a later section, we will examine the results of that election.

France has developed into a classic welfare state since World War II. For example, France has a universal national health care system and a generous, tax-subsidized retirement plan. In addition, the French minimum wage is nearly double that of the United States.

NATO

The North Atlantic Treaty Organization (NATO) is an international league that was founded in 1949. The league's original intent was to protect its member nations from Soviet aggression. Its original members included the United States and the nations of Western Europe. The organization proved to be effective during the Korean War and on other occasions. Challenges to NATO included the Soviet Union's formation of the Warsaw Pact in 1955 and the withdrawal of France from NATO in 1966. Following the collapse of the Soviet Union in 1991, several Eastern European states also joined NATO.

The costs for these policies are high taxes, high unemployment, and regulations that hinder the competitiveness of French companies.

Spread of Democracy

Nations including Germany, Italy, India, and Portugal embraced democracy after the Second World War. Some of these nations quickly stabilized and thrived economically as well as politically. Others experienced struggles along the way and endured conflict as various groups tried to prevent democracy from taking hold.

Greece was one of the nations that struggled to establish a successful democracy. This nation endured a civil war between 1944 and 1949 because Greek Communists attempted to seize control of the country. British and American support enabled the anti-Communist forces to prevail. Once the Communist forces had been defeated, Greece quickly joined **NATO** and sought to maintain close ties with the United States and Western Europe.

The struggle with communism became more than a conflict between nations. Communist political parties took root in many nations, including the United States. Few countries had to resort to an armed conflict as did Greece, but many countries experienced a philosophical struggle between democracy and communism.

Role of the United Nations

When the American, British, and Soviet leaders met to discuss strategy during World War II, they also agreed to form an international peacekeeping organization after the war. In 1945, diplomats representing fifty nations organized the **United Nations** (UN).

These nations founded the UN to ensure international peace. The role of this organization soon expanded to include seeking solutions to social, economic, and humanitarian problems around the world.

However, because the United Nations includes almost all the nations of the world, nations that cause problems also hold positions of status in the UN. For instance, during the Cold War the Soviet Union caused major problems in the world while at the same time possessing the power of veto in the UN Security Council.

The United Nations is required to address great moral issues that arise in the affairs of nations. Because of the diversity of nations and moral viewpoints represented, its approach to these problems is mixed. While the UN condemns atrocities like genocide, it also supports the right of mothers to kill their unborn children.

Section Quiz

1. Who led West Germany during the 1950s and played a key role in its "economic miracle" following the war?

2. Who became the president of France in 1958 and established the Fifth Republic?

3. What U.S. economic plan helped to stabilize Western Europe?

4. Why do French companies find it difficult to be competitive?

5. What Western nation fought a civil war in the 1940s to determine the success or failure of democracy?

★ From a biblical perspective, what is a key reason for the United Nations' inability to work toward solutions among countries with varying religious and ideological backgrounds?

II. Development of the Cold War

By the end of the Second World War, a different sort of war had begun. The United States and the Soviet Union emerged from the conflict as the clear world leaders. Although they had been allies in fighting against Hitler, their differences were so deep that both quickly realized they could not remain allies. Over the next four decades, Americans and Soviets fought what has been called the **Cold War**. The relationship between these nations was not outright war, but neither was it peaceful. Each side tried to dominate the other through the development of new weapons or through involvement in conflicts between other nations.

Differences Between Democracy and Communism

In order to understand the events that unfolded during the Cold War, one must first understand why the Soviet Union and the United States were rivals. The nations were driven by opposing worldviews. These worldviews differed most obviously in the following ways.

The United States and the Soviet Union were opposed economically. The United States promoted a capitalistic approach to the economy that allowed privately owned businesses to serve customers and pursue profits. The Soviet Union attempted to impose a central plan on its national economy. The state owned the industries and controlled all decisions for items produced. Since the Soviets placed a great emphasis on building a strong military, little was manufactured to meet the people's day-to-day needs.

Politically, the United States practiced a democratic form of government that stressed the role of the individual in the political process. The Communist Party controlled the Soviet Union, and the citizens had no say in their government.

Differences in economic and political systems alone are not enough to lead nations into war, however. The United States and the Soviet Union also differed religiously. Marxist-Leninists believed that capitalism was immoral and that it must be overthrown in a revolution that would establish socialist states. They taught that religion itself is evil because it drugs people into submission when they actually need to be stirred into revolutionary fervor. Americans, on the other hand, believed they were a Christian nation that needed to stand up to the atheistic Soviet Union. This was true of Fundamentalist preachers as well as politicians like Presidents Truman and Eisenhower.

Though Americans agreed that America was a nation under God (something Congress added to the pledge of allegiance under Eisenhower), it was not always clear who the American god was. The civic religion of Cold War America was empty of theological content. Americans were expected to have faith, but in whom was unclear. The key dogmas were the continuation of the American way of life, the free-market system, and personal peace.

Fall of China to Communism

In Chapter 17 you learned about the power struggle in China. After the Second World War, this struggle resumed. Communist leader Mao Zedong received support from the Soviet Union, and Chiang Kai-shek received aid from the United States. Mao Zedong

Guiding Questions

1. How did Western democracies and Communist regimes differ?
2. Why was the Communist Party able to seize control of China, and what were the consequences of the Great Leap Forward and Cultural Revolution?
3. What were the causes and consequences of major Cold War crises?
4. How did the rivalry between the superpowers affect the development of new military, nuclear, and space technology?

351

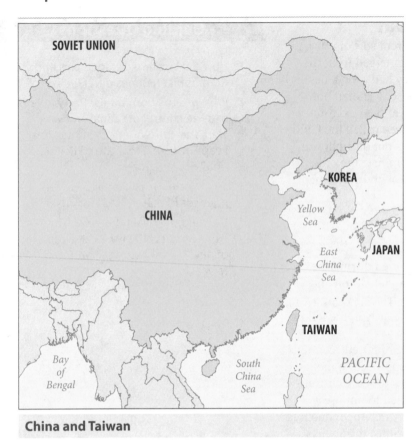

China and Taiwan

and the Communists made empty promises to the peasants and progressively gained enough popular support to drive Chiang's forces to an island off the coast of China in 1949. On the island of Taiwan, Chiang established the **Republic of China**, which has governed this island to the present.

China Under Mao

Mao's forces had seized the major cities in China by 1949 and had placed loyal Communists in key leadership positions. Even though China had received support from the Soviet Union in the 1940s, Mao's government developed animosity toward the Soviets. During the 1960s this hostility deepened and resulted in a diplomatic war of words, with each denouncing the other. In 1969 the tensions escalated into a border conflict, with the Russian and Chinese forces engaging in a limited war.

To revive the struggling Chinese economy, Mao developed a Soviet-style Five Year Plan in 1949. The Communist leaders sought to increase agricultural and industrial production. To accomplish these goals, they combined the farming regions into large collective units and controlled industrial development through a centralized economic plan. At best, the results were mixed.

In 1958 Mao announced a new economic plan known as the **Great Leap Forward**. Mao intended to double the production of steel and agricultural products from that of the previous year. To meet these ambitious goals, the Communist authorities compelled peasants to produce steel without proper equipment or training. The steel they manufactured often proved to be impure and useless.

Communist Chinese banner

The farm collectives also proved to be inefficient. Their ineffectiveness, combined with poor growing conditions, resulted in reduced harvests. As a result, famine swept across China.

Despite the famine, Mao continued to export grain to convince other nations that communism in China had produced a great bounty. The devastation caused by the famine and Mao's exportation of much-needed grain led to the deaths of twenty to thirty million Chinese people during the Great Leap Forward.

By the mid 1960s, Mao became convinced that the Chinese people had been influenced by ideas that would lead to the spread of capitalism. In order to remove these influences from Chinese society, Mao unleashed a social and political purge in 1966 known as the **Cultural Revolution.** This purge resulted in political chaos and economic upheaval for a decade.

Mao's young Chinese followers formed Red Guard groups. These gangs of extremists threatened all elements of Chinese society through their violent attacks on anything considered a threat to the Communist revolution. By 1969 Mao had to withdraw his support for these zealous followers and allow authorities to suppress them. However, the Cultural Revolution did not end until Mao's death in 1976.

China After Mao

Chinese leaders who succeeded Mao appeared to take a more practical approach to governing China. They allowed limited reform of the economy and reduced or eliminated some of Mao's repressive controls. Because of these economic reforms, many foreign companies built factories in China and created millions of jobs for the Chinese people.

However, economic reform did not lead to significant political reform. China remained a Communist country, and political freedoms remained very limited. In the spring of 1989, student protestors filled **Tiananmen Square** in the Chinese capital of Beijing. For several days the world watched broadcasts of peaceful protests for political reform. After initial hesitation by the Communist leaders, tanks arrived in the square, and the military violently ended the demonstrations. Troops killed more than two thousand people in the process of smashing this student movement.

Cold War Crises

At times, the United States and the Soviet Union came dangerously close to a major war. However, each time the two major powers averted direct conflict by compromise or limited war that could be contained in a particular region. We will briefly look at several of these crises.

Berlin Blockade

At the end of World War II, the Allies divided Germany into four zones. The British, French, and American forces occupied three of these zones. The Russians occupied the eastern zone. The German capital of Berlin lay in the Russian zone, and the Allies divided this city into four zones. The British, French, and American forces combined their zones to form the Federal Republic of Germany. The Russians established the German Democratic Republic from East German territory they controlled.

In 1948 the Soviets tested the resolve of the Allies by blocking all traffic through East Germany into West Berlin. This **Berlin Blockade** forced the Allies to make a difficult decision. In order to deliver much-needed supplies to West Berlin by road or rail, they would have to use military force. If they allowed the Soviet blockade to succeed, all of Berlin would face starvation or fall into Soviet control.

Berlin airlift: planes being loaded (above); *children waiting as planes fly into West Berlin* (middle); *planes lining up to unload supplies* (below)

353

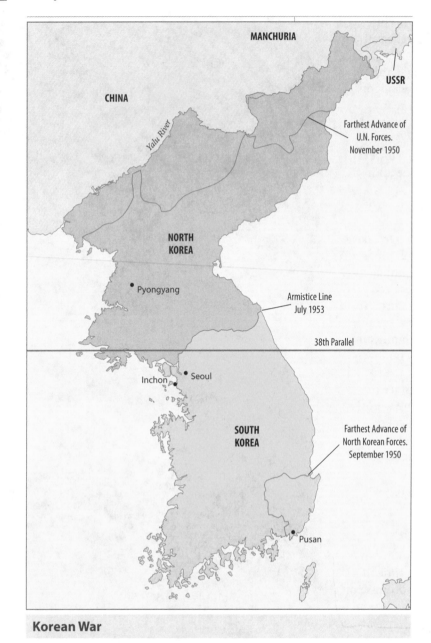

Korean War

However, the Allies devised an alternative plan that avoided both war and concession.

For eleven months, the United States and Britain delivered everything from coal to milk in a massive airlift. Unarmed cargo planes loaded with supplies landed in West Berlin every ninety seconds, twenty-four hours a day. The Soviets finally backed down and lifted the blockade to the German city. This struggle between the Allies and the Soviets ended without a shot being fired.

Korean War

The Allies also divided the Korean Peninsula between the Soviet Union and the United States following the war. The Soviets quickly built a strong Communist government and military and prepared to conquer all of Korea. In June 1950 the North Korean army invaded South Korea and overran most of the country in a matter of months.

In September, General Douglas MacArthur made a daring attack at **Inchon** (see map) with a UN force composed of a limited number of American and South Korean troops. MacArthur's forces drove the Communists deep into North Korea. The entry of over one hundred thousand Chinese Communist troops preserved North Korea from total defeat. This massive infusion of troops surprised the UN troops and forced them back across the **38th parallel** (see map) into South Korea.

Fighting continued until July 1953, when both sides signed an agreement to stop fighting. Neither side had won or lost. At best, communism in Korea had been contained. The Korean Peninsula remains divided to this day.

Cuban Missile Crisis

During the fall of 1962, the United States discovered that the Soviets had placed nuclear missiles in Cuba. Reconnaissance planes had photographed construction of several missile bases. These missiles posed a serious threat to American security. The United States promptly demanded the removal of these missiles and imposed a naval blockade to prevent access to Cuba.

America and the Soviet Union came dangerously close to engaging in a nuclear war during this two-week period in October. Complicating an already tense situation, a local Soviet commander launched a missile and shot down a U-2 spy plane flying over Cuba. The crash killed the American pilot, and tensions peaked on October 28. Following secret negotiations, the Soviets agreed to remove the missiles. However, American forces did not inspect the Soviet ships to verify the actual removal of the missiles. In exchange, the United States removed recently installed missiles from Turkey and promised not to invade Cuba.

U-2 spy plane

Vietnam War

Following World War II, the French tried to regain control of their colonies in Indochina, including Vietnam. However, a Communist leader named **Ho Chi Minh** resisted French efforts and declared Vietnam independent.

Vietnamese Communists ended French efforts by destroying the French army at the Battle of **Dien Bien Phu** in 1954. At the peace conference, diplomats divided Vietnam into the Communist north and the non-Communist south. However, Communists in the north began to coordinate with Communist agents in the south (known as the **Viet Cong**) in order to seize control of the whole country.

The United States and several other countries soon began to provide financial support to South Vietnam in order to prevent its fall to communism. Presidents Eisenhower and Kennedy also sent military advisors to train the Vietnamese forces.

U.S. presence increased dramatically under President Johnson beginning in 1964. Soon the government deployed over five hundred thousand American troops to Vietnam. Although U.S. forces won every battle against the enemy, many troops died and many Americans grew tired of the war. Improved military strategies probably came too late to renew support for the war. Critics questioned the integrity of Johnson's motives for increasing American involvement and the morality of the American presence in Vietnam. They also complained about real and perceived corruption in the South Vietnamese government. In addition, the media convinced many Americans that the United States was losing, and the war became very unpopular.

Richard Nixon became the president in 1968 and began to withdraw American forces from Vietnam and train the Vietnamese to defend themselves. Following the evacuation of American forces in 1973, the South Vietnamese forces slowed the Communist advance until 1975. However, Congress voted to reduce aid to the South Vietnamese during this critical period. Soon the well-supplied Communists conquered South Vietnam.

The cost to America had been high with the deaths of more than fifty thousand soldiers. In addition, the United States had spent one hundred and forty-six billion dollars to pay for this war. Following the failure to contain communism in Vietnam, America returned to a policy of isolation, and communism rapidly spread to nations in Southeast Asia and South America.

Rivalry for Technological Supremacy

After World War II, the rush for technological supremacy increased in intensity. The development of atomic weapons, jet engines, and rockets created great potential for good or for evil. The free world and the Soviet Union worked to get ahead of one another. Many assumed the winner of the technology race would become the dominant world power. However, the winning power turned out to be the nation with the stronger and more vibrant economy.

During the course of this race for technological supremacy, some people began to question the scientific achievements that resulted. Science and technology appeared to be working toward the destruction of mankind. For example, the development of germ warfare and a growing stockpile of nuclear weapons led many to despair of the future.

Ho Chi Minh

Loss of American Confidence

The United States of America had rescued the Allies in World War I. Its role in World War II was even more dramatic and led to the defeat of the Axis powers in multiple areas of the world. In 1950 America also rushed to rescue South Korea from a Communist invasion from the North.

Vietnam proved to be the war that resulted in a temporary loss of American confidence. Political decisions denied American soldiers the opportunity to win the war, and the American public questioned the role of the United States in fighting communism in distant lands.

The resulting lack of confidence led American leaders to appease the Soviets. For example, America began to sell grain to the Soviet Union as a gesture of good will. In addition, American leaders met with the Soviets and signed treaties in an attempt to end the arms race and lower the level of tension between the two superpowers.

Military

Both the United States and the Soviet Union developed improved versions of military weapons, including tanks, planes, submarines, and ships. In addition, radar system technology advanced and became able to detect enemy vessels much farther away.

Since the United States and Britain had developed a technological edge on the Soviets, they had to constantly guard against spies who worked for the Soviet Union. Soviet military advances often looked suspiciously like those developed in the free world.

Russian Air Force MiG-31 (above); *American B-2 Spirit stealth bomber* (right)

Nuclear

The United States became the first nation to harness the power of the atom, but Russia and other nations quickly developed their own nuclear weapons. During the Cold War, governments developed missiles with single and then multiple nuclear warheads. In addition, improved atomic bombs increased the amount of damage that one nation could inflict on an enemy target.

An early example of nuclear rivalry appeared when the Soviet Union exploded its first atomic bomb in 1949. The United States responded by working to develop the much more powerful hydrogen bomb. However, the Soviets soon developed their own hydrogen bomb.

This ongoing struggle to match or exceed one another was known as the arms race. Over the span of the Cold War, the United States and the Soviet Union developed the technology and stockpiled more than enough weapons to destroy one another. Known as mutually assured destruction (**MAD**), this strategy contributed to American and European appeasement. It also led to the signing of treaties designed to reduce the number of nuclear weapons. The Soviets took advantage of this perceived weakness and continued to seize territory.

Space

The Soviets took the lead in the race to place machines in space. In 1957 Soviet scientists launched *Sputnik*, the first man-made satellite. While the American government hurried to catch up in this race, the Soviets made another leap forward by launching the first man into space. From this point on, Americans determined to win the race to send a mission to the moon.

While the Soviet Union had initially led in the space race, the United States quickly outpaced Soviet efforts, rapidly developed the necessary technology, and launched the first of several successful

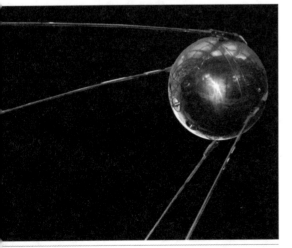

Replica of Sputnik 1

trips to the moon in July 1969. The Soviets soon abandoned their efforts to travel to the moon and concentrated on building a space station.

In addition to manned flights into space, the United States and other countries developed satellites for communication. Satellites also enabled nations to spy on their enemies without the risk of being shot down. This technology had many civilian uses as well, including satellites designed to record weather conditions.

Apollo 15 *Lunar Module Pilot James Irwin salutes the U.S. flag.*

Satellite

Section Quiz

1. Briefly describe the results of Mao Zedong's Great Leap Forward.
2. Why did Chinese Communists kill students in Tiananmen Square in 1989?
3. Who won the Korean War?
4. At what battle did the Vietnamese destroy the French army?
✶ How do Communist values differ from those of Western democracies?
✶ In what ways was the American civil religion better than Soviet suppression of Christianity? In what ways was it worse?

Apollo 15's *Command/Service Module* Endeavour *as seen from the Lunar Module* Falcon, *during rendezvous*

■ III. Transition in the Third World and the Middle East

As the Cold War progressed, Western nations continued to stress freedom and democracy. Men and women in the third world increasingly adopted this emphasis. If nations like Great Britain and France were so pleased with democracy and freedom, they asked, why couldn't the colonies have the freedom to become independent democracies?

Indian Nationalism

Indians had pressed the British government for independence over many years. Britain responded by gradually granting India a measure of self-rule through provincial councils. However, the people wanted to achieve independence at a faster pace than the British were willing to concede. Several Indian revolutionaries resorted to violent confrontations with the British. However, one man rejected violence and played an important role in India's independence through methods that were more peaceful.

Guiding Questions

1. How important was Indian nationalism during this period, and why did the British partition this region into India and Pakistan?
2. What role did World War II play in the rise of nationalist movements in Africa and Southeast Asia?
3. How did African and Asian countries achieve independence?
4. What international conditions influenced the creation of Israel, and why has there been persistent conflict between Israel and its Arab neighbors?

Mohandas Gandhi

The Third World

During the Cold War, the regions that remained neutral and did not ally themselves with the free world or the Communist powers became known as the **third world**. These regions included Latin America, South America, Africa, the Middle East, and Southern Asia.

Challenges Faced by Newly Independent Nations

List four challenges faced by newly independent nations.

Mohandas Gandhi (1869–1948) led a movement known as **passive resistance** to achieve Indian independence. Rather than fight against British rule, Gandhi encouraged his many followers to resist the British through strikes, refusal to pay taxes, and other nonviolent means.

After years of Indian resistance, the British finally granted India full independence in 1947. However, independence did not end the turmoil. A supporter of Hindu nationalism assassinated Gandhi in 1948. India continued to struggle with internal violence and occasional wars with its neighbors.

To minimize the growing hostility between Hindus and Muslims in India, the British partitioned India into two nations, India for the Hindu population and Pakistan for the Muslim population. Despite the efforts to avoid violence, rioting broke out between Sikhs, Hindus, and Muslims and about half a million people died.

In addition to the violence, nearly twelve million Sikhs, Hindus, and Muslims moved between these newly created nations. Violent clashes have continued, and these countries have endured many deadly struggles between various ethnic and religious groups.

Rise of Nationalist Movements

World War II led many colonial powers to realize that the citizens of their foreign empires had the right to be free just as they had fought to remain free of fascist control. In addition, the African colonies had contributed men and materials in support of the Allied cause. Following the war, these colonies expected to receive their freedom. The European nations gradually granted independence to their colonies. As a result, over the next thirty-five years, nearly one hundred and twenty nations emerged from Africa, Asia, and the Middle East.

Africa

Ghana became the first African nation to achieve independence. The British government had already recognized that the colonies needed to be developed and that the Africans needed to have a greater voice in the functioning of the colonies. Because Ghana had an educated population, it appeared to be an ideal colony to start this process.

In preparation for Ghana's independence, the British announced a general election in which Africans could vote and run for offices in a national assembly. In 1951 Kwame Nkrumah and his Convention People's Party captured the national assembly in a landslide victory. On March 6, 1957, Ghana became the first African colony to develop into an independent African nation. Within a few years, the majority of African nations had gained their independence.

However, not all colonies gained independence peacefully. In colonies with large populations of European settlers, the transition to independence often involved armed conflict. For example, the European population in Southern Rhodesia declared independence from Great Britain in 1965, fearing that Britain would force them to accept majority rule. In the early 1970s, a guerilla war began. Finally, in 1979 the Africans gained the right of self-government, and Southern Rhodesia became Zimbabwe.

At first, gains made by independence were remarkable, and many of the young nations seemed to prosper. The governments

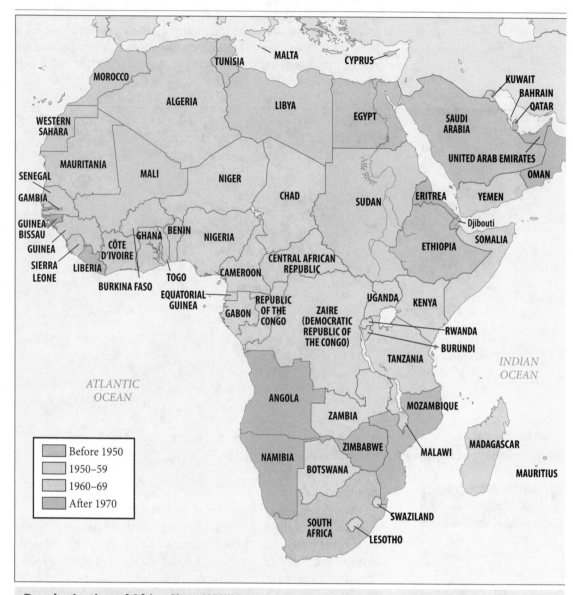

Decolonization of Africa Since WWII

set up schools and health-care clinics. However, over time, conditions began to deteriorate. Europeans had designed the economic structures to function in a mercantilist rather than a free market economy.

In addition, many of the early African leaders became convinced that socialism held great promise for bringing their people out of poverty. Thus, even well-intentioned leaders often set up policies that hampered their countries' growth. Sadly, not all leaders cared for the welfare of their people. Corrupt leaders often channeled a great deal of wealth into their personal bank accounts rather than using it to benefit their people.

African nations also found themselves caught between the United States and the Soviet Union. Soviets often took advantage of the weakness of these young nations and tried to spread communism across Africa. America responded by trying to prevent the spread of communism.

Often the United States government supported African dictatorships if they aligned with the West against the Soviet Union.

As a result, many dictators received supplies of cash and arms that enabled them to maintain a firm grip on their people. However, following the Cold War, many of these dictatorships collapsed as aid to African countries became subject to humanitarian treatment of the people.

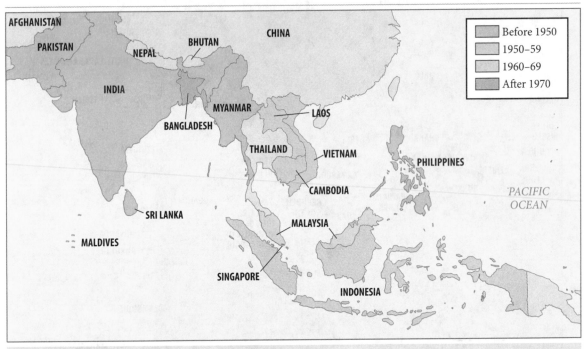

Decolonization of Southeast Asia Since WWII

Clashes Between Islam and the West

Muslims viewed the creation of modern Israel as intolerable. Muslim leaders claim Palestine as Muslim land and have repeatedly vowed to exterminate the Jews. In addition, Muslims recognize the Dome of the Rock in Jerusalem and the Al Aqsa Mosque on the Temple Mount in Jerusalem as sacred Muslim sites. Thus, Muslim leaders see the Jewish presence in Israel as defiling their land and their holy sites.

The West's support for Israel led to violent clashes with Islam, beginning with the Iranian hostage crisis in 1979. Muslim militants invaded the American embassy in Iran and took fifty-three Americans hostage, holding them captive for over a year. After the election and inauguration of President Reagan, the militants freed the hostages. This proved to be the first of many Muslim attacks on Americans.

Southeast Asia

We have already examined developments in India, Pakistan, and Vietnam. In addition, several other regions that had been colonized during the nineteenth century achieved independence following World War II. For example, the United States had prepared the Philippines for eventual independence, and this occurred in 1946. Native peoples across Southeast Asia formed national governments and regained their independence over the next twenty years (see map).

Rebirth of Israel

After the Roman legions destroyed Jerusalem in AD 70, the Jews had no homeland and spent centuries scattered throughout many nations. However, during the late nineteenth century, Jewish leaders began to work toward establishing a homeland. At the beginning of the twentieth century, Jews returned to Palestine in small numbers and purchased land.

Creation of Israel as a Modern State

In 1917 British Foreign Secretary Arthur Balfour issued a policy statement declaring that the British government favored the idea of a homeland for the Jewish people in Palestine. Known as the **Balfour Declaration**, it became the first official recognition by a world power that the Jews needed a land to call their own.

The British had governed Palestine as a mandate following World War I. However, by 1947 British forces realized they could no longer restrain the Jewish immigration and the growing Arab resentment. The British decided to partition Palestine into a Jewish state and an Arab state.

The British Mandate expired on May 14, 1948. On May 13 Jewish leaders proclaimed independence and named their new country Israel. The United States immediately recognized Israel as a country and provided military aid. Surprisingly, Stalin and the Soviet Union also recognized the nation of Israel.

Arab Response

Arab forces from Egypt, Syria, Jordan, Lebanon, and Iraq attacked Israel on May 14 and started the **1948 Arab-Israeli War**. After a year of fighting, both sides signed a ceasefire. Arab nations continued to support attacks on Israel and planned another major assault in June 1967. Egypt, Jordan, and Syria prepared to invade Israel with the assistance of several other Arab countries. However, the Jewish forces struck first and quickly destroyed most of the tanks, planes, and other weapons that were waiting to invade from Egypt and Syria. In what is known as the **Six-Day War**, Israel smashed the imminent Arab threat and seized control of several key areas that greatly enhanced Israel's security.

May 16, 1948, edition of the Jewish newspaper The Palestine Post, *soon renamed* The Jerusalem Post

A burnt-out Syrian (Soviet T34/85) tank in the path of the Israeli advance

Section Quiz

1. What method did Mohandas Gandhi use to pressure the British to grant India independence?

2. Why did Britain partition India into India and Pakistan?

3. What nation governed Palestine from the end of World War I until 1948?

4. What was the Arab response to the creation of Israel as a nation in 1948?

★ What problems did African states encounter upon independence?

★ What religious reasons cause Muslim leaders to reject Israel's right to exist as a nation in the land often referred to as Palestine?

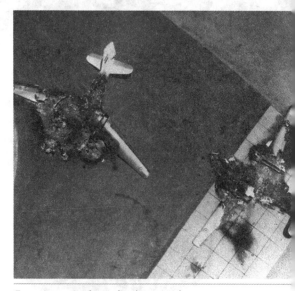

Egyptian warplanes lie destroyed on the tarmac after an Israeli Air Force preemptive strike.

Guiding Questions

1. What strong leaders helped dissolve the Soviet Union?
2. Why did the Soviet and other Communist governments collapse?
3. How did the Soviet Union splinter into various states?
4. What impact did the collapse of the Soviet Union have on the growth of Christianity in these areas?

Czech students holding a Czechoslovak flag as other Prague residents surround Soviet tanks in August 1968

Afghan soldier aiming an American-made stinger missile at enemy aircraft

■ IV. Collapse of the Soviet Union

In hindsight, it seems that the Soviet Union was destined to fall. Like other empires from the past, the Russians and their allies had seized more territory than they could successfully govern. In addition, the Soviet Union was composed of many nationalities and ethnic groups with little in common. Considering that only 5 to 10 percent of the people became members of the Communist party, it is astonishing that the Soviet Union survived until 1991. However, almost no one predicted the rapid demise of the Soviet Union during the 1970s and into the 1980s.

Soviet Aggression

By the end of the 1960s and on into the 1970s, freedom appeared to be on the decline, and communism appeared to be winning the Cold War. However, the election of strong leaders, including Margaret Thatcher and Ronald Reagan, resulted in a dramatic reversal during the 1980s.

The 1970s

The invasion of Czechoslovakia in 1968 provides a clear example of Soviet aggression. Alexander Dubček (DOOB chek) became the leader of Czechoslovakia in January 1968 and began to restore rights to the Czech people. He loosened control of the media, allowing free speech, and began to privatize the economy. This reform angered the Soviets, and they demanded that these changes cease.

When the Czech government refused to submit to the Soviet threats, the Russians and their allies sent a large armed force to crush resistance in Czechoslovakia in August 1968. Despite protests by Czechs and Western governments, no serious attempt was made to liberate Czechoslovakia. The Soviet troops remained until 1990.

The Soviet Union also supported North Vietnam's attempt to defeat the U.S.-supported government in South Vietnam. With the departure of American forces in 1973, communism gained an immense victory and succeeded in humiliating the United States. As America turned to isolationism, the Soviets became more bold in their spread of communism throughout Africa and Latin America.

The 1980s

The Soviets engaged in aggression again when a large Russian force invaded Afghanistan in 1979. On the pretense of bringing stability to this country, the Soviet Union sent over one hundred thousand troops to seize control. However, the Afghans vigorously resisted the Soviet occupation. With the United States providing weapons and financial support, the Afghans fought the Soviet troops to a stalemate. Although several hundred thousand Afghan fighters and civilians died because of the Soviet invasion, the Russians found victory to be elusive. Facing growing losses with no prospect of victory, the Soviet forces withdrew in 1989.

Strong Leadership in the West

In 1979 **Margaret Thatcher** led the Conservative Party in Great Britain to victory. She returned many nationalized industries to the private sector and tried to reverse many of the socialist programs that had weakened the British nation. In addition, she supported the anti-Communist strategy of a newly elected American president and forged a strong alliance with the United States during her eleven years as prime minister of Great Britain.

Ronald Reagan became the fortieth president of the United States in 1980. His strong leadership turned a struggling America into a political, social, and economic force that influenced the world. Reagan rejected the commonly accepted concession that the free world must peacefully coexist with communism. Instead, he focused the resources of the United States in an effort to overthrow this oppressive system of government. Through alliances with other conservative leaders such as Margaret Thatcher, he led an effective campaign to plant or restore democracy in many countries.

In addition, his policy of peace through strength led to the rebuilding of America's military might. In a speech made in 1983, President Reagan called for a space-based defensive system that would protect the United States from foreign missile attacks. Critics called Reagan's **SDI** (Strategic Defense Initiative) program Star Wars, but programs such as this convinced the Soviets that they could not compete with America. This realization contributed to the unraveling of the Soviet Union and led to its rapid disintegration.

While the Soviet Union supported the spread of communism in other countries, dissatisfaction and unrest were building in Soviet-dominated countries of Eastern Europe. Poland and the growth of the Solidarity Free Trade Union clearly demonstrated this unrest. Led by an electrical technician, **Lech Wałęsa**, Polish workers formed an anti-Communist movement that combined labor interests, the Roman Catholic Church, and Polish nationalists to oppose Soviet domination. Wałęsa endured job loss and imprisonment to lead the **Solidarity** movement and work toward Polish independence, which was achieved by 1989. Pope John Paul II also lent his support to this movement in 1987.

Margaret Thatcher

President Reagan speaking at the Brandenburg Gate in West Berlin

Lech Wałęsa

Mikhail Gorbachev

Fall of the Soviet Union and Division Along National Lines

The Soviet Union used force and military threats to enslave millions and hold an artificial empire together. However, the Soviet Union had to accept grain shipments from the United States and steal military technology from America and other countries in order to survive. Socialism and communism are not self-sustaining, and nations that embrace these forms of government cannot survive without the aid and support of others.

Collapse of the Soviet System

Following Stalin's death in 1953, **Nikita Khrushchev** ruled the Soviet Union until 1964. His policies became unpopular, and Kremlin leaders voted him out of office while he was out of the country on vacation. Khrushchev was succeeded by several aging Russian leaders. Meanwhile, a younger leader rose through the ranks of the Kremlin. Upon the death of the Soviet leader in 1985, **Mikhail Gorbachev** emerged as the leader of the Soviet Union. He assumed power without violence or opposition.

For decades the Soviet government had emphasized building a strong military. During these years the people had endured rationing of food, clothing, and other material goods. Gorbachev tried to revive the Soviet Union by ushering in a period of political and economic restructuring. He allowed private ownership of businesses and released thousands of political prisoners. In 1987 Gorbachev moved the Soviet Union closer to democracy by calling for multi-candidate elections. In 1990 the people elected him as the first president of the Soviet Union.

Because of these dramatic changes, the Communist Party lost control of the Soviet Union and additional changes could not be prevented. As the people realized that their government had been lying to them for years, they revolted against the Communist system and demanded freedom from Soviet domination.

States Formed from the Former Soviet Union

Division into Many States

The people of Romania violently opposed their Communist rulers and overthrew them. Bulgaria, Czechoslovakia, East Germany, Hungary, and Poland also broke away from their Soviet masters and declared independence. By 1991 the Soviet Union and the Eastern bloc had ceased to exist.

New Opportunities for Christians

With the fall of the Soviet Union, many changes occurred in Eastern Europe. Among those changes were religious freedoms that the Communists had withheld for over seventy years.

Freedom to Worship

While the level of religious persecution had fluctuated over the years, Communists consistently discouraged or prohibited Christians from publicly assembling to worship. Often believers had to meet in barns, forests, or fields in order to hold a church service. Yet, despite the discomfort and danger associated with public worship, Christians continued to meet whenever possible to worship and to encourage one another.

With the collapse of the Soviet Union, Christians were able to meet in public and worship without fear of arrest or harassment. Believers in Eastern Europe thronged to churches to take advantage of this new freedom.

Freedom to Evangelize

In addition to the freedom to worship, Christians could now witness to their neighbors and family members without fear of arrest and possible imprisonment. Many Christians had faithfully witnessed under the Communist regime, but they did so at great personal risk. This new freedom enabled Christians in many Eastern European countries to spread the good news of the gospel without government interference.

Missionary Outreach

Missionaries from the West could now obtain visas and minister in former Communist nations. This new freedom allowed Christians from the United States and elsewhere to take the gospel to remote regions of the former Soviet Union and shine the light of God's Word across this vast region.

Section Quiz

1. What country did the Soviets invade and try without success to conquer over a ten-year period?

2. What program did President Reagan propose that convinced the Soviet Union that it could no longer compete with the United States?

3. What Soviet leader came to power in 1985?

4. What impact did the Soviet emphasis on a strong military have on the civilian population?

★ How did the Soviet Union respond to the Czech government's attempt to restore basic rights to its people?

★ Why did the reforms supported by Gorbachev lead to the collapse of the Soviet Union?

CHAPTER REVIEW

People, Places, and Things to Know

Konrad Adenauer
Charles de Gaulle
Fifth Republic
Liberal Democratic Party
Marshall Plan
Common Market
NATO
United Nations
Cold War
Republic of China
Great Leap Forward
Cultural Revolution
Tiananmen Square
Berlin Blockade
Inchon
38th parallel
Ho Chi Minh
Dien Bien Phu
Viet Cong
MAD
Sputnik
Mohandas Gandhi
passive resistance
third world
Balfour Declaration
1948 Arab-Israeli War
Six-Day War
Margaret Thatcher
Ronald Reagan
SDI
Lech Wałęsa
Solidarity
Nikita Krushchev
Mikhail Gorbachev

■ Making Connections

1. Why was the economic recovery of Europe urgent following World War II?

2. How did Japan recover rapidly from the devastation of World War II?

3. Why did Britain and France resort to high tax rates?

4. How do Communist states and Western democracies differ regarding ownership of property?

5. Why did Mao Zedong instigate the political purge known as the Cultural Revolution? What happened as a result of this purge?

6. Why did the United States retreat from the war in Vietnam?

7. Why are spy satellites more effective and safer than spy planes?

8. How did Ronald Reagan and Margaret Thatcher play a leading role in the collapse of the Soviet Union?

■ Developing History Skills

1. On the map on the facing page, locate the following countries that received Soviet aid or came under Soviet domination.

   a. China   d. North Korea
   b. Czechoslovakia   e. North Vietnam
   c. East Germany

2. How did President Reagan's SDI proposals play a role in ending the Cold War?

■ Thinking Critically

1. How is the Islamic threat that emerged toward the end of the Cold War similar to the Soviet threat? How is it different?

2. A growing number of historians credit Mikhail Gorbachev with dismantling the Soviet Union. Evaluate this view in light of what you have learned in this chapter.

■ Living in God's World

1. During the Cold War, many liberal theologians spoke out against the arms race as un-Christian and immoral. Write a brief newspaper editorial taking the opposite position on biblical grounds.

2. Imagine that you are the newly elected president of a recently independent colony. Write a report detailing how you plan to learn from the mistakes of other colonies liberated in the twentieth century.

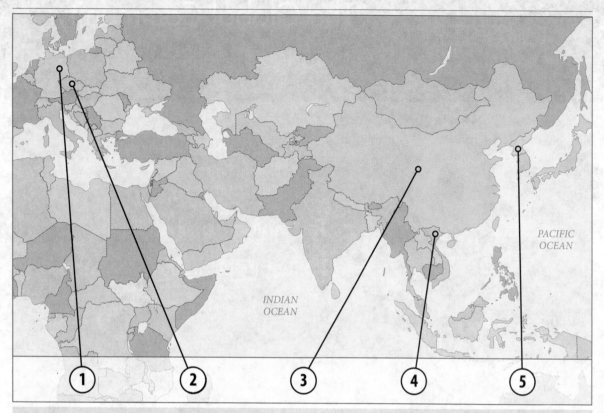

The Soviet Union's Far-Reaching Influence

CHAPTER 20

The Global Community
1945 – 2012

- Environmental Trends
- Global Economy
- Technology and Culture
- Political and Religious Trends

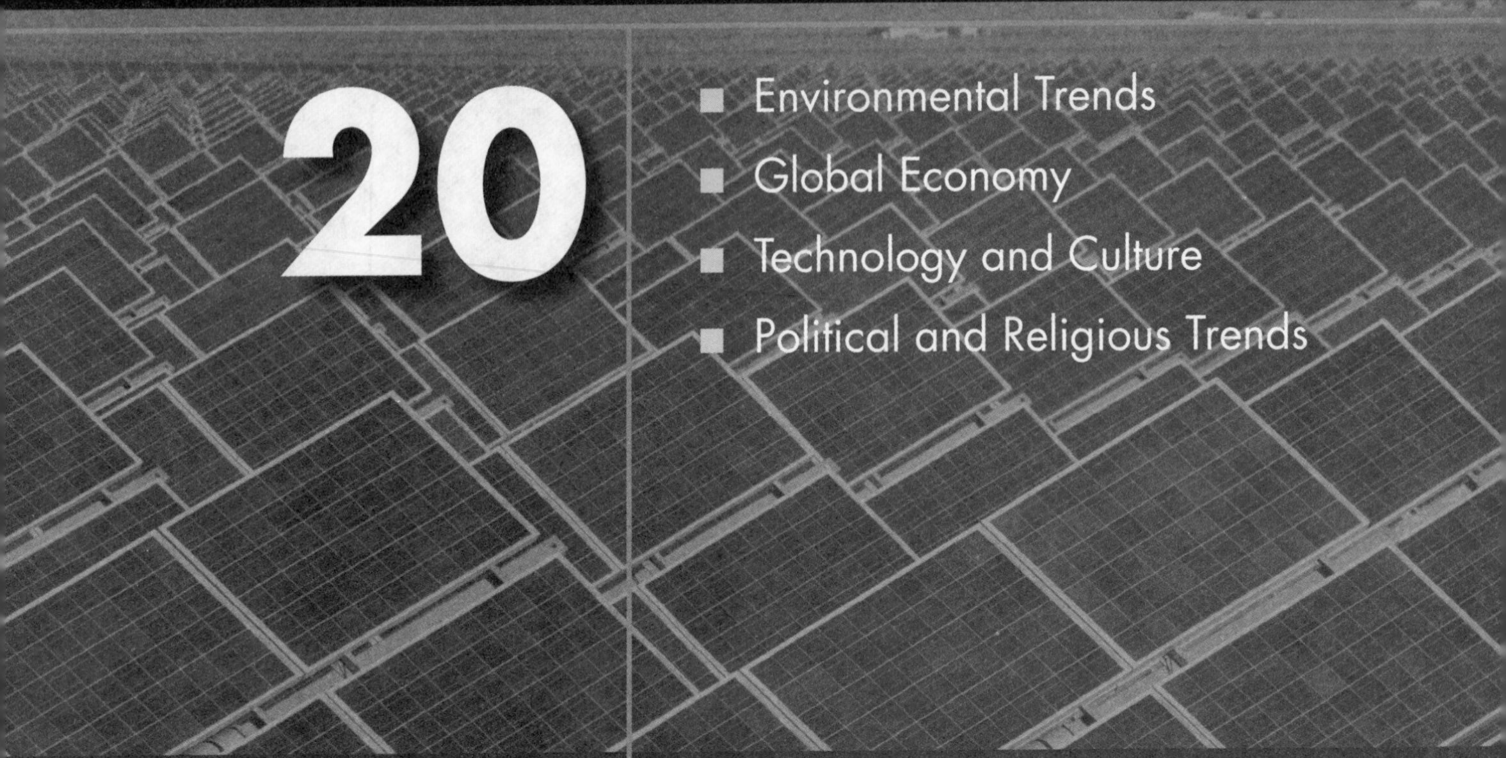

1960 – 2015

Iran is taken over by radical Muslim forces 1979

Central American Common Market is formed 1960s

Saddam Hussein attacks Iran 1980

1960	1965	1970	1975	1980	1985

Development of the Internet for military use 1960s

Iran holds fifty-two Americans hostage 1979–81

Big Ideas

1. How does the Bible's teaching about Creation, Fall, and Redemption shape your thinking about culture and civilization?
2. Why are covenants God made with Israel important for understanding world history?
3. In what way was the incarnation of Christ the turning point of world history?

The world is changing at a rapid pace. It is essential for Christians to understand some of the trends of this change and to make wise choices as stewards of what God has entrusted to us. Some trends seem to be positive, while others give much cause for concern. Through all the changes occurring around us and those that have yet to occur, Christians have the promise that Christ is always with us and will be with us until the end of time.

We began this book by referring to Paul's words in Acts 17 stating that God made the world and all the resources that we find on our planet. We end our study by examining some of the opportunities and challenges that your generation will face, including the spread of the gospel so that all men might not only "seek the Lord" but also find Him.

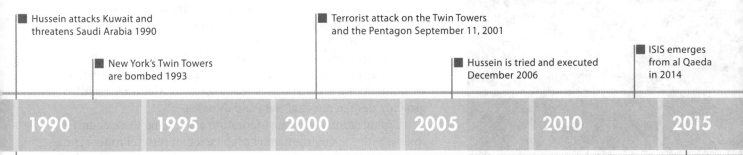

Hussein attacks Kuwait and threatens Saudi Arabia 1990

New York's Twin Towers are bombed 1993

Terrorist attack on the Twin Towers and the Pentagon September 11, 2001

Hussein is tried and executed December 2006

ISIS emerges from al Qaeda in 2014

| 1990 | 1995 | 2000 | 2005 | 2010 | 2015 |

Afghanistan comes under the Taliban's control 1990s

World population surpasses 7.4 billion in 2016

Guiding Questions

1. What are population shifts?
2. How has urban life developed?
3. What are the theories of climate change?
4. What are some issues related to energy resources?
5. What is man's role in the environment?

■ I. Environmental Trends

The earth, with its billions of human inhabitants and varied species of animal life, continues to experience changes in its environment. These alterations are reflected in shifting population numbers, continued movement to cities, and the growing need to manage finite resources.

Population Shifts

The human population is projected to reach eight billion by 2024, and it may reach 9.5 billion by 2050. Some areas of the world maintain a stable or gradually declining population, while others have a rapidly increasing population.

Stable or Declining

Most nations in Europe are experiencing a decline in population due to low birth rates. Large numbers of immigrants have slowed this decline, but many European states continue to experience a reduction of population. North America also has a low birth rate. However, the migration of foreign-born individuals to the United States has enabled this nation to maintain a stable population.

In our study of history, we have seen that population growth and movement to urban areas have resulted in significant changes. Eventually, a society's culture alters because of these changes. For example, the shrinking of Western culture in relation to the world's population is gradually resulting in a post-Western culture, one that is influenced more and more by emerging cultures from Latin America and Africa.

Nations that are maintaining a stable population are learning to manage environmental problems that accompany an industrial society, including various forms of pollution. Even though these states maintain a stable population, their influence in the world tends to diminish because of the growth of other regions.

Nations that experience a declining population tend to have significant problems. For example, they do not produce enough children to maintain a population capable of providing a future labor force and solving environmental issues. Over time, immigrants used to meet labor needs will dominate these states. Declining states will cease to play any significant role in the international arena. They may even be absorbed by other countries.

Growing at Varying Rates

A growing percentage of the world's population will live outside of the countries traditionally considered advanced. While the long-term effects of this population shift are impossible to determine, significant change is to be expected.

Regions such as Latin America and Asia, especially India and China, have produced the largest and fastest growing populations. In addition, the populations of many states in Africa are rapidly growing despite regional wars and diseases.

Urbanization and industrialization are forcing these countries to deal with the environmental problems that result. Proper sanitation and safe drinking water are essential to prevent the spread of disease. Increased use of coal and oil has also created significantly more pollution. Many emerging nations struggle to balance growing industry with protecting the environment.

Tokyo

Mumbai

Growth of Urban Life

More and more people are moving to urban centers in order to find employment. Therefore, the world's largest cities will need to provide an infrastructure to handle tens of millions of people in each city. The task will be daunting.

In 1900 the world's largest cities were located in Europe or North America. Currently, eight out of ten of the largest cities are in Asia or Latin America. The emerging megacities are located in India, Brazil, China, Mexico, and Africa.

In 2014, 54 percent of the world's population lived in cities. Scholars predict that by 2025 at least 60 percent of people will dwell in urban areas. Not only is the world population growing, it is also migrating.

Climate Change?

You learned in Chapter 5 about the Medieval Warm Period that began in the eleventh century. This period resulted in increased farming and a multiplied food supply. Later in that chapter, you learned about a cooling period in the early fourteenth century that led to famine and great loss of life.

One lesson we can learn from these periods and others like them is that the earth's climate experiences cycles of change. Some periods are warmer and allow greater food production, while others are cooler and reduce food production. These cycles occur naturally.

Recently, the topic of climate change has intensified because some insist that man is causing **climate change** and that dire consequences are just over the horizon. Many of those who embrace this view demand a consensus among scientists.

To reach answers regarding the issue of climate change, we need to ask several questions. First, is the earth warming beyond normal cycles? Second, if the earth is warming, is that a bad thing? Third, if the earth is warming, has man done anything to cause it? Finally, are the proposed measures to curb climate change sensible?

Shanghai

Energy

When God created the earth, He filled it with resources that could be used to meet many needs, such as production of energy. Whether the resource is coal, oil, the sun, or nuclear materials, man has the responsibility to use these fuels wisely for the betterment of mankind and man's dominion over the earth.

Coal

Coal is often used to produce electricity. The coal is crushed and burned in a furnace under a boiler. Water is turned into steam, and the steam spins large turbines that turn generators and produce electricity.

As of 2012, about 29 percent of the world's electricity was produced by burning coal. As of 2013, power plants in the U.S. produced about 38 percent of the nation's electricity by burning coal. Coal continues to produce the least expensive energy.

Wind

Wind power is converted into electricity by the use of wind turbines. Wind has also been used to power mills and pump water in the past.

Nuclear

Nuclear energy is used to heat water and produce steam for the production of electricity. Currently the U.S. produces about 19 percent of its electricity in nuclear power plants.

Nuclear power is also used to power submarines and some ships, such as aircraft carriers.

Solar

Light and heat from the sun are used to produce electricity through heat engines and solar panels. Solar heat engines use the sun's heat to turn water into steam and produce electricity. Solar panels turn the sun's light directly into electricity.

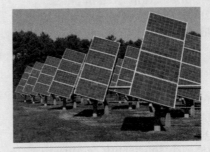

Water

People can use water to produce electricity by channeling the water restrained by dams

through tubes. The rushing water turns turbines that are connected to generators.

At this time, about 20 percent of the world's electricity is produced by water-powered turbines.

Oil and Natural Gas

Oil can be processed into many products, including gasoline or heating oil. Gasoline is most often used for automobiles. Diesel is used to power cars, trucks, and locomotives. Oil and natural gas are used to heat homes or produce heat in power plants to turn water into steam and produce electricity.

Oil pumpjack

Fracking drill rig on the prairie at dusk

In other words, do the benefits outweigh the costs? What will be the world economic impact of these measures? The answers to these questions will help us determine support for or opposition to the proposals that some scientists and government leaders are currently advocating.

Energy Resources

While man has discovered many energy sources, oil remains one of the main sources of energy for transportation, heat, and production of electricity. Even though oil is available in many regions of the world, most nations import much of their oil from the volatile Middle East. These imports grant significant importance to an area dominated by Islam. Since oil continues to produce most of the energy consumed in many countries, those who provide this resource will continue to exercise a great influence over the nations that import it.

A polar bear on the pack ice north of Svalbard, Norway

The rapidly growing economies in China and India have also increased the demand for oil. The level of demand fluctuates depending on economic factors including recessions and discovery of new supplies.

Many nations have expressed the goal of energy independence, or the ability of a nation to produce energy without importing resources. However, opposition to domestic drilling and to increased use of nuclear energy in some countries makes the goal of energy independence difficult if not impossible to achieve. France is one of a handful of countries that produce most of their electricity with nuclear power plants.

Man's Role in the Environment

With all the debates about man's role in the climate and in the change that man may or may not be causing, the Christian should remember at least two things. First, we find the Creation Mandate in Genesis 1. God gave human beings the earth to use wisely as stewards. This authorizes them to maximize the usefulness of God's creation.

Second, the Lord commands the Christian in Matthew 22:39 to love his neighbor. Christians can demonstrate love by carefully developing resources to provide the greatest number of people with such basic needs as affordable food and clean water.

We should also use resources to conserve human life. Scientists accomplish this task by developing improved medicines and medical care as well as removing pollutants from the air and water. Careless destruction does not accomplish these goals, but careful management of the environment for the good of humanity does.

Section Quiz

1. In the coming years, a growing percentage of the world's population will live outside of _____.

2–4. List three energy sources and briefly describe how they are used to produce energy.

★ Why are most nations in Europe experiencing a decline in population? What has offset this decline?

★ Briefly describe man's role in the environment based on Genesis 1:28 and Matthew 22:39.

Guiding Questions

1. What has caused the development of the global economy?
2. What are some examples of regional trade zones?
3. What are the advantages and disadvantages of the global economy?

A Walmart supercenter in Xiamen

Euros

■ II. Global Economy

Today a person can go almost anywhere in the world and find his favorite soft drink or fast food. In addition, products previously available only in a distant market can be purchased locally because of our global economy.

Causes

While the global economy began to develop following World War II, its growth has accelerated in the last two decades. Many recent events have made possible a truly global economy. In Chapter 19 you learned about the fall of communism in Eastern Europe. This political change dramatically increased opportunities for trade. Improvements in transportation and trade agreements have made it possible to ship products across many national boundaries. In addition, technology has contributed to the efficiency of trade on a global level. Finally, sustained peace among many nations of the world allows global trade to flourish.

Examples

Organizing regions into large trade zones has taken several forms. We will look at two examples.

Free Trade Areas

Many nations have established economic trade zones in order to increase trade. Members of these trade blocs agree to remove tariffs and quotas (amounts of products that other countries can sell to the members of these trade zones). **Free trade areas** exist in many regions, including parts of Africa, Latin America, Southeast Asia, and the South Pacific.

Single Market

Several regions have developed economic and monetary zones that cross national boundaries and include multiple states. This **single market** enables states to trade with one another without restriction. The single market has resulted in greater wealth for the member states. We will briefly examine three examples of this system.

The **European Union** (EU) is an economic and political alliance of twenty-eight nations across Europe. This organization built upon the European Economic Community described in Chapter 19. The EU has developed a single market using standardized laws that enable free movement of people, products, and funds throughout the member states. At the present, twenty-three states are using the **euro** as their currency.

Several Central American states formed the **Central American Common Market** in the early 1960s. This organization has sought to increase trade between member states. However, conflict between El Salvador and Honduras, two of the member states, erupted in 1969. In addition, ongoing political turmoil in this region has diminished the effectiveness of this economic effort.

Eight West African states currently form the **West African Economic and Monetary Union**. Their organization strives to promote economic cooperation and the use of a common currency, the **CFA franc**. This union also works to develop products that are competitively priced for the global economy.

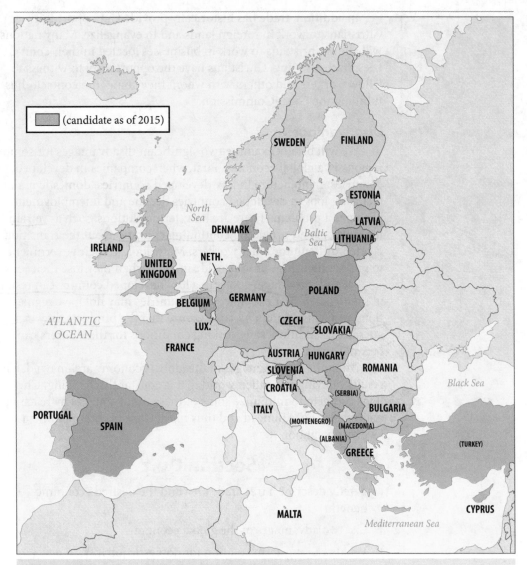

map legend: (candidate as of 2015)

Member Countries of the European Union

Evaluating the Global Economy

There are many steps involved in developing a global economy. Some of these steps have positive results. However, the global economy also creates challenges that affect job opportunities as competition increases.

Advantages

In the global economy, companies build factories in countries where the cost of labor, capital, and technology is lower. This strategy enables corporations to produce goods at a lower cost and remain competitive. In addition, small companies have almost unlimited potential for growth because they can offer their products to customers around the world. Increased sales can quickly build small industries into large corporations. Furthermore, mass production for a global customer base can lead to more products available at lower costs.

The global economy also provides another means to carry out the Creation Mandate of maximizing the use of God's creation. Free trade enables utilization of resources and allows the creativity of man to have greater expression as he develops products to meet needs.

In addition, trade has historically provided an opportunity for Christians to work in foreign lands and to evangelize. Many nations will allow Christians to work in businesses located in their countries. In this setting, Christians have the opportunity to witness to fellow workers and others with whom they come into contact, thus fulfilling the Great Commission.

Disadvantages

We will briefly examine two significant disadvantages for some regions in a global economy. First, when companies in developed countries manufacture in less-developed countries, domestic manufacturing jobs in developed countries decline and unemployment becomes a problem. There are long-term solutions, such as retraining workers and providing continuing education, but the transition is often difficult for older workers. Many look to their government to protect their jobs or to provide income when they lose their jobs.

Second, producing goods in a less-developed country can result in safety issues. For example, such countries may not have regulations and legislation in place to ensure that the products they make are safe. In addition, safe working conditions for the laborers can become an issue.

Often the disadvantages of the global economy are unavoidable results of living in a fallen world that is constantly changing. Christians can help to minimize some of these disadvantages by reaching out to help those in need and thus fulfill Christ's commandment to love our neighbor.

Section Quiz

1. Briefly describe a free trade area and the desired economic benefit.

2–3. List two advantages of the global economy.

4. What is a long-term solution for domestic job loss?

★ In what ways has the West African Economic and Monetary Union sought to improve economic conditions in West Africa?

★ Why has the Central American Common Market enjoyed less success than the EU?

■ III. Technology and Culture

Technological advances seem to occur on a daily basis in the modern world. No sooner has a consumer purchased a computer or cell phone than a newer version becomes available on the market. However, it is important for us to examine the revolution in technology and observe how it affects our culture.

Promise

The list of technological advances is long and growing longer by the day. The possibilities of technology seem to be endless. We will briefly examine four areas where technology has improved the quality of life.

Medical Advances

DNA studies have enabled scientists to better understand diseases and to develop drugs to overcome several of them. In addition,

Guiding Questions

1. What are the potential benefits of technology?

2. What are the perils of technology and its impact on culture?

A young boy born with a right hand malformation tries on his new 3D-printed hand given to him by the Association for the Study and Assistance of Child Amputees (ASSEDEA).

researchers have developed vaccinations to cure or prevent diseases such as polio and smallpox. Advances in medical technology include laser surgeries and other procedures to destroy tumors or repair injured organs through tiny incisions. These procedures protect the patient from many surgery-related infections and enable more rapid recovery.

Timesaving Devices

Household appliances, including washing machines, dishwashers, and vacuum cleaners, have enabled people to quickly do jobs that previously consumed many hours. Automobiles make it possible for people to travel great distances in less time. These timesaving devices have provided people with more leisure time. Some would argue that they have also improved our quality of life.

Communication Advances

Telephones, cell phones, e-mail, and social networking sites form a partial list of modern communication tools. Many people are able to communicate almost instantly because of these advances. Businesses can communicate in real time in all parts of the globe. This rapid communication cuts costs and enables a global reach for businesses. Missionaries can communicate with their supporting churches in real time and rapidly share their needs, prayer requests, and answers to prayer. Families can converse over long distances easily and economically.

Information Explosion

Many Internet sites provide free access to a wealth of material that was previously available only in print at specific libraries. Now you can view a newspaper from another part of the world or read a book from your computer or hand-held device. Information becomes available much more rapidly than a person can examine it. We are truly experiencing an explosion of information.

Peril

While technology holds great promise, it also generates concerns that Christians should address. We will look at a few of these concerns.

Technology

List the promises and perils of technology.

Promise	Peril

The Internet

Of the many inventions that have influenced our lives, perhaps no system has had more of an impact than the Internet. The Internet began in the 1960s as a U.S. government-funded project to enable the military to continue to communicate following a nuclear attack. The military believed that as long as the computer networks remained operational, communication would be possible. It is doubtful that anyone envisioned the incredible influence this technology would have on the modern world.

Stem Cell Research

Technology has enabled scientists to produce human embryos. Some scientists want to experiment with the **embryonic stem cells** to find cures for many diseases. It is important to note that during this process the scientist destroys the embryo. Many Christians oppose this practice because life begins at conception and an embryo is a developing person. This would mean that the destruction of the embryo is essentially murder.

Supporters of research on embryonic stem cells argue that this research is vital to curing a variety of crippling diseases. However, opponents point out that research on **adult stem cells** does not present the same moral dilemma. In addition, they note that this research is already being used to treat a growing number of diseases.

Guiding Questions

1. What are some modern political trends?

2. Why is Islam spreading around the world?

3. How has Christianity spread in the global south, and how have Christians there responded to persecution?

Medical Advances

Medical technology tends to obscure a sense of our own mortality. For example, people living in 1900 were more aware of death and were tempered by its reality. Technology also affects the doctor-patient relationship because the doctor tends to rely more on technology than on the patient's description of symptoms. Medical personnel also use technology for sinful purposes, including abortion and embryonic stem cell research.

Timesaving Devices

While technology has provided many timesaving devices, many people tend to consume their time using these devices. As a result, little time remains for thinking about important matters. We often fill our leisure time with things that add little or nothing to our lives. One of the keys to a proper use of technology is to control the technology rather than allowing technology to control the user.

Communication Advances

Constant communication interrupts work and lowers productivity. It also robs us of time for deliberation and quietness. Excessive communication often results in less thoughtful, reflective, and substantive communication.

Information Explosion

Christians should be concerned about the deluge of information with which the Internet bombards them. It is often difficult to filter out what is important and what is unimportant. In addition, it can be challenging to determine the accuracy of this information. Another result of this information explosion is easy access to harmful and sinful materials.

Mass communication—most notably TV—tries to grab the largest market and thus reduces the quality of public discourse. Since careful evaluation of important issues does not "sell," public discourse often degenerates into sound bites and sensational reporting.

Section Quiz

1–2. List two areas where technological advances have improved human life.

3–4. List two perils of technology.

✶ What role does TV play in the quality of public discourse?

✶ Briefly evaluate the perils of stem cell research.

IV. Political and Religious Trends

Political and religious trends can affect one another. For example, democracies tend to tolerate or embrace religious freedom. Communist or Islamic governments often deny religious freedom. However, Christianity continues to grow in many societies that persecute Christians. This trend has been true throughout the history of the church, and it remains true in many oppressed nations today.

Political

Muslim terrorists have been at war with the West, especially with the United States, for at least three decades. The war began with the taking of American diplomats as hostages in Iran during the Carter presidency. It continued with attacks on American forces in Lebanon, Saudi Arabia, and other countries.

The war dramatically accelerated with the attack on the Twin Towers in New York City and the Pentagon in Washington, D.C. American leaders tended to ignore the growing threat, but the attack on September 11, 2001, (9/11) forced the United States and other countries to respond with military action and take the battle to the enemies of the free world.

In addition, Communist China has quickly developed into a wealthy and powerful force in Asia. We will briefly examine the economic restructuring of China following the death of Mao Zedong that resulted in this transformation.

The Rise of Terrorist States

Following years of rule by a pro-Western, brutal dictatorship, Iran came under the control of radical Muslim forces in 1979. To demonstrate their hatred of the United States, they held fifty-two American diplomats and their staff hostage for over four hundred days from late 1979 to early 1981. In the years since then, Iran has been a major supporter of terrorism throughout the Middle East and other countries. In addition, its outspoken hatred of Israel combined with a growing nuclear threat continues to have a destabilizing influence on this region.

Iraq, under the dictatorship of **Saddam Hussein**, also became an important state in the Middle East. Initially, Hussein allied himself with the West against the common enemy of Iran. He attacked Iran in 1980 and engaged in a war that led to over three hundred thousand deaths but ended in a stalemate.

Hussein abandoned any pretense of support for the West in 1990 and invaded his neighbor Kuwait. He seized Kuwait's vast oil reserves and threatened to march on into Saudi Arabia. After American and allied forces halted his advance, Hussein's military was quickly routed and sent back to Iraq in 1991. Despite economic sanctions, U.N. resolutions, and warnings by the United States, Hussein continued to develop offensive weapons, to provide financial support for suicide bombers, and to refuse to allow inspections of sensitive nuclear facilities. To end Iraq's growing threat, a U.S.-led military coalition invaded Iraq in 2003. U.S. troops captured Hussein in December 2003. After a lengthy trial in an Iraqi court, the new Iraqi government executed him in December 2006.

Afghanistan is a rugged, landlocked country that lies east of Iran. During the 1990s, this region came under the control of a radical Muslim group called the **Taliban**. This regime provided a safe haven and base of operations for the Saudi extremist **Osama bin Laden**. He built a terrorist network known as **al Qaeda** that operated out of Afghanistan. Bin Laden aggressively supported attacks on the United States, including the bombing of the Twin Towers in New York City in 1993.

However, Osama bin Laden became infamous for his role in the destruction of the Twin Towers

Twin Towers burning after being struck by planes on September 11, 2001

379

and an attack on the Pentagon on September 11, 2001. President George W. Bush quickly rallied support for an invasion of Afghanistan when the Taliban refused to turn bin Laden over to international authorities. U.S. and allied forces promptly routed Taliban and al Qaeda forces, removing them from power. Bin Laden went into hiding and eluded American forces until authorities discovered his location at a compound in Pakistan. U.S. Naval special forces entered the buiding at night on May 2, 2011. Bin Laden died in the resulting firefight and was buried at sea.

The Rising Influence of China

China has transformed from an isolated nation with a predominantly agricultural economy to a rapidly growing economic world power. From 1952 to 1978, China's GDP (gross domestic product) remained stagnant. At that time, Communist leaders began to adopt economic reforms that encouraged a measure of free enterprise.

As a result, China's GDP rose dramatically from around nine billion U.S. dollars in the 1970s to over nine trillion dollars in 2013. A recent slowing of China's GDP growth is due, in part, to major economic downturns in the world economy. However, China's financial strength, combined with a large military force, has made China a key player in most economic and political decisions. China is becoming a superpower.

Religious

In Chapter 1 we examined the foundations upon which Christ built His church. In Chapter 2 we studied the formation and growth of Islam. While other religious movements have appeared in history, these two have ebbed and flowed throughout history and our study in this book.

Growth of Islam

You learned in Chapter 2 that the Muslim advance was halted at the Battle of Tours in 732. In the centuries that followed, Islam was very much present in the world, but it seemed to have lost its fervor. This situation changed with the rise of a zealous Sunni Muslim in Saudi Arabia during the eighteenth century. Muhammad ibn Abd-al-Wahhab was a Muslim scholar who utterly opposed changes to historic Islam. He advocated the violent suppression of these changes.

The **Wahhabist** movement (so-called by its enemies) gained prominence in Saudi Arabia. This movement has used the vast wealth generated by oil sales to spread the literal application of Islam to many parts of the world. Wahhabists attack Muslims who reject their violent teachings with as much hatred as they do non-Muslims. As a result, many Muslims fear and quietly oppose the Wahhabist interpretation of Islam.

In addition, Saudi Arabia has exported terrorism and hatred to many countries in the Middle East, Southeast Asia, and Africa. Saudi money has also paid for the construction of mosques in many of these regions. The leaders of these mosques are required to promote Wahhabism. Furthermore, many Muslim religious schools, called **madrasas**, use educational material produced in Saudi Arabia

GDP

Gross Domestic Production is a measure of a country's total economic output for a given year.

Madrasa students reading Qur'an passages to the imam

Palestinian Hamas militants

that teaches Wahhabist intolerance and hatred for anything that is not purely Islamic.

The latest form of Islamic extremism with Wahhabist-like qualities to emerge is **ISIS** (Islamic State in Iraq and Syria) which has rapidly grown out of the civil war that is raging in Syria. This group is also known as **ISIL** (Islamic State in Iraq and the Levant) which reflects the goal of this radical group to seize control of Turkey, Israel, and other nations that comprise the Levant (lands along the eastern Mediterranean Sea). They have used extreme forms of violence to terrorize their enemies and gain the world's attention. These Islamic extremists have also expressed a desire to establish a caliphate.

Islam also continues to grow through large families and conversions. Since Muslim couples are encouraged to have many children, their influence grows in every nation where Muslims have settled.

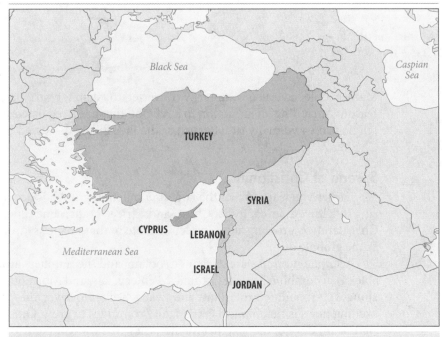

The Levant

Esposito

"Jihad as struggle pertains to the difficulty and complexity of living a good life: struggling against the evil in oneself—to be virtuous and moral, making a serious effort to do good works and help to reform society. Depending on the circumstances in which one lives, it also can mean fighting injustice and oppression, spreading and defending Islam, and creating a just society through preaching, teaching, and, if necessary, armed struggle or holy war.

"The two broad meanings of jihad, nonviolent and violent, are contrasted in a well-known Prophetic tradition. It is said that when Muhammad returned from battle he told his followers, 'We return from the lesser jihad [warfare] to the greater jihad.' The greater jihad is the more difficult and more important struggle against one's ego, selfishness, greed, and evil. In its most general meaning, jihad refers to the obligation incumbent on all Muslims, individuals and the community, to follow and realize God's will: to lead a virtuous life and to extend the Islamic community through preaching, education, example, writing, etc. Jihad also includes the right, indeed the obligation, to defend Islam and the community from aggression. Throughout history, the call to jihad has rallied Muslims to the defense of Islam."

John L. Esposito, *What Everyone Needs to Know About Islam* (New York: Oxford University Press, 2002), 117–18.

Cook

". . . [T]he basic point [is] that the internal jihad has no reality whatsoever— that it is a theoretical, scholarly construct for which we have little to no practical evidence. . . . [One author] carefully compares jihad theory to practice. But with internal jihad there is no practice, just theory. Others have fallen into this error as well. They comprise two basic groups: Western scholars who want to present Islam in the most innocuous terms possible, and Muslim apologists, who rediscovered the internal jihad in the nineteenth century and have been emphasizing it ever since that time as the normative expression of jihad—in defiance of all the religious and historical evidence to the contrary. The motives of the first group are well intentioned, probably undertaken with the goal of furthering interreligious dialogue and skirting an issue that has long been used by polemicists as a vehicle for attacking Islam."

David B. Cook, *Understanding Jihad* (Oakland: University of California Press, 2005), 40.

Note: Cook also finds fault with those who believe that since Islam historically spread by the sword that modern-day Islamic terrorists stand within the mainstream of Islamic tradition regarding jihad. The use of martyrdom or suicide bombers and the targeting of non-military targets are two significant departures from the jihad tradition (see pp. 141–46).

1. Summarize the views of both Esposito and Cook.

2. Explain how you would go about evaluating which view is more accurate.

Many people have also voluntarily converted to Islam for various reasons, including an attraction to a religion that has a regulated religious life and many rituals, such as the Five Pillars discussed in Chapter 2.

Spread of Christianity

Earlier you learned that the largest population growth is occurring in Latin America, India, China, and Africa. At the same time, Christianity is growing at an accelerated rate in these regions known as the **global south**.

Accurate numbers are difficult to obtain, and the numbers available often combine Roman Catholics, Pentecostals, and Mormons along with mainline Protestants and Evangelicals. However, the exciting news is that biblical Christianity continues to grow. One significant development is that missionaries are now coming from the global south to evangelize the traditionally Christian-influenced nations of the West.

Christianity is spreading throughout Latin America. Distinct from Roman Catholic and traditional Protestant churches, Evangelical and Charismatic congregations are growing and multiplying in many Latin American countries.

The expansion of Christianity in Africa provides another clear example of growth. There were an estimated ten million Christians in Africa in 1900. By the year 2000, the number had increased to around three hundred and sixty million, and the growth continues. Some speculate that the number of Christians may nearly double to more than six hundred million by 2025.

China provides yet another example of the phenomenal growth of Christianity. Some estimate the number of Christians in China in 1949 to have been between three and five million. The Christian population in China has now passed one hundred million, but precise numbers are impossible to obtain.

Persecution of Christianity

Christianity in the global south is growing in spite of and during a period of intense persecution in many regions, including Southeast Asia, China, and some states in Africa. Many political leaders view the spread of Christianity as undesirable and a threat to their humanist goals.

Believers in African countries such as Nigeria, Egypt, and the Sudan live in constant danger of persecution or forced conversion by Muslim groups. Many have been required to renounce their faith or suffer imprisonment or death. These believers can readily identify with the Apostle Paul's words in several of his letters, including his epistle to the Philippians and the references to being "bound" or imprisoned as a result of faithfully presenting the gospel (1:12–14).

As Christianity has spread throughout Southeast Asia, believers there have encountered violent opposition and even execution. In Indonesia, for example, Christians on the Malaku islands have endured massacres and forced expulsions by Muslim forces. Some

A Chinese Soldier of the Cross

Wang Mingdao (1900–1991) is one of many Chinese Christians whose life is worthy of study. Wang's ministry started with a Bible study in a tiny hut, and he soon became a popular speaker in many Chinese cities. Wang established the Chinese Tabernacle in Peking on August 1, 1937. One week later the Japanese marched into this city. He refused to join a puppet Japanese religious organization and gained the respect of the Japanese invaders by his consistent stand.

In 1949, when the Communists gained control of China, they tried unsuccessfully to get Wang to join their Three-Self Reform Movement that referred to Christianity as a tool of imperialism. Despite a growing threat of imprisonment, he continued to hold evangelistic meetings in Beijing. The authorities finally arrested Wang and his wife in 1955.

For two months, carefully coached cellmates terrified Wang about methods of persecution he might endure. He finally broke and confessed his "guilt."

The Chinese released Wang, but he felt that he, like Peter, had betrayed his Lord. Wang refused to follow through with the Communists' demands. As a result, authorities arrested Wang and his wife again in 1958. However, this time Wang withdrew his earlier confessions. The Communists responded by brutalizing Wang over the next twenty-two years. However, he remained true to his faith in Christ. Authorities released his wife in 1975 and Wang in 1980. His testimony encouraged many other Chinese to boldly stand for Christ in Communist China.

of their leaders have described this as a means of the Lord purifying His church, and they bravely continue to witness.

Christians in China have also learned to thrive despite ongoing persecution by the Chinese Communists. As the Chinese church continues to grow, the Communists fear the potential influence of Christians. Communist officials have responded with brutal tactics in an effort to destroy home churches and drive people away from local congregations.

As the Chinese church matures, many of its leaders are demonstrating a determination to serve no matter what the cost. In addition, they demonstrate evangelistic zeal by sending missionaries to foreign countries where Western missionaries cannot go.

Section Quiz

1. What two American cities were attacked on September 11, 2001?

2–3. Wahhabism first appeared in what country? What is the most recent example of Wahabbist-inspired Islamic extremism?

4. What is the name for a Muslim religious school?

5. In what areas is Christianity growing at an accelerated rate?

★ Why is Islam growing rapidly?

Making Connections

1. Why are people continuing to migrate to the cities?

2. What lesson can we learn from studying the history of climate change?

3. How is a declining population a disadvantage?

4. How should the earth's resources be used?

5. How could a global economy contribute to peace between nations?

6. How is technology being used for sinful purposes?

7. Where is Christianity spreading most rapidly?

8. What is the Muslim response to the growth of Christianity in many areas of the global south?

9. How has Christianity in China been affected by the Communist takeover in 1949?

Developing History Skills

1. Using the information in this chapter and any additional research you may wish to do, write a one- or two-page paper on the uses of water, wind, or solar energy in human history.

2. Using the information in this chapter and in previous chapters (2–5, 11, 15), trace the history and expansion of Islam.

Thinking Critically

1. In light of Christ's command to love one's neighbor, evaluate the demands of many environmentalists that more expensive sources of fuel be developed in order to reduce pollution.

2. How might you take advantage of the global economy in the coming years to help spread the gospel?

Living in God's World

1. Write a brief essay titled "Technology: My Generation's Blessing and Burden."

2. Suppose you are a historian who has been asked to address a conference of professional historians. You have titled your address "Has the Human Race Outgrown the Christian Religion?" Write a brief speech that seeks to answer this question.

People, Places, and Things to Know

climate change
free trade areas
single market
European Union
euro
Central American Common Market
West African Economic and Monetary Union
CFA franc
embryonic stem cells
adult stem cells
Saddam Hussein
Taliban
Osama bin Laden
al Qaeda
Wahhabist
madrasas
ISIS
ISIL
global south
Wang Mingdao

GLOSSARY

A

Abbas: Second founder of the Safavid Empire

Abbasid: Muslim caliphate under which Islam experienced a renaissance

Aborigines: European name for natives of Australia

Abrahamic Covenant: Covenant that revealed God's plan to redeem humans, enabling them once again to have dominion as God intended

abstinence: No drinking of alcohol

abstract expressionism: Form of painting developed by American painter Jackson Pollock; created by randomly splashing wet pain on the canvas with brushes

Adenauer, Konrad: German chancellor under whose leadership West Germany experienced an incredible recovery

adult stem cells: Cells that can be extracted from juvenile and adult tissue

Age of Reason: The seventeenth and eighteenth centuries in Europe

Akbar: Grandson of Babur who continued the brutal conquest of India; expanded the Mughal Empire to the west, east, and south to central India

Albert the Great: Dominican friar who played an important role in introducing Muslim documents to medieval universities

Alexander II: Russian ruler who abolished serfdom (r. 1855–81)

Allah: Name of the Muslim god which is an Arabic word meaning "the god"

Allies: Alliance of Russia, Serbia, and France in World War I; alliance of Britain, France, and Poland (and later the U.S. and the Soviet Union) in World War II

al Qaeda: A terrorist network that operated out of Afghanistan

Anabaptist: Those who baptize again

anarchy: Radical concept of society without government

Anatolia: Land east of the Byzantine Empire

anatomy: The structure of humans, animals, and plants

ancestor worship: The practice of praying to dead family members

Angkor Wat: One of over one thousand temples built in Ankor (Cambodia)

animism: Belief that spirits live in physical objects

Anti-Comintern Pact: Agreement between Germany and Japan prior to World War II

anti-Semitism: Hostility toward Jews

Antoinette, Marie: Political and financial collapse occurred during her reign; wife of Louis XVI

appeasement: Avoiding conflict by making concessions

Arius: An early church teacher who claimed that Jesus was not God

Arkwright, Richard: Became one of the most famous entrepreneurs; got the government to protect several inventions with a patent

astrolabe: Used by sailors to measure the angle between the sun or a star and the horizon at a specific time of day or night

Atahualpa: Emperor of the Incan Empire

Augustine: Christian church leader in Hippo (North Africa) who wrote *The City of God*

Australia Day: The day the First Fleet arrived in Australia (January 26, 1788)

Axis powers: Alliance of Germany, Japan, and Italy in World War II

Aztecs: An Indian society that was characterized by war and warriors

B

Babur: Founder of the Mughal Empire in India

Bacon, Roger: Made significant contributions in the areas of physics, geography, and optics

Baghdad: The new capital of the Muslim Empire under the Abbassid dynasty

baillis: Royal officials who collected taxes for the king and ensured justice in carrying out laws

Bakunin, Michael: A Russian radical that supported anarchy; known as the Father of Anarchism

Balfour Declaration: The first official recognition by a world power that the Jews needed a land to call their own

Balkans: A large region in southeastern Europe

bank: Term derived from "banca" ("bench"), which was a meeting place for transacting financial business and from which a banking system developed

barbarians: A Roman name for peoples not part of Greek or Roman culture

barrios: Neighborhoods of poor people in Latin American cities

Battle of Badr: Where Muhammad's army defeated the people of Mecca (prior to Mecca's submission to Muhammad)

Battle of Leignitz: Where Poles, Czechs, and Germans tried to stop the Mongols

Battle of Lepanto: Where an alliance of Catholic nations defeated the Ottoman naval fleet

Battle of Plassey: Where British commander Robert Clive defeated a much larger Indian force whose leader supported the French

Battle of the Bulge: Hitler's failed attempt to break through a lightly protected section of the Allied line

Belgian Congo: The territory in the interior of Africa along the Congo River

Bell, Alexander Graham: Patented the telephone

Berlin Blockade: The Soviets' blocking of all traffic through East Germany into West Berlin; ended due to a massive airlift of supplies by the United States and Britain

Berlin Conference: Where European powers established key agreements in phase two of the Scramble for Africa

bin Laden, Osama: Saudi extremist that built a terrorist network known as al Qaeda

Bismarck, Otto von: Appointed by King Wilhelm I as the chancellor of Prussia; became the driving force behind political unification of the German states

Black Death: A plague during the Middle Ages

Black Sea: Sea between Southeastern Europe and Western Asia

Blaxland, Gregory: Crossed the Great Dividing Range in Australia with two companions

Bolívar, Simón: Best known for his role in leading the Spanish colonies in their struggle for independence

Bolsheviks: Radical Russian political group led by Lenin that supported the violent overthrow of the monarchy

Bonaparte, Louis Napoleon: Elected as president of the newly formed French Second Republic in 1848; followed his uncle Napoleon Bonaparte's example and declared himself president for life; gave himself the title of emperor in 1852

Bonaparte, Napoleon: Took advantage of the chaos in France and used his power to take control of the government

Bougainville, Louis Antoine de: French explorer who claimed several islands for the French, including Tahiti

bourgeoisie: Capitalists

Boxer Rebellion: A period of unrest in which the Boxers, a secret society in China, killed missionaries, other foreigners, and Chinese Christians

Boyle's law: Chemistry law about gases

Boyle, Robert: Christian who wrote *The Skeptical Chymist* and contributed to chemistry with his work on gases that produced Boyle's law

British East India Company: Maintained the appearance of working under Mughal rulers until 1857, when they exiled the last Mughal emperor and imposed direct rule

British North America Act: Created the dominion of Canada with four provinces: Ontario, Quebec, New Brunswick, and Nova Scotia

Brunelleschi: Designed the dome for the Cathedral of Florence

Buddhism: Religion founded on the four noble truths

Bushido: Unwritten Japanese military code of the samurai

Byzantine: Pertaining to the Eastern Roman Empire

Byzantine Empire: The old eastern portion of the Roman empire

C

cabinet: System of representative government that developed in England

caliph: Islamic leader; title Abu Bakr took after Muhammad's death, from an Arab word that means "to succeed"

Calvin, John: Leading figure in the Reformation who wrote *Institutes of the Christian Religion*

camel: A unique four-legged animal designed especially for a desert environment

Canberra: Capital of the Commonwealth of Australia

Cape of Good Hope: Southern tip of Africa

Capet, Hugh: The count of Paris who founded a new royal line in France

capital: Supplied by bankers or wealthy investors to entrepreneurs to help them get their business started

caravel: A ship used for European exploration

Cartier, Jacques: French explorer sent by the king to find riches and a water route to China; discovered the St. Lawrence River

cash crops: Crops that could be sold for cash or supplies

Castiglione: An Italian author who wrote *The Courtier*

cast iron: Formed when iron ore and a small amount of carbon and silicon are heated to about 1200°C

cathedrals: Large and impressive churches

Catherine the Great: Reigned in Russia and increased the power of the Russian monarchy (r. 1762–96)

caudillos: South American leaders who established dictatorships

Cavour, Camillo di: Proved to be the most successful at uniting Italy; prime minister of the Kingdom of Sardinia

Central American Common Market: Formed by several Central American states to increase trade between member states

Central Powers: Alliance of Germany, Austria-Hungary, and the Ottoman Empire during World War I

CFA franc: The common currency of the West African Economic and Monetary Union

Chalmers, James: Missionary to Papua New Guinea who was killed by the natives

Chamberlain, Neville: Prime minister of England who led the European nations in a policy to avoid war by means of appeasement

Champlain, Samuel de: French explorer who discovered two of the Great Lakes (Ontario and Huron); also known as the Father of New France

Charlemagne: Became the sole ruler of the Frankish kingdom

Charles I: English king who like his father James I asserted the divine right of kings and struggled to defeat Parliament's efforts to deny him absolute power (r. 1625–49)

Charles II: Took the English throne after Cromwell's death (r. 1660–85)

Charter Act: Parliamentary decree that gave the British crown control over the British East India Company

Chartism: Movement in England in the 1800s that called for universal manhood suffrage and elections by secret ballot

Chaucer, Geoffrey: English poet who wrote *The Canterbury Tales*

Chengzu: Became the third emperor of the Ming dynasty after defeating the second emperor, Huizong, in a civil war

Chinese Communist Party: Radical element of the Kuomintang party

chivalry: A code or strict set of rules for a knight

Christ: Literally means "the anointed one" and refers to Jesus

circuit courts: Developed by Henry II; judges heard cases in a particular province (circuit) of England

city: A cultural institution in which humans who share certain core values work together to improve their quality of life

city-states: Cities that have their own governments, independent of those of other cities (even those within their own nation)

civilization: Human culture as it is lived in cities or under the influence of cities

civil religion: The use of religion to promote the goals of the state

Cixi, Empress Dowager: Adopted Guangxu, the token ruler, and served as the actual ruler of China for the first fourteen years of Guangxu's reign

clan: Largest family group in Africa

climate change: Related to global warming; the theory that the earth is warming and that this is due to man-made emissions

Clive, Robert: British commander who defeated a much larger Indian force whose leader supported the French

Clovis: Leader of a Frankish kingdom that used military force and other means to combine several kingdoms

Code Napoleon: Result of the codification of French law

Cold War: Political rivalry and conflict of ideas that stopped short of actual war between the U.S. and the U.S.S.R. (1945–1991)

colonialism: Conquest of one or more nations by another nation

Columbus, Christopher: Italian explorer, financed by Spain, who believed he could get to the East by sailing west

Committee for the Abolition of the Slave Trade: A group of Quakers and Anglicans who united their efforts for the opposition of slavery

Committee of Public Safety: A committee to manage the government that soon gained absolute authority in revolutionary France

common law: Uniform laws for all of England

Common Market: Another name for the European Economic Community; an organization that promotes economic cooperation in Europe

Commonwealth of Australia: Made up of six states—Queensland, New South Wales, Victoria, Tasmania, South Australia, and Western Australia—and two federal territories

communism: Economic system in which property is commonly and not privately owned

compass: An instrument that uses lodestone, a magnetic material, to find direction

Confucius: Chinese teacher that developed a philosophy based on relationships

conquistadors: Men sent from Spain to find gold, conquer the people, and convert them to Roman Catholicism

Constantine: Roman emperor who converted to Christianity

Constantinople: Ancient city of Byzantium that Constantine transformed into the new capital of the eastern portion of the Roman Empire

Constitution: The working document outlining the pattern of U.S. government

Cook, James: English captain who became the most famous explorer of the Pacific

Copernicus: Presented his view that the earth revolved around the sun, not the sun around the earth

Corn Laws: British parliamentary law that made food in England expensive

Cortés, Hernando: Spanish conquistador that massacred the Aztecs

cottage industries: Locations where wool was spun and woven to make cloth, providing income for the family

cotton gin: Enabled a few men to separate the cotton fibers from the seeds quickly

Council of Nicaea: A council of church leaders that met in the year 325 to consider the deity of Christ

Council of Trent: Met several times over a twenty-year period and wrote a statement of Roman Catholic beliefs and practices

Creation Mandate: God's command to humans to exercise dominion over the earth; found in Genesis 1:28

Creoles: People of pure Spanish or Portuguese descent born in the Americas

Cromwell, Oliver: Led Parliament's army against the king's forces and defeated them

crop rotation: Farming practice in which different crops are grown in a field to maintain the soil's fertility

Crowther, Samuel Ajayi: The first African bishop in the Anglican Church; translated the Bible into the Yoruba language

Crusades: A series of military expeditions originally intended to liberate the Holy Land and defeat infidels

Cubism: Art style after World War I that showed subjects in geometric shapes and from several perspectives at once

Cultural Revolution: Mao Zedong's social and political purge that resulted in political chaos and economic upheaval for a decade

culture: The physical and mental environment developed through human thought and labor

Curie, Pierre and Marie: French physicists who pioneered work in radioactive matter

Cuzco: The capital of the Incan Empire

D

da Gama, Vasco: Portuguese explorer that sailed all the way to India

Dale, Sir Thomas: Strong English leader that turned the Jamestown settlement into a thriving colony

Damascus: The new capital of the Muslim Empire under the Umayyads

Dante Alighieri: Italian who wrote the *Divine Comedy*

Darwin, Charles: Provided the foundation for an evolutionary theory to explain the origin and changes of life; assumed a natural explanation for man's origins

Davidic Covenant: Revealed that David's descendants would play a key role in fulfilling the three promises of the Abrahamic Covenant

da Vinci, Leonardo: The Italian artist of the Renaissance who is well known for *The Last Supper* and the *Mona Lisa*

D-day: The day when the Allies launched a massive invasion of France along a fifty-mile front on five beaches (June 6, 1944)

dead reckoning: Method in which sailors decided what they thought their location was, estimated their speed, looked at the map, and aimed for a compass heading that they believed would get them to their goal

December 7, 1941: Date the Japanese launched a surprise attack on the American naval base at Pearl Harbor, Hawaii

Decembrist Revolt: Rebellion in Russian started by a small group of nobles and army officers who sought to replace Nicholas with his brother in order to establish a constitutional monarchy

Declaration of the Rights of Man: Document signed by the National Assembly in 1789; demanded the end of many of the abuses suffered by the French people and advocated ideals such as not doing anything that harms others

de Gaulle, Charles: President of France who established the Fifth Republic

Descartes, René: Philosopher who did not trust any path to truth except human reason, which is a form of rationalism

Dias, Bartolomeu: Portuguese explorer that rounded the tip of Africa without realizing it

Diaz, Porfirio: Elected in Mexico based on his promises of a constitutional democracy and prosperity; transformed his government into a dictatorship

Dickens, Charles: Wrote about the negative aspects of the Industrial Revolution, including the slums where many workers lived

didgeridoo: Musical instrument played by Australian Aborigines

Dien Bien Phu: Battle in 1954 in which Vietnamese Communists defeated French forces

Diocletian: Roman emperor under whom the last and most widespread Roman persecution of Christians occurred

Directory: A five-man committee the formed the new government of France after the Reign of Terror

Disraeli, Benjamin: British prime minister who supported a bill that doubled the number of men who could vote

divine sovereignty: God's complete and permanent control over this world

donatario: A Portuguese noble that ruled in the New World; a hereditary privilege

Dostoyevsky, Fyodor: Author who provided readers with a glimpse into Russian society; embraced Eastern Orthodoxy and opposed the anarchists and atheists

Douglass, Frederick: A former slave in America; persuasive spokesman for abolition

Drake, Sir Francis: English explorer who sailed around the world

Dreyfus Affair: Episode in France during the 19th century in which a Jewish officer was falsely accused and imprisoned (example of anti-Semitism)

E

Edict of Milan: A decree by Constantine that put an end to almost three hundred years of Roman persecution

Edward III: English king who also claimed the right to the French throne

effigy mound: An earthen mound in North America that was made in the shape of an animal or object

Einstein, Albert: Made tremendous contributions to science with his theories on the relationship between matter and energy ($E = mc2$); father of modern physics

Eisenhower, Dwight D.: American general that led a force of 160,000 during the invasion of Sicily

embryonic stem cells: Cells that can be extracted from an embryo

empiricism: Belief that man can find knowledge only through experience

English Bill of Rights: Set limits on royal power, granted the English people basic civil liberties, and prevented future rulers from being Roman Catholics (1688)

English Civil War: War in which Oliver Cromwell led Parliament's army against the king's forces and defeated them

entrepreneurs: Businessmen who sell inventions or start businesses for financial gain and accept risk of personal loss

Erasmus: Highly regarded and influential scholar of the Renaissance who mastered Latin and Greek

Eratosthenes: Early Greek astronomer and geographer who determined the distance around the earth with great accuracy

established church: A church recognized and supported by the colony's government

Estates General: An assembly composed of representatives of the three estates in pre-Revolutionary France; the only political body in France with the authority to reform the tax system

Ethiopia: Name assigned by the Greeks to the African kingdom of Aksum and other regions in Africa

Euclid: Mathematician who wrote *Elements* and was also known as the Father of Geometry

euro: The common currency of the European Union

European Union: An economic and political alliance of twenty-eight nations across Europe

excommunication: A dismissal from the Roman Church denying any opportunity for salvation

existentialism: Philosophy that stressed a person's uniqueness, free choice, and the consequences of those choices

exported: Sent out of the colonies

Expressionism: Art style after World War I that emphasized how the artist felt about his subject

F

factories: Large buildings that are centrally located for most efficient production of goods

Factory Act of 1833: Placed limits on child labor

Fante Confederation: African organization formed in 1868 by African pastors and teachers to maintain self-rule

Federal Reserve: American agency that controls the U.S. money supply and works to protect the American banking system

Ferdinand, Francis: Archduke who was heir to the throne of Austria-Hungary and was assassinated in 1914

Ferdinand (King): Ruler of Spain who, with his wife, financed Christopher Columbus's voyages

feudalism: System in which local rulers controlled large estates called manors and the people served their local ruler in exchange for a place to live on the estate

Fifth Republic: Government established by Charles de Gaulle, president of France

First Consul: The position Napoleon used to become dictator of France

First Estate: The upper tier of the French social ladder which included archbishops and bishops

First Fleet: Sailed to New South Wales with a majority of convicts onboard to start a colony

Five Civilized Tribes: Tribes in the American Southeast that maintained peaceful relations with the Europeans and adopted some European ways; included the Cherokee, Chickasaw, Choctaw, Creek, and Seminole tribes

Five Pillars: Central Islamic practices of affirming Islam, performing daily prayers, almsgiving, fasting, and making a pilgrimage to Mecca

flying buttress: External support of a Gothic cathedral

flying shuttle: Invention that enabled weavers to combine strands of cotton into cloth more quickly

1453: Year in which Ottoman forces defeated and pillaged Constantinople

Fowler, John: Developed one of the first known self-propelled steam engines

Franco, Francisco: General in Spain who overthrew the republican government and imposed a fascist dictatorship

free trade areas: Areas where member countries can trade without tariffs and quotas

Frumentius: A slave who rose to favor with the king of Aksum and introduced Coptic Christianity to the people

G

Galilei, Galileo: Used the newly invented telescope for his observations

Gandhi, Mohandas: Led a movement known as passive resistance to achieve independence in India

Garibaldi, Giuseppe: Formed an army known as the "Red Shirts" and conquered the island of Sicily in 1860

Garrison, William Lloyd: American abolitionist; editor of the newspaper *The Liberator*

gathering-based economy: Economic system that allowed more Africans to access wealth by harvesting the continent's natural resources

gauchos: Cowboys in Argentina

Ghana: Coastal kingdom in western Africa

Ghiberti: Sculpted the door for the baptistery of Florence

Gladstone, William: Disraeli's political opponent who stressed domestic reform during his terms as prime minister

global south: The regions of Latin America, India, China, and Africa

Glorious Revolution: Change of power in England in 1688 without resorting to war

Goforth, Jonathan: Missionary to China whom the Boxers attempted to murder

Gold Coast: A name for Western Africa that derives from the gold trade that occurred at its coasts

Golden Horde: A Mongol empire based in western Asia and founded by Batu Khan

Gorbachev, Mikhail: Emerged as the leader of the Soviet Union in 1985; assumed power without violence or opposition

gospel: The message that Jesus died for the sins of humans and has been raised again to save them forever

Gothic: New style of architecture developed during the thirteenth century

Grand Canal: Restored by Chengzu to functionality; extends more than eleven hundred miles

Great Awakening: Spiritual movement that brought many to salvation, started many churches, and prepared the American colonies for independence

Great Depression: An economic downturn in the U. S. during the 20th century; affected many other nations

Great Dividing Range: A range of steep rock faces and giant gorges that kept the colonists near the coast of Australia for several years

Great Famine of 1315: Calamity that struck a large area of Europe caused by much rain, rotting crops, and a lack of salt to preserve meat

Great Leap Forward: New economic plan announced by Mao Zedong; inefficient and resulted in famine

Great Powers: Major European nations

Great Yasa: Law code by Chinggis Khan that dealt with every area of life

Greek fire: A chemical weapon used by the Byzantines against their enemies; chemical mixture that burned on impact and spread when doused with water

Guangxu: Boy adopted by Empress Dowager Cixi who, once he began to rule, worked to modernize China and develop a constitutional monarchy similar to the one developed in Japan

gunpowder: Combination of ingredients, including saltpeter, that forms an explosive powder

Gutenberg, Johannes: Invented the movable-type printing press

H

hacienda: A large country estate in Latin America

Hadith: Collection of writings about Muhammad's life, including what he said, what he did, and what he approved

Halley, Edmond: English astronomer that recorded the position and motion of hundreds of stars

hara-kiri: Ritual suicide practiced by Japanese warriors

Hargreaves, James: Invented the spinning jenny

Harvey, William: Englishman who discovered that blood is pumped by the heart, travels through the body in blood vessels, and returns to the heart in the circulatory system

Hegira: Muhammad's flight from Mecca to Medina

Henry II: Strengthened English royal authority by expanding the use of royal courts; developed circuit courts

Herschel, Sir William: Spent much of his life contributing to the field of astronomy; discovered the planet now known as Uranus; built telescopes to sell

Heyerdahl, Thor: Norwegian explorer who proposed that the first Polynesians came from South America rather than Asia and proved that it was possible to travel in a balsa boat from Peru to the Pacific island of Tuamoto

high islands: Pacific islands of volcanic origin whose height enables agriculture to grow and humans to reside on them

Hippocrates: A Greek physician who was also known as the Father of Medicine

Hirohito: Emperor of Japan that also played an active role in military decisions during World War II

Hitler, Adolf: Led the Nazi Party and used the political process to gain control of the German government

Ho Chi Minh: Vietnamese Communist leader; resisted French colonialism and declared Vietnam independent

Holocaust: The German attempt to destroy all of the Jews in Europe

Hong Xiuquan: Took a name meaning "Heavenly King" to reflect his claims that he was the younger brother of Jesus Christ; developed a cultic political movement

Horton, Africanus: Disproved the claims that the black man was racially inferior; wrote *West African Countries and Peoples: A Vindication of the African Race*

Huguenots: French Protestants during the Reformation

humanities: Subjects such as literature, philosophy, art, history, grammar, and speech that covered a wide spectrum of human interests and experiences

Hundred Days' Reform: Began by Guangxu with the goal of implementing sweeping political, legal, and social changes in China

Hundred Years' Wars: Series of battles to settle the issue of English control of land in France

Hussein, Saddam: Dictator of Iraq that invaded Kuwait; captured by U.S. troops; executed by new Iraqi government

Huss, John: A pastor in Bohemia influenced by Wycliffe's teachings who was burned at the stake

I

image of God: Set of qualities possessed by all humans that reflect God

imam: Literally means "leader" and refers to a political and religious leader of Shia Islam or a religious leader of Sunni Islam

Imperial City: Built in the Ming dynasty's capital, Peking

imperialism: Dominance and power asserted by one nation over less powerful nations

imported: Brought into the colonies

Inchon: South Korean city that was the site of a daring attack by a UN force composed of American and South Korean troops

Index of Prohibited Books: List of books that were declared heretical by the Roman Catholic Church

indictments: A list of accusations

indulgence: A document issued by the Church of Rome granting pardon from the punishment of certain sins

Industrial Revolution: Name for the eighteenth and nineteeth centuries due to great changes in manufacturing

infidels: Unbelievers

infrastructure: Network of facilities and structures needed for travel and communication

Innocent III: Increased papal power to its highest point

Inquisition: A Roman Church court set up to find and punish heretics

Interdict: A papal declaration by which people are denied access to most of the sacraments

internal combustion engine: An invention that produced power inside the engine

International African Association (IAA): Supposedly humanitarian organization run by King Leopold of Belgium but one that actually encouraged the harsh treatment and torture of African slaves

Iroquois Confederacy: Group of six tribes who spoke the common language of Iroquois

Isabella (Queen): Ruler of Spain who, with her husband, financed Christopher Columbus's voyages

ISIL (Islamic State in Iraq and the Levant): Islamic terrorist group whose goal is to seize control of Turkey, Israel, and the other nations that make up the Levant (lands along the eastern Mediterranean Sea)

ISIS (Islamic State in Iraq and Syria): Islamic terrorist group that grew out of the civil war in Syria; uses extreme violence to terrorize enemies and gain attention

Islam: Literally means "submission"; the religion founded by Muhammad

Istanbul: Name for Constantinople after the Ottoman Empire took over

J

James II: Became king after the death of his brother, Charles II (r. 1685–88)

Jamestown: An English colony in North America

Jenner, Edward: Englishman who developed a vaccine for smallpox

Jesuit: A Catholic monastic order formed during the Reformation to stop the spread of Protestantism

Jesus of Nazareth: Name of Jesus recorded in Scripture to designate the place where He spent most of His earthly life (see Matt. 2:23 and Luke 2:39)

jihad: Islamic holy war

Joan of Arc: Peasant girl who rallied the French during the Hundred Years' War

Judaism: The religion of the Jews that developed during the five centuries BC

June 6, 1944: Date the Allies launched a massive invasion of France along a fifty-mile front on five beaches; known as D-day

June 28, 1914: Date of the assassination of Archduke Francis Ferdinand, heir to the throne of Austria-Hungary

jury: Legal process developed in the Middle Ages whereby a group of local citizens made lists of accusations before a circuit judge arrived to hear them

K

Ka'bah: A stone building in Mecca that was once used for pagan rituals but is now a sacred Muslim site toward which all Muslims pray

Kai-shek, Chiang: Leader of the Kuomintang party in China following the death of Sun Yat-Sen

kamikaze: Term meaning "divine wind" that referred to seemingly miraculous storms that protected Japan from Mongol invasion

Kay, John: Invented the flying shuttle

Kellogg-Briand Pact: An agreement signed after World War I by which nations agreed to settle their disputes by negotiation rather than force

Khan, Batu: A grandson of Chinggis Khan who led an invasion into eastern Europe

Khan, Chinggis: A Mongol title meaning "Great Ruler," and the title given to the Mongol Empire's founder

Khrushchev, Nikita: Ruled the Soviet Union following Stalin's death; was voted out of office when his policies became unpopular

Kikuyu: An African clan that did not worship many gods, but believed in one god, Ngai

Kilwa: Key port through which Zimbabwe's gold was transported north

Kuomintang: Nationalist Chinese Party in the early 1900s

L

Lalibela: A Coptic holy city in Ethiopia that contains churches carved in rock below ground level

landscapes: Paintings that feature nature scenes

Lao-tzu: Developed the teachings of Taoism

Las Casas, Bartolomé de: Spanish Roman Catholic friar that came to the Americas to serve as a missionary to the Indians

Lateran Treaties: Agreements between Mussolini and Vatican City that ended the pope's opposition to Italy's unified government

Latin America: Another name for the regions of South America and Central America

Lavoisier, Antoine: The Father of Modern Chemistry

laws of gravity and motion: State that gravity keeps the planets in their orbits

League of Nations: An organization proposed by Woodrow Wilson that was supposed to bring about international cooperation

Lenin, Vladimir: Communist leader who came to power in the Russian Revolution and signed a treaty with the Germans which took Russia out of World War I

letter of credit: Enabled people to travel without carrying large sums of money

liberal arts: Studies taught in medieval universities for the nobility

Liberal Democratic Party: Party that ruled Japan until political scandals led the Japanese to replace it with a coalition government

Line of Demarcation: Line drawn on the map by the pope that was supposed to determine where Spain and Portugal could claim land

Livingstone, David: Most famous European explorer in Africa; presented the need for missionaries in Africa

Locarno Pact: An agreement Germany signed with France and Belgium recognizing its present borders with those two nations as permanent

Locke, John: Believed that rationalism was insufficient and argued in favor of empiricism

Louis XIV: French king who was one of the most successful monarchs of his time

Louis XVI: French ruler during the political and financial collapse that led to the French Revolution; husband of Marie Antoinette

low islands: Pacific coral islands that have little fresh water and few places where humans can live

Luftwaffe: Germany's air force in World War II

Luther, Martin: Wrote the Ninety-five Theses and translated the whole Bible into German

M

MacArthur, Douglas: American general in the Pacific theater of World War II

Macemba: African king of the Yao tribe who wrote eloquently to the German authorities and refused to submit to a treaty with them

Machiavelli: Worked for the government in Florence, Italy; observed political events in Europe and wrote *The Prince*

MAD: Acronym for mutually assured destruction; contributed to American and European appeasement

madrasas: Muslim religious schools that use educational material produced in Saudi Arabia that teaches Wahhabist intolerance and hatred for anything that is not purely Islamic

Magellan, Ferdinand: Explorer whose crew sailed all the way around the world; was killed in the Philippines before the end of the voyage

Magna Carta: Document limiting royal power that English nobles forced King John to sign

Mahmud II: Came to power in the Ottoman Empire during a period of decline and political instability; laid the foundation for a modern Turkey (r. 1808–1839)

Mali: Kingdom in western Africa

Manchu dynasty: Seized power from the failing Ming dynasty

manor: An estate on which most people lived under feudalism

Maoris: Tall, fierce natives of New Zealand who resisted Dutch attempts to land

Marn Grook: Game developed by Aborigines that has elements of football or soccer

Marquesas: A set of islands in the Pacific discovered by Mendaña that were named after the viceroy of Peru

Marshall Plan: Distribution of funds from the United States enabled Europe to rapidly rebuild and retool for a strong economic recovery

Martel, Charles: Ruler of the Franks (French) that led an army to stop the advance of the Muslim forces in Europe

Martín, José de San: Best known for his role in leading the Spanish colonies in their struggle for independence

Marx, Karl: Student of philosophy and history who wrote the *Communist Manifesto* with Friedrich Engels

Massachusetts Bay Colony: Settlement of Puritans in the New World

Maxim gun: A rapid-firing gun used by the Europeans in World War I

Maxwell, James: A Scottish scientist who made major contributions to the fields of physics and astronomy

Mayas: An Indian civilization in Central America that consisted of many independent city states

May 8, 1945: Date the Germans unconditionally surrendered; known as V-E Day for the victory in Europe

mayor of the palace: The leading palace official under a Frankish king

Mazzini, Giuseppe: Italian that formed a group called Young Italy for the purpose of accomplishing Italian unification

McCormick, Cyrus: Invented a horse-drawn reaping machine

Mecca: City that was a central place of Arab worship and was also Muhammad's birthplace

Meiji: Japanese emperor who led the transformation of Japan from a feudal society to a modern state

Meikle, Andrew: Developed a threshing machine

Mendaña, Alvaro de: Explored the Pacific islands

Medina: A small oasis where Muhammad and his followers fled

Medieval Warm Period: The warming of the climate in Europe in the beginning of the eleventh century

Mehmet II: Brought an end to internal strife in the Ottoman Empire (r. 1451–81)

Melanesia: Group of Pacific islands that includes Papua New Guinea, the Solomon Islands, and Fiji

Menelik: Ethiopian ruler who replaced his poorly trained volunteer army with well-equipped and well-trained soldiers; built factories to build modern military equipment

Mensheviks: Moderate Russian political group that sought change through peaceful methods

Messiah: Literally means "the anointed one" and refers to Jesus

mestizo: A person with Indian and Spanish parents

Michelangelo: Renaissance artist best known for his painting on the ceiling of the Sistine Chapel in Rome

Micronesia: A region of Pacific Islands that are small and low; means "tiny islands"

middle class: A group in feudal society composed of those who lived in towns; included the merchants, bankers, craftsmen, and other skilled laborers

Middle Kingdom: Chinese name for their land

Midway Island: Location of an important naval base during World War II

Mines Act: Barred women as well as boys under the age of ten from working in the mines

Ming: Chinese dynasty that sought to remove all traces of Mongol rule; restored native Chinese rule

Mingdao, Wang: Chinese Christian who suffered under the Chinese Communists and died in 1991

Moffat, Robert: One of the earliest missionaries from the British Empire to serve in Africa; translated the Bible and other works into one of the African languages

Mona Lisa: Famous painting by Leonardo da Vinci

monotheism: The belief in and worship of one God

Montezuma: The Aztec ruler

Montgomery, Bernand L.: British general who defeated the German forces that threatened British control of Egypt

More, Thomas: Served on King Henry VIII's court and wrote *Utopia*

Morse, Samuel: Patented the first known telegraph; developed the code to use with the telegraph machine

Mosaic Covenant: Covenant with the children of Israel that promised God would make them His own special nation and would protect them if they promised to obey God's laws

mother country: European country that practiced imperialism

Mound Builders: Indians who built earthen mounds

Mughal: The last Mongol empire; located in India and founded by Muslim leader Babur who conquered a large region in northern India

Munich Conference: Conference where British and French leaders gave in to Hitler's demands for the Sudetenland

Musa: The most famous ruler of Mali; also converted to Islam

Muslims: Followers of Islam

Mussolini, Benito: Formed the Fascist Party in Italy and gradually transformed Italy into a dictatorship

N

National Assembly: Members of the Third Estate in the French Revolution who convened and signed the Tennis Court Oath and the Declaration of the Rights of Man

nation: A very large group of people who share the same language, family history, land area, and culture

nationalism: Intense devotion and loyalty to one's own people and country

nation-states: Nations having their own governments, independent of other nations

NATO: North Atlantic Treaty Organization; formed in 1949 to oppose Soviet aggression

Nazi: The National Socialist German Workers' Party led by Adolf Hitler

Nero: Roman emperor who began the first official Roman persecution of Christianity

Nestorians: Taught that Jesus was both God and human but was not a single person

New Covenant: Covenant given in Jeremiah 31 that is actually a renewing of the previous covenants

New Holland: Tasman's discoveries in Australia that were claimed by the Dutch East India Company

New Laws of 1542: Laws passed to protect the Indians and mestizos from some of the abuses they suffered

New South Wales: Land in Australia that Captain Cook claimed for England

Newton, John: A former slave-ship captain who became a Christian in 1748; wrote the hymn "Amazing Grace"

Newton, Sir Isaac: Discovered concepts that have become known as the laws of gravity and motion

New Zealand: Set of islands inhabited by the Maoris

Nicholas I: Came to power in Russia in the midst of revolt (r. 1825–1855)

1948 Arab-Israeli War: Started when Arab forces from Egypt, Syria, Jordan, Lebanon, and Iraq attacked Israel on May 14; ended in a ceasefire after a year of fighting

Ninety-five Theses: Points of disagreement with the Roman Catholic Church written by Martin Luther

O

Old World: A term for Europe

Operation T-4: The Nazis' code name for their program that killed thousands in the name of euthanasia

opium: An addictive drug that British merchants brought to China in order to gain a favorable balance of trade

Opium Wars: Result of the mounting tension between British merchants who wanted to continue the opium trade and the Chinese government's efforts to bring an end to it

Ottoman Empire: Emerged during the beginning of the fourteenth century in the land east of the Byzantine Empire called Anatolia

P

Pact of Steel: Military alliance between Hitler and Mussolini

Pan-Arabism: Movement started by Arabs to seek a united state of Arabia and an Arab League that would spread from the west coast of northern Africa to Saudi Arabia

papal: That which is related to the pope, as in "papal authority"

paper: Formed from a mixture of fiber, rags, and water; first developed in China

Paracelsus: Scientist who stated that the body is mostly chemicals and should be treated with chemicals

Paris Peace Conference: Conference after World War I where five treaties were formulated, including the Treaty of Versailles

Parliament: Began as a group of advisors for the king and became a formal legislative body composed of the House of Lords and the House of Commons

Parliament Bill of 1911: Changed the balance of power by no longer allowing the House of Lords to veto laws passed by the House of Commons

passive resistance: Resisting foreign rule by nonviolent means (e.g., strikes, not paying taxes)

Pasteur, Louis: A French chemist who made many important discoveries that prevented several diseases

pasteurization: A process developed by Louis Pasteur in which milk and other liquids are heated in order to slow the development of disease-causing microbes

patent: Set of government-issued rights granted to an inventor to prevent others from copying and selling his invention for a certain amount of time

Paton, John: Scottish missionary to the islands of the South Pacific

Patrick: Missionary to Ireland during the 4th century AD

Peace of God: A church decree making church property off limits during fighting among knights

Pearl Harbor: American naval base in Hawaii that was bombed by the Japanese (December 7, 1941)

Pedro I: Crowned emperor of an independent Brazil

peninsulares: Spaniards born in Spain

Perry, Commodore Matthew: Visited Japan with his fleet and pressured the Japanese to open to trade

perspective: A technique for adding depth to paintings

Petrarch: A pioneer of Renaissance humanism and a central figure in Italian literature; known as the Father of Humanism

Phillip, Arthur: Captain of the First Fleet and later the governor of New South Wales

Phillip II: Developed a strong monarchy in France and improved the effectiveness of the royal government by sending out royal officials

Pilgrims: English people who came to the New World to escape persecution, to establish a place to bring up their children, and to advance missions

Pizarro, Francisco: Spanish conquistador who made himself ruler of the Incan empire but was killed by those of his own country

pogrom: A sweeping, targeted, and repeated attack on Jews in Russia

Polynesia: Group of Pacific islands located between the Hawaiian Islands, Easter Island, and New Zealand; means "many islands"

polytheism: The belief in and worship of many gods

pope: Term that literally means "papa" and gradually became a title of the bishop of Rome

porcelain: Product developed by the Chinese through the process of shaping kaolin clay into objects and then hardening them by heat

power of the purse: Parliament's power to grant or withhold approval of new taxes

predestination: God's deciding one's destiny before birth

Prester John: Mythical king in Africa who was thought to be a Christian

pretend retreat: Military tactic by which an enemy pretends to abandon the fight in order to draw its opponents out in the open

Prince Henry: Portuguese ruler who sent out sailors and ships to explore the coast of Africa in the fifteenth century

printing: Developed by the Chinese using woodblocks and later moveable type

proletariat: Communist term for laborers who rebel against the middle class and the bourgeoisie to make a classless society

Protectorate: Government founded by Oliver Cromwell after the English Civil War

Protestants: People who chose to follow Scripture and leave the Roman Catholic Church

Pueblos: Name for many of the Indians that lived in the Southwest region of North America

Puritans: English people who settled the Massachusetts Bay Colony in order to establish a society based on biblical principles

Q

Qing: Dynasty that weakened and brought China under European and Asian domination

Quetzalcoatl: An Aztec god whom the Aztecs were expecting to return

Quirós, Pedro Fernández de: The young navigator who joined an expedition led by Mendaña in search of the Solomon Islands; took command of the ships when Mendaña died

Qur'an: Sacred Islamic book that records Muhammad's visions

R

Ramadan: The holy month of Islam

rationalism: Belief that the path to truth is through human reason

Reagan, Ronald: The fortieth president of the United States; turned a struggling America into a political, social, and economic force that influenced the world

realism: Replaced romanticism as a new art form; pictured everyday life in realistic detail

reaping machine: Enabled farmers to cut wheat much more quickly

Reconquista: Roman Catholic seizure of Spain and Portugal from the Muslims

Reform Act of 1867: Granted voting privileges to all male homeowners

Reform Bill of 1832: Entitled the middle class in Britain to vote

Reign of Terror: A period of mass executions during the French Revolution

Reinsurance Treaty: Bismarck's secret treaty with Russia

Renaissance: A revival of learning in the beginning of the fourteenth century

Republic of China: Established on the island of Taiwan by Chiang Kai-shek

Risorgimento: Resurgence; contributed to the Italian movement for nationalism

Romanesque: An architectural style of the early Middle Ages that used elements of Roman styles of architecture

romanticism: Western style of art, music, and literature characterized by an emphasis on the mysterious and supernatural, a longing for the Medieval Age, and a love for freedom, nationalism, emotion, and nature

Rome-Berlin Axis: Alliance formed by Mussolini and Hitler

Rommel, Erwin: German general sent by Hitler to rescue the Italians in Egypt; defeated by General Bernard L. Montgomery

Russo-Japanese War: War in which Japan astonished the European states by quickly and decisively defeating the Russian army and navy

S

Safavid dynasty: Founded by Shah Ismail I (1501–1722)

Sahara: A desert that covers most of Northern Africa

Sahel: A narrow strip of land in Africa between the Sahara Desert and the rain forests

samurai: A Japanese warrior

Santa Cruz: Attempted settlement by Mendaña in the South Pacific islands; means "holy cross"

Sassanid: Another name for the revived Persian Empire

Saul of Tarsus: Began as an opponent of Christianity (see Acts 8) but was later converted to Christianity (see Acts 9), followed by a life of devoted service to Christ and the church

savannah: Flat grasslands in Africa

Schlieffen Plan: Germany's two-front war strategy during World War I in which Germany would quickly conquer France and then fight Russia

Scramble for Africa: The rush for European conquest of Africa

scurvy: Disease that many sailors contracted because of a lack of vitamin C in their diet

SDI: "Strategic Defense Initiative"; space-based system that would protect America from missile attacks

Second Empire: Established in 1852 by Louis Napoleon Bonaparte when he gave himself the title of emperor

Second Estate: Second-highest level of French society before the French Revolution; contained the aristocracy

Second French Colonial Empire: Began in 1830 with the invasion of Algeria in North Africa; stemmed from a desire to have colonies

secularism: A society that is free from religion

seed drill: Invention that efficiently placed seeds in rows across a plot of land

seed of the serpent: Reference to those who would reject the Messiah (see John 8:44)

seed of the woman: Reference to those who would accept the Messiah; ultimately a reference to Jesus

Sepoy Mutiny: An uprising of Hindu and Muslim soldiers hired by the British in India; began because of a rumor that the cartridges for a newly issued rifle had been greased with either pork or beef fat

sepoys: Indian soldiers hired by the British

September 1, 1939: Date that Germany invaded Poland

September 2, 1945: Date the Japanese and Allied representatives signed the documents that formally ended Japanese involvement in World War II; known as V-J Day

serfs: Peasants who made up much of the Russian population and lived in a condition of virtual slavery

shading: A technique for adding dimension to figures in artwork

Shah Ismail I: Founded the Safavid dynasty

shaman: A man in Mongol religion who is believed to have power over spirits

Shang: The first dynasty in Chinese history

Sharia: Islamic law

Shiite: Literally means "follower" and refers to Muslims who insist that the right to rule was limited to descendants of Muhammad

Shintoism: A Japanese religion that taught nature worship, the deity of the emperor, and patriotism

Shoah: The name many Jews use to refer to the Holocaust; means "calamity" in Hebrew

shogun: The title of a Japanese clan's leader; means "great general"

siege warfare: Method of conquest in which enemy forces surround a city and mount repeated attacks

single market: A system of economic cooperation that enables states to trade with one another without restriction

Sino-Japanese War: War in which Japan easily defeated China, humiliated the Manchu government, took possession of Korea, and received Taiwan along with other Chinese territories

Sistine Chapel: A famous building in Rome whose ceiling was painted by Michelangelo

Six-Day War: War in which Israel smashed the imminent Arab threat and seized control of several key areas that greatly enhanced Israel's security

smallpox: A disease that killed or left people terribly scarred

Smith, John: Strong English leader that turned the Jamestown settlement into a thriving colony

Smoot-Hawley Tariff Act: Established the highest tariff (duty or tax on foreign products) in U.S. history

socialism: Economic system in which the government owns businesses

Solidarity: Labor movement led by Lech Wałęsa to help achieve Polish independence

Solomon Islands: Pacific Island chain discovered by Alvaro de Mendaña

Song: Dynasty of the northern kingdom of China that ruled during a time of strong economic growth

Songhai: Kingdom in western Africa that was located between Mali and Ghana

South Australia: New colony founded by explorers who traveled southwest from Sydney around the coast

spheres of influence: Established by European nations as they claimed Chinese territory for themselves

spinning jenny: Invention that could rapidly spin spools of cotton thread into yarn

Spinoza: Dutch philosopher who applied rationalism to the Bible and thought almost everything in Scripture was contrary to reason

Sputnik: First man-made satellite; launched by the Soviets in 1957

stalemate: Wartime condition in which two opposing forces have no major gains on either side

Stalin, Joseph: The second dictator of the Soviet Union; continued and intensified oppression of religion (1879–1953)

Stanley, Henry: A Welsh reporter that found David Livingstone at Lake Tanganyika

steam engine: Provided the necessary power to pull heavy loads in the form of tractors and locomotives

steam tractor: A self-propelled tractor that could plow fields and dig drainage canals

Sucre, Antonio José de: Fought alongside Bolívar for Venezuelan independence and then went on to free Ecuador from Spanish dominion

Sudetenland: An area of Czechoslovakia that came under Hitler's control with the approval of British and French leaders but without the Czech government's input

suffrage: The privilege to vote in elections

Sunni: Literally means "adherent" and refers to Muslims who believe that any worthy Muslim could become the ruler of Islam

Swahili: A trade language in Africa built upon the Bantu language

Sydney Cove: Location of the first English colony in Australia

T

Table of Nations: Another name for Genesis 10, which lists the descendants of Shem, Ham, and Japheth and the nations that descended from them

Tahiti: An island claimed for France by Bougainville

Taiping Rebellion: An uprising led by Hong Xiuquan that British and Chinese forces were able to quell

Taizu: Founded the Ming dynasty and established a pattern of absolute rule that his successors followed for the next three centuries

Taj Mahal: One of India's greatest pieces of architecture; built during the Mughal rule

Taliban: A radical Muslim group

Tamerlane: Mongol leader who was lame but became a powerful conqueror

Taoism: A passive Chinese religion that emphasizes living in peace and harmony with nature

Tartars: The European name for the Mongol forces that invaded eastern Europe

Tasman, Abel: Dutch explorer who sailed from southern India in search of the mythical unknown southern land; discovered Australia, Tasmania, and New Zealand

Tasmania: Island discovered by Abel Tasman

technology: Putting knowledge to effective use

temperance: Drinking in moderation

Ten Commandments: Ten laws showing Israel how to love God and other humans

Tengri: The name of the Mongol god, meaning "the great god of heaven"

Ten Hour Bill: Restricted women and children to working a ten-hour day in any British industry

telegraph: Enabled people to write messages to others who lived far away

telephone: Enabled people to speak to others who lived far away

Tenochtitlán: The Aztec capital

Thatcher, Margaret: British politician who led the Conservative Party in Great Britain to victory in 1979; an ally of Ronald Reagan during the Cold War

The Last Supper: Famous painting by Leonardo da Vinci

Theodosius I: Roman emperor who made Christianity the only recognized religion in the empire

Theresa, Maria: Monarch of Austria (r. 1740–80)

threshing machine: Enabled a few men to separate the wheat from the husks and stalks quickly

Third Estate: Lowest level of French society before the French Revolution; contained the middle class, artisans, townsmen, and peasants

Third Reich: A new German empire constructed by Hitler

Third Republic: French government that captured and deposed Louis Napoleon

third world: Regions that remained neutral during the Cold War

38th parallel: Line of latitude used to divide Korea into North and South

Thirty Years' War: Began as a revolt by the Bohemians against loss of religious liberty, but soon became a major conflict between Catholic and Protestant forces in Europe

Tiananmen Square: Site of a student protest in China in 1989 that was violently ended by the military

Timbuktu: Important city in western Africa located on the Niger River

Tojo, Hideki: Japanese general that played a central role in expanding the power of the military in Japan and supporting Japanese conquest; maintained a strong loyalty to the emperor

Tolstoy, Leo: Described the difficulties of life in Russia; wrote the novel *War and Peace*

total war: War in which all of a country's resources are devoted to destroying the enemy; war in which there are no limits on targets or the kind of weapons used

town charter: A legal document issued by the king that listed privileges of the town's inhabitants and freed them from most feudal duties

trade winds: Winds blowing from east to west that brought European explorers across the Atlantic Ocean

transubstantiation: Roman Catholic doctrine that the bread and wine of the Lord's Supper change into the very body and blood of Christ

Treaty of Kanagawa: Signed by Japan and the United States in 1854; opened Japan to trade with other nations

Treaty of Tordesillas: A final agreement by Spain and Portugal that moved the Line of Demarcation

Treaty of Versailles: Treaty between the Allies and Germany that contained harsh demands and blamed Germany for World War I

tribe: Consisted of two or more African clans living together and sharing a common language, beliefs, and customs

Triple Entente: Loose confederation between Russia, England, and France prior to World War I

Truce of God: A church decree restricting fighting among knights to certain days of the week

Tull, Jethro: Developed a seed drill

Ture, Samori: Developed a modern army with current weapons to defend the Wassoulou Empire

U

Umayyad: Muslim dynasty that moved the capital of the empire to Damascus

United Nations: Organized by diplomats representing fifty nations; founded to ensure international peace

United States of America: Nation that developed from the original thirteen colonies

V

vaccine: A weakened form of a disease exposed to a person on purpose to prevent his getting a serious form of the disease

vernacular: National language, such as French or German

Vesalius, Andreas: Developed his work on human anatomy by dissecting human bodies

viceroy: Ruler of a Spanish colony who represented the king of Spain

Victor Emmanuel II: King of Sardinia who became the first king of a united Italy in 1861

Victoria: Colony in Australia named for the Queen of England

Victoria Falls: Discovered by Livingstone as he followed the Zambezi River

Viet Cong: Vietnamese Communist agents who tried to take over South Vietnam

Voltaire: Wrote volumes of literature to describe and endorse Enlightenment ideals

W

Wahhabist: Movement that gained control of Saudi Arabia and used the vast wealth generated by oil sales to spread the literal application of Islam to many parts of the world

Wałęsa, Lech: Led an anti-Communist movement that combined labor, the Roman Catholic Church, and Polish nationalism to oppose Soviet domination; helped achieve Polish independence

War for Independence: Delivered the colonists in North America from English rule

Wars of Apostasy: Abu Bakr's campaign against Arabs who sought independence after Muhammad's death

Washington Naval Conference: Meeting of several nations that agreed to limit the number of warships each could build

Wassoulou: Empire in Africa led by Samori Ture that resisted European colonization

Waterloo: Site of the battle in which the armies of Prussia and Britain defeated Napoleon and his forces (1815)

Watt, James: Made important improvements in the design of the steam engine that increased efficiency

Weimar Republic: German government after World War I; organized at Weimar

Wesley, John: One of the greatest preachers in Britain during the eighteenth century; organized his converts into Methodist societies, with laymen serving as leaders

West African Economic and Monetary Union: Organization of Western African states that strives to promote economic cooperation and the use of a common currency

Whitefield, George: An eighteenth-century British preacher with an international ministry

Whitney, Eli: Invented the cotton gin

Wilberforce, William: Christian in the English Parliament who led the effort to abolish slavery in the British Empire

Wilhelm I: King of Prussia and later the first king of Germany

Wilhelm II: Ruler of Germany who dismissed Bismarck and allowed the Reinsurance Treaty to expire

William and Mary: Signed the English Bill of Rights in 1689 in exchange for the English throne

William the Conqueror: Laid the foundation for a strong monarchy through his conquest of England

Wright brothers: Made their first successful flight on December 17, 1903

Wycliffe, John: A pastor, teacher, and theologian in England that produced the first Bible in the English language

X

Xavier, Francis: Jesuit missionary to Japan who sought to convert the people to Roman Catholicism

Y

Yahweh: Name for God used in the Hebrew Bible

Yat-Sen, Sun: Leader that worked to bring reform to China; struggled to bring unity to China through the Kuomintang, or Nationalist, Party

Yoruba: African language into which Samuel Ajayi Crowther helped translate the Bible

Young Italy: Italian nationalist group founded by Giuseppe Mazzini

yurt: A movable house used by the Mongols

Z

Zedong, Mao: Led the Chinese Communist Party and stirred up peasant revolts in order to undermine the conservative government of Chiang Kai-shek

Zen Buddhism: Version of Buddhism that teaches intense mental concentration and self-control

Zheng He: Chinese admiral of a great convoy with an army and crew that may have numbered almost thirty thousand; presented gifts to foreign rulers and brought back treasures

Zimbabwe: An empire that developed from the city of Great Zimbabwe in southeast Africa in the 1300s

Zollverein: Economic union of German states in the nineteenth century that resulted in German unification

Zwingli, Ulrich: Swiss reformer who studied and accepted Martin Luther's teachings

INDEX

PHOTO CREDITS

Ray Hems; **174t** © Heritage Images/Corbis; **174b** "Captainjamescookportrait" by Nathaniel Dance-Holland/Wikimedia Commons/ Public Domain; **175l** "'Death of Captain Cook', oil on canvas by George Carter, 1783"/ Wikimedia Commons/Public Domain; **175r** © Corbis; **176tl** © Reuters/CORBIS; **176bl** Lynn Gail / Media Bakery; **176br** "Bark Painting LACMA M.2009.127.8"/Wikimedia Commons/Public Domain; **177t** The Sydney Morning Herald/Fairfax Media/Getty Images; **177b** "Arthur Phillip" by Francis Wheatley/ Wikimedia Commons/Public Domain; **178t** © iStock.com/Ida Jarosova; **178b** © Boginda | Dreamstime.com; **179t** Auscape/Universal Images Group/Getty Images; **179c** © Joshua Cortopassi | Dreamstime.com; **179b** © iStock. com/Totajla; **180l** © iStock.com/Dirk Freder; **180c** © hotshotsworldwide / Fotolia; **180r** © iStock.com/Craig Dingle

Chapter 11

184–85bg, 187 edge © frenta / Fotolia; **185i** © iStock.com/sinopics; **187l** "Wucai ewer BM Franks 853" by Marie-Lan Nguyen/Wikimedia Commons/CC By 3.0; **187r** "Chinese - Vase with Court Scene and Three Star Gods - Walters 492349 - Side A"/Walters Art Museum/ CC By-SA 3.0; **188tl** "Qiu Ying - Fishing under Chinese Sweet Gums - Google Art Project"/ Wikimedia Commons/Public Domain; **188tr** Universal History Archive/Universal Images Group/Getty Images; **188br** © iStock.com/ Aleksander Mirski; **189tl** © Keren Su/Corbis; **189tr** © iStock.com/Songquan Deng; **189br** © claudiozacc / Fotolia; **193t** Martin Siepmann/ image / imageBROKER / SuperStock; **193b** "Benjamin-Constant-The Entry of Mahomet II into Constantinople-1876"/Wikimedia Commons/Public Domain; **195** © iStock.com/ prmustafa; **197** Aleksandar Todorovic/Bigstock. com; **198** © iStock.com/Holger Mette

Chapter 12

204–05bg, 209 edge "Episode of the September Days 1830 (on the Grand Place of Brussels)" by Egide Charles Gustave Wappers/Wikimedia Commons/Public Domain; **205i** "Ingres, Napoleon on his Imperial throne"/Wikimedia Commons/Public Domain; **206** Heritage Images/Hulton Archive/Getty Images; **207l, 216b** Art Archive, The / SuperStock; **207r** "Élisabeth Vigée Le Brun - Marie-Antoinette au livre - 1785"/Wikimedia Commons/Public Domain; **208** SuperStock / SuperStock; **210** © Don Troiani/Corbis; **211** "Napoleon I. BomannMuseum@20150903"/Wikimedia Commons/Public Domain; **212** © Gianni Dagli Orti/Corbis; **213** "Battle of Stoczek" by Jan Rosen/Wikimedia Commons/Public Domain; **215** "Portrait of Otto Eduard Leopold von Bismarck" by Franz von Lenbach/Wikimedia Commons/Public Domain; **216t, 217t, 217b** DeAgostini / SuperStock

Chapter 13

220–21bg, 225, 231, 235 edge, 233 Library of Congress; **221i** Katja Kircher / MediaBakery; **222l** Science & Society Picture Library/SSPL/ Getty Images; **222r** Robert Bird / Alamy; **223b** "Batteuse 1881"/Wikipedia/Public Domain; **224tl** Stock Montage/Archive Photos/Getty Images; **224tr** © Corbis; **224bl, 232b** North Wind Picture Archives via AP Images; **224br** Henry Guttmann/Hulton Archive/Getty

Images; **225bg** "Gloucestershire Steam & Vintage Extravaganza 2013 (9447054942)" by Barry Skeates/Wikimedia Commons/CC By 2.0; **225i** "John Fowler001"/Wikipedia/ Public Domain; **226tl** "Portrait of James Watt" by Henry Howard/Wikimedia Commons/ Public Domain; **226tr, 227** Science and Society / SuperStock; **226bl** "Shuttle with bobin" by Audrius Meskauskas/Wikimedia Commons/ CC By-SA 3.0; **226br** Joyce Landis; **228** Library of Congress, LC-DIG-nclc-01342; **229** "Sweeper and doffer boys in Lancaster Cotton Mills. Many more as small. Lancaster, S.C. - NARA - 523120" by Lewis Hine/NARA/Wikimedia Commons/Public Domain; **230** Library of Congress, LC-DIG-nclc-02103; **232t** ACME Imagery / SuperStock; **234t** Everett Collection Historical / Alamy; **234b** "Olaudah Equiano - Project Gutenberg eText 15399"/Wikimedia Commons/Public Domain; **235t** "William Lloyd Garrison by Southworth and Hawes, c1850"/Wikimedia Commons/Public Domain; **235b** "Frederick Douglass as a younger man" by J.C. Buttre/Wikimedia Commons/Public Domain

Chapter 14

238–39bg, 250, 254 edge "East and West shaking hands at the laying of the last rail" by Andrew J. Russell/Wikimedia Commons/ Public Domain; **239i, 240t** Heritage / SuperStock; **240b** Art Archive, The / SuperStock; **241** © Underwood & Underwood/ Corbis; **242** Topical Press Agency/Hulton Archive/Getty Images; **243t** "Benjamin Disraeli CDV by Cornelius Jabez Hughes, 1878"/ Wikimedia Commons/Public Domain; **243b** John Jabez Edwin Mayall/Hulton Archive/ Getty Images; **244t** "Portrait of Napoleon III" by Franz Xaver Winterhalter/Wikimedia Commons/Public Domain; **244b** © iStock.com/ duncan1890; **245** Library of Congress; **246** "Dickens Gurney head" by Jeremiah Gurney/ Wikimedia Commons/Public Domain; **247l** "Leo Tolstoy 1897, black and white, 37767u" by F. W. Taylor/Wikimedia Commons/ Public Domain; **247r** "Young Women from the Village" by Gustave Courbet/Wikimedia Commons/Public Domain; **248** "James Clerk Maxwell profile"/Wikimedia Commons/ Public Domain; **249l** Roger Viollet/Getty Images; **249r** "Portrait of Charles Darwin" by George Richmond/Wikimedia Commons/ Public Domain; **251t** Library of Congress, LC-DIG-ppmsc-05542; **251b** Car Culture/ Car Culture ® Collection/Getty Images; **252t** "Wrightflyer" by John T. Daniels/Wikimedia Commons/Public Domain; **252b** "Samuel Morse with His Recorder" by Mathew Brady/ Wikimedia Commons/Public Domain; **253** "Alexander Graham Bell in colors"/Wikimedia Commons/Public Domain; **254l** Imagno/ Hulton Fine Art Collection/Getty Images; **254r** © GraphicaArtis/Corbis

Chapter 15

260–61bg, 274, 276, 278 edge © iStock.com/ slpu9945; **261i** Library of Congress; **263tr** © Voisin/phanie/Phanie Sarl/Corbis; **263bl** Hasnuddin/Shutterstock.com; **263br** wk-1003mike/Shutterstock.com; **264** © volff / Fotolia; **266tl** Iberfoto / SuperStock; **266tr** © photoromano / Fotolia; **266bl** "George Baxter, The Reverend Robert Moffat, 1 April 1843"/

Wikimedia Commons/Public Domain; **273** Photo 12/Universal Images Group/Getty Images; **274l** ©2009 JupiterImages Corporation; **274r** Pantheon / SuperStock; **276l** Library of Congress, USZC4-4609; **276r** Culture Club/ Hulton Archive/Getty Images; **277t** Volodymyr Burdiak/Shutterstock.com; **277b** © Michal Bednarek | Dreamstime.com

Chapter 16

282–83bg, 291, 296, 298 edge © Marina Ignatova / Fotolia; **283i** © Underwood and Underwood/National Geographic Creative/ Corbis; **285** "Bonaparte Before the Sphinx" by Jean-Léon Gérôme/Wikimedia Common/ Public Domain; **286t** "Mahmoud II. Litho" by Josef Kriehuber/Wikimedia Commons/ Public Domain; **286b** "Troika" by Vasily Perov/ Wikimedia Commons/Public Domain; **287** "The Decembrist revolt at the Senate Square on December 14, 1825." by Vasily Timm/ Wikimedia Commons/Public Domain; **288** Heritage Images/Hulton Archive/Getty Images; **289** Heinz-Dieter Falkenstein / age fotostock / SuperStock; **291l** © iStock.com/ vishureddy; **291r** Dchauy/Shutterstock. com; **293l** "Ganga canal" by BOMBMAN/ Wikimedia Commons/CC By 2.0; **293tr, 293br** © Sadık Güleç | Dreamstime.com; **295** National Archives; **296–97bg** Public Domain; **296tl** Private Collection / © Look and Learn / Elgar Collection / Bridgeman Images; **296tr** The Granger Collection, New York; **296br, 301** Library of Congress; **297bl** "James Curtis Hepburn"/Wikimedia Commons/ Public Domain; **297br** Overseas Missionary Fellowship/Public Domain; **298b** "The Ci-Xi Imperial Dowager Empress (5)"/Wikimedia Commons/Public Domain

Chapter 17

306–07bg, 315 edge National Archives; **307i, 317l, 319** Print Collector/Hulton Archive/Getty Images; **308** "Punch - The Dogs of War" by John Tenniel/Wikimedia Commons/Public Domain; **309** "Robert Koch BeW"/Wikimedia Commons/Public Domain; **310** "The Austro Hungarian Empire Before the First World War Q81810"/Imperial War Museums/Wikimedia Commons/Public Domain; **312** Popperfoto/ Getty Images; **313tl** "1st Aero Squadron Salmson 2A2"/Air Service, United States Army/ Wikimedia Commons/Public Domain; **313tr** © Bettmann/CORBIS; **313bl** "German sub-marine stranded 1921"/Library of Congress/ Wikimedia Commons/Public Domain; **314l** BACM Research; **314r** Library of Congress, LC-USZ62-54961; **315** Library of Congress, LC-DIG-ggbain-35451; **317r** "Nicholas II of Russia in his coronation robe" by Aleksandr Makovsky/Wikimedia Commons/Public Domain; **318t** "Stalin between 1930 and 1936"/ Wikimedia Commons/Public Domain; **318b** "Adolf Hitler cropped restored"/German Federal Archives/Wikimedia Commons/CC By-SA 3.0 DE; **320t** ullstein bild/Getty Images; **320c** © Hulton-Deutsch Collection/CORBIS; **320b** © AS400 DB/Corbis; **322** "Einstein 1921 by F Schmutzer"/Wikimedia Commons/ Public Domain; **323t** "The Scream" by Edvard Munch/Wikimedia Commons/Public Domain; **323b** "Portrait of Pablo Picasso" by Juan Gris/ Wikimedia Commons/Public Domain; **324tl** © Richard T. Nowitz/Corbis; **324tr** "6268 Dessau"